HENRY BROUGHAM

Henry Brougham
1778–1868
His Public Career

ROBERT STEWART

THE BODLEY HEAD
LONDON

*The publisher acknowledges subsidy
from the Scottish Arts Council
towards the publication of this volume*

British Library Cataloguing
in Publication Data
Stewart, Robert, *1941–*
Henry Brougham 1778–1868: his public career
1. Brougham, Henry Peter, *Baron Brougham and Vaux*
2. Lawyers—Great Britain—Biography
3. Statesmen—Great Britain—Biography
I. Title
941.07'3'0924   DA536.B7
ISBN 0–370–30271–0

© Robert Stewart, 1985
Set in Linotron 202 Baskerville
by Wyvern Typesetting Ltd, Bristol
Printed in Great Britain for
The Bodley Head Ltd
30 Bedford Square, London WC1B 3RP
by The Bath Press, Avon
First published 1986

CONTENTS

Acknowledgments, vii

Illustrations, ix

1 The Scotch Provenance, 1

2 Political Apprenticeship, 28

3 Member for Camelford, 55

4 Out of Parliament, 84

5 The Game of the Country, 99

6 Whig Frontbencher, 120

7 The Queen's Attorney, 140

8 'A Most *Powerful* Man', 160

9 The Schoolmaster Abroad, 183

10 Canning and Coalition, 205

11 Pride and Fall, 230

12 The Woolsack: I, 253

13 The Woolsack: II, 277

14 'A Grotesque Apocalypse', 303

15 A Political Ishmael, 325

16 Recessional, 345

Notes, 362

Biographical Notes, 389

Select Bibliography, 392

Index, 399

ACKNOWLEDGMENTS

To assist me in the research to write this book both the British Academy and the Twenty-Seven Foundation awarded me a grant, for which I am happy publicly to thank them. Without their support the book would probably not have been written.

I am also delighted to record my gratitude to James Michie, an old friend, who first suggested the book to me and whose editorship has been the very model of tact, intelligence and unobtrusive encouragement.

LIST OF ILLUSTRATIONS

Between pages 86 and 87

Plate 1 The Trial of Queen Caroline by G. Hayter (1820)

Plate 2 Portrait of Sydney Smith by H. P. Briggs (1833 or 1840)

Plate 3 Portrait of Francis Jeffrey by A. Geddes (1820 or 1826)

Plate 4 Portrait of Francis Horner by H. Raeburn (1812)

Plate 5 Portrait of Henry Brougham by J. Lonsdale (1821)

Plate 6 'Patent Penny Knowledge Mill', *Maclean's Monthly Sheet of Caricatures*, October 1832

Between pages 214 and 215

Plate 7 Drawing of Henry Brougham by C. H. Lear (1857)

Plate 8 Manuscript letter from Brougham to John Allen (1835)

Plate 9 'To the Temple of Fame', *Punch*, 23 October, 1858

I

The Scotch Provenance

'By God! Brougham is Chancellor.' So the Earl of Sefton, in November 1830, expressed to Thomas Creevey his surprise that their old friend, Henry Brougham, had accepted the Woolsack in Lord Grey's reform government.[1] A day earlier Sefton had assured Creevey that it would end in Brougham's taking the Rolls and that Brougham, bellowing that he *ought* to be offered the Seals, had sworn he 'wd. kick them out of the window rather than desert his Yorkshire friends by taking a peerage'.[2] Only four months had passed since Brougham, the tribune of the people, the scourge of judges on the northern circuit and the most formidable debater in the House of Commons, had, in what he called the proudest moment of his life, been elected, without spending a penny of his own, as the member for Yorkshire. Election by Great Britain's largest and, so men believed, most independent electorate, the freeholders of Yorkshire, had confirmed Brougham's standing as the most important liberal politician in the country. Reformers in every part of the land, their spirits revived by the electoral blow dealt to Toryism in the summer of 1830, looked to him as their parliamentary champion. Now, to their disappointment (to the satisfaction, however, of the more respectable portions of the community), Henry Brougham was no more. In his stead, removed to another place, was Lord Brougham and Vaux.

Astonished as some men were that Brougham had lowered himself, others wondered at his having climbed so high. Lord Grey's cabinet, although not exclusively aristocratic like Pitt's of 1804 or Perceval's of 1809, was a splendid representation of the Whig family compact. Brougham, a middle-class Scotch lawyer, never quite overcame his distaste for the pretensions of high Whiggery; yet, although Lansdowne House, staid rendezvous of Whig front benches, remained wary of outsiders, Holland House threw wide its doors to men of wit and information. Grey himself in 1809, before his youthful zeal had given way to idle patience, hailed radical Brougham as the 'first man this country has seen since Burke's time'.[3] The Whigs were accused of

I

having used Burke's gifts without rewarding him for them, but Burke's talents were not obviously suited to ministerial office. In an age when Addington and Canning became prime minister it would be silly to exaggerate the jealousy of the ruling political circles. Sydney Smith's jibe that in England it was considered an impertinence for a man of less than two or three thousand a year to have an opinion on important matters was blunted by the fact that, chiefly through the operation of the nomination boroughs, the two great parties in the state, Whig and Tory, were alliances between men of birth and men of intelligence. In the pre-reform era, when the back benches were littered by elder sons with little interest in politics and less knowledge of public affairs, a clever young man on the make met little competition. If he could speak and had something to say he was certain to win notice.

Brougham's antecedents were, at any rate, far from ordinary. His father, a squire who wore his hair powdered and tied, dressed immaculately in cut-away coat and white waistcoat, and carried with him always a tall, gold-headed cane, had inherited the modest estate in Westmorland in which stood Brougham Hall, a massive-walled, 12th-century fortress built to secure its owners against the hostility of their border neighbours and commanding a view of the mountains along the lakes of Ullswater and Derwent. ('Brough' is Old English for 'fort' and the name 'Brougham', pronounced as one syllable, means 'homestead by the fort'.) His great-uncle, on his mother's side, was William Robertson, Scotland's most renowned historian, principal of Edinburgh University and leader of the Moderate party in the Church of Scotland. Fortunately for Brougham, his father removed to Edinburgh and it was there, on 19 September 1778, that Brougham was born. His family had little money, but they were in touch with the educated elite of Edinburgh and that kind of access counted for more in Great Britain than mere wealth. Brougham was born just at the time when the middle rank of society, shortly to be eulogized by James Mill in his *Essay on Government* as 'the chief source of all that has exalted and refined human nature', was about to enter into its political and social inheritance. He had only to survive for his light to shine.

For a boy of Brougham's transcendent intelligence and precocious intellectual appetite, Edinburgh, then bathed in the sunset rays of the Scotch Enlightenment, was a blissful place in which to grow up. The accumulation of wealth in Glasgow, derived from the 18th-century colonial trade in tobacco, had spread prosperity throughout the lowlands, while the influence of French thought, assisted by Scotland's ancient ties with France, did not struggle, as it did in England, to make itself felt. Scotland was at the forefront of the age, no longer distracted by the quarrels of the 17th century (Jacobinism was a spent force) nor wracked by the enmity, which deeply coloured French intellectual life, between Church and State. Natural science and revealed religion were not in dispute; pure and practical reason marched hand in hand. As much as the philosophers, David Hume and Adam Smith, and the writers, Scott and Burns, did scientists contribute to the last flowering of Scotch culture. The faculties of law and medicine were the pride of Edinburgh's university. The air which Brougham breathed was infused with the spirit of rational inquiry. Brougham lived until 1868, but he remained throughout his life a representative of the 18th century, immune to both the adolescent yearnings of Romanticism and (except for a half-hearted flirtation with Owenite spiritualism) the 19th-century regression into religious enthusiasm. Hence Brougham's contemptuous dismissal of Rousseau, a man rendered distasteful by his morbid introspection and his private dissipations and a thinker unfitted for political or economic writing by his failure to grasp that the representative system of government was the great improvement of modern policy. Can Brougham ever have read the *Discourse on Inequality*? He *did* read the *Confessions* and discovered in them Rousseau's masterpiece, though a masterpiece only because its magical prose turned a base, low life into art.

> The subject is not only wearisome generally, revolting frequently, but it is oftentimes low, vulgar, grovelling, fitted to turn us away from the contemplation with aversion, even disgust . . . We stand aghast after pausing, when we can take breath, and can see over what filthy ground we have been led, but we feel the extraordinary power of the hand that has led us along . . . No triumph so great was ever won by diction. The work in this respect stands alone; it is reasonable to wish that it may have no imitators.[4]

Men who looked only at Brougham's personal quirks, or at his somewhat erratic political progress, were quick to accuse him of inconsistency and unreliability. In the things that mattered Brougham never wavered. His attachment to Newton and Voltaire, twin pillars, as he thought, of modern European civilization, never loosened. In his eyes it was the condemnation of English culture that as late as the mid-19th century Newton remained unhonoured by a single public monument and Voltaire, in the places where he was read at all, was still dismissed as a mere religious scoffer. Through Scotland Brougham received the 18th-century European inheritance: a belief in the expediency of reason and the possibility of human improvement and the conviction that those two elements were, or at least could and ought to be, joined, so that right thinking should issue in right action.

Brougham gave to his maternal grandmother, the sister of Robertson, credit for all his success in life: 'she instilled into me from my cradle the strongest desire for information, and the first principles of that persevering energy in the pursuit of every kind of knowledge which, more than any natural talents I may possess, has enabled me to stick to, and accomplish ... every task I ever undertook'.[5] He recorded, too, his debt to Robertson, who supervised his reading of the classics from an early age. The Robertsons had wonderful material to work upon. Brougham uttered clearly intelligible words at the age of eight months and two weeks and he learned to read by the age of two. His mother remarked that from mere infancy he showed a marked attention to everything that he saw and, afterwards, to everything that he heard. He was blessed with a most retentive memory and a fund of energy—his capacity for work, right to the end of his long life, never failed to excite the awe of all who knew him — which were joyfully applied to the acquisition of knowledge. It was not then the habit to pamper children. Thomas Arnold, at the age of three, was given the twenty-four volumes of Smollett's *History of England* as a reward for the accuracy with which he had related the stories attached to paintings and portraits of successive reigns. Even so, it was an exceptionally mature and self-confident boy of thirteen who wrote such a letter as this, sent by Brougham to Robertson in January 1792:

> You will perhaps remember that you allowed me to translate either Livy or Florus. I pitched upon the latter—not that his style appeared to me any way superior to that of the other; but as I had read, partly at Edinburgh and partly here [Brougham Hall], almost the whole of the first five books of Livy ... it naturally occurred that there would be less field for exertion in translating an author with whose works I was acquainted, than in trying one

whose works were quite new to me. Besides, I was confirmed in my choice when I recollected that *you* seemed to give the preference to Florus. That author, though concise and nervous, is not the less elegant and instructive. Full of vigour, and just, in his descriptions relating the conquests of Rome in that rapid manner, as it were, in which they were acquired. As he writes in a very peculiar stile, so I thought that by a literal translation his elegance would be lost. I have endeavoured, therefore, by taking a little freedom, to transfuse his beauties into the English language, without impairing the sense.[6]

When that letter was written, Brougham had already left Edinburgh High School and was about to matriculate at the university. Henry Cockburn, the memorialist, who was a year behind Brougham at the High School, recorded that it was notorious for the severity of its masters and the riotousness among the boys, with whom coarseness of language and manners was the fashion.[7] Brougham looked back upon his school days as time fruitlessly spent, at any rate the first four years under the harsh discipline of the under-master, Luke Fraser. It was in Fraser's form that Brougham, displaying the tenacity of purpose, fearlessness of authority and delight in pugnacious argument which remained his distinguishing traits, made what Cockburn called his 'first public explosion'.

He dared to differ from Fraser, a hot, but good-natured old fellow, on some small bit of latinity. The master, like other men in power, maintained his own infallibility, punished the rebel, and flattered himself the affair was over. But Brougham reappeared next day, loaded with books, returned to the charge before the whole class, and compelled honest Luke to acknowledge that he had been wrong. This made Brougham famous throughout the whole school. I remember as well as if it had been yesterday, having him pointed out to me as 'the fellow who had beat the master'.[8]

Fraser taught only Latin. For Brougham's last two years at the High School, under the learned and patient rector, Dr Adam, Greek was added. When Brougham entered his form in 1789, revolution had just broken out in France and Brougham was delighted to hear Adam, a Whig admirer of the revolution, intersperse his comments on the classical texts with congratulatory remarks upon political events across the water. (He later recorded his surprise that Adam was able, considering the Tory grip on the Scotch professions, to get away with his remarks.) Although he passed out of the High School as dux, or head of the class, Brougham had no memory of distinguishing himself there. More useful were the months spent out of school during a protracted period of illness, the first of the recurrent bouts of psycho-somatic languor and fever which afflicted him for most of his life. Left to his own lights, he read continually and tried his hand at composition. Out of school, also, he instructed himself in modern languages and mathematics. One afternoon, when he was about twelve years old, a cousin came upon him walking with a volume of Laplace in the original and wondered 'what sort of lad this must be who not only studied mathematics for pleasure, but through the medium of a foreign tongue'.[9]

Brougham went up to the university a prodigy. He was avaricious of knowledge. He had developed powers of intellectual resource. He had already decided that learning and information, however gratifying to the private imagination, were to be placed in the service of public action. Brougham's university years were the making of him. The university was then passing through the most brilliant period in its history. Dugald Stewart in moral philosophy, Playfair in mathematics, Black in chemistry and Robertson himself, principal when Brougham matriculated in 1792, lent the institution such lustre that in the last years of the 18th century and well into the 19th it was fashionable for English gentlemen to send their sons north for their university education. At Cambridge and Oxford wealth and rank were obstacles to the acquisition of knowledge, the sons of noble families being exempt from examinations—as if, Denis le Marchant, the diarist and for a time private secretary to Brougham, remarked, ignorance were essential to nobility.[10] William Lamb, the future Lord Melbourne, Lord John Russell and Viscount Palmerston, all cabinet colleagues of Brougham in Grey's reform ministry, were sent to Edinburgh, Russell's preference for Cambridge being overridden by his father because 'there was nothing to be learnt at English Universities'.[11] Cambridge especially was notorious for the licentious and ruinously expensive manner of its undergraduates, many of whom made the form sheets for Newmarket their chief study. How different the atmosphere was at Edinburgh! 'I may truly say,' Sir James Mackintosh, who went up in 1787, wrote, 'that it is not easy to conceive a university where industry was more general, where reading was more fashionable, where indolence and ignorance were more disreputable. Every mind was in a state of fermentation.'[12] Mackintosh found fault with the excessive love of speculation, which exhausted strength in vain leaps and sacrificed accurate and applicable knowledge to flights of imaginative logic, and he attributed to this baneful metaphysical air at Edinburgh his life-long tendency to indolence. No doubt some minds, encouraged early to believe that words alone matter, not facts, never quite grow up. Brougham, at any rate, was in no danger from the metaphysical sickness. Francis Horner, Brougham's pre-school playmate and bosom friend both at the High School and the university, observed the development of his powers closely: 'He is an uncommon genius, of a *composite* order, if you allow me to use the expression; he unites the greatest ardour for general information in every branch of knowledge, and, what is more remarkable, activity in the business, and interest in the pleasures of the world, with all the powers of a mathematical intellect.'[13]

Brougham went up to the university, at the usual age of thirteen, to read Humanity and Philosophy, the name given to the arts curriculum then prevailing in Scotch universities. It encompassed ancient languages, rhetoric, logic, moral philosophy, mathematics, natural philosophy, astronomy and political economy, a curriculum far more modern than any to be found in England. Brougham first made his mark as a mathematician and natural philosopher, delighting Playfair with his independent inductive discovery of the binomial theorem and setting himself to master the fluxional calculus. In 1795, the year in which he completed the course, he sent off to the Royal Society the first of two papers describing experiments upon light and colour which, he believed, made small additions to Newtonian optics. In 1798 he became one of the youngest men ever to have a paper read before the society. It was entitled 'General Theorems, chiefly Porisms, in the Higher Geometry' and, although not so original as Brougham fancied, was, like the two optical essays, published in the society's transactions. Brougham regretted only that the secretary of the society required certain parts of the optical experiments to be omitted, on the ground that they belonged rather to the arts than the sciences.

This was very unfortunate; because, I having observed the effect of a small hole in the window-shutter of a darkened room, when a view is formed on white paper of the external objects, I had

7

suggested that if the view is formed, not on paper, but on ivory rubbed with nitrate of silver, the picture would become permanent; and I had suggested improvements in drawing, founded upon this fact. Now this is the origin of photography; and had the note containing the suggestion in 1795 appeared, in all probability it would have set others on the examination of the subject, and given up photography half a century earlier than we have had it.[14]

Brougham's interest in mathematics and the natural sciences never waned: without it it is inconceivable that he should have been so ardent a promoter, thirty years later, of the Mechanics' Institutes, or that he should have played a decisive part in the founding of both London University and the Useful Knowledge Society. Men have different ways of relaxing. Throughout his life Brougham's was to retire at the end of the parliamentary session to Brougham Hall and immerse himself in mathematical *divertissements*.[15] 'I heard from Brougham yesterday,' Lord Lyndhurst wrote in 1854. 'He has hurt his leg, and is repairing it, as he says, by the differential calculus.'[16] But neither his capacious mind nor his extraverted personality suited Brougham to a life of scholarly concentration upon a single subject. Loving Newton, he wished to emulate Voltaire. His mind was drawn towards public affairs and a public career.

* * *

For sons of the middle ranks of society the law, of the genteel professions the one least dominated by the gentry, provided the surest access to public eminence. In 1795 Brougham settled down to drudge work in the faculty of law, passing four or five hours a day in absorbing Voet and the *corpus juris* with a steadfastness that Francis Horner would never have expected 'if I had not known from observation of some years standing, that Brougham has a mind capable of any exertion that he chooses to put it to'.[17] With Horner, Francis Jeffrey, Cockburn and John Murray, Brougham formed a select coterie of students of uncommon intellectual activity, broad tastes and high purpose. Together they spent the years from 1795 to 1800 consciously preparing themselves for a life of high achievement and useful service. Self taught to a remarkable degree, they gladly imposed upon themselves an arduous schedule of reading and writing. The broad scope of their interests—literature, politics, history, philosophy, law, mathematics, chemistry and physics—is striking enough; more impressive is the patient deliberation with which they strove to bring order and system out of the chaos of their promiscuous reading. They translated the classics, they made notes of their impressions, they analysed styles, they practised writing in various manners. Above all, they sifted what they read and subjected everything to minute criticism, meeting daily to exchange views and test one another's opinions.

The fruits of Brougham's study were gloriously displayed in the several societies which were the ornament of the university. Brougham himself founded the Edinburgh Academy of Physics in 1796 and with Horner and John Thomson, later Professor of Pathology at the university, helped to establish the Chemical Society three or four years later. Above all, he, Horner and Jeffrey restored to the Speculative Society the high reputation which it had won in the first days of its existence as the leading literary society in the town. The 'Spec' was founded by a group of undergraduates in 1764 for improvement in literary composition and public speaking. By the time that Brougham was invited to join its select company, the membership had been raised from twenty to twenty-five. Fines were still imposed for late arrivals at, or absence from, its weekly meetings, but the original injunction against the introduction of political questions had been largely circumvented, although it was not formally rescinded until 1826. In his three years as an ordinary member of the Speculative Brougham read papers entitled 'The Effect on Scotland of the Union with England', 'The Balance of Power', 'The Indirect Influence of the People' and 'The Influence of National Opinion on External Relations'. The society's proceedings were just then conducted by a formidable array of future political luminaries— including three Englishmen, Robert and Charles Grant and Lord Henry Petty, the eldest son of the Marquis of Lansdowne—and Brougham quickly excited his colleagues' admiration by the breadth of learning and felicity of expression which adorned his papers and also by the energy and readiness which he exhibited in debate. 'There is perhaps,' Brougham wrote in his *Colonial Policy,* 'no principle more universal in its influence over the mind of man, or more conspicuous in its effects on his conduct, than the desire of being distinguished among his fellows.'[18] The society's debates became a contest between the old Tory guard and the Whiggish Young Turks who, led into battle by Brougham, turned the Speculative into a mock parliament. Cockburn, who joined the society in 1799, paid tribute to Brougham's ascendancy in its proceedings:

9

Brougham, in particular, whose constitutional keenness made him scent the future quarry, gave his whole soul to this preparatory scene, and often astonished us by the vigour with which, even to half a dozen lads, he could abandon himself to his subjects, and blaze as if he had been declaiming against Cicero in the forum.[19]

Years later, when Cockburn had learned to excoriate Brougham, it remained his opinion that it had not fallen to his lot to hear three better speeches than he heard as a young man at the Speculative—Jeffrey's on national character, Horner's on the immortality of the soul, and Brougham's on the power of Russia.[20] Brougham's oratorical successes did not come easily: they were the reward for diligent study of the ancient orators, especially Cicero and Demosthenes, and frequent visits to the Court of Session and the General Assembly to hear the most praised advocates and preachers of the day. Caring little for the merits of their arguments, he concentrated upon analysing the effects of their mannerisms and noting the differences between written and spoken rhetoric.

No constitution, however sturdy, could withstand without relief the demands which Brougham placed upon it. Brougham brought to his pleasures the same inexhaustible energy that he brought to his work. He was acknowledged the best of companions, childishly given to extravagant display and immoderately fond of high jinks, but withal affectionate and easy-going. Brougham's sharp tongue and outspoken manner clouded many of his friendships, but men's anger was seldom proof against the dissolving influence of his amiability. Calling on him one day in 1840, Henry Crabb Robinson found it strange that in his presence 'I forgot all my grounds of complaint against him'.[21] 'No human being probably has uttered a greater number of severe expressions of his fellow-creatures,' James Stephen wrote in 1838, 'and I believe at the same time there is hardly any man who has shown more constant and affectionate regard to the interior circle which enjoys his real and abiding good-will.'[22] It was so with Brougham from the beginning. A companion on one of the frequent walking trips in which Brougham delighted described the excursion as 'one of the most delicious jaunts that ever was jaunted'.[23] Only the return to Edinburgh brought an end to eight days of laughter. Excessive and continued drinking was so pervasive among the professional and upper classes of Scotland that Dean Ramsay devoted a chapter of his *Reminiscences* to the subject, and many a day's studious slogging ended in Brougham's taking the lead in 'very riotous and unseemly proceedings'.[24] After imbibing at Apollo's Club, he and his companions (an entirely different set from Horner and Jeffrey) would parade noisily about the streets of the New Town, wrenching brass knockers from the doors of houses and tearing out the handles of the bells. Brougham also indulged a young man's fancy for turns of extravagance and luxury, perfuming his rooms to suffocation when giving grand dinners and smoking hookahs while taking hot baths (one night he nearly drowned after falling asleep). Perhaps he was most famous for his habit of laying bets as to how he would arrive at a race-course—once in a wheelbarrow, once in a coffin, another time in a basket on a friend's shoulders. All this might be mere gossip, worth forgetting, were it not that Brougham's fondness for light-headed pleasures never left him, so that his political progress suffered from stupid men's failure to perceive that a penchant for low fun is the frequent and entirely compatible companion of the most enlarged intellect.

In February 1800, having returned with Charles Stuart from a six-month tour of the Western Isles and Scandinavia (during which he paid close attention to fossil remains and mineralogy), Brougham began to prepare for his bar examinations. 'I am slowly and heavily inhaling Scots law,' he wrote to John Allen, the Edinburgh doctor recently installed as librarian at Holland House, 'and mean to pass in Summer, as does Horner.'[25] Stuart, who described Brougham as 'the cleverest man he ever knew, but the least steady', was pleased to find him applying close, despite the fact that within a few weeks of their return Brougham was writing to him of his increasing discontent both with Edinburgh and 'this cursedest of cursed professions'.[26] Hateful the preparation might be, but Brougham was always thorough in what he undertook; although he never became a really sound lawyer, he had, in his student days, as even his critic, Lord Campbell, ac-knowledged, 'so far *legalised* his mind that ever after, *pro re nata*, he could understand, get up, and plausibly discuss any question of law which came in his way, however abstruse and however strange to him'.[27]

Brougham was called to the bar, or passed advocate as the Scotch phrase has it, in June 1800. He then made a strange decision. Eager to escape from the trammels of a legal career by making his way in politics, he nevertheless forswore the course customarily taken by newly-passed advocates who wished to gain notice by oratorical display, namely to be ordained a ruling elder in the Kirk Session and then returned as a lay member of the General Assembly. There indeed was a grand and serious forum for the Nestor of the Speculative. Instead, Brougham went immediately on the summer circuit. Equally surprising, in view of his need of money to achieve his object of establishing himself in London, was his decision to accept as clients only persons who were too poor to pay for legal representation. Brougham's first circuit has passed into the lore of the Scotch bar for his relentless baiting of Lord Eskgrove, the judge of assize. Eskgrove was a considerable lawyer, of sound and broad knowledge, who behaved like a buffoon on the bench, demeaning judicial proceedings with his coarse humour. He rambled at length and, wishing to be the sole star in his firmament, liked counsel to be passive. Accordingly he was enraged by the eloquence, energy, sarcasm, resource and all the 'discomposing qualities' of Brougham.[28]

We may need to look no further than Brougham's solicitude for the down-trodden to explain his readiness to accept a run of unpaid briefs. Or the explanation may be more mundane: the heavy Tory hand which lay upon Scotch public life made it difficult for a senior barrister of Whiggish taint, almost impossible for an untried advocate just out of law school, to get briefs at all. Scotch liberalism lay dormant at the turn of the century. Scotland's electorate was smaller than 3,000 and its forty-five members were, with rare exceptions, safely returned in the Tory interest by Pitt's right-hand man, Henry Dundas, the first Viscount Melville. Yet for all the surface calm, Scotch public life was exasperated by hatreds and the charities of private life were soured by political enmities. Although Jacobinism was dead and gone, fears engendered by the French Revolution revived the word as a term of abuse to be laid against anyone professing liberal opinions, however modest. Melville, as Cockburn wrote, was the Pharos of Scotland: who steered upon him was safe; who disregarded his light was wrecked.[29] By 1793, when the Terror was working its vengeance in France, even Adam had prudently abandoned his habit of enlivening the ancient texts with contemporary analogies. In 1796 Henry Erskine, the brightest ornament of the Scotch bar and the only one of the marked Edinburgh Whigs to be cordially received in private Tory circles, was removed from his position as Dean of the Faculty of Advocates after presiding at a public meeting to petition against the war with France. From that day until 1814 not a single public meeting was held at Edinburgh. Attendance at one would have been fatal, branding a person as a

Jacobin. Scotch society was oiled by patronage and the patronage was practically engrossed by the Tories. On Brougham, as on many of his contemporaries—juniors who came to the bar between 1790 and 1805—this pervasive Toryism worked its influence in several ways. It helped to direct his opinions down a liberal path, the law being, at any rate, the only profession in Scotland to preserve a Whig tradition. It quickened his desire to try his luck in London. And it left him idle, or, since he seldom was idle, it left him free to write.

When Brougham's first summer circuit was over, he returned to Edinburgh, articled himself to a Writer to the Signet (a solicitor who performs in the supreme courts in Scotland) and waited for employment at the Court of Session. He discovered, however, that his circuit exhibitions did not bring him business. Day after day was passed lounging in the company of Jeffrey and Horner in the Outer House, the famous chamber which gave off the courts. There Brougham and his friends railed at their enforced exclusion from the Inner House and dreamed of the day when judges like Braxfield should no longer sentence a man like Muir to long years of transportation by misrepresenting liberal hopes as seditious plotting. (Neither Jeffrey nor Samuel Romilly, who watched Muir's trial in 1793, ever forgot it or mentioned it without horror.) The Outer House, as Cockburn described it, was a scene full of lively interest.

It is filled, while the courts are sitting, by counsel, and all manner of men of the law, by the public, and by strangers, to whom the chief attraction is the contemplation of the learned crowd moving around them. For about two centuries this place has been the resort and the nursery of a greater variety of talent than any other place in the northern portion of our island. It has seen a larger number of distinguished men—it has been the scene of more discussed public principles, and projected public movements—it has cherished more friendships. When Jeffrey sat on its remoter benches, and paced its then uneven floor, so did Scott, and Cranstoun, and Thomas Thomson, and Horner, and Brougham, and Moncrieff, and many others who have since risen to eminence. These men had before them the figures and the reputations of Blair, and Erskine, and Charles Hope, and Clerk, and other seniors, on whom they then looked with envy and despair. But they had the library, and each other, and every enjoyment that society, and hope, and study, or gay idleness, could confer.[30]

Brougham was less enamoured of the place's charms. After six months he was writing to James Loch that Parliament House work was abominable and that he envied his cousin's ten-day excursion to London. A month later he was again bemoaning his fate. 'The Law is more and more horrid every day—and the Parlt. house is still more odious than the study part of Law. Nothing but absolute necessity can keep me at it—I mean the total want of a substitute for it.'[31] In April Brougham decided not to go the circuit again. 'I do not know what he does,' Andrew Clephane wrote to Loch, 'for when I call on him I find the Book on which he pretends to read always open at the same place. I rather think he sleeps a great deal. Whether it be that his Clerk, from whom he expected so much, has really no business to give him, or does not choose to employ him, is more than I can say, but true it is that he has never had but one Cause from him.'[32] Brougham's first year as an advocate was probably the most inactive of his life. Finding no outlet for his ambition, he fell into despondency. When James Loch announced that he was going to read for the English bar, Brougham expressed his astonishment. 'My opinion is that both professions are disagreeable and bad—but especially the Scots—as it keeps you quite out of all chances of rising in other ways—and is in itself extremely slow and uncertain.'[33]

* * *

How to rise in other ways? The question preoccupied Brougham's mind. The answer was to write a book. In the last months of 1801 he decided to publish a survey of the history of colonialism and its current status among the European powers. Brougham's chief contributions to the Speculative's debates has been concerned with foreign topics and on one occasion in 1799 he and Jeffrey had entertained the society with an animated discussion of colonial establishments. Moreover, his reading of the French *philosophes* had acquainted him with the physiocrats' attacks on mercantilist theory, while attendance at Dugald Stewart's lectures had exposed him to Adam Smith's epoch-making, but not yet conquering, political economy. Brougham did not, therefore, simply cast about for a marketable subject with which to gain the world's attention. But to write for no other reason than the love of writing was foreign to his imagination: in his view, by competing for the Academy's poetry prize at the age of seventeen and making the bold attempt at a tragedy a year later, Voltaire had betrayed how powerful was the sentiment of ambition in his nature.[34]

An Inquiry into the Colonial Policy of the European Powers, Brougham's master-piece as an author, was an astonishing virtuoso performance for a man still not twenty-five years of age. The book comprised two large octavo volumes of dense argument and copious information, yet within a year of beginning it—a year, too, by no means entirely devoted to it—Brougham was sending proof pages to his friends for comment. Single-mindedness of purpose kept him at his desk. For weeks on end he laboured from early morning until two or three o'clock the following morning, going out only to pay one visit to the Speculative, to attend the funeral of his great-uncle, Robertson, and to deal with trifling matters of legal business that came his way, enduring the toil 'as cheerfully as if it were all pleasure or exercise, and more cheerfully than if I had a wife to go to bed with at that late hour'.[35] Marriage was a grave mistake for a young man with worldly aspirations, Brougham pointed out in a jaunty letter to James Loch:

> I was sorry to see by the newspapers that a connection of your Uncle's had died at the Park. It struck me it might be the lady who they said two years ago you was going to be married to—in which case I heartily condole with you, because I imagine a shock of that kind must be very severe in the mean time—but in the main—tho' you may think it cruel, I rejoice at any event which keeps a man out of matrimony. I daily see men born for great things—give themselves up to little things—turn domestic and leave not only the pleasures of freedom, but its views and prospects.[36]

The *Colonial Policy* was published in the spring of 1803. Brougham professed not to be sanguine of its prospects and turned aside Loch's suggestion that he be on the spot on publication day.

> In fact, my expectations from it are very low; it will sell, I daresay, and I shall fulfill my end in writing it by getting a little good money to pay off some scores (for, *entre nous*, of the £700 which my foreign expedition cost me, only £600 are paid, and the two years after my return cost me above three). But as for any chance of preferment— why, Adam Smith was only made Commissioner of the Customs, and my utmost chance is a gauger [an excise man] or doorkeeper to the board—in the proportion of merits. Indeed, there is a very

prevalent idea (not always false) that authors can't act or speak. If my work ever attracts any notice, every one would take the odds that I never had been out of my closet and could fill no active post whatever, so that, I suspect, I might rather lose than gain by it in this point of view.[37]

Before the book was on the stalls, Brougham heard from Longman, the publishers, that orders were coming in and within a few weeks of its release he reported that it was selling vastly well in Scotland.

I rejoice to find that merchants, Americans and West Indians, and travellers praise the accuracy of my facts. My constant opinion of the success of the book, I am sure, will be realised. It will be slowly read and be a long while neglected, but in the end I think the matter it contains will keep it up. I find here nobody has the spirit to give any general opinion at all, for fear they may discover ignorance of Political Economy. Those who talk upon it are lavish in their praises of subordinate parts, and of the historical branch. Jeffrey, I am glad to find, is a convert to my general doctrine, and he is the only man I have taken the trouble to converse with about it—being in a state of unaccountable indifference and absurd confidence which I never expected would seize hold of me . . . I had a very civil sort of a letter from [Charles James] Fox, who promises candidly to examine my opinions, but says, if I differ from him on the Slave Trade—he is incorrigible there.[38]

Despite having sent a copy to Fox, the leader of the Whig opposition in the House of Commons, and one to Sir Joseph Banks, his father's old friend and president of the Royal Society, Brougham fretted that he had not done enough to push the book: 'I have given no preface, of course no dedication, and a very unintelligible introduction, at least, one which a reader who has not looked at the table of contents will not soon comprehend. My sections are perhaps too long for the *Vulgus*— the first two of the first book are stiff reading.'[39]

Stiff reading the *Colonial Policy* remains. Prolix and ill-organized, it ought to have been pruned to half its length. Nevertheless, the reviews were favourable—'certainly sufficient to satisfy a greedier man'[40]— and by the end of the year the Edinburgh quota of the first printing was all sold. Sir James Mackintosh, the member of parliament whose stout reply to Burke in the *Vindiciae Gallicae* had earned him an honoured place in the Whig intellectual pantheon, pronounced the

Colonial Policy to be the best discussion of political economy since Adam Smith's *Wealth of Nations,* published nearly thirty years before;[41] and Sydney Smith recommended it to Caroline Fox, sister of Lord Holland, as the work of a young man of considerable talents.[42] One way and another the publication brought Brougham to the attention of the leaders of the Whig party. On the other side of politics, too, it caught the eye of a man with whom Brougham was soon to work closely. William Wilberforce declared the book to be 'manifestly the *launcher,* and a capital one too, of a shrewd man of the world'.[43] Francis Horner, remembering that Lord Liverpool had written himself into notice by a puny, but seasonable, pamphlet on the rights of neutrals, expected the *Colonial Policy* to make valuable connections for Brougham and trembled at the prospect of an active scene's being opened up to him. Horner acknowledged that Brougham's information on political subjects was now immense and that his talents were equal to the most effective use and display of that knowledge. But, his ardour being so urgent, he might be wanting in prudence. 'That he would ultimately become a leading and predominant mind, I cannot doubt; but he might attempt to fix himself in that place too soon, before he had gone through what, I presume, is a necessary routine of subordination.'[44]

Brougham chose the subject of his launcher well. Great Britain was at war with her greatest colonial rival and the two questions which dominate the book—slavery and free trade—were matters intimately associated with the very existence of a large trading empire. Thanks to the efforts of Pitt and Wilberforce those questions had been brought into the full light of political discussion. Little progress had been made, however, and when Brougham's book was published Great Britain was still a slave-trading nation whose commerce rested on mercantilist and protectionist assumptions.

The *Colonial Policy* is a speculative treatise in the tradition of Scotch philosophical history: like Smith, Ferguson and Robertson, Brougham looked to history-writing to yield general truths useful to his own day. Men who came to the book without any knowledge of its author may well have concluded that a new Tory star was in the ascendant. Not only was the chief purpose of the first volume to defend colonial empires against the folly of the physiocrats, who were wrong to believe that colonial rivalries led to war (Brougham does not analyse the long Anglo-French wars of the 18th century), that colonies wasted revenues of the mother country, and that monopolies hindered trade, but Pitt's sinking fund was stoutly defended and his declaration of war against revolutionary France in 1793 vindicated. More surprisingly, Brougham asserted the necessity of putting down Toussaint l'Ouverture's slave rebellion in Santo Domingo, for reasons which he had earlier expressed privately to James Loch:

> I have of late been going through the West Indies, and am astonished to see our government delay one moment in assisting the French, or any state that chuses to quell the Hispaniola Negroes; it is like refusing to help your neighbour (with whom you have an old quarrel) when his house is on fire and to windward of your own; or can government be so very ignorant as not to know that a Colony (somewhat divided) would be a much less dangerous neighbour than an independent state, even putting the nature of the Negroes out of the question?[45]

Most of the second volume is a neutral appraisal of the great powers' policies in the Caribbean sugar islands. Only in the very last section did Brougham, forgetting that he was trying to be an historian, unleash an attack on both the slave trade and the institution of slavery itself. West Indian society was scarred by two overriding evils: the cruel treatment of the slaves and the ease with which the African trade kept up the planters' stock of them. The one evil fed the other. 'If a man cannot buy cattle, either from the dearth or want of the article, he will breed. Although this plan must immediately diminish his profits, he will also be careful of the lives and health of those beasts which he already possesses.'[46] Since the planters would not take the long road to stable prosperity, when wealth could be quickly gained at whatever future cost, the imperial legislature must act. It was cant to argue, as many conscience-stricken Englishmen did, that the mother country had no right to interfere in the domestic affairs of the colonies. Slow the progress might be—Brougham had no truck with those who would sport with immediate emancipation—but the day of reckoning was not far off and it was the duty of the government, by wise and liberal legislation, to look forward to it.

> The avarice of Europeans may for yet a few generations wallow in the blood-stained spoils of African labour; until, in the fulness of time, the great event which has for ages been slowly preparing,

shall be accomplished; and the African warriors, gradually civilized in the fruitful islands of America, shall obtain quiet, and, may we not add, rightful possession of those plains which have been cultivated by the toils and sufferings of their fathers.[47]

All the while that Brougham, with resolute speed, was writing the *Colonial Policy*, he was also caught up in the excitement of launching the *Edinburgh Review*, a signal event which ended long years of periodical stagnation, both in Scotland and England, and which heralded the rise of that most characteristic Victorian institution, the serious quarterly review. The *Edinburgh* was the child of that set of young lawyers and free-thinkers of whom the chiefs were Jeffrey, Horner and Brougham. For ten years they had been daily engaged—at Edinburgh's societies, at oyster cellars, at their own houses, at the Outer House—in the discussion of politics and literature, treating all manner of things, Lady Holland learned from Sydney Smith, 'with a freedom impossible in larger societies, and with a candour which is only to be found where men fight for truth and not for victory'.[48] Smith, who had enlivened their gatherings with his flippant wit since his arrival in Edinburgh as tutor to Michael Hicks Beach in 1798, first suggested the idea of starting a new review. But the moving spirit was Jeffrey, who remained its editor from the publication of the third number in 1803 until 1829. Smith, who made endless sport of the Scot's inability to take a joke without a surgical operation, hid his seriousness behind a mask of mocking word-play, and Brougham mixed high purpose, quick temper, horse-play and consuming ambition in a way disquieting even to his close friends; Horner (whom Smith nicknamed 'the Knight of the Shaggy Eye-brows') and Jeffrey were formed from a different mould—solemn, proud, painstaking and cautious. What united the four was a common passion to learn and a common resolve to inform.

No critical journal had been published in Scotland since the first *Edinburgh Review* had folded after only two issues in January 1757. Existing reviews, in England as well as Scotland, restricted themselves to short, lifeless pieces which were little more than booksellers' puffs. None of them aspired to air public measures, mark the advance of science or bring into play enlarged views of literature and literary criticism. An untilled field therefore awaited cultivation. How better for young men of elastic minds and combative spirit to fill the hours of enforced idleness than to broadcast the seeds of their private enlightenment, to bring their animated discussions into the open, thereby reviving the habit of public polemic and offering a challenge to the complacency of Scotch Toryism?

Brougham's co-operation was essential to the success of the new journal. Jeffrey, five years older than Brougham, had the sweetness of temper and the patience to supervise the undertaking and his range of reading in the higher branches of literature was matched by an exquisite taste and a sure judgement. He had, moreover, some experience of reviewing. But the *Edinburgh* was intended to be more than a literary magazine. Political economy, natural philosophy and mathematics were to come within its broad compass and, while Horner commanded political economy as much as Brougham, in scientific matters Brougham was indispensable. When, early in March 1802, he was told of the scheme that Smith, Jeffrey and Horner were hatching, he entered into it warmly. It was settled that the first number should appear in June; it was not ready until October and one cause of the delay was Brougham.

Less than a month after the founding meeting in March, Jeffrey wrote complaining to Horner that Brougham, who had originally agreed to write two articles for the first number, was talking of having no connection with the review. In his memoirs Brougham explained that he was reluctant to take part in the venture until both Jeffrey was formally given sole charge of it and it was established with the publishers that the review was to be quite independent of the booksellers. Sydney Smith, in an informal way, had taken the job of editing the first number and it was natural that Brougham should place less confidence in him than in Jeffrey. No doubt, too, he was genuinely concerned that no external restraint should be placed upon the reviewers' freedom. But he may also have been hurt, not only by being brought late into the discussions about the prospective review, but also by being excluded from the editorial management of it. Smith had persuaded Jeffrey and Horner that Brougham was too 'violent and unmanageable' to be given any direct influence over the review.[49] He was relegated to the role of prince among the mere contributors. By September Horner was able to write to John Allen, then in Paris, that 'Brougham is now an efficient and zealous member of the party';[50] indeed, when promised articles failed to arrive, Brougham came to the rescue by contributing six articles to the opening number—three on various 'Travels', one on the sugar colonies, one on optics and one on Hutton's theory of uniformitarianism in geology. He continued to chafe at his secondary role, however, and in January 1803 he vented his spleen on James Loch.

> My first *tome* [*Colonial Policy*] was nearly ready when that d——d, blasted, b——g, brutal *Review* stopped it for a whole calendar month . . . I had to contribute (Oh! Nefas) a hundred pages of print, tho' I am not one of the editors—they gave their tens and twenties and I had literally to *write*, I may say, the whole. And then, to crown all, a supply came from an unexpected quarter and I had only 70 pages printed.[51]

Brougham fully earned Jeffrey's praise as 'the surest and most voluminous of men'.[52] His contribution to the second number consisted of four articles on mathematical subjects and one on the politics of European cabinets. Eight articles, a prodigious output in only three months, followed in the third number, published in the spring of 1803. By then Brougham's patience had nearly run its course. In May rumours reached Horner that he was projecting a rival publication. The rumours were groundless, but matters came to a head in the last week of June, when Brougham, in a letter which he himself called 'infernally long', unburdened himself to Horner. Smith was the object of his attack: he knew plainly from what 'revd. quarter' the prejudices against him flowed, a quarter, too, to which the review was 'indebted for nothing but its worst parts'. Smith was entrusted with authority while he, Brougham, was 'only consulted when so many pp. were required within a certain No. of hours and then *worked out* with very little ceremony'. Smith must be made clearly to understand that Brougham was to have as much of the management as if he had been one of the original set, or he would cease to contribute.[53] Horner, who might have known his man better, advised Brougham not to exert himself to be a mere 'headman of a village'. Brougham's reply was a terse statement of the ruling motive of his career: 'You are wrong; always be a headman of your own village—unless you are thereby prevented from getting to the head of a larger town or city.'[54]

Brougham was certain of victory. He was the review's chief contributor, unrivalled even by Jeffrey in the speed and facility with which he could get up an article. 'I am in the greatest distress for MSS.,' Jeffrey wrote to Loch in 1804, 'and if it were not for my reliance on Brougham, I should have no help of salvation.'[55] Jeffrey capitulated, not only bringing Brougham into full participation in the running of the review, but, at Brougham's insistence, removing

Smith from control of the scientific department and placing John Allen in charge of it. From that moment Brougham's will dominated the *Edinburgh*. 'I am but a feudal monarch at best,' Jeffrey wrote a few years later to Horner, 'and my throne is overshadowed by the presumptuous crests of my nobles.'[56] He might better have said 'noble', for it was no secret that 'the Sieur Brougham', as Smith came to call him, was the mightiest of Jeffrey's subjects. When, in 1811, Brougham was preparing to review a publication adverse to the reputation of Charles James Fox, he sent a copy of it to Grey, inviting the Whig leader's remarks. 'It is too delicate to trust even Jeffrey with, so I intend to give him general reasons for begging he will leave it wholly in my hands. And I know he will as a matter of course.'[57]

The first number of the *Edinburgh* sounded with the strident force of a trumpet-blast, and, however guardedly Jeffrey and the others might avow that their object was simply their own amusement and improvement, they could not but be gratified by the extraordinary success which attended the review from the beginning. Both the substance and the manner of its articles produced a startling effect. The seriousness of its tone, the freedom of its opinions, the very length of its articles, and, most originally, the awesome authority and destructive cleverness with which it dared to expose cant, dulness and inaccuracy effected a revolution in periodical publishing.

Brougham and Sydney Smith were the principal perpetrators of the review's spicy, intrepid style. When, years later, Harriet Martineau chastised Smith for having broken hearts and discouraged talent by the cruelty of the review's notices, he gave her an unrepentant reply.

> We *were* savage. I remember how Brougham and I sat trying one night how we could exasperate our cruelty to the utmost. We had got hold of a poor nervous little vegetarian, who had just put out a poor silly little book; and when we had done our review of it, we sat trying to find one more chink, one more crevice, through which we might drop in one more drop of verjuice, to eat into his bones.[58]

A journal written in this audacious spirit, removing as it did the mask from hypocrisy and treating established institutions and ideas, not with hostility, but with marked impartiality and scepticism, was bound to excite alarm and jealousy in the ruling classes. The *Edinburgh* was assailed in Canning's *Anti-Jacobin* and Horner recorded in his journal that 'the severity, in some of the papers it may be called scurrility, has given general dissatisfaction'.[59] Even Samuel Romilly, the radical Whig member of parliament and tireless campaigner for the liberalizing of the criminal law, had his gentle spirit disturbed by the glee with which the reviewers pinioned their victims: 'The Editors seem to value themselves principally upon their severity, and they have reviewed some works, seemingly with no other object than to show what their powers in this particular line of criticism are.'[60] Yet the sharp tone of the review served to bring into wider notice the rare excellence of its substance. At the end of its first year in circulation, Sydney Smith had the pleasure of informing Jeffrey 'that it is the universal opinion of all the cleverest men I have met with here, that our Review is uncommonly well done, and it is perhaps the first in Europe'.[61]

* * *

Among the motives which had given rise to the *Edinburgh* Jeffrey cited 'some personal, and some national, vanity'.[62] Yet by the end of 1803 the set in which Brougham had grown to manhood was breaking up, as one after the other nearly every one of its members except Jeffrey made his progress to London. It may seem strange that men so proud of their Scotch inheritance and so eager to reform Scotch institutions should flee in such numbers from the undoubted charms of Edinburgh. Romilly, enchanted by Edinburgh's natural beauty, judged it to be the finest town imaginable, but for its climate, in which to pass one's life.[63] Sydney Smith, who never lost the memory of happy days spent amid odious smells, barbarous sounds, bad suppers and excellent hearts, found the romantic grandeur of its ancient buildings and the regularity of its modern ones 'uncommonly beautiful'.

> I left Edinburgh with great heaviness of heart: I knew what I was leaving, and was ignorant to what I was going. My good fortune will be very great, if I should ever again fall into the society of so many liberal, correct and instructed men, and live with them on such terms of friendship as I have done . . . at Edinburgh.[64]

Smith was an English visitor to Edinburgh and an Anglican clergyman. When his tutorship was up, it was entirely natural that he should take a living in England. The rest of the happy band—Murray, Allen, Horner, Brougham and most of the lesser lights—left by their own choice.

Edinburgh at the turn of the century was not a mere provincial capital. It was a metropolitan city with a European reputation, lent distinction by its university, its supreme court of justice and the annual convocation of the Scotch Church. To a rare degree men of letters and the law mingled on cordial terms with the representatives of the higher gentry. Pride in its eminent men and distance from London (even after Palmer's accelerated coach services in the 1780s the journey took sixty hours) had enabled Edinburgh to resist the gravitational pull of London. Yet even as the city was passing through its golden age, the men who were contributing to its lustre, and who were conscious of it, knew also the melancholy truth that the splendour was about to fade. Hardly had Burns died than his glory, as Cockburn lamented, began to contract, because the sphere of the Scotch language and the course of Scotch feelings and ideas were rapidly being abridged.[65] Cockburn remembered his school days, when an English boy at the High School was a strange monster to be mocked. But by the beginning of the 19th century the habit of reading English books and listening to English discourse was spreading, and although the Scotch dialect remained ingrained in the common people, it receded with great speed among the gentry. Brougham never quite lost his Caledonian burr, but before he left Edinburgh it had become the fashion for Scotch boys of the educated classes to eradicate their native accent in order to make their way in the world. Francis Horner was sent to study with the Reverend John Hewlett in Middlesex for two years, and Hewlett was pleased to inform his father, just before Horner returned to Edinburgh to read for the Scotch bar, that 'the principal object for which your son came to England has been accomplished'. He had 'got rid of the Scotch accent and pronunciation, and acquired the English so completely as not to be distinguished from a native'.[66] Even Cockburn was unable to resist the Anglicizing tide. In 1823 he helped to found the Edinburgh Academy in the New Town, and since its purpose was to train Scotch boys to compete with English ones for posts in the empire, there was to be 'a Master for English, who shall have a pure English accent'.[67]

Samuel Johnson's barb that 'the noblest prospect that a Scotchman ever sees is the high road that leads to London' wounded Scotch vanity because it was true. Especially was it true of the law. The legal profession in Scotland did not offer the fortunes to be made on the English circuits, nor the practicable seat in the House of Commons, nor the lofty peaks of the English judiciary. The Scotch judiciary had no lord chancellor, no Master of the Rolls, no Chief Justice. The head of the Scotch hierarchy was the lord advocate for Scotland, a member of the imperial government. The highest local eminence to which a Scotch lawyer could aspire was the Deanship of the Faculty of Advocates. Alexander Wedderburn, Pitt's lord chancellor after 1793, Thomas Erskine, lord chancellor in the Whig ministry of 1806–07, and John Campbell, a year younger than Brougham and made lord chancellor in 1859, all abandoned the Scotch bar where they were trained in order to catch at the prizes which an English career offered.

From the moment that Brougham passed advocate in 1800 he tormented himself and his friends with his anxiety to escape from Edinburgh and the Scotch bar. Neither the labours devoted to the *Colonial Policy* nor the establishment of the *Edinburgh Review* brought him peace of mind. In the late summer of 1802, when both enterprises were fully occupying him, he worked himself into a frenzy of discontent.

I am absolutely ashamed [he wrote to Loch on 20 August] and (for the first time in my life) uneasy at sitting down to what used always to be the greatest pleasure—writing to you. You must have thought my long silence strange indeed; but the fact is, I have been in many respects so very uncomfortable, that I knew anything I might scrawl must he extremely uninteresting, and besides, I believe that laziness had in some degree taken possession of me, which generally attends a mind ill at ease . . . I am either tossed about and harassed by a thousand perplexities, or sink into a deceitful and dangerous calm. In short, I am completely discontented, as I have long been, with all the prospects in this place, and I much fear that I shall find it impossible to make the exchange I so much desire—what that change should be, is another question. The English bar is in a very great degree tedious, and, to say the least of it, somewhat uncertain. I look forward with no small horror to five years' dull, unvaried drudgery, which must be undergone to obtain the privilege of drudging still harder, among a set of disagreeable people of brutal manners and confined talents; any opening abroad seems a matter of extreme difficulty at present, at least to one who has no sort of interest. The army is indeed a resource, but it is the last, and only for incurables; besides I have been too long of thinking of it.

For the same reason the East Indies seems out of the question;

and any civil appointment as secretaryships, etc., in the West Indies is, I suppose, as difficult to be procured as one in Europe. As to places at home, I don't know whether the present order of Ministers employ commis, etc., but if they do, to me it won't much signify; so that, altogether willing as I am to labour, I see no change of employment. Such and so melancholy are all my prospects. I leave you to judge whether study, to which I constantly fly for occupation, can be of any great relief. It is, however, cheaper than dissipation, and is attended with some improvements which may enable one to profit by the chapter of accidents; but in that I don't much confide.[68]

The colonial and diplomatic services were, in John Bright's famous phrase, gigantic systems of outdoor relief for the sons of the aristocracy and Brougham had, as he said, 'no sort of interest'. Applications to Lord Hawkesbury, foreign secretary in Addington's government, and Sir Joseph Banks failed to turn up anything in the diplomatic line, and the year 1803 opened with Brougham still sulking: 'I know I shall rise near the top in the end, but as for the meantime I shall be contented if I do not sink to the muddy Bottom of Scots Law.'[69]

The rest of the year was spent in finding out from Horner and Loch how much it cost to live in London, what the expenses of chambers were, and what opportunities the capital provided for entertainment—'except dissipation and publick places'. The opposition of his father, who would have to foot the bill if Brougham removed to London to read for the English bar, had also to be overcome. Brougham complained that his father was 'the damndest lazy man to deal with in the way of business', going generally upon the maxim that everything might as well be done tomorrow as today. 'The very reverse is always my principle, so that matters are often at a dead stop between us.'[70] The real trouble was that his father, with a large family to consider, was entirely dependent on the few hundred pounds of income which his Westmorland estate yielded annually, but at last his resistance was broken and on 14 November 1803 Brougham's name was entered at Lincoln's Inn. Jeffrey, who alone of his contemporaries could not imagine living anywhere but Edinburgh, was made forlorn by the dissolution of the intimate society to which he had for ten years acted as mentor, and consoled himself with believing that the emigrants had all made a mistake: 'we have here capabilities of happiness that will not so easily be found anywhere else'.[71] 'I despair,' he wrote to John Allen at the beginning of 1804, 'of finding any substitute for those quiet and confidential parties in which we used to mingle, and play the fool together.'[72]

Jeffrey's cup of happiness wanted nothing more than the pleasures of private study and the confidences of private friendship to fill it. His cautious, pessimistic nature shrank from taking the high risk. Brougham's ambitions soared too high to be contained within the circle of domestic or fraternal affections. Brimming with self-confidence, he set out, where his reputation had gone before, on the road to London.

2

Political Apprenticeship

Brougham's mother, the niece of William Robertson, was Scotch and according to Cockburn Brougham's upbringing 'worked Scotland indelibly into his bones'.[1] Cockburn, therefore, never forgave him for abandoning his interest in Scotch affairs. Lord Campbell, too, chastised him for forgetting that he owed to Edinburgh the education which enabled him to surpass the senior wranglers and double-classmen of Oxford and Cambridge.[2] There was another way of looking at the matter. In an essay published in *The Spirit of the Age*, Hazlitt remarked that Brougham, born in Edinburgh of an English father, was a Scot only by adoption. His real roots lay in Westmorland. However much Brougham may have looked upon himself as Scotch, one thing is certain. He was inhibited by no consciousness of provincial inferiority. From the moment that he took up residence in London in January 1804 he set about insinuating himself into the capital's society.

The metropolis did not bewilder Brougham by its size; nor did its novelty arouse his apprehensions. Much as he delighted in country rambles, he had formed thoroughly urban tastes. Soon after taking up lodgings in the West End, he wrote to Charles Stuart to chide him for remaining in the rural isolation of Richmond Lodge.

> I never made any way in the pursuits of a man, I mean intense study, without an abandonment of all rural propensities, to which, I fancy, I had a more early and more strong predilection than even you.
>
> Study—labour of the mind—carried to such an excess as to become labour of the body also. This is the business of every man under forty; this is the sweetest of all works; this is the most light of all burthens; the most invaluable of all blessings. It is a good independent of all the ills of life, supremely and principally our own, subject to no fates, times, or seasons, pleasant in itself, and quickly and surely returning a plenteous harvest.

Beware of the new and senseless slang which is creeping in; don't undervalue a man because he is well informed and laborious minded; don't say 'he is a coarse headed fellow', 'has no fineness of intellect' etc. etc. etc. All this is founded on a truth—but it is of most dangerous application and may be twisted into an apology for all manner of idleness and lasciviousness and waywardness of taste.[3]

Brougham's broad humour and liberal sympathies saved him from becoming a pedant or a prig, but scorn of idleness, love of learning and suspicion of country life were ill-suited to an easy familiarity with the shire-happy gentlemen who formed the backbone of both the Whig and the Tory parties. A few years after settling in London Brougham joined a shooting-party in Norfolk, with untoward results. He set fire to the powder horn, singed his eyelashes, and then provoked the Duke of Argyll and Lord Ponsonby to loud laughter by his endeavour to explain the mishap on philosophical principles. John Ward, who told the tale, drew the moral that 'we Edinburgh-bred gentlemen ought not to meddle with field sports'.[4]

Brougham's ostensible purpose in settling in London was to read for the English bar; his real purpose was different, and from the very outset he was 'wholly absorbed in political schemes, with the view of bringing himself into action'.[5] Somewhat surprisingly, perhaps, he was first drawn into the Evangelical, largely Tory, circle of the 'Clapham Sect' Saints. Research for his *Colonial Policy* had made him an expert enemy of slavery in the West Indies and the Scotch clergy, as Thomas Babington remarked in 1792, were abolitionists almost to a man.[6] By temperament, however, Brougham was worlds removed from the Saints, whose every action was impelled by a sense of Christian mission. Brougham was a believer all his life, but his belief rested on his inability to discover an intellectual ground for unbelief. There is no reason to suppose that faith ever stirred his emotions or directed his mind. Horner was made gleeful by the thought of his joining in family worship at the home of James Stephen. 'Would not you have given all your hopes of heaven (not a great price on your part),' he wrote to Jeffrey, 'for a sight of Brougham upon his knees?'[7] On the other hand, Brougham felt no impulse to ridicule another man's religious convictions.

I think he who attacks Christianity [he wrote to Leigh Hunt in 1812] does a great & serious injury to mankind. I say so independent of all faith or reasonable belief in that system—and I hold that a pure & philosophical Deist may in perfect consistency reprobate & deeply lament whatever tends to vilify Christianity in the eyes of the world. First, because so long as the bulk of mankind believe it, he who *laughs & rails* at it is guilty of the same offence with him who should laugh & rail at our near relatives—and expose them to *us*, who see them with the blindness of affection. But next, because I am firmly convinced that the real good operated by that religion is a thousandfold greater than its abuses have worked, and lastly because it really approaches as near to pure theism as the bulk of men can go, in their present state of information.[8]

Brougham was accustomed to hear Edinburgh sceptics scoff at the doctrines of Christianity; William Wilberforce's saintly character, adduced by some as an argument for Christianity, he put down to all that was good and amiable in the man despite his creed. Yet, when he met Wilberforce's hard-headed colleagues, Henry Thornton and Zachary Macaulay, and found them to be warmed by the glow of Christian zeal, 'it did strike him there must surely be more in it than the Edinburgh wits dreamed of'.[9] Wilberforce struck the right note when, after an Abolition Committee dinner in July 1804, he described Brougham as 'very unassuming, animated, and apparently well inclined to religion'.[10]

Neither the uncongenial religious fervour nor the Toryism of the Saints dampened Brougham's enthusiasm to co-operate with them in the campaign to abolish the slave trade. The circumstances in which he first met Wilberforce are not known. His arrival in London coincided with the revival of the Abolition Committee's efforts, stifled since 1797, to get an anti-slave trade bill through the houses of parliament. In February 1804 Wilberforce had begun work on a tract to be circulated among members of parliament before the new measure should be brought forward. But before he had completed it, Brougham had been enlisted by the Abolition Committee and the job of writing the pamphlet was handed over to him. It was published as *A Concise Statement of the Question regarding the Abolition of the Slave Trade* and distributed to members before the first reading of Wilberforce's bill on 30 May. The pamphlet was so cogent a summary of the abolitionist argument that Pitt flourished it in his hand while speaking in the debate. Three years later Brougham wrote to John Allen that 'it would probably be thought very nearly allied to vanity, or fanaticism, if I were to express any portion of the excessive pride and exultation which I feel when I recollect that two several motions were made by the enemies of the Abolition (G Rose & Dent) for delaying the debate in consequence of the impression which this same pamphlet produced'.[11] Brougham took part, with Wilberforce, Thornton, James Stephen and Zachary Macaulay, in drafting the bill and during its passage through the Commons dined daily with the inner circle of the Saints. The bill was accepted by the Commons, but was thrown out in the Lords.

Early in August Brougham set out, disguised as an American with an American passport, on a hazardous tour of war-torn Holland, Germany and Italy. He was seized by the desire to catch a glimpse of Napoleon, and after one or two perilous escapades he managed to land sight of him at a village near Cologne. But the chief object of the tour was to inquire into the state of the abolition question in Holland, or, as Wilberforce somewhat grandly put it, to enlighten the minds of the good people of Holland.[12] A powerful anti-slavery movement existed in Holland and Brougham was gratified to discover that his views were already well known, thanks to the Dutch translation of the *Colonial Policy* and his pamphlet. Armed with letters of introduction from Lord Harrowby, secretary of state in Pitt's government, he was able to have long conversations with government ministers and leading abolitionists. He reported to Wilberforce that the Dutch government, which had suspended its slave trade for the duration of the war, was willing to progress to immediate and permanent abolition in return for a pledge from the English government that the Dutch colonies, chiefly Guiana, would be restored to Holland at the end of the war. Wilberforce, accustomed by years of struggle to disappointment, found Brougham's sanguine view of the prospects for a speedy abolition somewhat innocent. Pitt was, indeed, unwilling to give the Dutch the pledge which they required, but Wilberforce told Harrowby that Brougham's reports from Holland did him credit, that he was 'a man of great energy, who has his wits about him, and good wits too', and that, if negotiations with the Dutch were to be started, Brougham was the fittest man to conduct them.[13]

Brougham was in Holland for only a few weeks. The remainder of the year was passed in Italy, seeing the sights and sending reviews for the *Edinburgh* to Jeffrey. In one forty-eight-hour period in Venice, he wrote an article on the armies of Europe (without the aid of his library), spent one night at the theatre and devoted a morning to the inspection of St Mark's and the Ducal Palace.[14] 'I know,' Wilberforce once wrote to him, 'that you never plead *alibis*, if I may so express it, or conceive it is any reason why you may not do a twentieth thing that you already have nineteen others on your hands.'[15]

When Brougham returned from the continent at the beginning of 1805, London society was entirely taken up with the Melville scandal. Lord Melville, Pitt's wire-puller in Scotland, had, during his tenure of the admiralty, either by connivance or neglect allowed his paymaster to invest admiralty funds in private speculations. No money was lost to the country and Melville survived a vote to impeach him in the House of Commons. Nevertheless, his career had suffered a fatal blow and he never held public office again. Brougham believed that the failure to impeach him was a grave error. The public had incurred risk. Moreover, even if money had been gained for the government, the public would still have been the loser, since the very success of the enterprise would make it an attractive precedent. Brougham shed no tears for Melville, for years the scourge of Scotch liberals: dirty fingers would not do in England.

> But those who love Dundas [Melville] with *the pure affection which I bear him*, must feel a mixed sensation—a little sorrow for the country, and an infinite satisfaction for the fate of the man. I feel truly savage upon the whole affair, and only lament most sincerely, as every admirer of Pitt must do, that he has been so long coupled with such a nasty dog.[16]

The reference to Pitt is not altogether curious. It is true that on a short visit to London in 1798 Brougham had denounced the Foxite secession from parliament with the ardour of a true Whig appalled at any relaxation of the opposition to Pitt's government: 'I begin to fear for the cause. God grant that we may not live and die under the present system of things—but I am much afraid.'[17] But undergraduate enthusiasms are often short-lived and in his first twelve months away from Edinburgh Brougham had moved chiefly in Tory circles. At the beginning of 1805 he was not certain in which direction his political future lay. Like Disraeli in the 1830s he was eager, first of all, simply to get into parliament. Nor should it be supposed that it was utter apostasy for a radical to form a Tory attachment. The early 19th-century party structure did not resolve itself into a simple opposition of liberal Whigs against reactionary Tories. Pitt had made his early reputation as a reformer and on two questions at least in which

Brougham had instructed himself—slavery and free trade—there was no reason to expect more from the Whigs than the Tories. Brougham had praised Pitt in his *Colonial Policy*. More recently he had defended his sinking fund in an article in the *Edinburgh* which subjected an economic treatise by Lord Lauderdale, the friend of Grey and Holland and the unofficial leader of the Scotch Whigs, to severe criticism. Like all contributions to the *Edinburgh*, the article was anonymous, but everyone knew Brougham was the author and it dismayed the Whig leaders. No doubt Lauderdale was out of his depth in political economy, yet it is hardly surprising that some readers, like Creevey's radical friend, Dr Currie, should see more than scholarly disagreement in Brougham's strictures. Currie told Creevey that Brougham, having been taken up by Wilberforce, was ingratiating himself with the Tories. 'He is a notorious prostitute, and is setting himself up for sale. It seems Ld. Lauderdale offended him by refusing to be introduced to him, but it is to pay court to Pitt, depend on it, that he writes as he does . . . You may mention this to Mr. Grey.'[18]

Horner was perplexed by the game that Brougham was playing, since he could not believe that between Brougham and the Saints there could be any real community of sentiment.[19] Henry Thornton, after only a few months' acquaintance with Brougham, reached the same conclusion and advised Wilberforce to be wary of his protégé. 'It is my clear and deliberate opinion, that Brougham tho' clever and in some respects useful to our cause and also to the Government is so rash, so unreasonable in his expectations and above all has such accommodating principles that he is neither a very pleasant, a very safe, nor a very creditable instrument.'[20] Wilberforce put a higher estimate on his value. He knew that Brougham's influence made the *Edinburgh* an abolitionist journal. It was Brougham who got Wilberforce to write a slashing piece on the subject for the October number of 1804. He himself wrote another for the July number of 1805 and thereafter scarcely an issue appeared without some reference to the matter. Brougham may also have persuaded Wilberforce that he was more of a Tory than he was. Wilberforce sent copies of Brougham's Lauderdale article to Pitt, and when, in the autumn of 1805, he recommended him for a diplomatic post, he told Pitt that Brougham was not only a young man of 'uncommon talents and address', but also 'so long the advocate for your Government in Edinburgh'.[21]

Brougham flirted with Toryism, or at least with the Tories, for some time. As late as May 1806, he applied, through Wilberforce, to the great Tory boroughmonger in the north, Lord Lowther, for the nomination to one of the Lowther family's seats, then vacant, in Westmorland. Had Lowther shown any interest in the proposal, Brougham might have begun his parliamentary career as a Tory. Perhaps, as it has been suggested,[22] it was accident that he cast his lot with the Whigs. Yet it is difficult to imagine that Brougham, who had grown up resentful of the Tory hegemony in Scotland and whose Edinburgh associates had almost all been of a liberal disposition, would have found a comfortable, or permanent, home in the Tory party. Pitt, despite Wilberforce's hints, did not bother to make his acquaintance. John Wilson Croker, the high Tory member of parliament and contributor to the *Edinburgh*'s great rival, the *Quarterly Review*, put the matter in its true light in a letter to Brougham in 1839.

There are two great antagonistic principles at the root of all government—stability and experiment. The former is Tory, and the latter Whig; and the human mind divides itself into these classes as naturally and as inconsiderately, as to personal objects, as it does into indolence and activity, obstinacy and indecision, temerity and versatility . . . I don't believe that any circumstances could have made you a Tory or me a Whig. We might very easily have been thrown into those parties. You might have attached yourself to Pitt, and I might have been a humble follower of Fox, but amongst our more homogeneous associates, we should have been considered as 'crotchety, troublesome fellows', always hankering after the opposite doctrine.[23]

* * *

Throughout 1805 and 1806, all the while that Brougham was on the look-out for a Tory appointment or a Tory parliamentary nomination, he was assiduously cultivating Whig friendships. His fame as an *Edinburgh* reviewer and his intimacy with Horner, Smith and John Allen meant that he did not want for introductions. Nor did he shrink, with Horner's diffidence, from forming a connection with the Whig aristocracy. Like Jeffrey, he had associated sufficiently with men of rank and pretension to feel himself their equal 'in everything intrinsic and material'.[24] If anything, he suffered from an heroic self-confidence. Smith, writing to Jeffrey early in 1805, remarked that Horner, who in a few years in London had won golden opinions for his upright and shining talents, verified his observation that the world did not so much dislike originality, liberality and independence as the insolent arrogance which usually accompanied them. 'Now Horner pleases the best judges, and does not offend the worst. He will entirely excell [sic] Brougham.'[25]

Brougham was an intellectual Pooh-Bah, possessed, in John Morley's cruel phrase, of an 'encyclopaedic ignorance'.[26] He liked to hold the centre of the stage and he did not always wear his learning like a pocket-watch. On one occasion, when he was lord chancellor, he dined in the company of Lord Grey and Lord Sefton at the house of the brewer, Fowell Buxton. The guests were given a tour of the brewery, where Buxton's employees were on hand to explain its workings. Brougham, however, took the business into his own hands and explained everything—the mode of brewing, the operation of the machinery, right down to the feeding of the cart-horses. At the British Museum, too, he once took over from the curator who was guiding him through the mineral collection 'and dashed off with as much ease and familiarity as if he had been a Buckland or a Cuvier'.[27] Brougham never knew when to keep quiet, and however severely rebuffed, he was never bowed. No wonder Macaulay described him as 'a kind of semi-Solomon' who half knew everything from the cedar to the hyssop.[28]

Many years later, when Brougham was estranged from the Whigs and was doing all he could to blacken their reputation in the public prints, he wrote that Horne Tooke, a conscientious radical and eminent economist whom the Whigs should have nursed, was kept at a distance from them by his unwillingness to measure his importance by the place he held in the estimation of some powerful lord.[29] Nor did Brougham stoop, but by ease of manner, animated conversation and frank good nature conquered. In an age when political alliances were contracted in the salons of the great houses, his gregariousness, grating to the fastidious, endeared him to the pleasure-seekers who made the nightly round of dinners. With Wilberforce, he was one of the last, before the fashion went out in England, to sing after dinner. His mimicry was so accurate that Kemble declared it would have made him his fortune to have got him on the stage for a season.[30] And Viscountess Eversley, the daughter of Samuel Whitbread, recalled a breakfast at which he held a group of young ladies spellbound by a lecture on the habits of bees 'which he made as charming as a fairy-tale'.[31]

Brougham was elected to Brooks's, the Whig club, and to the 'King of Clubs', a literary dining club of almost exclusively Whig member-ship; he was introduced to Lady Spencer's soirées, much attended for the brilliant conversation of the hostess and of political service to Brougham, since Lord Spencer was a Grenvillite who was to serve in the Talents ministry of 1806–07; and soon after the Hollands returned from a continental tour in the spring of 1805, his name appeared for the first time in the Holland House dinner books. Holland House, described by Macaulay as 'that venerable chamber, in which all the antique gravity of a college library was so singularly blended with all that female grace and wit could devise to embellish a drawing-room', was just then entering into that splendour which made it, for a generation, the first house in Europe. It gained its reputation by the constant, almost servile, attendance of men like Brougham. Barred from most of the great houses by reason of her divorce from her first husband, Lady Holland took her revenge by drawing the most eminent wits and poets to her dinner table. Over her guests Lady Holland exercised a capricious tyranny; and as many as made their way to Kensington to suffer her quizzing were led there by the finished and discreet conversation of her husband. Lord Holland, an accomplished amateur scholar and a man of so sunny a disposition that he always came down to breakfast like a man upon whom a sudden good fortune had just fallen,[32] was the bearer of the Whigs' proudest name and, after Fox's death in 1806, of the party's tradition of civil liberty and religious toleration. It was no small matter for Brougham's future that, as Sydney Smith reported to Sir James Mackintosh, Lady Holland had 'taken hugely to the Edinburgh Reviewers'.[33] Even more important was the good opinion of Lord Holland, the owner of slave-worked estates in Jamaica, but an unyielding advocate of abolition, and a member of the small inner circle which framed Whig policy and directed the party's behaviour.

* * *

On the night of 21 January 1806, Brougham was huddled with Horner and James Loch in a corner of the House of Commons' gallery, all of them waiting to see if a Whig amendment to the speech from the throne would bring down the Tory government. It failed. Then, two days later, Pitt died, exposing the weakness of a ministry which he alone was large enough to shield, and the Whigs, after more than twenty years in opposition, were led into office by Lord Grenville and Charles James Fox. Brougham at once took up Lord Holland's suggestion that he write a pamphlet puffing the new ministers and repudiating Pitt's conduct of foreign affairs. In the *Inquiry into the State of the Nation at the Commencement of the Present Administration* Brougham turned round on opinions expressed in his earlier writings and denounced Pitt's foreign policy in all its works. He also took the opportunity to put forward arguments for parliamentary reform, relief for the Irish Catholics (who were barred from holding political or civic office) and a modification of the country's protectionist tariff structure. If he hoped to be protected by anonymity he was duped. Wilberforce, applying on Brougham's behalf for the Lowther seat in Westmorland a few months later, was obliged to acknowledge that the pamphlet cast doubts upon the aspiring candidate's Toryism.

During the first six months of the new government's existence, Brougham acted as a go-between for the ministry and the Saints, carrying the abolitionists' views to Lord Holland and informing Wilberforce of the progress that the question was making in cabinet.[34] In August he received additional evidence of Whig confidence when he was appointed secretary to Lord Rosslyn and Lord St Vincent on their special mission to Portugal, the purpose of which was to investigate the state of Portugal's defences against what was believed to be imminent, Napoleon's invasion of the country. It came to nothing, alarms at Napoleon's intentions proving in the end to be groundless. Brougham took the opportunity, however, to talk to Portuguese ministers about the slave trade and, in order to encourage the Whig cabinet not to tarry in its plans to introduce an abolition bill, reported that the Portuguese were only waiting for a lead from England.[35] The mission also served to bring him into proximity with Lord Rosslyn, a crony of Grey and one of Scotland's most influential Whigs. He carried out his duties with initiative, thoroughness and despatch and he was able to write to Lord Holland that he and Rosslyn had lived together on the most agreeable terms.[36] Unfortunately for Brougham, the mission also instructed him in the thoughtless ways of the rich. He was then a man of modest income, living off the earnings of his pen, yet he never recovered the expenses which he incurred in honouring bills run up by the British consul at Oporto. 'It was a little hard,' he remarked in his memoirs, 'not only to do the work, but to pay for the secret service of this LIBERAL Government.'[37]

Lord Rosslyn returned to England some weeks before Brougham. In the middle of October Brougham wrote to him from Lisbon asking for accurate information on the prospects of a dissolution of parliament. 'That point interests me very nearly; for though I have some assurances that I shall be brought in at the election, yet if I am off the spot and have not warning of it, I know how little such promises avail.'[38] Brougham seems earlier to have told Horner that his application for a Westmorland seat was approved by Fox, Grey and Holland,[39] and if that were so, he had reason to suppose that the Whig leaders were eager to bring him into parliament at the first opportunity. It would be surprising if in casual conversation they had not expressed the desire to see him one day on the Whig benches, although it is scarcely credible that they looked forward to his sitting there under the watchful eye of Lord Lowther. There is no evidence that he had received the direct promise of a seat at the elections of 1807; nor does it make sense to suppose that his absence from London until the end of November should have constituted an insuperable barrier to his standing for parliament in the following spring. Brougham's statement to Rosslyn was an early instance of his habit of spreading half-truths (or half-lies) in order to pose as an injured party. In the event he was not brought in and his exclusion from parliament made him angry: 'But Secretaries of State and such great folks don't much think of other people in the lower departments of Government; and still less do they trouble themselves with thinking of absentees *hors de vue*.'[40]

Brougham wanted patience. He was not yet thirty, he had no money to contribute to the enormous cost of contesting or buying a seat, and he had done little to impress himself upon the Whig leaders as a reliable member of their ranks. It is worth recording, however, that Horner, a stern critic of Brougham's arrogant impetuosity, on this occasion agreed with him that absence from England had kept him out of parliament. 'Had he been here . . . his activity would have carried his object through all obstacles. It cannot be long, however, before a good opportunity will occur; he is too well known now for him to be suffered to lie unemployed: and that is the scene, I am sure, where he may be employed to the best advantage.'[41]

Brougham remained out of parliament until 1810. Much of his time was taken up by the law. After the fall of the Talents government in March 1807, and the return of the Tories to office, he entered the chambers of Nicholas Tindal, afterwards Chief Justice of Common

Pleas, but then practising as a special pleader under the bar.[42] Brougham acted occasionally as a special pleader; and as a Scotch barrister he gained some business by arguing Scotch appeals in the House of Lords. In May, 1808, he told Grey that the law was becoming easier and less disagreeable every day and that 'in a year or so more, I doubt not, I shall know more about it than is requisite'.[43] In truth, he never mastered the subtleties of the English law, especially the law of property, beyond what was requisite. There can be little doubt that had he possessed an independent income he would never have pursued his legal career: his mind, having caught the bug of politics, was not in it. When a relative inquired of Tindal whether Brougham was giving body and soul to his profession, Tindal replied that he knew nothing of his soul, 'but his body is very seldom in my chambers'.[44]

Brougham earned his living from 1807 to 1809 by writing, both for the *Edinburgh* and for the Whig daily press. In the spring of 1807 the Whigs decided to organize a propaganda department for the forthcoming elections to ensure that the correct line be taken by the various Whig newspapers. A room was hired in Ryder Street to serve as the headquarters of the press campaign and Lord Holland, to whom the responsibility for this delicate operation fell, entrusted the day-to-day management of the office to Brougham. Though still smarting from his failure to be given a seat, he threw himself into the work, as Holland later acknowledged.

> His extensive knowledge and extraordinary readiness, his assiduity and habits of composition, enabled him to correct some articles and to furnish a prodigious number himself. With partial and scanty assistance from Mr Allen, myself and two or three more, he, in the course of ten days, filled every bookseller's shop with pamphlets, most London newspapers and all country ones without exception with paragraphs, and supplied a large portion of the boroughs throughout the kingdom with handbills adapted to the local interests of the candidates, and all tending to enforce the principles, vindicate the conduct, elucidate the measures, or expose the adversaries of the Whigs.[45]

It was exhausting work supplying the five Whig dailies with fresh articles every day. Writers had to be cajoled; editors had to be soothed; rivalries among the papers had to be adjudicated; and articles had to be read carefully, corrected, and then copied in longhand to be distributed. Lord Holland, John Allen and Sydney Smith came up to Brougham's expectations, but most of the writing was done by Brougham himself. So was much of the research. 'I have been for the whole of this morning,' he wrote to Allen early in June, 'hunting for the Irish statute to answer the most impudent paragraph in the Courier of last night. It shall be done by tomorrow.'[46] Neither Horner nor Sir Francis Vincent, under-secretary at the foreign office during the late Whig government, fulfilled their promises to furnish him with pamphlets. 'Vincent says every other day he is coming to town. His last excuse is a *friend being unwell* . . . When all his relatives & friends are either buried or recovered we shall have him in full inactivity at Mrs B's, or in his own home.'[47]

When the elections were over, in the first week of June, the 'Castle of Indolence', as Brougham, disappointed of helpers, called the Ryder Street room, was shut up. Throughout the two months his spirits had never drooped and Grey wrote to him that he was 'lost in admiration of your activity'.[48] Brougham's grubbing raised his standing in the party, but he found it distasteful, 'dirty work, like most works of necessity'.[49] Nevertheless, as the elections were drawing to their close and it was clear that the Tories were confirmed in office, he suggested to Allen that a constant and heavy fire against them be kept up in every direction.[50] For the next couple of years he continued to supply paragraphs to the *Morning Chronicle*, the most important of the Whig dailies, and to write anti-government pamphlets. His interest still lay chiefly in foreign affairs and early in 1808 he published pamphlets on Great Britain's relations with the continental powers and on the orders-in-council; he also supervised the joint production of one on Portugal and Brazil.

Brougham had misgivings about earning a reputation as a paid hack who turned out whatever the Whig party asked. At the beginning of 1807 he had refused to write a defence of the Whig government's domestic policies, because he did not support the budget and he saw no other proposals which demanded an elaborate defence. He explained himself to John Allen.

It may be said, 'Why have you an opinion of your own upon such matters? Or make exceptions when you affect to support a party in general?' I am not so romantic and foolish as to think that, *in a party*, every man is bound to make exceptions in favour of his own opinions . . . But there is all the difference in the world between a regular coadjutor and a private, individual, insulated defender. What is known, and established, and respected as the duty of the former, gets a very scurvy name in the latter . . . There is no chance, I fear, of my share in the pamphlet being ultimately concealed. It might, if it involved a compromise of my opinions, greatly injure the portion of good fame which I have from accidental circumstances been lucky enough to acquire and that I fear is much too small to bear any diminution . . .

My repugnance to assume the station of a pamphleteer is by no means diminished. I know it to be a very subordinate one in itself, perhaps even inferior to my pretension. Stamp a man with this profession and he will never be anything better. Now as it never was *my* profession I am averse to adopt it now, without some obvious purpose of doing good to the cause.[51]

Why did Brougham stifle his scruples and write the 1808 pamphlets? The obvious reason is that he needed to earn money. But in addition he may have been willing, for a time, to adopt the only means, however injurious to his finer feelings, by which he could hope to move the Whig party in the direction he wished it to follow. It was in the year 1808 that he first revealed himself in radical colours and first gained a reputation beyond the select company of the higher political and literary world.

* * *

The occasion of Brougham's rise to public prominence was the intensifying trade war between Great Britain and France. It had begun in the spring of 1806, when Napoleon closed the ports of Prussia to British ships. By the middle of 1807 French victories in the field had secured Napoleon almost the whole of the European coastline. He was therefore in a position to enforce the Berlin decree of November 1806, and prevent all British goods, whether carried in British or neutral ships, from entering the continent. By the autumn of 1807 the British government was contemplating, as an extension of the original order-in-council of the Talents government, an order to make it obligatory that all goods entering European ports, whether carried by British or neutral ships, should pass through Great Britain. Such a step was bound to inflame American opinion, already worried about the damage inflicted on American trade by the European war. In September Brougham wrote to Grey that the Yorkshire merchants were in great anxiety lest a dispute with America should ruin them.[52] In October he published an article in the *Edinburgh Review* in which he warned the government that to issue comprehensive orders-in-council would lead to war with neutral America. The orders were published in November and the United States' immediate reply was to place an embargo on American shipping to Great Britain and prohibit the import of a large class of British goods into America. Brougham at once returned to the charge in the January issue of the *Edinburgh*. He exposed the government's hypocrisy in alleging that the orders were meant as a retaliation against Napoleon's continental system: their real purpose (the government was unable to deny it) was not to prevent neutral trade with Europe, but to garner some of the profits from that trade. And worse than the intention of the orders was the effect which they would inevitably produce, namely the disruption and diminution of British trade.

The effects of the Anglo-American dispute were felt most severely in Lancashire. Lancashire, the home of the infant industrial revolution, produced almost all of Great Britain's staple export, finished cotton. The import of raw cotton from the American South fell from 143,000 sacks in 1807 to only 23,000 in 1808. Under the unreformed electoral system the cotton towns of the north had no voice in parliament. When, therefore, the orders-in-council came to be debated in the House of Commons, the merchants and traders of Manchester and Liverpool, eager to have their case against the orders heard, turned to the man who had put it so forcefully in the pages of the *Edinburgh Review*. They engaged Brougham as counsel and won the right to have their suit pleaded, with evidence, before the bar of the House. Brougham put all his debating power into the attack. Petitions were got up, witnesses gathered and trading statistics amassed. For three weeks Brougham examined witnesses in the House of Commons, and in a long winding-up speech on 1 April he lacerated the government for its folly. Before the orders-in-council British goods had been able to pass into Europe in neutral ships armed with false sailing papers; now the orders enabled Napoleon to seize all ships on the ground that they *must* have passed through a British port.

Brougham's plea for the immediate repeal of the orders went unheeded. But for nearly a month he had commanded the attention of a full House of Commons and packed galleries. Not yet a member of parliament, he had nevertheless delivered his first major speech there.

More important, he had made a popular name for himself among the mercantile middling class of British society. When the case was ended, the petitioners met in a body to pass a vote of thanks to him and he reported to Grey that they had departed from London 'all tolerably well satisfied'.[53]

It was thanks to Brougham's efforts that the Whigs henceforth made opposition to the government's trade restrictions an item of their policy. The party followed where he led and his initiative greatly strengthened his standing with both its conservative and radical wings. It also led to an immediate increase in his legal business. The presentation of the government's case against the cotton merchants, as it were the examination of witnesses and the presentation of evidence for the defence, had been entrusted to James Stephen, a fellow Saint but no friend of Brougham, whose book on the sugar colonies Brougham had savaged in the first number of the *Edinburgh Review*. It was known to everyone that, despite the outcome of the debate, Brougham's performance had marked a distinct triumph over Stephen's feeble defence of government policy. The result was that Stephen, hitherto the leading advocate of the commercial interest at the Cockpit (the Westminster court which heard admiralty and prize cases), found his fame eclipsed by that of Brougham and new briefs given to his young rival. Brougham, who took immoderate delight in small triumphs of that kind, fairly crowed of his success to Grey.

> The Londoners also invited me to practise in the Cockpit, where they have the whole business in their hands, and have adopted me as Stephen's successor . . . Stephen is more outrageous than ever. He has completely quarrelled with me, first for saying what I did, and next, for not preventing it being published. He says it is an incendiary and pernicious speech, and can only do mischief. But the real truth is that he does not like being attacked, and he finds Perceval [the chancellor of the exchequer] is the only man who defends him. His witnesses all failed, and did more good to us than to the ministry, which exasperates them the more; and George Rose [treasurer of the navy] goes about saying he blames him greatly for not stopping me at every other sentence.[54]

Having tasted applause in a semi-legal arena, Brougham was eager to have his first go on an English circuit. The obvious choice was the northern circuit, not only because he had now made valuable connections with Lancashire folk, but also because it was there that the

largest profits were made and the highest reputations won. Techni-
cally, he was not eligible for admittance to the bar until November
1808, but he hoped, by means of a special motion at Lincoln's Inn, to
be called in July and thus to go the autumn circuit.

> I set out with too slender a provision of law, no doubt, and may very
> possibly never see a jury until I have to address it, my stock of
> practice being so slender that I never yet saw a *nisi-prius* trial. But
> the points of law are few on a circuit, and by good fortune none of
> any difficulty may fall on me, and . . . I may push through the thing
> with a little presence of mind and quickness.[55]

Brougham's hopes were disappointed when the government, piqued
at his assault on the orders-in-council, sent down the attorney-general
and solicitor-general to Lincoln's Inn, where they were successful in
getting the motion on his behalf defeated by one vote. Everyone,
Brougham told Grey, called it a vile political job scarcely ever
attempted before. 'They luckily cannot easily prevent me next term;
but I am infinitely injured by the delay, besides the foretaste it gives
me of what I have to expect in future when I shall stand in need of a
silk gown.'[56]

Brougham took the setback, itself nothing more than being told not
to jump the queue, irrationally hard. Nursing his slighted pride with
self-pity, he gained solace from puerile dreamings of revenge.

> I am sorry to inform you [he wrote to John Allen] that the Saint,
> Parke, hath prevailed and smote me hip & thigh. I am refused, and
> must be patient. I scarcely expected anything else, indeed it would
> have been the first time in my life that I owed anything to favour or
> connivance, having always found extra-difficulties where other
> people met with extra-helps, and being always rather thwarted
> than assisted even by my own relations, in respect of everything
> professional, for which I may perhaps live to take my revenge one
> day both on them & on St Parke & shall feel that as agreeable at
> least as succeeding by their aid.[57]

* * *

Brougham's championship of the commercial and industrial interests, those interests which were to sustain the liberal reform movements of the next forty years, proclaimed no unrestrainable radical

tendency. He had been offered a brief and he had accepted it. The Whig leaders, happy to beat the government with any stick, applauded his effort. A few months later, however, with some flourishes of democratic rhetoric in the *Edinburgh*, Brougham brought down a storm upon his head.

As soon as the orders-in-council business was out of the way, he turned his attention to the state of affairs in Europe, where the most pressing issues were coming to be the progress of the insurgent Spanish constitutionalists and the French threat to Spanish independence. In the first of two articles in the *Edinburgh*, published in July and October of 1808, he analysed the prospects of a successful Spanish resistance to the armies of Napoleon. There was nothing very exceptional in his pessimistic conclusion (he did not share Lord Holland's hero-worship of the French emperor) that Spain was too weak to stay the power of French arms and that Great Britain had no assistance to offer. In urging that the proper policy for Great Britain was to continue to sue for peace, however, Brougham was aligning himself with the left wing of the Whig opposition and, by implication at least, endorsing their discovery that the warlike stance of the Whig leaders constituted a desertion from Foxite principles. Grey was deeply pained by the inference in Brougham's article that the late Whig government had faltered, after the death of Fox, in its quest for a negotiated peace. 'To be accused of abandoning when in power,' he wrote in a letter of reproach to Brougham, 'the principles I had maintained in opposition, is a severe charge from an enemy; but for a friend to entertain, and to think it necessary to promulgate, that opinion, must inflict a much deeper wound.'[58] Brougham replied that he had imagined no distinction between the views of Fox and Grey and there the matter ended.

The passions stirred by Brougham's second article, the celebrated 'Don Cevallos' review, were not so readily stilled. The review, which arose from a recent publication by the Spanish first secretary of state, asserted that the source of Spanish weakness lay in the social and political structure of the kingdom. The preponderance of an effete and selfish aristocracy enfeebled the country. Nor was that all. In a remarkable passage the reviewer gave his opinion that only a thorough popular revolution could save Spain and—here was the offence—that the success of such a movement in Spain would sound as a clarion call to English democrats. Who, Brougham asked, had led the fight against Napoleon in Spain?

The people, then, and of the people, the middle, and above all, the lower orders, have alone the merit of raising this glorious opposition to the common enemy of national independence. Those who had so little of what is commonly termed *interest* in the country, those who had *no stake* in the community (to speak the technical language of the aristocracy), the persons of *no consideration* in the state—they who could not pledge *their fortunes*, having only lives and liberties to lose, the bulk—the mass of the people—nay, the very odious, many-headed beast, the multitude—the mob itself—alone, uncalled, unaided by the higher classes—in spite of those higher classes, and in direct opposition to them, as well as to the enemy whom they so vilely joined—raised up the standard of insurrection—bore it through massacre and through victory . . . Happen what will in the sequel, here is a grand and permanent success—a lesson to all governments—a warning to all oligarchies—a cheering example to every people.

What then of England, where a Tory government was driven by its war against France to succour the growth of democracy in Spain?

This system of liberty will grow up with the full assent and, indeed, the active assistance of the English government; and, what is of far greater importance, with the warm and unanimous approval of the English people. And who then shall ever more presume to cry down popular rights, or tell us that the people have nothing to do with the laws, but to obey them—with the taxes, but to pay them—and with the blunders of their rulers, but to suffer from them? What man will now dare to brand his political adversary with the name of a revolutionist—or try to hunt those down, as enemies of order, who expose the follies and corruptions of an unprincipled and intriguing administration? These tricks have had their day—a day immeasurably disastrous in its consequences to England and to Europe. Their impudence has at last been exposed; they have ceased to blindfold the multitude; and we can once more utter the words of *liberty* and *people*, without starting at the echo of our own voices, or looking round the chamber for some spy or officer of the government . . . The *Spanish* revolution comes most opportunely . . . to awaken in this country all those feelings of liberty and patriotism which many had supposed were extinguished since the *French* revolution; and to save our declining country, by the only remedy for its malady—a recurrence to those wholesome popular feelings, in which its greatness has been planted and nursed up.[59]

To publish such language in 1808, when the taint which the French revolution had cast on reform sentiments had hardly begun to be washed away, and to publish it in the respectable pages of the *Edinburgh Review*, was a deliberate provocation. The Cevallos article was the joint production of Jeffrey and Brougham, but the evidence, both from the style of the passage itself (especially the piling of sarcasm upon sarcasm, so favourite a device of Brougham) and from private letters, is that the offending or, as Jeffrey called them, 'mischievous' words were Brougham's.[60]

The passage dismayed Tories; it disconcerted the Whigs. Jeffrey learned that in Edinburgh alone about twenty-five persons of consideration had forbidden the review to enter their doors again and Sydney Smith reported that titled persons of all parties were returning their volumes of the *Edinburgh* to the booksellers and fumigating their bookshelves.[61] The Earl of Buchan, a friend to reform in the 1790s, placed the issue on the floor of his lobby, then kicked it into the middle of the street, where it lay to be trampled into the mud. Most significant of all, Walter Scott, who earlier in the year had ceased to *write* for the magazine because of an unfavourable review of *Marmion*, now resolved never to *read* it again. Instead, he and a few Tory friends came together to establish the *Quarterly Review* as an antidote to the *Edinburgh*. The reaction from certain Whigs was hardly less restrained. Horner described the passage as 'reprehensible in tone and spirit'[62] and, as Brougham later recalled, it offended Grey and Holland House as much as it did the Tories.[63]

Why did Brougham publish the words? He had, of course, allowed his pen to run away with him before, most notoriously in an article which mistakenly and dismissively discredited Young's theories on the undulation of light, even though he had not troubled to repeat the experiments himself. At the beginning of 1808, too, he had published a scornful, sarcastic review of Byron's *Hours of Idleness*, exposing the inflated claims which Byron made for his *juvenilia* to the ridicule they deserved and consequently (no small service to English literature) calling forth Byron's maturing powers in *English Bards and Scotch Reviewers*. Men had come to expect rash outbursts from Brougham. Horner, estranged from him and jealous of his versatility, put the Cevallos article down to recklessness. Brougham, he remarked, was throwing away in 'dashing declamations' what should have been the fruits of his careful study of politics and his first-hand observation of Spanish affairs.[64]

We may suppose that Brougham's purposes were more studied. His private language was as vehement as his public voice. 'One thing is clear to me,' he wrote to John Allen a month before the review appeared, 'that the success of the Spands. is the downfall of our government, *constituted as it now is.* There is an end to the high aristocratic tone of the upper orders, & the whole discredit brought on democracy by the Reign of Terror (in France) is wiped away.'[65] Since Brougham never, at any point in his career, advocated a radical reform of parliament, his remarks on Spain may be taken as an example of the habit of English liberals to applaud popular movements abroad and stifle them at home. On the other hand, the great ends to which Brougham devoted his life, the widening of educational opportunity especially, were inspired by the desire to give the lower orders of society greater scope for self-improvement and self-management. In the autumn of 1808 he appears to have had two objects before him: to prosper the cause of the left wing of the Whig opposition and, partly as a corollary, to turn the *Edinburgh* into an instrument of political warfare.

From the resignation of the Fox–Grenville ministry in March 1807 down to 1830 the Whigs remained in opposition. 'Nought's permanent about the human race,' Byron wrote, 'except the Whigs *not* getting into place.' No bright flame of popular passion illuminated the Whigs' fall from favour, only the embers of a dying quarrel. Having failed to gain George III's consent to a small measure of Catholic relief (the right of Catholics to serve in the army and navy), they left office rather than promise not to raise the question again. They would not have their freedom hemmed in by regard for a dubious royal prerogative. No doubt they were right not to lower the standard which the Rockingham Whigs had raised in the 1760s, but the price they paid, the return of the Tories under the Duke of Portland, was high; and the meek manner of their going suggests that they were happy to find a high constitutional principle with which to cloak the nakedness of their ideas. Uncertain how to sue for peace without seeming unpatriotic and largely untouched by the social and economic changes coming over the country, the Whig leaders hesitated to challenge the moratorium on innovation and reform which was the Tory response to the French revolution.

Yet there was a distinct revival of radical aspirations in the years 1808 and 1809. The roots of the revival lay in the shock given to educated opinion by the Melville scandal of 1805; and the confidence of the people in the integrity of their rulers was further undermined by the inquiry, in 1809, into the allegation that the Duke of York had allowed one of his mistresses to sell commissions in the army. Meanwhile the war against France was going badly. Sir John Moore's march into Spain to assist the Spanish insurrectionists ended in the disastrous retreat to Corunna; the hopes that Germany was being roused to resistance were dissipated by Napoleon's victory at Wagram; and the expectation that Great Britain would single-handed strike a mighty blow against France by the capture of Antwerp died, along with hundreds of British troops, in the pestilent marshes of Walcheren. Crisis succeeded crisis without the Whigs, directed in the Lords by the cautious Lord Grey and in the Commons by the slovenly George Ponsonby, making any headway. In these circumstances a knot of radical opposition members came to distance themselves more and more from the official leadership of the party. Their ranks included a number of men justly renowned for their intelligence, their knowledge, and their courageous perseverance in the pursuit of legal and parliamentary reform. Foremost among them were Samuel Romilly and Samuel Whitbread, the latter, Lord Grey's son-in-law, brooding sulkily at being passed over by Ponsonby for the leadership of the opposition in the House of Commons. By 1809 the independent behaviour of Whitbread and his discrete band of followers had earned them the designation of a faction and the name, borrowed from the French revolutionary left, of the 'Mountain'.

When the *Edinburgh* was established in 1802, the intention of its founders was to keep it free of political and, *a fortiori*, party controversy. Like John Wilson Croker, for thirty years the chief contributor to the *Quarterly*, they were no friends to making the review a political organ: solid literature and science were the substance of a review; the rest was mere 'leather and prunella'. 'In short, a review should be a *review*, and a review of the *higher* order of literature, rather than the ordinary run of the topics and publications of the idle day.'[66] It was also a cardinal precept that articles should actually review the books at hand, not use them as pegs on which to hang an essay. Had these high principles not been more honoured in the breach, the 19th-century reviews would not have come to occupy their lofty Victorian eminence. They gained a stature unknown before or after,

49

graver than their Augustan predecessors and far more substantial than their 20th-century successors. The *Edinburgh*, in initiating the review-like essay and the essay-like review, was, Bagehot wrote looking back on it, 'in this country the commencement on large topics of suitable views for sensible persons'.[67] The reviewers served readers who possessed both the time and the inclination to read and reflect upon articles upwards of 15,000 words in length. The existence of a market for journals which brought together under one cover learned discussions of literary, scientific, theological, philosophical, historical and political questions is one mark of the gulf which separates the Victorian from a later age. Constricted within narrower confines, the reviews would not have commanded the attention which was paid to them. On the other hand, there can be little doubt that the popularity of the *Quarterly*, the *Edinburgh* and the *Westminster* owed much to their becoming the acknowledged, although never the official, organs of Toryism, Whiggery and Benthamite radicalism.

That the *Edinburgh* and its rivals should take on a deeper political colouring as the 19th century advanced was, of course, a reflection of the deepening and the widening of partisan public debate in the country, especially after the close of the Napoleonic wars in 1815. But the reviews made their own contribution to that increase of public responsibility and no one worked more consciously to assist it than Brougham. Many years later, during the debates on the great reform bill, he held up the pre-reform press as the only institution which had been able to dictate to the government, 'since nothing else could speak the sense of the people'.[68] It is curious, therefore, to find him expressing anger at Jeffrey's decision to review Cobbett and asking John Allen to dissuade him from taking such an imprudent and useless step. The effects of a weekly paper could not be combated in a quarterly publication and the attempt would involve the *Edinburgh* in a 'degrading controversy' and 'bring it many steps down from its literary & speculative character'.[69] Cobbett was an acute case and Brougham's anger may have arisen (he does not say so) from the fear that Jeffrey would place the *Edinburgh* on too anti-radical a footing. He undoubtedly felt, too, that if anyone were to review Cobbett, he, not Jeffrey, was the man to do it. But Cobbett was not an isolated case. At the beginning of 1808, the year in which Brougham was to write his forthright attack on the orders-in-council and the two Spanish articles, he asked John Allen to suggest some books for review, 'of course *not political*, for I have given Jeffrey notice that I have cut those subjects in so far as writing is concerned'.[70] Even more surprising, as late as 1814 Brougham was putting it about that an article which he had written on current French politics represented a deviation from his rule of handling general subjects only.[71]

In the minds of those people who lamented the new tone of the *Edinburgh*, a tone not simply more outspokenly partisan, but also more decidedly liberal, the culprit was Brougham. Brougham defended the *Edinburgh*, just before the Cevallos article appeared, by saying that it only seemed not to be impartial because the government was more often wrong than the opposition. Certainly the *Edinburgh* had none of the stridency of Canning's *Anti-Jacobin*. Even so, Smith and Horner repeatedly urged upon Jeffrey the need to keep Brougham in harness. Smith, indeed, praised Brougham's 1809 piece on the conduct of the war as 'long yet vigorous like the penis of a jackass', but he objected to its railing and ridiculing tone; and six months later he took offence at Brougham's 'violent tirade against the Ministry'.[72]

The attacks which rained upon Brougham all, in the end, resolved themselves into the accusation of impropriety. Horner charged him with printing in the *Edinburgh* those things which ought to be spoken in the House of Commons and Smith described him as 'bolting out of course' and behaving in 'an unwhiglike manner'.[73] What disturbed Brougham's Whig critics was not simply that he exceeded polite bounds in his jabs at Tory ministers, but that he was ready, as in the Cevallos article, to include the Whigs in his criticism. For all the cant about keeping the *Edinburgh* untainted by political partisanship, it was Brougham's very independence of thought which made Horner tremble whenever he opened a new copy of the review. Moreover, to say in the public prints what ought to be said in parliament was more than indecorous: it hinted at demagoguery and threatened the cherished Whig assumption that an uninstructed people could safely entrust its interests and grievances to its parliamentary champions. Brougham winced at the Whigs' smugness. After a visit to Cambridge, he described the Whig 'valuables' there in characteristically mocking language.

> The men whom they have shown me here . . . are all whigs, & valuables, talking as if there was no King in this world & no devil in the other, & indeed, appearing by their certain & infallible manner to have not the most remote suspicion that any human being exists who differs from themselves in the most trifling particulars on any

subject. In a word, they are 'right', and 'quite excellent', and 'exceeding good', and 'most valuable' and 'prodigious proper sort' of 'persons'.[74]

Brougham, endearingly, never became stuffy; he carried his youthful impishness into middle and old age. But it would be a mistake to interpret his impatience with the Whig valuables as the innocent irreverence of a young man unpolished in the ways of the world. The times were uneasy; radicalism, outraged by the Duke of York scandal and the human sacrifices entailed in the Walcheren expedition, was flaring its nostrils; Cobbett was making friends; and the *Examiner*, directed with reforming purpose and written with stylish verve by Leigh Hunt and his brother, had entered the polemical lists. Brougham watched Romilly's pleas for a mild reform of the criminal law turned down by the House of Commons and looked on with dismay at the Whig leaders' nervous refusal to join the Mountain in uncompromising denunciation of ministerial corruption and incompetence. He came to the conclusion that the Whig party risked becoming a relic of the past if it did not rally to its side that liberal opinion which, despairing of the party of Fox, would turn to the likes of Cobbett and Sir Francis Burdett.

Brougham wished to make the Whigs play the game of the country, to take the people into their confidence and listen to what it had to say. To accomplish his object he had to use what weapons were available to him. Until he entered the House of Commons, that meant using the *Edinburgh*. Most of Jeffrey's friends assumed that he bent Jeffrey to his will. It was not so. Bullying from Brougham did not inspire the ardency of the advice which Jeffrey gave to Horner on the eve of the parliamentary session of 1810.

Do, for Heaven's sake, let your Whigs do something popular and effective this session in Parliament. Cry aloud, and spare not, against Walcheren; push Ireland down the throats of the Court and country; and do not let us be lost without something like a generous effort, in council as well as in the field. You must lay aside a great part of your aristocratical feelings and side with the most respectable and sane of the democrats; by so doing, you will enlighten and restrain them; and add tenfold to the power of your reason, and the honour of your cause. Do you not see that the whole nation is now divided into *two*, and only two, parties—the timid, sordid, selfish worshippers of power and adherents of the Court, and the dangerous, discontented, half noble, half mischievous advocates for reform and innovation? *Between* these stand the Whigs; without popularity, power, or consequence of any sort; with great talents and virtues; but utterly inefficient, and incapable of ever becoming efficient, if they will maintain themselves at an equal distance from both of the prevailing parties. It is your duty, then, to join with that to which you approximate most nearly; or, rather, with that by whose aid alone you can snatch the country from imminent destruction. Is this a time to stand upon scruples and dignities? Join the popular party; which is every day growing stronger and more formidable. Set yourselves openly against the base Court party; bring the greatest delinquents to serious and exemplary punishment; patronise a reform in Parliament; and gratify what may be a senseless clamour, by retrenching some unnecessary expenditure. I doubt whether all this can now save us; but I think it quite certain that we shall have rebellion, as well as invasion, unless something be done upon a great generous system. Cobbett and Sir F. Burdett will soon be able to take the field against the King and his favourites; and when it comes to that, it will be hard to say which we should wish to prevail.[75]

Holding such views, Jeffrey was proof against the prim journalistic conservatism of Brougham's critics. In 1810 the political temperature was much higher than it had been in 1802, and with George III relapsing into mental instability, the regency of the Whigs' supposed friend, George, Prince of Wales, lay round the corner. 'Do you take the Catholics?' Jeffrey wrote to Brougham in March 1810, of the next issue of the *Edinburgh*, 'at all events I hope the responsibility and something else political—at such a moment as this it is really throwing away your great powers to employ them on anything else.'[76] The bias against politics in the review gradually subsided and it became more and more closely tied to the Whig party. In 1809 Grey expressed misgivings about Brougham's article on the war. 'If I were disposed to criticise severely, I should perhaps say that it was better as a political paper than as a critical review; but if this does not interfere with the general object of the publication, the objection is of no importance.'[77] Six years later Grey's reservations had entirely vanished. 'I have been regretting,' he told Brougham, when returning the sheets of an article on the income tax, 'that a fire has not been already opened, and steadily kept up from this battery, the only one from which our artillery can be expected to produce any real effect.'[78]

In retrospect, it is cause for some wonder that the battle to make the *Edinburgh* political had to be fought at all. It was politics which made the 19th-century reviews the national institutions that they were. As Croker pointed out to John Lockhart, the editor of the *Quarterly*, 'where would you have been *without* them?'[79] The great reviews were leavening agents whose effect was to assist in the raising of the tone of political debate in early 19th-century England. They upheld the notion that the rational discussion of public questions was not incompatible with polemical spirit. It was a splendid conviction and it is Brougham's due to be remembered for the part he played in sustaining it.

3

Member for Camelford

The year 1808 was Brougham's thirtieth, time enough, by the world's wisdom, for a man to be steadying his opinions and marking out a settled course. After one of his periodic outbursts of impatience with the Whigs, he received a piece of cautionary advice from Jeffrey. Since no possibility existed of raising a third party of any consequence, he ought to league himself wholeheartedly with the Whigs. 'The truth is . . . that *you are* of their party, and you only quarrel with them because they fall short of their profession and do not act up to their principles.'[1] Brougham's radicalism, nurtured by 18th-century modes of thought, had its source in the conviction, not so much that men had needs which were not being supplied, as that they had rights which were not being acknowledged. Like the Whigs, he showed in public no anger against English society and its institutions, no irreducible outrage at the poverty and despair of the downtrodden. No episode in the early 19th century revealed the confines of Whig liberalism more clearly than the Whigs' response to the Peterloo massacre of 1819. Great was their fury at the government. Why? Because lancers had slain innocents? Because a great open-meeting had testified to the suffering of the unfed and the unemployed? No, or at least only in small part. The Whigs rose up against the Tory ministers because they were robbing Englishmen of their ancient right to petition for the redress of grievance. No more than the Tories did the Whigs suggest means of removing the grievance. Their anger was self-preserving. By defending the rights of the petitioners they sought to proof the more intelligent of them against the seductive demagoguery of Orator Hunt and his accomplices. Whiggery's view of itself was impervious to the passage of time. As late as 1855 Francis Baring was able to describe the Whig party entirely in the language of *noblesse oblige*.

I mean . . . a body of men connected with high rank and property, bound together by hereditary feelings, party ties as well as higher motives, who in bad times keep alive the sacred flame of freedom, and when the people are roused stand between the constitution and revolution, and go with the people, but not to extremities; do them away and the fight between the Radicals and the Conservatives would begin in earnest.[2]

Whiggery, by that view, was no more than the outwork of the Tory castle.

Brougham had no fundamental quarrel with the defensive preoccupations of the Whigs. But he saw further than they did and he saw more clearly. His activity was miscellaneous, as Bagehot put it, because he was a 'Jonah of detail', a man whose mind was pricked by facts, not absorbed in a creed.[3] He wished the Whigs to give practical substance to their claim to be the 'friends of the people'. Therefore he found himself often in agreement with the Mountain. His difficulty was that he was not content to be a voice in the wilderness; he yearned for recognition and influence, thirsted for action and authority. Sterling reputations could be won on the left wing of the Whig party. Brougham had to suffer many an odious comparison with Horner and Romilly, whose integrity, adherence to principle, absence of rancour and fair-mindedness won canting praise from their opponents. But neither Horner nor Romilly progressed to parliamentary leadership. Each remained an eloquent, but back-bench, spokesman for a single cause, Romilly for relaxing the severity of the criminal code, Horner for modernizing the financial and trading institutions for the country. As such men usually are, they were fearless and unfeared, disrespectful of authority and respected by it.

Brougham's eye ranged wider and his ambition leapt higher: to be both a frontbencher *and* a tribune of the people, to play the party game *and* to play it for real stakes. No one who knew him can have supposed him easy to tame. Nevertheless, he appeared almost as a necessity. Now that Fox was dead, Sheridan a debt-ridden and alcoholic shadow of his former self, and Whitbread a brooding malcontent on his Mountain perch, the Whig party was bereft of speakers. Gilbert Elliot, member of parliament and heir to the earldom of Minto, was not alone in thinking that it would be 'downright waste in these times of severity [for Brougham] to confine his fine talents entirely to the law'.[4] Before Brougham had even entered parliament, George Tierney, Ponsonby's rival for the Whig leadership in the Commons, talked of his being appointed undersecretary at the foreign office in the next Whig government.[5] Brougham, for his part, courted the Whig lords and ladies, sometimes to the amusement of his friends. John Ward, a friend from Edinburgh days, gave Helen d'Arcy Stewart, better known as 'Ivy', an account of one of Brougham's flirtations.

> An't you quite charmed with Brougham and Lady Rosslyn? You would be still more so if you knew as I do how, upon their first acquaintance, the Countess hated the Critic, and the Critic despised the Countess. However, it seems that they have at last arrived at a due sense of each other's merits. His 'universality', about which we always used to joke with him, prevents me from being surprised at anything he does. Else it is comical enough to see the lawyer, the politician, the negotiator, the geometer, setting up all of a sudden for a man of gallantry. However, it is no bad arrangement—perfectly innocent I feel sure—the only object of each being to be flattered by the other and talked of by the world.[6]

Brougham's correspondence with the Whig magnates in these years—with Lauderdale, with Rosslyn and, above all, with Grey, whose friendship was now deepening into a cordial attachment—bears no trace of condescension from experienced statesmen to a fledgling colleague or from proud estate-owners to a Scotch scribbler. Brougham peppered Grey with his opinions and Grey replied with unfeigned interest. So little did Brougham feel a gulf between himself and the Whig aristocrats that he was soon following his natural bent and taking to lecture them. In October 1808, he sternly rebuked Lord Holland for proposing to pass another long season abroad in Spain. A step so ill-considered, taken during a critical phase of the war, when difficult days for the government lay ahead, would rightly cost him public popularity.

> Be assured that however popular the Spanish cause has been or may still be . . . this country does not require a man in your situation to run over to the patriots to shew his zeal for them . . . I must really speak plainly what I feel upon this matter. Your Uncle and Pitt are both dead, and your running away at the present moment is a mighty different matter from any other journey to the Continent that you have formerly made . . . You will say 'What signifies the foolish talk of the publick about one's conduct'? I say, it signifies nothing to a private man, and if you chuse to give up

politics altogether, you are right—but why do you go to the H. of Lords and make speeches and do a thousand other things which all lead to acquiring power, through popularity? I hold it to be quite an inconsistency, at one time to court publick opinion and at another to defy it. I speak what I have heard a thousand times last summer in town.[7]

Brougham returned to the charge three weeks later, adding that both Grey and Lauderdale opposed the foreign trip and warning that, if the Whig opposition broke up, Holland would have to answer for it.[8]

The Hollands ignored the advice and crossed the Channel. For some unaccountable reason, in the autumn of 1809, soon after their return, Brougham and Lady Holland fell out with one another. Perhaps, although Lady Holland declared herself at a loss to explain Brougham's absence from Holland House, it was something that Brougham said. Lady Bessborough had heard 'the protégé of Ld Holland, and apparent toad-eater and adorer of Lady Holland, abusing her violently'.[9] Brougham himself claimed that, although there was no quarrel nor anything like it, he had been 'compelled' to quit Holland House. When asked, he 'always let it appear that Lady Holland had declined my acquaintance, not I hers'. The most probable ground of her displeasure, he imagined, was the offence given her by his mother, who had refused, when the Hollands stopped by at Brougham Hall on their way south from Scotland, to allow the mother of a child born out of wedlock to cross her threshold.[10] Sydney Smith laid the blame on Brougham's ill manners and lamented that his wayward temperament had landed him in another scrape—'for I really like Brougham and regret most heartily that he will not walk thro' life in a straight path'.[11] Whatever the origins of the tiff, it was not easy for two persons so imperious and so sensitive to slight to make it up. Not until 1816 did Brougham again appear at Holland House and, as Lord Holland recorded, resume the habits of familiarity and intimacy without a word of explanation on either side, 'as if we had parted in the morning'.[12]

When the story of the quarrel was first making the rounds of London, Sydney Smith remarked that, having given up the Hollands, Brougham had necessarily given up the Duke of Bedford, 'for they go together'.[13] He could not have been wider of the mark. Brougham's estrangement from Lady Holland did not at all sully his friendship with her husband; nor did Lady Holland possess political influence capable of souring his relations with the Whig leaders. It was, indeed, the Duke of Bedford who, at the end of 1809, brought Brougham into parliament. In 1807, despite the ill treatment he had received in the *Edinburgh Review*, Lord Lauderdale had urged Grey to persuade Bedford to bring in Brougham. 'His activity would annoy them [the government] much; it is impossible to answer for a man's succeeding before he is tried, but I think he has a good chance.'[14] Two years later, Lauderdale again pleaded Brougham's cause as 'a thing of consequence to the Party'.[15] Grey and Holland put the proposition to Bedford. The Duke persuaded Lord Robert Spencer to surrender the representation of Camelford, in Cornwall, and the empty seat was offered to Brougham.

There were then three ways to come into parliament: by the patronage of a boroughmonger (or the treasury), by buying a seat (Curwen's act of 1809 outlawing the practice notwithstanding), or by open contest in a popular constituency. The second and third methods were beyond Brougham's means. Bedford offered him the first. For a radical to enter parliament by any means other than a popular contest was inauspicious, but by the standards of the time far from remarkable. Romilly, the purest of radicals and the least corruptible of men, thought the purchase of a seat preferable to nomination by a boroughmonger, since, even if the nomination were made without conditions, at the first critical moment the strings would tug. Even he, nevertheless, accepted the treasury seat of Queensborough in 1806: 'one who should carry his notions of purity so far, that, thinking he possessed the means of rendering service to his country, he would yet rather seclude himself altogether from Parliament than get into it by such a violation of the theory of the constitution, must be under the domination of a species of moral superstition which must wholly disqualify him for the discharge of any public duties'.[16] Brougham discovered in Bedford's offer no moral obstacles to overcome. There was only the practical difficulty of combining a parliamentary career with practice at the bar, risking what everyone knew would be certain success on the circuit by entering the hazardous arena of politics.

Brougham sent letters off in all directions, asking for the advice of all the Whig leaders before coming to a decision. He was fearful, as he had told Grey earlier, of turning out to be 'too much a politician for one set of men, and too much a lawyer for the other'.[17] He could not, however, afford to be in parliament without the income derived from the bar. Lord Rosslyn, who knew, no doubt, that Brougham wanted encouragement, not advice, sent him a dizzying reply.

You must first settle with yourself to what objects your inclination leads you, and how far your judgment will allow you to sacrifice solid advantage to the more brilliant allurements of power, and reputation, and distinction.

I have no doubt, that if you continue to work in your profession only, that you must make a great fortune, and come to the head of it; but, in so doing, you submit to great slavery, and you forego a great many of the greatest gratifications, to the enjoyment of which you are sufficiently alive. If you go into Parliament, and devote yourself to politics, which most probably you will then do, you have the most favourable opportunity opening to you from the present state of the House of Commons in general, and that of your own party in particular; and there is no office in the country to which you may not look in a short time without any presumption on your part, or any disposition to compliment on mine; but, in pursuing that line, you will probably be two-thirds of your life in opposition; and if your private fortune and expectations be equal to the expenses which now or hereafter you may wish to incur, you will, like Fox, be standing in the full enjoyment of high consideration and great fame.

I have not overlooked the middle course to which alone your letter points, and to that I should less object if I thought you were sure of being able steadily to pursue it, and not to be seduced into abandoning the profession entirely by the persuasion of your friends, and the temptations which the present state of politics must hold out to your vanity and ambition . . .

The whole circuit you will retain, and if you get to the head of it rapidly, which, if I am rightly informed, you may expect, the situation of Solicitor-General opens to you easily, and with few competitors . . . it is obvious enough that being once Solicitor-General, all the rest is smooth and easy.

. . . You will go into Parliament with advantages that no modern lawyer has tried; with a fund of political and commercial information more than adequate to the possible demand upon it, and sufficient to weigh down all those with whom you may have to contend. Your occasional preparation for parliamentary business will therefore be easy, and occasion less distraction . . .

You will now come in without any decided leader to the party, in a state of the House of Commons the most favourable to the display and the success of talents, with no very powerful opponent to bear you down; and with the opportunity (from the eagerness expressed by all your principal friends to have you there, perhaps more for their own purposes than considering your advantage) of seeming to sacrifice your own interest to the general cause of the party . . .

To conclude, I would advise you to accept, forming and declaring your resolution to adhere to your profession, and your intention to attend as constantly as your legal avocations would permit, but not beyond that point.

You have what I advise; but probably you will have decided before you receive this. I have only to add, that when you become Secretary of State, it will be prudent to *seal* your despatches. Your letter came to me open, and certainly unmarked by wax or wafer.[18]

On the day that Brougham received Rosslyn's letter he accepted the nomination to represent Camelford. He was thirty-one years old. He had been in London for only five years. He had just finished only his first year at the bar. What other man so young and so inexperienced in public affairs ever entered the House of Commons with such a reputation behind him and such expectations of future eminence before him?

A young man from whom great deeds are expected suffers great anxiety. Brougham did not enter the House of Commons to play a passive, or even secondary, part in its proceedings. He was therefore more apprehensive than others knew. He had scored a notable triumph when speaking at the bar of the House in 1808; finding the right tone as a member was a decidedly more difficult matter. For want of finding it, many a man of intellectual gifts and oratorical acumen has dug himself a parliamentary grave. Parliamentary reputations are most easily raised on obscure foundations. 'I should feel much more comfortable,' Brougham confided to John Allen, 'were I in the predicament of having already failed & having my way to fight up again. Nothing can be worse than beginning with a sort of character formed.'[19]

Brougham set out on a parliamentary career with two signal advantages. He had knowledge, and the thirst to gain more, in an age when, as he himself later wrote, the material out of which English statesmen were for the most part fashioned was an attendance upon debates in parliament and a study of newspapers in the clubs.[20] And his knowledge was at the service of a prodigious gift of speech. Parliamentary government, as Macaulay once said, is government by speaking. Not that flights of oratory are evidence of executive capacity, nor that they have but rarely a direct and immediate effect upon administrative action. We are tempted to look back upon the age of Pitt and Fox, of Canning and Sheridan, and imagine that the fate of governments hung in the balance while they crossed swords in the chamber. We remember the noble generosity of Burke at his best and forget that Burke, whom men called the dinner-bell of the House of Commons, was a parliamentary failure. Then, as now (it is the unavoidable consequence of the party system, hastily condemned by skin-deep democrats) the outcome of important divisions was nearly always a foregone conclusion. Speeches were intended, not so much to win over the hesitant, as to flatter the prejudices of party and catch the ear of the country. All the more remarkable was it, then, that Brougham should on two famous occasions—the repeal of the orders-in-council in 1812 and the repeal of the income tax in 1816—triumph over constitutional tradition and almost single-handed lead the Commons to inflict embarrassing and unexpected defeats on the government of the day.

Brougham's accomplishments were manifest. There were, nevertheless, obstacles to surmount. The House of Commons, composed as it largely was of the English aristocracy and its hangers-on, eyed with suspicion Scotsmen, lawyers and journalists. Disraeli wrote novels and, for a time in the 1850s, conducted his own newspaper, but he is the only man of letters in English history to have occupied the prime minister's office; Spencer Perceval, of whom Ward said that 'if he had not been bred a lawyer he would probably have risen to the character of a great man',[21] is the only law officer to have done so; and, if we exclude Bute, the only Scotch prime minister before the 20th century was Lord Aberdeen, and he was raised in England from the age of eight and educated at Harrow and Cambridge.

'I can scarce conceive,' Lord Shelburne once wrote, 'a Scotsman capable of liberality. That nation is composed of such a sad set of innate cold-hearted impudent rogues.'[22] Yet the House of Commons was not implacable in its hostility towards the Scotch. As Sydney Smith said, for Horner they suspended 'their habitual dislike of lawyers, of political adventurers, and of young men of *conseederable taalents* from the North'.[23] A man had only to show the good judgement to put aside things Scottish and the good taste to adopt the habits and manners of an English gentleman. He had, that is, to cease to be Scotch. It is all that an imperialist race ever requires and for Brougham compliance entailed no sacrifice.

To be Scotch and a lawyer was a double handicap. A friend listening to James Mackintosh making his maiden speech in the House of Commons heard all the country gentlemen round about 'damning him for a Scotch lawyer'.[24] The dislike of lawyers had ancient roots. James I issued a proclamation directing the electorate 'not to choose curious and wrangling lawyers, who seek reputation by stirring needless questions'.[25] It was not, either, a peculiarly English aversion. In 1802 a correspondent of Lady Melbourne reported the opinion of the French Girondist, Tallion, who 'said that the Lawyers had done all the mischief in the Assemblys by their Metaphysicks & Law-jargon, & *really* praised the English H of Commons for not listening to Erskine & his crew'.[26] Most barristers who made a name for themselves in politics—men like Pitt, Dundas and Melbourne— were men of independent means who entered parliament at a young age and, forsaking the circuit, never acquired legal habits. When Brougham entered parliament, Erskine's failure to adapt the brilliant manner of the advocate to the temper of the promiscuous and hostile audience in the House of Commons was fresh in the public mind. It seemed to confirm men in their conviction that a barrister, accustomed to weigh each argument in detail, to dwell upon technical points of law, and to treat all causes with equal gravity, was certain to bore the House, or, by falling into the trap of talking over it with the vulgarity of demeanour and lecturing air of the *nisi prius* advocate, to treat it as if it were an anxious and undiscerning jury. Lawyers, sprung usually from the middle classes, were experts intruding into a world of aristocratic amateurs.

A Lawyer art thou?—draw not nigh!
Go, carry to some fitter place
The keenness of that practised eye,
The hardness of that sallow face.[27]

Lawyers, or so it was held against them, argued from facts and figures; the House of Commons, in the age before the blue books transformed humbug into humdrum, liked men who argued from first principles, who pondered, statesmanlike, on universal themes.

For all that, the law remained the broadest gate through which entry into the purple might be gained by a man born outside it. Brougham, writing in the 1830s of the 'fixed and settled rule that there is in this country a line drawn between the ruling caste and the rest of the community', observed that 'out of a profession like the bar, intimately connected with politics, or out of the patrician circles, themselves the monopolists of political preferment', it was impossible for a man to rise in the political world.[28] Erskine's failure was spectacular, but hardly representative. He came from an arena in which he was acknowledged to be unrivalled into one where he was surrounded by equals and, in some instances, superiors. He had a scanty provision of political knowledge. Above all, he never gave his mind wholly to the art of parliamentary debating. None of this could be said of Brougham. He first made his mark in parliament and his success at the bar was built largely on the reputation which he gained there. Indeed, the ascendancy which he won in the House of Commons suggests that the animus of members of parliament was directed, not so much against lawyers, as against lawyers who continued to behave like advocates in their midst. It was misread, even by contemporaries, as a prejudice against all lawyers, because so few of them learned to play the game of politics by its own rules.

Then there was the third, most damning, liability, the association with journalism. On the eve of his parliamentary debut, Brougham wrote that he was so much accustomed to writing 'that I shall infallibly get into a preaching, dissertating, E. Review kind of manner if I do not look sharp'.[29] The real danger lay elsewhere, in the moral taint which infected the inhabitants of Grub Street. Neither Gladstone nor Salisbury, it is true, suffered from being regular contributors to the reviews, but by the middle of the century journalism had acquired a degree of respectability withheld from it fifty years earlier. Newspapers were then tied to governments, theatres and booksellers; puffing was the rule (Brougham on more than one occasion warmly praised his own publications in the *Edinburgh*); and the practice of 'suppression and contradiction' (by which a person was given the opportunity to pay to have a disagreeable item in a newspaper suppressed beforehand or gainsaid afterwards) was widespread. The efforts of men like the Hunts and Thomas Barnes to make the *Examiner* and *The Times* independent organs stood out as oases of integrity in a desert of skulduggery. The Duke of Wellington's refusal to have dealings with the 'gentlemen of the press' was not mere priggishness. Nor, however, was it simply a reflection of ethical fastidiousness. Political power lay in the shires; journalism flourished in the towns. Journalists were interlopers, urban meddlers in the world of high politics. Worse, they addressed themselves to the populace, thereby not only assisting in the development of a middle-class opinion which threatened the political authority of the landed interest, but encouraging the lower orders who read their reports in ale-houses and gin-shops to contemplate matters above their station. 'Your connection with any newspaper,' Walter Scott warned John Lockhart in 1839, 'would be a disgrace and a degradation. I would rather sell gin to poor people and poison them that way.'[30]

* * *

On 4 February 1810 Brougham was officially returned as member of parliament for Camelford. Two weeks later his father died and soon thereafter Brougham removed his mother permanently to Westmorland and established her in Brougham Hall. His direct link with Scotland was thus severed at the moment that his English parliamentary career began.

Brougham's maiden speech, delivered on 5 March in support of an opposition motion censuring Lord Chatham for a minor constitutional indiscretion, was a modest affair. It was, Horner assured Brougham's mother, in every respect parliamentary in its style of delivery and gave assurance of future success. 'It was well judged to begin with a speech which was *extempore*, and to give this proof of what he can do.'[31] Jeffrey, too, congratulated Brougham on beginning with perfect prudence and good judgement.[32]

For the next three months Brougham kept virtually silent—for the only time in his parliamentary life. On 15 June he rose to deliver his first important speech.[33] Although Wilberforce was still a member of the House, the abolitionist leaders chose Brougham to carry the banner in the next stage of their campaign. The act to abolish the slave trade, passed in 1807, was proving powerless to stop the traffic because the small fines imposed on those who contravened it acted as no deterrent. Brougham therefore proposed that slave-trading should be made a felony punishable by transportation and gave notice that he would be introducing a bill to alter the law in the next session. Campbell exaggerated when he wrote that Brougham came forward 'as if he had long been the acknowledged chief of a party' and by his speech 'conquered a commanding position in the House of

Commons'.[34] But he had deprived the Whig leaders of the opportunity to make the bill a party measure by not taking them into his
confidence, and it was singular for a member of only three months'
standing to take upon himself, without the official backing of his
party, responsibility for a major change in the law. Nor did he evince a
trace of diffidence towards his audience or the objects of his attack.
Who, he asked, were these slave-traders, who subjected human
beings to the horrors, and probable death, of the 'middle passage'?

> Traders, or merchants, did they presume to call themselves, and in
> cities like London and Liverpool, the very creations of honest
> trade? He would give them the right name, at length, and call them
> cowardly suborners of piracy and mercenary murder.

What did the Scriptures, which malicious men made out to be silent
on the subject, say of such evil-doers?

> 'Whosoever' (says the Scripture) 'stealeth a man, and selleth him,
> or in whose hands he shall be found, shall surely be put to death.'
> And what was our gloss or application on this divine text?
> 'Whosoever' (says the English law) 'stealeth a man, and tortureth
> him, and killeth him, shall surely—pay twenty pounds!'

The House was impressed by Brougham's pugnacity—the safe side,
Cockburn said, for all gentlemen to err upon.[35] 'I do assure you,'
Brougham wrote to William Roscoe, the Liverpool radical, 'that all
the abuse I lavished on slave traders (which was really very
unmeasured and only flowed from my feelings towards them) was
cheered the more warmly the more violently it was bestowed.'[36]
    That speech, which won Brougham his parliamentary spurs, was
his sole important contribution to the session of 1810. Privately he
was directing his mind towards domestic questions, hitherto kept in
the background by his interest in foreign and colonial matters. At the
beginning of 1810 he published an invective against Pitt in the
Edinburgh in language which Pitt's admirers found so disrespectful
that Melville wrote to Lord Grenville asking him to have Brougham
put out of parliament.[37] Brougham somewhat ingenuously told
Creevey that his attack on the 'Arch-juggler', as he called him, owed
nothing to 'any reason of party expediency or party concert'.[38] The
truth was that the almost religious veneration in which Pitt's memory
was held made it senseless to oppose the repressive policy at home, the

notorious state trials of the 1790s, and the war with France, without holding Pitt to account. Pitt's friends might find Brougham's remarks an 'unprovoked outrage on their feelings',[39] but it was precisely those feelings which needed dislodging. As Hazlitt, with Pitt in mind, remarked of the maxim that men were not to war with the dead, we ought not to trample on their bodies, 'but with their *minds* we may and must make war, unless we would be governed by them after they are dead'.[40] Pitt's reputation was inseparable from the policy which his successors had inherited. To defrock Pitt was an essential part of educating the nation. In combative spirit, Brougham informed Creevey that if any of their Whig friends took offence at his remarks, the offence 'could only have the effect of making one speak more loudly if possible'.[41]

The two most important domestic issues facing the Whigs in 1810 were Catholic emancipation—the catchphrase for the removal of the ban on Roman Catholics' holding political office—and parliamentary reform. On neither question had the party reached agreement on what should be done if, as expected, the authority of the Crown were invested in the Prince of Wales as Regent and they were invited to take office. On both questions Brougham took a decidedly moderate position, calculated to win Grey's approval and distance himself from the Mountain. He was, he told Allen, not one of that odious description of politicians 'who would give up principles to make a ministry, or would shew any anxiety to see new men without new measures',[42] but his principles were scarcely of the stuff of which martyrdom is made. Although he expressed to Lord Holland his opinion that the party would suffer great loss of character by the smallest abatement in its efforts on behalf of the Irish Catholics, he would go no further than to support their petitions to parliament.[43] To make Catholic emancipation a *sine qua non* of taking office was merely to ensure that the government would remain in the hands of Ireland's enemies, since the Crown objected to incoming ministers laying down conditions.[44] It is difficult to see how, by Brougham's reasoning, the Whigs were to be better friends of the Irish than the government. In addition his apparent solicitude for the constitutional sensibilities of the Crown married ill with his statement in the *Edinburgh Review* that the reform of parliament was required 'chiefly, if not entirely, that a barrier may be raised against the overgrown power of the Crown'.[45] Brougham had not advanced beyond the old Whig notion that the Crown was the chief enemy of the people to the radicals' understanding that the enemy was the unreformed House of Commons itself. Property, he believed, must be allowed to retain its just influence.

The natural influence of property is that which results spontaneously from its ordinary use and expenditure. That a man who spends a large income in the place of his residence—who subscribes handsomely for building bridges, hospitals, and assembly-rooms, and generally to all works of public charity or accommodation in the neighbourhood—and who, moreover, keeps the best table for the gentry, and has the largest accounts with the tradesmen—will, without thinking or caring about the matter, acquire more influence, and find more people to oblige him, than a poorer man of equal virtue and talents—is a fact, which we are as little inclined to deplore, as to call into question. Neither does it cost us any pang to reflect, that, if such a man was desirous of representing the borough in which he resided, or of having it represented by his son or his brother, or some dear and intimate friend, his recommendation would go much farther with the electors than a respectable certificate of the extraordinary worth and abilities of the opposite candidate . . .

In ordinary life, and in common affairs, this natural and indirect influence of property is vast and infallible; and nothing can conduce so surely to the stability and excellence of a political constitution, as to make it rest upon the general principles that regulate the conduct of the better part of the individuals who live under it, and to attach them to their government by the same feelings which ensure their affection or their submission in their private capacity. There could be no security, in short, either for property, or for anything else, in a country where the possession of property did not bestow some political influence.[46]

Such language was far removed from the inflated democratic rhetoric with which, just fifteen months earlier, Brougham had hailed the popular rising in Spain and looked forward to the spreading of its contagion to England. Brougham was susceptible to instant enthusiasms. At the end of 1809, for example, he greeted the unexpected victory of Lord Grenville, the leader of the Pro-Catholic Whigs, over the Tory, Lord Eldon, in the contest for the chancellorship of Oxford University with unreasoning rapture. 'Never was any victory more important or more ominous to the Court,' he wrote to Grey. 'It is better than a majority in Parliament, because it is more permanent and general; it gives "No Popery" a death-blow; Toryism and *twaddle*, and illiberality of every kind, such a shake, as it can scarcely recover.'[47] Men came to expect Brougham's ardour for a cause to wax and wane according to his mood and his circumstances. Parliamentary reform, at any rate, was not one of his pet causes. He wrote the Cevallos article when he was angry with the Whigs for not having brought him into parliament. Once in parliament, his opinions came to resemble theirs more closely. Thrown out again by the Liverpool electors in 1812, he rediscovered his radical voice.

Brougham himself, it needs to be said, put the matter differently. The 1810 session of parliament opened with Canning, his rivalry with Castlereagh having ripened into a public quarrel, removed to the back benches. Grey and Brougham looked upon Canning as the most profligate politician of the age. Yet the longer he remained in opposition the more difficult it would be to act separately from him. It was therefore, in Brougham's view, essential that Grey should take office as quickly as possible, in order to avert 'a coalition of this odious sort'.[48] What folly, then, to saddle the Whigs with an office-denying pledge to the Irish Catholics or a commitment to extensive parliamentary reform. Previous attempts at reform had failed because their promoters had fallen into the error, common to system-builders, of trying to do everything at once. Moderate reform promised to erect a barrier between the Whigs and Canning without forcing a breach between the Grenvillite right wing and the main body of the opposition. Piecemeal reforms could be accepted one at a time and yet by their cumulative effect disarm much of the fear which stood in the way of all innovation. In the circular which he distributed among opposition members in the spring of 1810, Brougham limited his proposals to three modest reforms: a bill to exclude junior officers of the Crown from the House of Commons, one to reform the Scotch county representation, and one to enfranchise copyholders in the English counties. Their object was to weaken the influence of the Crown. 'If you throw open thirty county elections,' he explained to Lord Grenville, 'you make a great step for a first beginning, a very great stride indeed . . . and this is enough at first.'[49] There, it appeared, for all Brougham's spasms of declamatory fervour, was the making of an English Whig.

* * *

In the course of the next two years Brougham consolidated the favourable impression which his initial endeavours had made upon the House and, by taking up a number of humanitarian causes, increased his stock of good will with the reforming portion of the public. His bill to make slave-trading a transportable felony received the royal assent early in the session of 1811 and on several other issues—flogging in the army, the law of libel, the repressive measures introduced to punish Luddite rioters, and the extravagant profits made by the tellers of the exchequer—he found himself in a minority composed chiefly of adherents to the Mountain. Brougham hastened to assure Grey that accusations of his being a Jacobin, or at least a mediator between the party leaders and the Mountain, were absurd. 'I don't believe (as far as my opinions signify) I ever thought of going beyond you.'[50] To the more approachable and more speculative Holland he spoke with less restraint. If men fancied that he was drawing apart from the party, they were misguided. 'What I most invariably have kept in my view, has been an adherence to the true principles of the Whig party & Mr. Fox . . . and if ever I may seem to have differed with the body of the party, it has been owing to the warmth with which I entertain those principles & feelings.'[51]

A politician who is out of step with his party commonly claims to represent its virgin conscience, but in truth what marked Brougham apart was less his opinions than his style. His instinct for attack, his readiness to embarrass the government at every opportunity, contrasted sharply with the insipid leadership which Tierney and Ponsonby gave to the opposition. To his dismay he learned, while on circuit duty in the spring of 1811, that the opposition front bench had voted with ministers to defeat Lord Folkestone's motion to liberalize the libel laws. The episode, he told Holland, bore 'a very unpleasant appearance'.

It has grieved me beyond expression to see the accounts in the newspapers of the division & debate on Ld. Folkestone's motion . . . if the leaders of the party really absented themselves or voted with the Govt. on purpose to discourage the motion & to manifest an indisposition towards such salutary & popular causes, I confess I should apprehend that an open splitting of the Whigs is near at hand, and that those strange *Whigs or Foxites* who love state prosecutions and neither care for the people nor can bear the occasional personalities of the press, and on account of such trifling inquiries hate the press itself, will find themselves deserted by the friends of liberty everywhere, and despised by the real thorough-bred courtiers. For after all, do what they will, they must prove at the best a second-rate kind of tories, & can't fail to be outwitted by your Jenksburies and Castlereaghs who are born & bred to the trade.[52]

The Whigs, Brougham argued, would find themselves stranded and impotent between a Tory party supported by the court and a radical party led by Sir Francis Burdett and supported by the people.

Whence arose the Whigs' short-sightedness? From the fear, Brougham believed, of offending the Prince of Wales. The Whigs, like the 'outs' in the 18th century, were trusting to the reversionary interest to bring them into office. Such blindness! The idle, profligate and tyrannical Prince, whose conduct was 'beyond every epithet of reprobation', would, once the business of making ministries was his, abandon the Whigs. In the meantime the opposition was handing over a host of popular issues, not got up by malcontents, but 'naturally suggested by the events of the day', to the Mountain and Burdett. They were falling deeper and deeper into the error of despising the people and forsaking their own inheritance.

These reflexions [Brougham wrote to John Allen] naturally arise out of the last two debates in the H of C, for you will observe that the Whigs abstaining from such things is by no means a reason with Burdett &c. to avoid them, and accordingly upon every occasion he contrives to do those things which the Party ought to have done. Folkestone's motion on the unjust sentences, and Burdett's on Flogging, are what I particularly allude to, and this night, Whit-bread, Burdett, Romilly &c. made an attack on Solitary confine-ment . . . There is clearly an individual case of oppression, and the abuse seems very general, so that a more truly Whig ground of proceeding cannot easily be supposed. One must think very strangely of the country indeed to be surprised at a man [Burdett] becoming popular who thus seizes every opportunity of doing those things which raised the Whigs formerly high in the public estima-tion . . .

If anything can exceed the childishness of this conduct it is the being offended at those who, when such motions are forced on them, feel it incumbent on them to support them & not to run away, & to make matters still more absurd, such exception is still taken at a time when no sort of concert prevails among the members of the party & no one of the leaders ever thinks of letting his sentiments be known upon any public or party measure.[53]

By thrusting himself forward in debate and taking a progressive line, Brougham exposed the supine leadership of Ponsonby and Tierney. Although Tierney is remembered for saying that the duty of an opposition was to propose nothing and oppose everything, Brougham was scarcely being unfair in complaining to Grey that Tierney behaved as if he were in the cabinet, forgetting always that 'an Opposition can hardly be too active or adventurous'.[54] There were times when Brougham's enthusiasm—self-seeking his critics called it—led him to overstep the mark. When in 1812, for instance, the government proposed to increase the excise duty on leather, and the shoemakers of Northampton placed their case against the proposal in Lord Althorp's hands, Althorp, having mastered the question, found to his surprise that Brougham intended to bring forward the question. Althorp asked him to yield. Brougham refused, and in the end it was Althorp who agreed to second Brougham's motion. Yet the authority and confidence with which Brougham handled a vast range of topics were marvellous to behold. He made himself fluent with the intricate subject of the droits of admiralty (the prizes derived from the sale of confiscated enemy ships) and, by showing that their value had risen to seven or eight million pounds during the long war against France, provided strong ground for his argument that it was a vile job to leave so vast a fund in the free gift of the Crown, especially when, as he broadly hinted in the House, part of the money was squandered on the Prince of Wales' shady entourage. 'There were names and possible cases held out in terrorem,' Horner wrote of Brougham's speech to John Murray, 'which may stop in the mean while some abuses of this fund that were perhaps meditated. I was told by some members who sat near Lord Yarmouth [first lord of the Admiralty] that the words mistress and minion were rung, till he looked black upon them'.[55] Brougham knew that Tierney and others were somewhat put out by his rise to prominence,[56] but the fault was theirs. As Horner rightly said, questions such as the droits of admiralty, pertinent to the Whigs' age-old campaign against the patronage and influence of the Crown, had been waiting for years to be treated by so able a hand.[57]

Larger matters claimed Brougham's attention. Nothing did more to raise his reputation, in parliament and in the country, than his successful defence of the Hunt brothers in a libel action of 1811 and his triumphant assault upon the orders-in-council in 1812. Each of them was a stunning personal achievement, representing, as each did, a popular victory over established authority. The one secured Brougham's place at the bar: never again did he want for lucrative briefs. The other secured him a permanent place in the annals of parliament and raised him to that eminence in the House of Commons which he occupied for the rest of his days there.

At the beginning of the 1812 session of parliament Brougham returned to the subject of the orders-in-council. By then a new element had been added to the debate about their economic usefulness, the prospect, namely, of their provoking war with the United States. In 1808 the American government had responded to the French and the British ordinances by placing an embargo on trade with both belligerents. Anglo-American trade fell sharply and American opinion, already inflamed by Great Britain's use of the press gang to enlist Americans in port in the royal navy and also by the searching of American ships for deserters and contraband, became increasingly bellicose. In these circumstances, powerful sections of American society, especially in the world of trade and commerce, were ready to take advantage of Great Britain's European preoccupations to satisfy their covetous longing to annex Canada and Florida (the possession of Great Britain's ally, Spain) to the United States.

War was far from inevitable. In 1811, the American government, in an effort to avert it, asked the British government to relax the orders-in-council. Brougham found, throughout the north of England, an almost unanimous desire on the part of commercial men to avoid war by restoring free trade between the countries. In the latter part of 1811 he organized the gathering of petitions against the orders and against the war in all the leading industrial towns of the north. When, therefore, he brought the matter before the House in the first week of March 1812, he was backed by the almost unanswerable weight of public opinion. As in 1808 the House had no choice but to grant his request that witnesses be heard. Proceedings began on 5 May and during the next six weeks—uninterrupted, at Brougham's insistence, even by the assassination of the prime minister, Spencer Perceval— the government, feebly defended by George Rose, watched helplessly as witness after witness and petition after petition declared against it. At last, near the end of June (too late to prevent war with America) the government yielded and announced the repeal of the orders.

Parliamentary history records few greater personal triumphs. A government, normally secure in its majority, faced by a fragmented and timid opposition, had been forced to capitulate, at the height of its war with Napoleon, on a major article of its commercial and military policy. Public opinion had gained one of its first direct victories over the legislature. And, as Castlereagh recognized, the landed aristocracy had suffered its first defeat at the hands of the new industrial interest. In an episode prophetic of the future, Brougham had led the Whigs away from their accustomed agriculturalist assumptions towards an alliance with trade. He had done it, too, by pushing against the conventions of polite politics. Whipping up opinion out of doors was unseemly in a respectable politician. (In 1809 Romilly, for all his devotion to the cause of parliamentary reform, declined an invitation to attend a public meeting on the subject from his 'very great aversion to acting any conspicuous part, or putting myself forward in any way, out of the House, upon any public measure'.)[58] Brougham acknowledged the support he had received from Lord Grenville and Alexander Baring, but no one disputed that the laurels of the victory belonged to him almost alone. Even John Ward, who had just quitted the Whigs to range himself under Canning's standard, was unwilling to stint his praise. 'Brougham,' he wrote to "Ivy", 'is at the height of human glory . . . His notions upon popular questions are not much to my taste, but I heartily rejoice at his prosperity. It is delightful to see the success of great talents and industry—particularly in the person of an old friend.'[59] Near the end of his life, Brougham looked back upon the repeal of the orders as the greatest achievement of his life, notwithstanding all that he had done for education, the slaves, charitable trusts and law reform. 'In these I had the sympathy and aid of others, but in the battle against the Orders in Council I fought alone.'[60]

Far less important in its consequences, but just as satisfying personally, was Brougham's successful defence of Leigh Hunt and his brother, accused by the Crown of libel after their paper, the *Examiner*, had reprinted from the *Stamford News* an anonymous article (written by John Scott) entitled 'One Thousand Lashes!!!'. Soon after his arrival in London Brougham had made the acquaintance of Leigh Hunt, and Hunt was not long in seeking his criticisms of his translations of Latin poetry. Brougham, for his part, encouraged the Hunts' endeavours to make the *Examiner* a muck-raking paper. 'I cannot but greatly applaud the boldness as well as the ability of your attacks upon the ruinous and unworthy conduct of our present rulers,' he wrote to Leigh Hunt on one occasion, 'and I am persuaded that the Press alone can now be looked to as the saviour of the Country, & the discussions in Parlt. *thro'* the Press.'[61] To counteract the influence of the radical press the government had recently revived the practice of filing *ex officio* informations against publishers. In the two years from 1808 to 1810 such files had risen to the unprecedented number of forty-two, although twenty-six of them were not, in the event, brought to a prosecution.

Scott's article was an attack upon the use of flogging as a punishment by the army. Great Britain lagged far behind Napoleonic Europe in the barbarous severity of its criminal law and alone of all European nations retained flogging in the services. Time and time again, Romilly had called the attention of parliament to instances of men dying from the infliction of hundreds of lashes. Yet parliament, fearful of bringing discredit upon the army in time of war, was reluctant to deliver the mildest of rebukes and shrank from the very discussion of the question. Grey warned Romilly that 'any measure which would draw the public attention to the subject was very objectionable'.[62] In 1810 Cobbett was fined £1,000 and sentenced to two years' imprisonment for remarks upon flogging in the *Political Register*. When the Hunts' trial came on at Westminster in January 1811, the verdict, therefore, was hardly in doubt.

The case drew forth all Brougham's powers. Here was the hated authority of the Crown, backed by the might of the law, shielding its inhumanity from the public gaze and perpetuating a vile cruelty by the cowardly resort to censorship. The information charged the Hunts with raising sedition and mutiny in the forces. Brougham was able to show that military men, men held in such great esteem as Brigadier-General Stewart and General Sir Robert Wilson, men whose ambition was scarcely to discourage the recruitment of soldiers or lower morale in the ranks, had published pamphlets calling for the abolition of flogging in language far stronger than Scott's. No action had been taken against them, nor against the beloved Pitt, whose speeches against the slave trade and the conditions of slave life in the West Indies must be held, if the charge against the Hunts were sustained, to have encouraged sedition and rebellion among His Majesty's slave subjects. That was the narrow ground of the defence, intended to absolve the Hunts of a seditious intent. But Brougham was not content to let the matter rest there. At stake was the liberty of the subject, at risk the right to free individual expression.

If there is a difference in the importance of different subjects—if one person naturally feels more strongly than another upon the same matter—if there are some subjects on which all men who, in point of animation are above the level of a stock or a stone, do feel warmly;—have they not a right to express themselves in proportion to the interest which the question naturally possesses, and to the strength of the feeling it excites in them? If they have no such power as this, to what, I demand, amounts the boasted privilege of free speech? It is the free privilege of a fettered discussion; it is the unrestrained choice of topics which another selects; it is the liberty of an enslaved press; it is the native vigour of impotent argument. The grant is not qualified, but resumed by the conditions. The rule is eaten up with the exceptions.

Then came the peroration, a scornful, sarcastic ridiculing of men stupid enough to imagine that it was public knowledge of the atrocity of flogging, not the atrocity itself, which endangered morale in the army.

The men therefore are to see their comrades tied up, and to behold the flesh stripped off from their bodies, aye, bared to the bone! They are to see the very ribs and bones from which the mangled flesh has been scourged away—without a sentiment of discontent, without one feeling of horror, without any emotion but that of tranquil satisfaction! And all this the by-standers are also to witness, without the smallest risk of thinking twice, after such a scene, whether they shall enter into such a service! There are no fears entertained of exciting dissatisfaction among the soldiers themselves by the sight of their comrade thus treated . . . all is safe; there is no chance of their being moved; no complaint, no indignation, not the slightest emotion of pity, or blame, or disgust, or indignation can reach their hearts from the spectacle before them. But have a care how, at a distance from the scene, and long after its horrors have closed, you say one word upon the subject!. . . because, if you should attempt to express your opinions upon that subject, a single word of argument—one accidental remark—will rouse the whole army into open revolt![63]

Lord Ellenborough, summing up in his accustomed forthright

manner, claimed the duty, under Fox's 1793 libel act, of informing the jury that it was his opinion that the Hunts were guilty of the seditious intention imputed to them in the charge. In so doing he perverted— and there were few men charitable enough to put the error down to his ignorance—the unmistakable meaning of Fox's act, that the judge should inform the jury of the nature of a libellous intention, while leaving the jury to decide whether the accused had had such an intention. Ellenborough's impudent conduct made Brougham's triumph the sweeter. In a remarkable show of independence the jury acquitted the Hunts.

> I am sure the enclosed accounts of Brougham's success this morning [Lord Rosslyn wrote to Grey] will give you pleasure; I can only add that he had no hope of a verdict, & that there seems to have been but one opinion . . . that it was a desperate case. It was a most violent & seditious passage in the *Examiner*.[64]

'I think it a great victory for the public,' John Murray wrote from Edinburgh to congratulate Brougham, 'for the prosecution of libels is carried too far, and it is a great object that it should be checked. You are the first person since Erskine who has done so, and you have now a much higher situation than any ministry could give you.'[65]

The verdict had few repercussions. Three weeks later Brougham was unsuccessful, as a special pleader at the Lincoln assizes, in his effort to defend the proprietor of the *Stamford News* charged with the identical offence. In 1814 parliament, in a gesture sublimely contemptuous of mercy or reason, limited the number of lashes to 300, but flogging was not abolished until 1868. Nor did the Hunts' acquittal strike a blow for the liberty of the press. Only a year after the flogging case, Leigh Hunt was again brought before Lord Ellenborough to answer for his mocking reply to the *Morning Post*'s fawning description of the fat, middle-aged Prince of Wales as an 'Adonis in loveliness'. Hunt gave an accurate picture of the prince— 'a violator of his word, a libertine over head and ears in debt and disgrace, a despiser of domestic ties, a man who has just closed half a century without one single claim on the gratitude of his country or the respect of posterity'—and even Brougham, whom Ellenborough most irregularly accused of being inoculated with all the poison of the libel, was unable, despite an eloquent passage fastening the words *effeminacy* and *cowardice* where no one could fail to apply them, to rescue him from the consequences of speaking the truth.

Brougham's friends in the Whig party rejoiced at his victory in the 1811 trial, but Brougham was saddened by the narrow view which they took of it. 'Tho' I have received abundance of personal congratulations,' he wrote to Lord Holland, 'it does so happen that I can find none of our friends (except the *Mountain*) who care a farthing about the cause itself.'[66] The distinction, he pointed out to John Allen, was quite marked. 'I was only mortified to find so many of the Whigs (I may say almost the whole regular party) regretting upon public grounds that which from kindness to myself they were disposed to congratulate me upon.'[67] A few weeks later the Whigs, as we have seen, failed to support Lord Folkestone's motion to restrain the Crown in its citing of *ex officio* informations for libel and in the 1812 session of parliament only eight members voted in favour of Burdett's bill to abolish flogging.

The flogging trials, resonant in their libertarian and humanitarian overtones, were ideally suited to Brougham's temper and style. Criticisms of his courtroom manner were frequent. James Losh, a Durham barrister and educational reformer who was to become a confidential friend and ardent admirer of Brougham, first heard him on the northern circuit in 1812 and found him 'vigorous and indeed eloquent, but somewhat too vehement for the Bar and defective also as not having a sufficient degree of calm statement'.[68] Horner, too, while praising the reach and compass of Brougham's mind and the industry with which he collected information, thought his arguments to be deficient in 'the best style of legal reasoning'. Brougham's success at the bar was nevertheless prodigious, more rapid and extensive, Horner believed, than that of any barrister at the outset of his career since Erskine.[69] From 1812 onwards his income from the northern circuit never fell below £8,000, making his practice one of the most lucrative in the profession. If, as a contemporary writer on legal affairs remarked,[70] the tendency of the times was for the courts to adopt enlarged and liberal principles of construction to the injury of strict technical rules, so that decisions were coming to be based less on principles of law and more on vulgar notions of equity, Brougham's success, however galling to plodders better versed in the fine points of the law, is not surprising. Whereas most lawyers in parliament carried a courtroom style into the House, Brougham treated the courts to displays of rotund parliamentary oratory.

Brougham's energy and eloquence had raised him, in just two years, to the front of the Whig ranks. He was reckoned as the most formidable of the candidates for the leadership of the opposition in the House of Commons. In a future Whig ministry he seemed assured of a leading place. The prospect of such a ministry, however, was fast receding. The Whigs had been disappointed by the failure of the Prince of Wales, on becoming Regent, to dismiss Perceval and install them in office. Invited to join Perceval's government, Grey and Grenville refused, on the ground that they were unwilling to work with ministers who had promised to remain silent on the matter of Catholic emancipation. Then, in May 1812, after Perceval's assassination, they again declined the offer of four or five places in a reconstructed Tory administration to be headed by Wellesley and include Canning. They would come in as a party or they would not come in at all. Brougham agreed that it was impossible for the Whigs to row in the same boat as Canning and Wellesley. 'Anything without the country,' he wrote to Creevey while the abortive negotiations were taking place, 'is real madness or drivling.'[71] But if the Whigs were to eschew coalition with the Tories on the one hand and by their pusillanimous conduct in parliament fail to make themselves into a popular party on the other, how were they ever to come into office? What was the object, from a party point of view, of bringing public pressure to bear on the government, of agitating the country so successfully as to compel the government to abandon the orders-in-council, if such efforts were not made the foundation for building a party so firmly established in popular support that the Court should be impotent against it? Ruefully Brougham concluded, in the *Edinburgh Review*, that

> the lot of the Whigs is merely to modify and palliate the mischievous proceedings of the Tories, by their opposition, and to come in, for a few months or weeks, once or twice in a reign, to carry through some great and salutary measure, which it goes against the consciences of the said Tories to adopt—and to go back again to the unpopularity of conscious virtue, which is so obviously their portion in this world.[72]

* * *

Disappointing the Whigs' exclusion may have been, but it was as nothing in comparison to the blow dealt Brougham by the Duke of Bedford. In the autumn of 1811 the Duke informed Brougham that he had decided to sell his nomination to the representation of Camelford at the next dissolution of parliament. Bedford's course was dictated by financial considerations. It owed nothing, as both he and Brougham were eager to make known, to political differences between them. Brougham remained thoroughly persuaded of the Duke's fairness and liberality. The timing of the announcement, however, was unfortunate. A month earlier Brougham had turned down an offer to come in for Worcester, partly from the apprehension that to fight a contested election there might, if he were defeated, put at risk his connection with Bedford and Camelford. By the time that Bedford made his intention known, another candidate had started on the Worcester interest.

Brougham had not far to seek for another invitation. After the repeal of the orders-in-council the towns of the north had held dinner after dinner to pay tribute to him. At one such dinner in August, organized at Liverpool by his Lancashire friends, William Roscoe, Dr Shepherd and Lord Sefton, it was proposed that he should stand at Liverpool at the coming general election. Brougham took time to consider the invitation. We may wonder at his statement to John Allen that few people would be less chagrined at being out of parliament than he,[73] but he was deterred, as Romilly had been a few years earlier, by the tumult and bribery which always accompanied a Liverpool election. On the other hand, Liverpool offered him a public platform and the certainty that his campaign would be closely reported in the national press.

> There is some good to be done [he wrote to Leigh Hunt] even in the present state of things by popular elections & by bringing together large bodies of men to hear peaceable, free & sound language. This is all I have to set agt. the great inconvenience of such elections & of the kind of seat one has, even after succeeding. But I really am much in debt to the Liverpool people for their friendly zeal, and I foresee it will be difficult to be off.[74]

More to the point, it was difficult to see where else he might stand, since the Whigs did not come forward with a pocket borough to replace Camelford. In the end the Liverpool committee decided to put up two candidates in the liberal interest, Brougham and Thomas Creevey, so that the battle for the town's two seats became a contest between them on the one side and, on the other, Thomas Gascoigne, standing in the 'corporation interest', and the Tory, Canning.

Sefton assured Brougham that he would be supported by

Gascoigne's voters,[75] Gascoigne having voted for the repeal of the orders-in-council, whereas Canning had opposed it. If, as General Tarleton, the sitting member who was squeezed out by the two Whig candidates, believed, the election was to be determined by the orders issue, Brougham's prospects appeared bright. There were, however, formidable difficulties in his way. He had made enemies of those persons, perhaps as many as 10,000, who were involved in the slave trade. As Brougham said many years later, the wealthy merchants hated him 'with a hatred hardly natural for branding them with the name and fate of felons'.[76] His candidacy also alarmed the Church-and-King party in Orange Liverpool; his advocacy of Catholic relief was well known and he was surrounded by men like Roscoe and Sefton who for a generation had been the leaders of the pro-Catholic element in the borough.

Brougham entered the fray in high spirits. 'I am in for it,' he wrote to Grey as soon as he had agreed to stand, 'and accordingly I shall go through it as if it were a matter of life and death.'[77] In the course of just three weeks, Brougham made 160 speeches. He struck terror in his opponents' hearts by the fierceness of his campaign and the volleys of declamation which he delivered against the Tories. Over and over again he appealed to the desire of the trading community for open trade and peace. On the fourth day of polling a dramatic turn occurred, when it was learned that Great Britain, by licensing privateers with letters of marque and reprisal, had entered into war with America in earnest. On the same day arrived the news that Moscow was burning. In the evening, before a crowd of several thousand, Brougham treated his supporters to a fiery philippic against Pitt, the begetter of war.

Gentlemen, I stand up in this contest against the friends and followers of Mr. Pitt, or, as they partially designate him, the immortal statesman now no more. *Immortal* in the miseries of his devoted country! Immortal in the wounds of her bleeding liberties! Immortal in the cruel wars which sprang from his cold miscalculating ambition! Immortal in the intolerable taxes, the countless loads of debt which these wars have flung upon us—which the youngest man amongst us will not live to see the end of! Immortal in the triumph of our enemies, and the ruin of our allies, the costly purchase of so much blood and treasure! Immortal in the afflictions of England, and the humiliation of her friends, through the whole results of his twenty years' reign, from the first rays of favour with which a delighted Court gilded his early apostacy [sic], to the deadly glare which is at this instant cast upon his name by the burning metropolis of our last ally! But may no such immortality ever fall to my lot—let me rather live innocent and inglorious; and when at last I cease to serve you, and to feel for your wrongs, may I have an humble monument in some nameless stone, to tell that beneath it there rests from his labours in your service, '*an enemy of the immortal statesman—a friend of peace and of the people*'.[78]

The speech, which 'shook the very square and all the houses in it from the applause it met with',[79] disconcerted many Whigs. Brougham was unrepentant. 'I prize it for the effect it produced,' he wrote to Leigh Hunt, '& the untoward circumstances under which I made it, or rather it burst from me, for it was the dictate of the moment . . . and I desire to be in every respect judged by that speech. It was made to a real popular assembly of 4 or 5000 people, all in a state of agitation & passion not to be described.'[80]

At the end of eight days' polling Brougham lay second, behind Canning but ahead of Gascoigne. In the end, however, Tory money and corporation influence were too powerful to be overcome and on the twelfth day Brougham and Creevey withdrew. To Creevey the result meant little: he was safely returned for Thetford. For Brougham it meant the abrupt termination of a parliamentary career so brilliantly begun. Defeat was all the more painful for being unnecessary. Roscoe's enthusiasm was almost certainly to blame. It was the double Whig candidature which brought Canning into the field. Left to fight against Gascoigne, alongside Tarleton, an independent but as anti-government as any regular Whig, Brougham's return would scarcely have been in doubt. He would have preferred to stand with Tarleton, but, as he told Grey, it was not for him to prescribe to the Liverpool committee. Horner was scathing in his condemnation of Roscoe and his colleagues, 'the most perfect specimens of wrong-headedness, men of a dissenting, provincial cast of virtue', who deemed it treachery to the cause to be content with half a loaf and would rather lose everything contending for the whole.[81] Brougham was given the opportunity to escape from the consequences of Roscoe's impetuosity. At the close of the fourth day, when he was running Canning close, his opponents suggested a compromise: Gascoigne and Creevey should retire to leave the spoils to

Brougham and Canning. Brougham rejected the suggestion out of hand. Neither he nor Grey would dishonour themselves by assisting Canning's return. Nor, in the despondency of defeat, did he waver. 'The more I reflect on it I rejoice the more that the unbending course was preferred to that which would have yoked me to a man so adverse in all points of principle.'[82]

4

Out of Parliament

The Liverpool contest drained Brougham of his energies and left him feeling ill for some weeks. It also gave him direct experience of the shameful working of the electoral system and turned his mind, fleetingly at least, in the direction of extensive parliamentary reform. Liverpool, he discovered, for all its reputation as a large, open borough, was every bit as closed a constituency as Camelford. In each place the same minute proportion of the electorate enjoyed the privilege of voting. Affairs at Liverpool were, indeed, the more sorry, since the bulk of the electorate consisted of freemen in thrall to the shipping and other powerful interests. The remedy, Brougham concluded, was a liberal addition to the electorate. It is doubtful whether he would have taken that view of the matter had the Whig freemen of Liverpool, those in servitude to the American traders and a portion of the country gentlemen, not been, as he allowed, outnumbered by the Tory freemen who owed their votes to the shipbuilders and the town corporation.

Brougham was angry with the Whigs. He did not cease to esteem the services which the Whig aristocracy had rendered, and retained the power to render in the future, to the cause of the people; nor did he wish to deprive the people of their 'natural & fit' leaders.[1] But the leading lights of the opposition—Tierney, Romilly, Horner and himself—had been thrown out of parliament at the late elections because the Whig boroughmongers had sacrificed the needs of the party to their own selfish concerns.

> Romilly, Tierney, Lamb, &c. being out of Parliament [he wrote to Lord Grey] is a great imputation on some of our friends. They must not hereafter talk of the fickleness and wrong-headedness of the people, nor even of the great sin of not being wholly party-men; for these professors of party-attachments have no sort of scruple to dissolve the regular Whig interest, or leave it with one single leader in the House of Commons, rather than forego the gratification of

84

giving some cousin or toad-eater a power of franking letters! This is their love of the Whig cause, and the constitution and the party.[2]

Many people expected that Brougham, smarting from defeat, would, as John Ward put it, 'turn downright Jacobin'.[3] Brougham pooh-poohed Ward's language, but he delivered veiled threats that he intended to take a more popular line. He drew Lord Grey's attention to the large, well-funded reform associations which were coming into existence in the northern towns. The prospects for good which these associations opened sweetened the pill of electorate defeat. 'I believe as much good may be done out of Parlt. as in it, and I don't deny that it is my intention not to be idle.'[4] To Creevey Brougham wrote in more honest and more splenetic vein. Having received from all the Whig leaders except Grey 'regular letters of dismissal, thanking me for past services', he had half a mind to take up parliamentary practice at the bar and thereby make enough money to buy his way back into parliament. It was, he knew, a dishonourable course of action. Nor had he ever contemplated it

till I began to get angry with the leading Whigs for their cool way of taking leave; as much as to say—it is out of the question our ever bringing you in again. This, and the knowledge of others, as Plumer &c. being brought in, has rather raised my spleen, and given me an inclination to go into that line [parliamentary practice] and make enough to buy a seat (with what I can afford to add, viz. £2000 or £2500), and then come in and enjoy the purest of all pleasures—at once to do what I most approve of in politics and give the black ones an infernal licking every other night![5]

Brougham was less than fair to the Whigs. Rosslyn and Lauderdale had, as soon as the 1812 elections were over, pressed his claim upon Grey and Grey did what little was in his power to find seats for the defeated candidates. Tierney alone was rescued by his efforts, but as he explained to William Lamb, who, like Brougham, had complained of the party's 'cold neglect', he was impotent to coerce boroughmongers who would not be moved by entreaty.[6]

Brougham's temper soon cooled. By the end of the year he was giving cordial assurances to Grey (who understood the importance to the party of keeping its most energetic member sweet) that he would welcome the opportunity to come in on the Whig interest whenever it should arise, albeit adding, with the unpleasantness of a blackmailer, that he could not answer for his frame of mind by the time of the next dissolution.[7] Brougham's behaviour in the next few years has been interpreted as marking a sharp veer to the left.[8] There is little convincing evidence of such a shift in his opinions. It is true that in the three years he spent out of parliament his attachment to Bentham and James Mill deepened, but most of the time was occupied in consolidating his position on the northern circuit, working with the anti-slavery society, and continuing to supply Jeffrey with articles for the *Edinburgh Review*.

Immediately after his defeat at Liverpool, Brougham was taken up by the veteran radical, Major Cartwright, a man of narrow views, but for forty years an unwavering advocate of parliamentary reform. Cartwright offered Brougham and Romilly the representation of Middlesex, as if, what was not so, it were in his gift, on the condition that they pledge themselves to support the introduction of the secret ballot, universal suffrage and annual parliaments. Cartwright argued that seven-year parliaments, which had existed since the septennial act of 1716, effectively disfranchised for a number of years a man who came of age early in the life of a parliament. Brougham and Romilly declined his invitation, pointing out that his logic led to the justice of monthly or even weekly elections.[9] Brougham told John Allen that he was fully aware of 'the nonsense that is talked on this subject & of the subordinate value of the question, compared with some others'.[10] The remark discloses the gulf which separated Brougham from the radicals. To them, whether fiery Cobbettites who ranted against 'The Thing' or learned Millites who spoke darkly of 'the sinister interest', all the ills of society were traceable to the unrepresentative, aristocratic constitution and none was curable until the poisonous root was destroyed.

In the autumn of 1812 Cartwright also engaged Brougham to defend a number of Manchester radicals accused of inciting Luddite riots. Brougham's advocacy gained thirty-eight of them an acquittal and he followed this success by going to York at the turn of the year to attend the Special Commission which was trying Luddites there. Brougham had made a name for himself by taking 'the sedition line' and the frequency with which he defended the civil liberties of the subject in court kept the polish on his radical reputation with the public. He, of course, knew that the appearance was often deceiving. Indeed, in a notable encounter with Lord Ellenborough in 1814 he was delighted to upbraid the Chief Justice for making the elementary

G. Hayter's oil painting of the House of Lords during the divorce proceedings against Queen Caroline. Brougham (*centre, standing facing the viewer*) is in conversation with Thomas Denman, while between him and Lord Grey (*standing with right arm extended*) sits Queen Caroline.

The four *Edinburgh Reviewers*
Top: Sydney Smith *Bottom:* Francis Jeffrey

Top: Francis Horner
Bottom: Henry Brougham

This cartoon is typical of the radicals' lampooning of Brougham's educational activities, condemned by men like Cobbett as schemes to indoctrinate the lower orders with Whig creeds.

mistake, during a trial for blasphemy, of identifying the advocate's opinions with those of his client. He accused Ellenborough of bullying and demanded a public recantation of the slur. Ellenborough, 'meek as a lamb' and, as Henry Crabb Robinson testified, 'evidently mortified', was compelled to climb down and avow that he had intended to make no insinuation against him.[11]

Episodes of that kind raised Brougham in stature at the bar. They point to no leftward lurch in his politics. The Luddite trials brought him up against the facts of industrial poverty and he prepared a report, early in 1813, on disturbances in the manufacturing districts. He presented it, however, to the *Whig* leaders and his remedy for working-class distress did not go beyond the acceptable nostrums of peace, retrenchment in government expenditure, and the lifting of the property tax imposed in 1797. The last of those was directed chiefly towards the relief of farmers; it had no direct bearing on the urban workers who earned too little to pay the tax. Brougham remained, in short, where he had always been, in the reformist wing of the Whig party. Yet there was some truth to his repeated avowals, in these years, that he had no claim on the Whigs' patronage, not being a regular party man. The reform programme which, had he been elected in 1812, he intended to bring forward in the new parliament, contained no reference to parliamentary reform. Instead it enumerated, in addition to bringing an end to the war with the United States, a reform of the tithe, a scheme for popular education, and a remodelled libel act to increase the liberty of the press. The appeal of those proposals lay beyond the party battlefield. They were calculated neither to attract the Whigs nor to embarrass the government, but to raise Brougham in the public mind as a national politician removed from the sham dogfighting in the House of Commons.

The elections of 1812 had increased the government's majority in the House of Commons, while the Whig front benches continued to show more interest in squabbling among themselves than in opposing ministers. Whitbread, whose virtues Brougham continued to preach to Grey, remained a disgruntled outcast, alienated from the party's inner circle by what Ward called his 'high popular doctrines'[12] and also by his resentment at their past conduct towards him. In the circumstances Brougham affected to disdain the petty proceedings of parliament. 'You know I care not two farthings one way or t'other,' he wrote to Creevey, 'and have far more liking—I should rather say far

less dislike—towards C[anning] than to many of our own friends—
the little Whigs who ruin the party . . . The Ministry being dished
over and over again has no effect in turning them out, because our
friends have lost the confidence of the people—a plant of slow growth
and almost impossible to make sprout again after it has been plucked
up and frostbitten—for example, by the Grenville winter.'[13] There
was something more than sour grapes to this outburst. On only one
issue, the emancipation of the Roman Catholics, did Brougham and
Canning find themselves on the same side of the political divide. Both
men, however, experienced the frustration of battling against the
entrenched elites who ruled their respective parties. Neither of them
ever felt entirely comfortable in the company of the landed
aristocracy. Had the ingrained habits of party not kept them apart
until a few months before Canning's death, their mutual, distant
admiration might have blossomed into a political alliance powerful
enough to have dominated post-Waterloo politics. Or would their
natures, alike proud and bent on domination, have made fruitful co-
operation between them impossible? Like Canning, Brougham was
exhilarated by the game of politics. It was useless for him, after the
Liverpool setback, to pretend otherwise. 'I wish you were not so
perverse and so *coquettish* about coming into Parliament,' Lady
Charlotte Lindsay, lady-in-waiting to Princess Caroline, chided him.
'I give you no credit for either your ambition or your politics being on
the decline.'[14]

For some time Brougham had been drawing closer to the Benthamite set. In 1811 he joined James Mill and others, mostly
Quakers, in establishing the Royal Lancasterian Society (after 1814
the British and Foreign School Society) to provide cheap primary
education for working-class children in London on the monitorial
method begun by Joseph Lancaster a few years earlier at his Borough
Road school. Brougham was brought into the movement by William
Allen, the Quaker with whom he had worked for several years in the
anti-slave trade campaign. There he made the acquaintance of
Francis Place, the Charing Cross tailor who was fast becoming the
moving spirit of radical politics in the metropolis. Place, like Mill a
disciple of Bentham, aspired to make the Lancasterian Society the
basis of a comprehensive system of primary and secondary education,
and although he had nothing but scorn for the know-nothing, time-
serving Whigs, Brougham impressed him as 'one of the few who see
the whole scope and extent of what it may lead to'.[15]

At about the same time, Mill introduced Brougham to Bentham. Bentham, of course, knew of Brougham by reputation, but he was ever shy of making new friendships and it was not until July 1812, after angling for an invitation for months, that Brougham at last sat down to one of the master's select suppers at Queen's Place Square, Westminster. Bentham then wrote of him that he was 'already one of the first men in the House of Commons, and seems in a fair way of being very soon universally acknowledged to be the very first'.[16] Two months later Brougham was out of parliament, disaffected and seemingly at loose ends. Mill, Bentham and Place sought to bring him more closely within their proselytizing circle. The attempt was doomed to failure. They found it impossible to closet so flirtatious a mind as Brougham's within the systematic confines of utilitarianism. Nor were they able to make Brougham look upon the Whigs as the enemy. Brougham's *amour propre* would not suffer him to accept the fawning attendance which Bentham asked of his acolytes, who were expected to refine his ideas, revise his texts, propagate his gospel, in short to form, as Francis Horner called the group, a 'Scribbling Shop'.[17] Nevertheless, the rapid ingenuity of his conversation and the practical bent of his liberalism commended themselves to Bentham and their friendship lasted, unimpaired save for one unpleasant disagreement near the end, until Bentham's death in 1832.

The first fruit of the Benthamite connection came in the spring of 1814, when events made it appear almost certain that a by-election was forthcoming at the Westminster constituency. Not long before Brougham had described the representation of the borough, with its large, relatively uncorrupted and sophisticated electorate, as 'the summit of popular ambition'. To possess it placed a man in a position to do infinite good.[18] At the beginning of 1814 the two sitting members were both radicals, Sir Francis Burdett and the naval hero, Lord Cochrane. When, in March, Cochrane was implicated, undoubtedly unjustly, in a stock exchange swindle, it was commonly expected that he would be expelled from the House of Commons. A vacancy would thus arise at Westminster. Long before events came to that pass the parties were busy in the field to find candidates to succeed him. The Whigs brought forward Richard Brinsley Sheridan, once a glittering ornament of their front bench, but now at the age of sixty-three having lost his oratorical sparkle. His swollen face bore the marks of debauchery and his involvement in the Drury Lane Theatre had left him debt-ridden. Worse, he was politically discredited by his devious part in the 1812 ministerial negotiations which left the Whigs high and dry and by his continued friendship with the turncoat Prince Regent.

Sheridan's candidacy rendered a Whig-radical alliance at the by-election impossible. On the radical side two names were canvassed from the beginning: Brougham and Major Cartwright. The choice lay with the Westminster Committee, the powerful electoral organization built up by Francis Place. Brougham, who was brought forward by Place and James Mill, had several advantages over the veteran reformer. He was young and had already proved his mettle in the Commons, whereas Cartwright was seventy-four and had never sat in the House. The Tories, moreover, decided not to put up a candidate, but to support Sheridan in an attempt to break the radical hold on the borough. Their decision ensured that the contest would be a close one. The radicals needed a candidate who could attract Whig votes. Brougham therefore looked a far better prospect than Cartwright, especially since it was known that the influential Russell-Cavendish section of the Whigs was resolved to desert Sheridan and support him.

Brougham's weakness was his ambivalent attitude to parliamentary reform. Francis Place laid down as a condition of adoption that the radical candidate pledge himself, in a written statement, to the three cardinal articles of the radical faith: the extension of the franchise to all taxpayers, the creation of equal electoral districts, and the introduction of annual parliaments. Place knew, of course, of Brougham's adamant opposition to the last of them, but by dangling the plum of Westminster before him he hoped to trap him into making a declaration from which he would find it difficult subsequently to retreat. Brougham produced a hedged statement which, without giving hostages to fortune, apparently satisfied Place, though Cartwright told a friend it was all moonshine.[19] In the end none of it mattered. The public, sceptical of the evidence brought against Cochrane at his trial and shaken by the severe sentence of a year's imprisonment, a fine of £1,000 and consignment to the pillory, rallied to his standard when the House of Commons expelled him on 5 July, after a debate enlivened by declarations from leading Whigs, notably Whitbread and George Ponsonby, that they believed Cochrane to be innocent. Feeling in the constituency ran so strong in Cochrane's favour that all the candidates withdrew from the race and he was re-elected unopposed.

For Brougham the result was, on the whole, satisfactory. A contest would have further damaged his standing in the Whig party by placing him in open competition with the party's nominee, Sheridan, however much some of the Whigs might have shared his amusement at the infinite folly of the party's discovering in the rat to Carlton House an old and trusted adherent of Charles James Fox.[20] Victory must sooner or later have exposed the duplicity of his compliance with the far-reaching constitutional reforms of the radicals. His dalliance with Francis Place, a man of vastly different antecedents and social milieu from his own, was from the beginning uncomfortable. Place, reared in poverty and as a young journeyman breeches-maker black-listed by employers for leading a strike, was, in effect, asking Brougham to give up the fashionable drawing-rooms of the great houses for the grimy, clamorous streets of working-class London. Brougham had not courted the radicals; they had made suit to him. He had neither the fixity of purpose nor the congenital anger at the existing order which enabled them to forgo the game of parliamentary 'ins and outs'.

The question which did fix Brougham's attention, the plight of the slaves, played no part in the Westminster manoeuvrings. Place and his committee were unmoved by it. Brougham, and the African Institution of which he was a director, had not, however, lost interest in the question simply because Great Britain had abolished the trade in slaves. Great Britain's example had not been followed by the other leading European colonial powers, France, Spain and Portugal. Brougham had sedulously carried on the war against the foreign slave trade in the pages of the *Edinburgh*, in issue after issue laying before his readers detailed accounts of the heart-rending cruelties and injustices perpetrated daily on the Caribbean plantations. It would scarcely be an exaggeration to say that by their unremitting assault on the English conscience his articles (and, later, his speeches in parliament) did more than anything else to prepare men's minds for the next great step needed, the step from abolition, as the campaign against the trade was called, to emancipation and the ending of slavery itself.

That day was still far off. In the meantime the Westminster by-election coincided with the long-awaited arrival of peace in Europe. In April armies of the grand coalition had occupied Paris and despatched Napoleon to the island of Elba. What brought rejoicing throughout Europe was cause for alarm and despair on the west coast of Africa. Peace meant a revival of the slave trade, which had been virtually suspended while the war lasted, thanks to Great Britain's supremacy on the high seas. France was the chief participant in the renascent trade. It was therefore the object of the English abolitionists to compel France to outlaw the trade in return for favourable peace terms. Wilberforce, a Tory through and through, was reluctant to put pressure on Lord Liverpool's government, but Brougham and Romilly were able to overcome his hesitancy and gain the approval of the African Institution for an aggressive public campaign. Addresses in favour of immediate abolition were presented to the Regent and voted in both houses of parliament, supported by petitions drawn from all over the kingdom. When, therefore, the articles of the preliminary peace treaty with France were published at the beginning of June, the abolitionists were disappointed to learn that France had agreed to abolish the trade only after a period of five years, ample time in which to stock her plantations with fresh importations from Africa.

It was fortunate for ministers that Brougham was out of parliament. Romilly's patient and reasoned advocacy was no substitute for Brougham's scathing tongue. Without Brougham to fire their courage, the Whig opposition lacked the resolution to make the inclusion of abolition in the peace treaty a party matter. Brougham denounced the treaty in the *Edinburgh* as 'this last disgrace'[21] to ministers' name and, with Romilly, he organized protest meetings at London and Edinburgh. The Edinburgh meeting was the first assembly to promote a public object to be held in Tory Scotland for twenty years. Reformers and liberals, whatever the direct influence of the meeting on government policy, were able to take heart from the revival of popular feeling to which the 10,000 signatures to the anti-slave trade petition there attested.[22] Throughout the country the petitioning movement gained 750,000 signatures.[23]

What settled the issue in the end was a somewhat bizarre intervention by Napoleon, who, in the course of his triumphant 'Hundred Days' return to France, announced that the slave trade, being carried on chiefly by British capital, was of little benefit to France. It was his last contribution to world history. In the final peace terms drawn up at the Congress of Vienna, the French delegation gave its consent to immediate abolition. Spain and Portugal thus stood as the only countries which still maintained the trade. Little more could be achieved by the abolitionists, especially with a Tory government reluctant to bring diplomatic pressure on its friends in office. Brougham's efforts to persuade the government to enter into contracts giving the powers mutual rights-of-search of ships suspected of illegally carrying slaves foundered on the refusal of the American government, made touchy by its recent quarrels with the British government on the issue, to consider such an agreement.

* * *

We may be sure that if Brougham had felt great disappointment at his failure to come in for Westminster, he would, as he had done in 1812, have hurled thunderbolts down on the Whigs who had not rallied to his standard and, probably, on the electorate for its stupidity in showing loyalty to Cochrane. He did not. In September he took his annual short break, visiting his mother at Brougham Hall and immersing himself in mathematical *divertissements* before setting out for Paris, where he intended not to trouble any men of science except Laplace and Cuvier, 'nor any politician at all'.[24]

Brougham had been to the continent three times before, but this was his first visit to France, the country which in after years he was to make his second home. In his youth he had been a friend to the French revolution and the years of anti-French propaganda had not blinded him to Napoleon's virtues, far short of Lord Holland's hero-worship though he fell. It was entirely to be expected that he should grasp the first opportunity of peace to see France for himself. He was able to spare only a fortnight away from his legal practice, but armed with introductions from the Duke of Wellington, then in Paris for the peace negotiations, he made profitable use of his time. He met a number of French deputies, attended two sittings of the French Institute (the counterpart to the Royal Society in England), and had long conversations on the state of France with the eminent French general, statesman, mathematician and military engineer, Lazare Carnot. His only real disappointment was not to make Laplace's acquaintance. Paris, he told Creevey, was *the* place to go and live. 'I say, after seeing all the rest of Europe from Stockholm to Naples, nothing is to be named in the same year with Paris for delights of every kind and sort.'[25] Returning to the grey, provincial life of the northern circuit required 'no small fortitude', although it was somewhat straining Grey's credulity to inform him that 'as for politics, Paris has made me quite indifferent to them, for I found (what I never could before) that I could enjoy life thoroughly without ever thinking of parties'.[26]

Shortly after his return from Paris Brougham fell dangerously ill. In March 1815 he abandoned the circuit. For four or five months his constitution was impaired and he was unable to write a single article for the June number of the *Edinburgh*. 'I can only give you a notion of how much I am altered,' he told Creevey in July, 'by saying that I have not made such an exertion in writing for three months as this letter is, and that I already *ache all over* with it.'[27] At midsummer he was so little recovered in strength that he left London for Brougham Hall, where, in a few weeks, a cure was effected, not so much, he believed, by the health-giving air of Westmorland, as by the investigations which he undertook into the cellular structure of bee-hives.[28] His physician was apparently unable to diagnose any physical cause of debility and Creevey hinted at hypochondria and, more alarmingly, insanity. Creevey was thus the first of Brougham's acquaintances, it would seem, to give voice to the notion that he was 'mad'. Brougham himself found the cause to lie in the strain which years of ceaseless activity had imposed upon his mental and physical resources.

The attack of 1815 was singular only in its severity and its duration. Brougham suffered from spells of illness, or exhaustion, or depression, many times before and after. Lord Littleton, who sat in the House of Commons from 1812 to 1835, had occasion to remark in his diary that all the leading men of his time, among whom he listed Liverpool, Canning, Huskisson, Peel, Romilly, Grey and Brougham, were 'the most wakeful and susceptible of men', possessed of 'highly mercurial temperaments'. Like Castlereagh they would come to a premature death, worn out by the fatigue to which they were impelled by the ardour of their minds.[29] Littleton pressed his case far. Romilly and Castlereagh, it is true, took their own lives and Liverpool and Canning succumbed to strokes in middle age. But Huskisson was accidentally killed by a railway engine and Peel was thrown fatally from his horse. Grey, Wellington and Brougham all lived into their eighties. Nor is there anything exceptionally illuminating in the connection which Littleton hinted at between the febrile working of the imagination and physical debility.

The nature of his illness Brougham described in an essay on Samuel Johnson.[30] Johnson, he wrote, habitually succumbed to the hypochondriac's morbidity of mind, languishing so deep in dejection and drained so thoroughly of all energy for the simplest of life's duties that his days were made a misery. To overcome the condition, which severely hindered his digestion, he had at various times recourse to bodily exercise, enforced mental labour and, late in his life, bouts of immoderate drinking. The malady was 'frightful' and, so Brougham's account runs, one 'altogether intolerable when it weighs down the spirits and faculties of him whose mental labour must contribute to the supply of his bodily wants'. He assured his readers that he was competent to speak of the matter.

I speak with some confidence on a subject which accident has enabled me to study in the case of one with whom I was well acquainted for many years; and who either outlived the malady, which in him was hereditary, or obtained a power over it by constant watchfulness, diligent care, and a fixed resolution to conquer it. As in Johnson's case, it was remittent, but also periodical, a thing not mentioned of Johnson's; for in my friend's case it recurred at intervals, first of six months, then of a year, afterwards of two and three years, until it ceased; and the duration of the attack was never more than eight or ten months. It seemed wholly unconnected with bodily complaint, though it appeared to interfere with the functions of the alimentary canal; and it was relieved by a strict attention to diet, and by great temperance in all particulars. There was, as in Johnson's case, no kind of delusion, nor any undue action of the imagination; but unlike his, it was wholly unattended with apprehensions or fears of any kind. There was also no disposition to indulgence of any sort except of sleep; and a particular aversion to the excitement of fermented liquors, the use of which indeed never failed to exacerbate the malady, as Johnson, too, from his confession to Mr. Boswell, appears to have found, after trying them in vain to alleviate his suffering. The senses were not at all more dull than usual, and there was as much relish both of physical and mental enjoyment. But the seat of the disease being in the mind, and in the mind wholly, independent of and unaffected by any external circumstances, good fortune produced no exhilaration, afflictions no sudden depression. The attack commenced sometimes suddenly, that is, in a few days, and not seldom was foretold by dreaming that it had begun. The course was this: the active powers were first affected; all the exertions of the will becoming more painful and more difficult. This inertness next extended itself and crept over the intellectual faculties, the exercise of which became more distasteful and their operations more sluggish; but the results, though demanding more time, were in no respect of inferior quality. Indeed, the patient used sometimes to say that when time was of no importance, the work was better, though much more painfully done. The exertions resolutely made and steadily persevered in, seemed gradually to undermine the disease, and each effort rendered the succeeding one less difficult. But before he became so well acquainted with the cure, and made little or no exertion, passing the time in reading only, the recovery took place nearly in the same manner as afterwards under a more severe regimen, only that he has told me that to this regimen he ascribed his ultimate cure after obtaining a constantly increasing prolongation of the healthy intervals. The recovery of the mind's tone always took place in the reverse order to the loss of it; first the power returned before the will; or the faculties were restored to their vigour, before the desire of exerting them had come back . . . Dr Baillie was at one time consulted, but declared that the mental and bodily regimen which had been adopted was the best that occurred to him; only he strongly recommended horse exercise, and an abstinence from hard work of all kinds, neither of which prescriptions, as I have since understood, were followed.

Dr Baillie was the physician who attended Brougham in 1815 and the unnamed acquaintance in the account was Brougham himself, a secret which he disclosed to his friend and 'fellow-sufferer', William Forsyth, in 1859.[31] In two particulars the account is misleading. By 'hypochondriac' Brougham clearly means 'psychosomatic': the disease was seated in the mind. And his periods of suffering were not 'wholly unattended by apprehensions or fears'.

Brougham suffered his first attack in 1801; the illness then recurred every two years down to 1821, when it transferred its visitations to the even years. By 1840 the disease (so Brougham calls it) wore itself out, 'partly by discipline'. For thirty years after the attack of 1815 his susceptibility to breakdown preyed upon his mind. In two curious letters sent from France to Sir Robert Peel in the early 1840s, one including a memoir in praise of the committee for the Society for the Diffusion of Useful Knowledge, the other enclosing a proposed criminal code as his 'legacy', Brougham confessed that, never being sure of his life, he always made his arrangements, before going abroad, as if he were never to return. 'Having a notion that I since 1815 have carried about with me a friendly power which will one day take me a very long journey in a very short space of time, I really always reckon on each night being my last. Possibly the symptoms are mistaken, but I still act *from habit.*'[32] Psychosomatic illness is frequently more painful for the friends of its victim than it is for the victim himself. Brougham, however, met the enemy with spirit. He neither wearied men with accounts of its ravagings, nor allowed it, except in the year 1815, to distract him from his work. At worst, it may have contributed to the somewhat manic fits of exuberance and sudden changes of course which his colleagues found unsettling and which encouraged them to brand him as a devious and unscrupulous self-seeker worthy of the soubriquet, given him by Creevey, of 'Old Wickedshifts'.

* * *

On 6 July 1815, Samuel Whitbread, leader of the disaffected left wing of the Whig party, died. Romilly, after his exertions on behalf of the slaves over the previous eighteen months, was enfeebled by a violent inflammation of the lungs. Neither man could be counted among the ranks of the 'regular' opposition, but they were two of the most persistent and effective critics of the government. Without them (though Romilly was not confined to his bed) the opposition was gravely weakened in the House of Commons. On 9 July Lord Grey asked the Earl of Darlington to fill the vacancy at the borough of Winchilsea, one of seven seats in the House recently purchased by Darlington, by offering the representation to Brougham. Brougham received Grey's letter informing him of the proposal at Walton, where he had that day journeyed from London to visit Lord Ossulton, an adherent of the Mountain. The journey left him unable to move, but he agreed to return to London to discuss the proposition with Darlington. The interview took place on 13 July and the business was quickly settled. 'You will marvel at my coming into Parlt.,' Brougham wrote to Creevey, then sojourning in Brussels, 'which I have been overpersuaded to do . . . The usual and unchangeable friendship of Ld. G[rey] obtained the seat, but I am not at all satisfied that I have done wisely in accepting it . . . All I can say to myself is that I *may* recover and be again fit for service, in which case I should think myself unjustifiable had I decided the other way. But 20 years hard work have produced their effect, I much fear, and left little or nothing in me.'[33]

Two months later Brougham's health was fully restored. He wrote five articles for the October number of the *Edinburgh*, then knuckled down to preparing a programme of reform for the coming session of parliament. The auguries were fair. Peace having descended at last, the Tory ministers, for the first time in twenty-three years, would have to face their opponents without the shield of war to protect them. And the Whigs were in want of a champion to lead the attack.

5

The Game of the Country

When despondency settled on Brougham it was the world that was out of sorts. Early in 1815, before the sun of Winchilsea had dispersed the cloud of Westminster, he informed Lord Grey that, lying as he did under the Whig party's interdict, only their personal friendship remained as a pretext for his connection with it.[1] Brougham's capacity for self-delusion prevented him from acknowledging that *his* suspect politics disconcerted the Whigs. The intellectual cannot maintain his independence of thought, nor the humanitarian the ardour of his aspirations, within the English party system. A politician, to win the visible rewards of his vocation, must seal up his compassion and narrow his mind. He must give up to party what was meant for himself. He may not, simply because his mind has been invaded by a fact or his imagination altered by a glance, give way to sudden shifts of feeling or opinion. He rises by making himself the instrument of party or, more broadly, of the collective will of the body politic. Wishing to be both prophet and politician, Brougham passed his days in restless dissatisfaction, churlish when confined by the harness of party, spiteful when broken free of it. In 1816 he attempted both to establish his *individual* popularity and weight in the country and to bring about a *parliamentary* alliance of forward-looking Whigs and moderate radicals under his leadership. The outcome was ordained. At the end of the year his hopes lay crumbled, and in their ruin may be read the failure, politically speaking, of his whole career.

The high enthusiasm with which Brougham greeted Europe's deliverance from war, and with it the transfer of the English political battle to a new ground, was founded on a not unreasonable hope that, as almost everyone on the non-government side of politics did hope, the Tory citadel, a safe stronghold for so long as Napoleon was the enemy, would fall to the assault of the enemy at home. Reformers had, of course, been gulled by many a false dawn before. In 1805 Creevey had been jubilant to discover in the exposure and impeachment of Lord Melville that 'a clamour for reform in the expenditure of the

99

publick money is at last found to be the touchstone of the House of Commons and of the publick'.[2] Ten dark years followed. In 1815, the war over, optimism revived. 'I cannot defer my congratulations on these important events,' Brougham wrote to Leigh Hunt of the final victory over Napoleon, 'so useful to the cause of constitutional liberty & improvement. The immediate & great reduction of the power of the crown may fairly be expected to arise from peace & the lopping off of so much patronage & the cessation of the alarm (so useful to arbitrary power) in which we have been kept for the last 20 years.'[3]

The war had raised the national debt to £860,000,000. The charge on it of £46,000,000 alone amounted to more than twice the sum of government expenditure in 1793. Few Whigs or radicals agreed with Alexander Hamilton that a national debt, certainly not one of such unprecedented magnitude, was a national blessing. Like Hamilton's opponents in the United States, they looked upon it as a national evil, raising up a moneyed aristocracy, hangers-on of the Crown—the THING, Cobbett called it—whose interests were fatal to the prosperity and the liberties of the people. The war had tied the fundholder to the government; it had also greatly increased the size of the bureaucracy, both at home and in the colonies. It had, in Whig eyes, raised once more the spectre of arbitrary government, sustained by placemen and a standing army and oiled by patronage and corruption. War and the expensive machinery of government which conducted it were symbiotically linked. Hence the Whig cry became 'peace, retrenchment and reform'. The cry did little more than dress up the old Whig grievance against the influence of the Crown in new language, but it was a cry that Brougham was ready to adopt.

> I should really like to see the eyes of our countrymen opened to their real situation after so victorious a war, as in the end it proved, and a good foundation laid for making them hereafter less prone to hostilities. Must we always be so knit to the continent, even after our own dangers are terminated, that every quarrel of the German princes about territory or precedents shall draw us into a new war? Can't the people learn to hear of wars & rumours of war without running out to fight, whether they have any concern in that business or not? . . . I am sure to exaggerate the necessity of retrenchment in all the items of our ruinous establishments is quite impossible, whether we regard *liberty* or *property*.[4]

Throughout the autumn of 1815 Brougham prepared an opposition strategy for the coming parliamentary session. His programme, which he supplied in generous outline to men representing all shades of anti-government opinion, fell under three heads. In foreign affairs it was futile to make a frontal attack on the victorious ministers, but the public should be roused to view with foreboding a peace settlement which enthroned despotisms in foreign capitals and pledged English arms (an army of occupation 149,000-strong in France) and diplomacy to their support. Englishmen must be warned of the danger of being drawn into another war, especially one on behalf of the French Bourbons whose restoration had been imposed upon a people ill-disposed to have them back, in the defence of principles—legitimacy and the right of the despotic powers to intervene in foreign countries to suppress liberal nationalist movements—which were offensive to every freedom-loving Englishman. At home the one thing needful was a sustained campaign against the size and expenditure of government. The heavy weight of taxation, above all the property tax, must be cut down. 'Until the peace establishment is brought as low as it can be, the country can never have a chance with the Crown, nor indeed with the tax-gatherer.'⁵ Third, the opposition would do well to take up a range of reforms not traditionally part of the party struggle, but of great immediate interest to the country and ultimately of benefit to the party which had the foresight and the will to pursue them: reform of the prisons, provision for the education of the poor, reform of the tithe, and liberalization of the law of libel.

The fault in the programme lay not in what it proposed, but in what it failed to propose. The prosperity of the British economy during the latter years of the war was somewhat artificially founded. Naval supremacy had secured for the country a predominance in world trade. The voracious demands of war had greatly stimulated industrial production and provided an expanding labour market. Landowners had grown fat on the profits from land which in peace-time had been considered too poor to be tilled. The inconvertible currency introduced by Pitt in 1797 had raised agricultural and manufacturing prices to record levels, and for so long as the war maintained both nearly full employment and relatively high wages, high prices inflicted little suffering, comparatively, on the mass of the population. Short-lived was the rejoicing, therefore, when the nation discovered that the end of the war entailed the collapse of the war economy. The faltering economy of the post-Waterloo years, years which are among the bleakest in modern English history, raised class antagonisms to a rare pitch. Demand fell; landowners withdrew acre after acre from tillage; manufacturers reduced their stock of labour; prices plummeted; and discharged veterans of the war swelled the numbers thrown out of work, causing wages to sink still lower. Only one class was able to defend itself: the landed interest which supplied the House of Commons with five-sixths of its members and was thus able to secure the price-maintaining Corn Law of 1815 and, as it proved, to get rid of the property and income tax. The needs of the people, ill-housed, ill-fed and ill-paid, went unprovided and their pleas for justice, driven as they were into rioting, unattended. The Whigs fixed their sights on the familiar enemy, the Crown and its minions, and failed to see, or, seeing did not like to acknowledge, that what was needed was not fewer sinecures or the diminution of direct taxation, but an electorate more representative of the population and measures to lift the burden of poverty from its shoulders. It was not primarily shackles on the press, nor a standing army, nor a large foreign and colonial establishment which oppressed the millions. On the real causes of their suffering the Whigs, and Brougham with them, were silent.

Whatever its shortcomings from the point of view of the mass of the population, Brougham's plan of campaign had much to recommend it as a parliamentary strategy. By concentrating his fire on the Crown and the Tory ministers he appealed to the main body of the Whigs. Abolition of the income tax and reform of the tithe were magnets to draw the votes of the independent country gentlemen whose support was essential to the survival of any early 19th-century government. And by adding a list of reforms with a broader social and libertarian appeal (though it could scarcely be denied that the want of education and the stringent libel laws were as much bulwarks of the ruling oligarchy's power as bloated defence and colonial establishments) Brougham sought to gain allies among the Mountain and the Benthamite radicals.

Brougham took pains to assemble an anti-government coalition in parliament. He primed the Whig leaders of his intentions and received from Grey the assurance that his line was 'the only one from which our artillery can be expected to produce any real effect'.[6] As important as Grey's blessing was the co-operation of the Mountain and the radicals. For one thing, Brougham had his eye on the Westminster constituency, where Lord Cochrane's elevation to the Lords on the approaching death of his father was certain, in the near future, to leave a vacancy. For another, he knew from past experience that however warmly the right-wing Whigs might applaud his schemes, especially if the result was to unseat the government, the brunt of each night's debating in the House would have to be borne by the left-wingers. To the latter, therefore, he let it be known that the 'earwigs', as he called the Whigs proper, were the least part of his concern. 'I really wd. fain hope that Tierney and Abercromby at length will see the folly of their temporising plans, and will act always and systematically as they did during part of last session,' he wrote to Creevey, who after two years was still in Brussels playing truant from English politics. 'But nothing must be left to chance, and . . . I am quite determined (tho' ready to meet them half-way for peace and union sake) that the game of the country and the people shall be played in good earnest—if not with their help, without it—by God's blessing.'[7] Brougham's pleadings failed to bring Creevey back to London, but he lined up the most important members of the Mountain, especially Henry Bennet and Lord Folkestone, and he secured the extra-parliamentary assistance of Francis Place and James Mill, by whose offices it was settled that the session would open with Burdett and himself making common cause against the government.

There remained the question of the Whig leadership in the House of Commons. Officially it was in the hands of George Ponsonby; practically it was in abeyance. While he was alive, Samuel Whitbread, though perpetually at odds with the party, had filled the gap left by Ponsonby's indolence. Whitbread's death in July 1815 brought the matter once more into prominence. Brougham's suggestion was to give the lead to Lord George Cavendish, scion of the illustrious clan of Devonshires, not, he argued, because Cavendish was anything more than a time-serving backbencher, but because his large house in Burlington Place would serve as a rendezvous for the party, a thing much more needed than a leader. This was disingenuous, as was Brougham's representing to Grey that Cavendish had the backing of the Mountain. Sometime before the 1816 session began Brougham regained the habit of frequenting Holland House and, although by the end of the year Lady Holland was writing to Grey that she and Brougham were again 'the best friends in the world',[8] it seems that Brougham was concerned not to strain his precarious alliance with the radicals by appearing too fast with the Holland House set. Nothing could be more unpropitious, he told Creevey, than 'carrying on the party by a *coterie* at Lady Holland's elbow, which cannot be submitted to for a moment.'[9] The high Whig associations and somewhat hedonistic manners of Holland House were distasteful to the more resolute radicals, but to put up Cavendish, every inch as well-born as Lord Holland, as a counterpoise was to gain nothing. Bennet, who told Creevey that the Mountaineers resented the proposal, was outraged.

> Some talk of Ld. George Cavendish, which I resist, because I think his politicks are abominable and his manners insolent and neglectful; but also because the Cavendish system, with the Duke of Devonshire at the head, is not the thing for the present day. They are timid, idle and haughty: the Duke dines at Carlton House and sits between the Chancellor and Lord Caithness, and I have no doubt will have, one of these days, the Ribband. Then the Archduchess (as they call him) is a great admirer and follower of Prinnie's [the Prince Regent], and *presumes to abuse the Mountain.*[10]

Brougham would not have put the objection to Cavendish less sharply, had it not suited his purpose to install a puppet as nominal leader, while the effective command should fall to himself. It suited no one else's purpose and the session opened with Ponsonby lounging in his accustomed place.

Brougham began by attacking the government's relations with the autocratic European powers in a series of speeches delivered in February. It was an insult to the British people that Napoleon should have been defeated in order to allow Ferdinand VII to trample on the liberal aspirations of the Spanish patriots; it was a dereliction of duty not to demand payment of the interest owed to Great Britain by Austria; it was monstrous that British troops should help to secure Charles X on the throne, when the French administration was destroying the liberty of the press, emasculating the chamber of deputies, and acquiescing in Roman Catholics' destruction of Huguenot property and murder of hundreds of Huguenots. On 11 March Brougham delivered a blast against the army estimates which he later described, for reasons which it is impossible to guess, as his greatest parliamentary success.[11] It was, certainly, a bold speech and it was loudly cheered. Brougham demanded that the British garrisons, superfluous in peacetime, be withdrawn from Malta and Gibraltar, that the Ionian islands and the newly-acquired possessions in the Caribbean, rich only in patronage, be given up, and that a liberal policy towards Ireland be initiated in order to permit the removal of the 25,000 English troops stationed there. Why, he asked, was the government recruiting twice as many guards, ludicrously named Household Troops as if the monarch required protection from his subjects, as Pitt had found sufficient in the distracted year of 1792? Castlereagh had said that it was unfair to make soldiers return immediately to civilian life. Was it the foreign secretary's opinion that the soldier's status was higher than the private civilian's? It was not the view of the constitution. Standing armies had no place in a country which cherished its liberties. He was therefore proud to support the motion, introduced by the Whig, John Calcraft, to reduce the estimate from £385,000 for 8,100 guards to £192,000 for about 4,000 of them.

> I have done my duty—I have entered my protest. It cannot be laid to my charge that a force is to be maintained in profound and general peace . . . It is not my fault that peace will have returned without its accustomed blessings—that our burthens are to remain undiminished—that our liberties are to be menaced by a standing army, without the pretence of necessity in any quarter to justify its continuance. The blame is not mine that a brilliant and costly army of Household Troops, of unprecedented numbers, is allowed to the Crown, without the shadow of use, unless it be to pamper a vicious appetite for military show, to gratify a passion for parade, childish and contemptible, unless, indeed, that nothing can be an object of contempt which is at once dangerous to the Constitution of the country and burthensome to the resources of the people.[12]

The government was secure from defeat on foreign questions. Brougham's motion calling on it to publish the iniquitous Holy Alliance gained only 30 votes. Calcraft's motion fared little better. Brougham's purpose, in driving home the message that the foreign office was cloaked with the repressive continental powers, was to polish his liberal reputation in the country and to give substance to his main charge against the government, that its huge establishment was in part made necessary by the unwillingness to disengage Great Britain from its alliance with European despots.

> I have been extremely occupied [he wrote to Leigh Hunt] in the fight against arbitrary power, in its two worst shapes, the military establishment & the Income Tax. I think we have given the first a blow & the second a compleat defeat, or what in the end will prove

such if the country backs us. My voice has been directed to this & to rouse the popular feeling, which alone can keep the House right . . . The govt are sorely pressed and I have great hopes that they will be beaten out of their measure.[13]

In the wake of his success in overthrowing the orders-in-council in 1812 Brougham had suggested to Grey that the opposition's next target should be the income tax, which was as unpopular among the agriculturalists as the orders had been with the trading community. 'I don't mean that things should be undertaken from mere love of popularity, but it is a good assisting reason, when they are excellent in themselves.'[14] The question was not again raised until Brougham was back in parliament, by which time the case against the tax had become stronger, since the opposition could accuse the government of breaching parliamentary and public trust by seeking to perpetuate in peacetime a financial innovation which had been introduced by Pitt as a temporary war expedient. The income tax, being assessed only on real property, fell chiefly on landowners, who, despite high corn prices, were suffering from a reduction in demand and, more seriously, from the necessity of paying in a greatly depreciated currency money due on loans and mortgages taken out during the boom years of the war. Even so, the country gentlemen who belonged to no party and who constituted perhaps one-third of the House of Commons were difficult to move against the King's government, especially on a financial measure which, if it were defeated, would deprive the exchequer of some £15,000,000. As in 1812 Brougham and his supporters—chiefly Alexander Baring, his ally three years earlier, and Charles Western, the spokesman for the Whig backbench agriculturalists—organized the collection of petitions from all parts of the country. So spontaneous was the feeling in the counties against the tax that little management from the centre was required. Liberals were especially delighted by the anti-tax meeting held at Edinburgh in February, the first 'respectable' meeting for a political object in Scotland for twenty years, one 'justly considered by the prophetic as a striking indication of the tendency of the public mind'.[15]

Repeating his tactics of 1812, Brougham used every parliamentary means at his disposal to delay the passage of the tax bill (which proposed to retain the tax at half the wartime rate of 10 per cent) for several weeks, long enough for the cry of distress from the shires to reverberate in the House of Commons. Lord Liverpool, the prime minister, was sufficiently apprehensive to let it be known that a defeat would force ministers to resign. The government whips predicted a ministerial majority of forty, and even the opposition expected to fall twenty votes short of victory, but in the days when a three-line whip was a thing never yet heard of such calculations were far from reliable, so that on the evening of 18 March the House filled with members in an unusual state of excitement. They had not come to debate. Everything to be said had already been said. Petition after petition had been paraded into the chamber. When Sir William Curtis came forward with the last of them, signed by 12,000 persons, including eminent bankers and merchants, from the City, the House clamoured so loudly for a division that not a single voice could be heard above the din. At last, shortly after 11 o'clock, Brougham rose. He waited for the hubbub to die away, then slowly read the words of Pitt's act imposing the tax 'for and during the continuance of the war, *and no longer*'. 'The shout which these words raised I shall never forget,' Brougham wrote nearly fifty years later.[16] The House proceeded immediately to a division, and when the tellers announced the figures, a majority of 37 against the tax, exultant cheers from the opposition benches crowded against Brougham's ears. He had stood on these giddy heights once before; he was never again to reach them.

The majority against the government came quickly to be known as 'Brougham's 37', after a brand of snuff called Hardham's 37, and within a few days Brougham was caricatured offering a pinch of it to the Prince Regent. On the morning after the triumph a number of Whigs gathered at Brooks's to make their plans for coming into office. Brougham, blood-headed, left the meeting to call on Francis Place—strange company to seek out in the hour of triumph, for Place, of all the radicals, had been the most outspoken opponent of the campaign against the income tax. Place listened, in amazement, to Brougham's declaration that he meant the next day to go to the House, furnish it with Castlereagh's circular letter saying that the government would resign if beaten, and then offer himself to the nation with the words, '*I am willing to take the charge of this Government, to reform the Parliament, and to change the whole of the present ruinous system*'.[17]

Having scotched the government, the opposition strove to harry it to its death. Two nights after the income-tax division, ministers were again placed in a corner, assailed from all sides for proposing to raise the salaries of the two secretaries to the admiralty. Men believed at the time that Brougham, made heady by late events, saved the government by a blundering excoriation of the Prince Regent. Why, he asked, was this government behaving with such profligacy? The answer was that behind it, sustaining it, stood a corrupt Court, presided over by the Prince Regent, a monster whose degeneracy and venality exceeded even that of the Stuarts, who entertained no scruples of religion, who experienced no tenderness of conscience, who lurched from one wasteful expenditure to the next, unable for a moment to suspend his thoughtless amusements, and who now, surrounded by mercenaries and unable to trust to the attachment of the nation, had the temerity to ask the House of Commons to lavish on his favourites money extracted from the pockets of the suffering people of England. What Brougham said was true and not a man heard his words who did not know them to be true. But the language was scarcely parliamentary; it was assuredly not Whiggish; and it was out of all proportion to the particular matter before the House.

When the figures were announced the government was relieved to discover that it had escaped, in a small House, by a vote of 159 to 130. It is by no means certain that, had the vote gone the other way, ministers would have given up the seals of office. Nor is it certain that they were saved by Brougham's ill-timed candour. Charles Wynn, the Grenvillite, professed to know of five members who switched their votes and twenty-seven more who abstained from voting as the direct consequence of Brougham's intemperance.[18] Thomas Whishaw, the 'Pope' of Holland House, was sceptical of such reports.

> Your conjecture [he replied to a friend] as to the impropriety and impolicy of Brougham's personal attack on the Regent was perfectly correct. It alienated a great number of the new adherents of the Opposition, disgusted several of the old ones, and is considered as having lost them the question on Wednesday night. This is extremely doubtful, because weak and timid people are glad to avail themselves of *any* pretexts in such cases; but certainly Brougham's imprudence afforded them very plausible reasons for declining to act with a party avowing personal hostility to the Sovereign. This unfortunate mistake has been the general subject of conversation ever since.[19]

Romilly grieved to see Brougham loaded with the reproaches of his friends and unfairly made a scapegoat for the Whigs not getting place. But even he, a warm admirer of Brougham and no stranger to the faults of the Prince, thought Brougham's outburst injudicious and his language better fitted to describe the Emperor Tiberius. What a pity it was that 'his want of judgment and of prudence should prevent his great talents, and such good intentions, from being as great a blessing to mankind as they ought to be'.[20]

Brougham himself was defiant. With feigned penitence he offered himself in sacrifice to Grey, saying that he would leave parliament if by that means alone the injury he had done the party could be repaired. His true feelings found vent in a letter to Leigh Hunt.

I should hardly have troubled you now, but for the interesting state of affairs, & the opportunity which it has given me of speaking out my mind at length upon the scandalous & unfeeling profligacy of *the Court*. I did so last night in a way to give much pain I verily believe to many persons—to the objects of attack certainly—but I find also great discontent among many of the opposition, who tho' they received every word I said with a full chorus of cheering, & tho' the cheers continued in peals for some moments after I sat down, yet discovered in half an hour after that a few timid & trimming tories whose votes they had reckoned upon, took fright & went away, or at least *gave* my attack on the Court *as their reason* for going. The offence of lessening our minority was thus imputed to me & to hear them talk you'd think I had kept them out of place. I care not even if I had done so—and as for a few votes, much better let wholesome truths be told to Parlt. thro' the press (our grand & guardian power) to the people than have a dozen more of our adversaries now & then vote with us. What I spoke I spoke deliberately, & with the design of its exciting a sensation throughout the country, whether it pleased the party or not. I thought it right to give you this explanation in case the sort of clamour now raised reaches you that the concluding sentences of my speech spoilt the division, for be assured they who are the loudest *now* in saying so, were the loudest in cheering that peroration in their places.[21]

The letter had its intended effect. Three days later Hunt lauded the peroration in the *Examiner* as 'a conclusion every way worthy of that gentleman, whether as the supplier of Mr Whitbread's place, as a patriot, as an orator, as a thorough observer of the signs of the times, as a man of taste and spirit, moral and political'.[22]

Praise came, too, from another radical quarter, for Place saw in

Brougham's indifference to Whig sensibilities reason to believe that it might actually be possible to wrench him away from the party and place him at the head of the radical forces in parliament. He wrote to Brougham on 23 March.

I can hold may tongue no longer, but must congratulate you on your manly English speech; my admiration alone would not however have caused me to trouble you with uncalled-for advice, but when you are in everybody's mouth, when all minds are employed upon you, I must tell you what passes, and advise you also.

My shop is in some degree a centre of communication, where all manner of persons bring all kinds of information, and where every one talks as he pleases. Those who really love their country expect to see you in the exalted station to which their hopes have raised you, and treat with scorn the insinuations and assertions of those whom the obsequious practice of late days and a hatred of liberty have caused them to utter . . .

You, I hope, are not made for mediocrity—you have indeed stepped out, and taken the lead from those who cannot but envy and must soon hate you; yourself a distinguished and marked object to them. To you mediocrity cannot now belong; above it or below it you must be placed, either the great, the leading man, or nothing. You have in fact placed yourself in the most arduous of situations, assailed by friends and foes, by friends who hope for you, who fear for you—by enemies who dread you and hate you . . . None but a strong-minded man, none but a man possessing vast powers, could have possessed himself as you have done of the ear of the whole people of England; none but the best constituted mind can keep that possession, none but a man who is eminently useful can long retain it, none other deserves it.

Your enemies, the enemies of England, are calculating on your retrograding, as they call it, into the gentleman; do it, and they will be the first to howl against you for having done it. Persevere, I beseech you, for this disgraced and too servile people, in whom, however, still resides the latent spirit and love of liberty which, in trying times and on many great emergencies, has brought them through with honour.[23]

Place, for all the artful flattery contained in this letter, represented Brougham's higher conscience, a conscience which spoke of a nobler

calling than party politics. What were party victories in the House of
Commons if patriots, if friends of the people, had to retrograde into
Whig gentlemen—Brougham knew *their* worth—to win them? The
defeat of the income tax was not really a party victory at all. It was the
House of Commons bending to the deliberately expressed will of the
political nation. So widespread was the odium in which the tax was
held that members who normally supported the government felt
compelled to desert it. They did not thereby signify their desire to be
led by Brougham or to cast their lot with the Whigs. The episode was
portentous, but its portents were of things which would run far deeper
than the scramble for spoils between rival parties within the landed
establishment. Brougham understood the direction in which the tide
of public opinion was beginning to flow. Hence his frequent avowals
that he cared nothing for the Whigs, only for the country. Hence also
his Herculean labours, outside parliament, on behalf of the slaves, the
uneducated, the defenceless to whom the courts offered no succour.
Brougham longed to be borne to greatness by the popular current.
But Place was able to appeal to only one side of Brougham. The
popular current ran too wide to be narrowed into the channels of the
party: forced into them, it lost its strength. Yet left free, what did it
gain a man? What did it gain a people? What deserts did it irrigate? In
England things were accomplished by party. Brougham poured scorn
on the place-hunters; but it was the hunters he despised, not the
places. Francis Place hated both.

Brougham pecked away at the government for the rest of the
session. He also made his debut as a law reformer. His libel bill,
introduced in May, proposed to make the truth admissible as
evidence in justification by the defence and to strip the Crown of its
power (a power it was not slow to use) to file *ex officio* informations.
Necessary though the reforms were, the House of Commons showed
no interest in the bill and Brougham was compelled to abandon it.
Like Whitbread before him, he discovered, not for the first time, that
the Whigs proclaimed themselves to be the champions of the people's
liberty, but would not stir to prosper it. Like Whitbread, too, he
discovered that to lead the opposition attack almost single-handed for
a whole session was not to gain the confidence or the gratitude of the
party. Brougham spoke nearly 160 times in the course of the session,
Ponsonby less than half that number. 'Our friend Brougham,' Bennet
wrote, 'has done everything this year with no help, for there is literally
no one but Folkestone who comes into the line and fights.'[24] Lord

Liverpool paid him an implied tribute when he complained, in March, that the government was exposed to 'the most acrimonious, systematic, and persevering Opposition that I ever recollect to have been seen in Parliament'.[25] Yet by the end of the year Brougham's progress towards the leadership of the party had taken a step backwards. He had also come, once and for all, to the parting of the ways with the radicals.

From the beginning Brougham knew that attempting to bring together the disparate elements of the anti-government ranks was a formidable undertaking; he foresaw, too, 'a rupture with Grey as by no means an unlikely result of doing my duty and taking my swing'.[26] There was no falling out with Grey, but the right wing of the party was alarmed by Brougham's forthrightness. It was partly that he attempted too much. 'If he would stint himself to doing twice as much as two of the most active men in London,' Sydney Smith observed to Lady Grey, 'it would do very well.'[27] Charles Western put the point more gravely.

> As to the general proceedings of the Opposition, I can say little. There is no superior *mind* amongst us; great power of speaking, faculty of perplexing, irritation and complaints, but no super-eminent power to strike out a line of policy, and to command the *confidence* of the country. Brougham has shown his powers rather successfully, and exhibits some prudence in his plans of attack; but I cannot discern that superiority of judgment and of view (if I may so express myself) which is the *grand* desideratum.[28]

Western was the very type of the back-bench squire, anti-Tory (or at least anti-Court) in his prejudices, conservative in his instincts, without whose allegiance no future Whig government could stand. Brougham worked closely with him in the campaign against the income tax, and adopted the attitude of his class in a well-considered speech on the distress being suffered by the farming community. Western's financial difficulties were real: he expected to receive no midsummer rents that year. Brougham's harangue against the Prince did not simply wound his feelings of delicacy; it was handing the government an easy means of escape and throwing away the opportunity to force real retrenchment upon it that made him angry.

> I have often marvelled at the *want* of sense, discretion, judgment and common sense that we see so frequently accompany the most

brilliant talents, but damn me if I ever saw such an instance as that I have just witnessed in your friend Brougham. By Heaven! he has uttered a speech which, for power of *speaking*, surpassed anything you ever heard, and by which he has damn'd himself past redemption. You know what my opinion of him has always been: I have always thought he had not much sound sense nor too much political integrity, but he has outstripped any notion I could form of indiscretion; and as to his politicks, they are, in my humble opinion, of no sterling substance (but that between ourselves). He has been damaging himself daily, but to-night there is not a *single fellow* that is not saying what a damn'd impudent speech that of Brougham's—four or five driven away—even Burdett says it was too much. He could not have roared louder if a file of soldiers had come in and pushed the Speaker out of his chair. Where the devil a fellow could get such lungs and such a flow of jaw upon such an occasion as this surpasses my imagination.

I was sitting in the gallery by myself, and he made my head spin in such a style I thought I shd. tumble over. He quite overcame one's understanding for a time; but when I recovered, I began to think—this will *never* do—impossible—I will go down and see what the other lads think of it: perhaps my nerves are a little too sensitive. I soon found, however, that everybody was struck in the same way, and even more. Now, when I say that he has damaged himself past redemption, I mean as a man aspiring to be Leader, for to that his ambition aspired, and for that he is DONE NOW.[29]

Brougham's defence of the landed class failed to gain him the adherence of regular members of the opposition like Western; it also opened a wide breach between him and Francis Place. Place wished to retain the income tax because, falling as it did on the rich owners of property, it went a little way to offset the enormous weight of indirect taxation exacted from the poor. In the first half of the 19th century taxes on food and tobacco supplied nearly 60 per cent of government revenue. And Adam Smith's argument that taxes on necessities were passed on to the workers in the form of higher wages was belied by the rising unemployment and falling wages of the post-Waterloo years. Even worse, in Place's view, was the long speech of 16 April in which Brougham defended the 1815 corn duty as an essential palliative for the farmers and recommended a thorough, Malthusian reformation of the system of poor relief in order to ease the burden of maintaining the poor which, as the law stood, fell on the rate-paying landowners.

Radicalism entered a new phase after the war. Leadership of the movement, among the dispossessed, passed from respectable reformers like Major Cartwright to William Cobbett and 'Orator' Hunt, men whose demagoguery was distasteful to the intellectually fastidious Benthamites. Place thought Cobbett too ignorant to understand that the common people must ever be imbeciles who were lost without the leadership of men of money and influence.[30] Cobbett and Hunt, in seeking to liberate the working population from dependence upon the middle class and its parliamentary spokesmen, were dooming it to impotence. Hence his interest in detaching Brougham from the Whigs and placing him at the head of the 'genuine' reformers. But Place, as much as James Mill and Bentham, liked to rub aristocratic noses in the dirt. He suspected Brougham's fascination with the *haut monde* of Holland House and Lady Jersey's salon. Brougham even voted, to the radicals' disgust, for the £60,000 grant which parliament awarded to Princess Charlotte for her wedding outfit. That Brougham, who had recently been appointed the Queen's attorney-general, should naturally take Charlotte's side in the painful domestic quarrels of the royal family, and that the Whigs, eternally out of favour with the Regent, should pin their hopes of office on the heir presumptive, did not mitigate the offence. Nor did Brougham's indignant departure from a meeting of the Westminster electors, rather than be placed in the company of 'Orator' Hunt, do anything to allay Place's fear that he could not be brought to mix openly and frankly with the people. Brougham defended his action, taken when Hunt launched into a tirade against the Whigs as anti-reformers and place-hunters, to Leigh Hunt.

> The blackguard conduct of Hunt at the Westr. meeting failed entirely as it merited. All the reputable part of the meeting were disgusted & highly approved of our withdrawing. Burdett's conduct in not silencing the fellow is generally reprobated. Indeed, it was very bad & he is damaged by it.[31]

That was not the radicals' view of the affair and Brougham lowered himself further in their estimation when, in May, he declared in the House of Commons that the English constitution, despite one or two blemishes which needed removing, had never been in a better state.

When the session ended Brougham was too tired to go the northern circuit. Instead he took himself off to Switzerland and Italy and remained out of England until the beginning of 1817. As always, he fretted about politics at home. In September he wrote to Bennet from Milan to ask whether a dissolution were in the offing. Bennet passed the letter to Place, who gave a withering reply to Bennet's inquiry whether Brougham might be brought forward at Westminster. It was, Place wrote, out of the question after his 'absurd conduct' of the last session. He had shown too much reserve, both in his relations with the Westminster electors and in his attachment to annual parliaments and 'suffrage as extensive as direct taxation'. 'The electors suppose his object is to obtain the Seals under the Princess if she should become Queen, and they say they will not be made a stepping-stone for him to mount. They say if Brougham is looking to the Court for preferment he has been consistent, but then he ought not to expect to be taken up by the people.'[32]

In the winter of 1816–17 the economic crisis in the country deepened. A failed harvest sent wheat prices soaring to 103s. a quarter by December, twice what they had been just six months earlier. Discontent led to the Spa Fields riots of December and a disquieted propertied class took further alarm from the attempted assassination of the Prince Regent in February. The government suspended habeas corpus and passed a bill so restrictive of public meetings that the Cambridge Union, the Academical Society of Oxford and the Manchester Literary Society all shut up shop, while a magistrate banned the meeting of a mineralogical society on the ground that its studies might lead to atheism. The Whigs opposed the government's repressive legislation and settled themselves comfortably into their protective bunker between government and the people. The Mountain scurried to join them. Events stripped away the veneer of Brougham's radicalism and exposed the gulf which for a time he and the Benthamites had tried to pretend did not exist between them. At the opening of the 1817 session of parliament Brougham was pleased to report that differences within the Whig opposition had faded away: 'we are firmly united on almost every point . . . at once fighting against the Crown and putting down the pernicious and insane rabble, equally the enemies of us and of the people'.[33]

The session had not proceeded far when the rupture with the Westminster radicals became public. On two or three occasions Brougham treated the House to unhedged denunciations of those people who would answer the agitation in the country with schemes of manhood suffrage, annual parliaments and the secret ballot. His apostasy was not allowed to go unremarked. Place exposed Brougham in his new broadsheet, called *Hone's Register* after its publisher, William Hone. He also gave to Lord Cochrane, the member for Westminster, a copy of Brougham's 1814 statement to the Westminster Committee pledging himself to support the very reforms he now so scornfully repudiated. Cochrane read the statement to the House of Commons on 17 February. Brougham made no mention of the episode in his memoirs; indeed the memoirs pass over his flirtation with the radicals in the years between 1814 and 1817 as if it had never happened, as if he had acted throughout as a regular (and misused) adherent to the Whig cause. The episode was embarrassing. Brougham's blustering reply to Cochrane, that he would not turn from his public duty merely to maintain a childish appearance of consistency, did not dispel the impression that he had been a reformer when the representation of Westminster beckoned and an anti-reformer when the chance disappeared.

Brougham had acted the star part in the 1816 session of parliament, only to find himself despatched by the radicals and distrusted by the Whigs. His endeavour to build a broad anti-government front came to nothing. He had therefore to make his peace with the Whigs. The best plan for the 1817 session, he told Grey, was to leave things alone and not seem anxious, although even while recommending this course he was unable to conceal his temper.

> Indeed it would be very difficult to *be* very anxious—about what our friends do. Any efforts one makes only slacken people, and make them angry or suspicious; and they really treat you for trying to serve them as if you were serving yourself. I think Burke once remarked that no man ever busied himself for the party without incurring this suspicion; but now they wish you not to do anything, from a shabby fear of its keeping them out of place—place of all things![34]

In the succeeding weeks Brougham partly redeemed himself in his critics' eyes by his temperate stand against the extreme parliamentary reformers and by a wide-ranging speech on manufacturing distress, in which he anticipated liberal Tory policy in the 1820s by calling upon the government to relax the country's tariff barriers, to let in Baltic iron and timber and French wine, and, by abandoning the execrable doctrine of legitimacy and the fawning love of Ferdinand VII, to sacrifice the antiquated prejudice against colonial independence and open up the vast continent of South America to English manufactures.[35]

When Ponsonby died suddenly in the summer of 1817 it was nevertheless taken for granted by everyone, including the Mountain, that Brougham's indiscretions, as they were called, disqualified him for the leadership. Whishaw saw that Brougham must, by degrees, become the *efficient* leader and so be a source of weakness to the party.[36] In the event the choice fell on Tierney. Tierney's selection blurs the image of the Whigs as an exclusive family compact, for like Ponsonby he was born of Irish parents (though they sent him to Eton) and his fortune, inherited from his father, came from trade. He had not risen above those natural deficiencies by parliamentary brilliance. True, he had made himself into the most knowledgeable debater on economic subjects on the Whig benches, and in the 1816 session of parliament he had matched Brougham's persistence, night after night, in attacking the government's financial proposals. Yet he was held to want fire. And there were other marks against him. A bad liver kept him for long periods away from the House; his anti-Foxite past was not forgotten; and his defects as a speaker were highlighted daily by being set against the eloquence of Romilly and Brougham. Romilly, financially dependent on his law practice, was unavailable and Brougham would not do. So Tierney, whom the Mountain made sport of and called 'Mrs Cole',* came to the leadership by default. The party looked forward to making the best of a bad job. 'I think that the good old lady can be kept in order,' Bennet wrote to Creevey, 'and tho' she be timid and idle, yet she is very popular in the House, easy and conciliatory; in no way perfect—in many ways better than any other person.'[37]

Tierney was reluctant to act as the avowed leader and although Brougham effaced himself during the 1818 session, partly to allow Tierney to put himself forward, it was decided at the end of the session that formal recognition of Tierney's position was required. What

---

* Creevey explained the nickname: 'The reason I call Tierney by the name of "Cole" is this. It used to be his constant practice in making his speeches in Parliament to bear particular testimony to his own character—to his being a "plain man", "an honest man", or something of that kind. Having heard him at this work several times, it occurred to me that he had formed himself upon that distinguished model Mrs Cole, an old lady in one of [Samuel] Foote's farces, who presided over a female establishment in Covent Garden. Mrs Cole was always indulging herself with flattering references to her own character . . . Brougham was for many years quite enamoured of the resemblance of the portrait. He christened Abercromby Young Cole, and the whole shabby party "the Coles".' (*Creevey Papers*, i, 327n.)

followed amounts to the first *election* of a party leader (though Grey remained the leader of the whole party in both Houses) in English history. A meeting of about forty Whigs at Brookes's club on 12 July agreed that Tierney should be formally appointed leader. A letter inviting him to take the office was then circulated among members of the party for their signatures and within a month 113 of them, by signing the requisition, pledged themselves to follow Tierney's command.[38] The novelty of the proceedings struck Creevey's funny bone. The party deceived itself if it believed 'the leader of the Whigs to be an article that can be created by election, or merely giving it that name. A man must make himself such leader by his talents, by his courage, and above all by the excellence and consistency of his publick principles.' By administering 'a kind of Luddite test' the party had rashly bound itself to its captain for better or worse. 'I am sure no one can laugh more heartily than Tierney himself in his sleeve as *Leader of the Whigs.*'[39]

Brougham was canvassing in Westmorland, where he was standing for election, while these proceedings took place. He sent a letter entirely approving of Tierney's election to Lord Sefton and Sefton read it to the meeting at Brooks's in order to allay misgivings that Brougham, by setting himself up as the *de facto* leader, might make Tierney's life a misery. Brougham also worked to bring young John Lambton, heir to the earldom of Durham, round to supporting Tierney. It was no light task. Since entering the Commons in 1813, Lambton had revealed that root-and-branch propensity of mind which was to endear him to the reformers and to earn him the soubriquet, 'Radical Jack'. His nature, frank, ingratiating, impetuous, quick to take offence, was of the same mould as Brougham's. They fell into confidential friendship, and when he was on the northern circuit Brougham was always made welcome at Lambton Castle. In 1818 Lambton was in no mood to have Tierney foisted upon the party. He objected to Tierney's 'wavering and indecisive system' and he told Grey that this sentiment was so widespread in the party that he, Lambton, had been suggested as an alternative.[40] When, in July, he received the requisition asking Tierney to accept the leadership, he would not sign it, for reasons which he gave to Robert Wilson.

I have refused to sign the requisition to Tierney as I do not care to submit to the cavalier mode of dictation assumed by the meeting with whom it originated. They never thought me worthy of being communicated with previously, and after having named whom they pleased they write to me to sign the requisition—without even saying what the requisition is, in what terms it is couched, or who the gentlemen were who thus arrogated to themselves the right of naming a Commons leader to the Whig party.[41]

Lambton's pretension to leadership (he was only twenty-six), his readiness to imagine himself slighted and his peevish language are so reminiscent of Brougham that it is amusing to find Brougham taking the part which Grey had so often played to him, mollifying Lambton and seducing him into compliance with the party's wishes. Lambton had been helping Brougham in his Westmorland canvass and had taken him to Lambton Castle to recover from the exhaustion of the campaign and the disappointment of defeat. To Brougham, therefore, it naturally fell to plead Tierney's cause to Lambton.

It was generally felt that something should be done—and they said IF all agree, as may be expected, then Tierney is a fair experiment to try. Your misconception is in supposing the *resolution* to be taken first—and then all of us asked to accede to it . . . Don't, therefore, my Lambton, talk of the thing being first cut and dried and then people being consulted, for it really and indeed is not so. Certainly nobody thinks Tierney unexceptionable. All of us feel as you do on the subject, but they feel what I wish to God you would, and what I really hope and trust you may, that it is a necessary step and must be taken with all its risks and evils *in the choice of difficulties*.

Your non-adhesion is very unfortunate. It acts as a damper and will annoy Tierney, as well as injure materially the success of the measure. Pray therefore do consider it again . . . Again and again I beseech you not to play the Achilles and let your wrath disturb the operations of our army.[42]

Brougham was fond of Lambton. He did not need to *think* in order to want him in the Whig eleven. It happened also, nonetheless, that the Whig party, with which Brougham's political lot seemed now to be irrevocably cast, would more readily take the direction in which he would point it if its councils were leavened by men of the stamp and opinions of Lambton.

6

Whig Frontbencher

One of the first things that Brougham did on his return to Westminster in 1816 was to draw the attention of the House of Commons to the deplorable want of education among the 'lower orders' of society. It would be wrong to suppose that parting company with the radicals implied any slackening of his resolve to improve English society. At the same time as he was making his peace with the Whigs he was laying the foundation of his most far-reaching and lasting contribution to English life, the diffusion of education among classes of people whom most of his colleagues would happily have left in ignorance. Brougham loved knowledge for its own sake. It distressed him that generation after generation of the labouring poor went to their graves unvisited by science and literature. But he was not blind to the usefulness of education. It was the means by which a man raised himself in the world. And he saw, earlier than most of his contemporaries, that an industrial society could not prosper without an educated labour force. Long before Robert Lowe, soured by the enfranchisement of the urban worker in 1867, spoke complainingly of the need to teach the new masters their letters, Brougham understood that national affairs could no longer be satisfactorily conducted if the public remained uninformed. The game of aristocratic politics, he told Lord Lansdowne in 1817, was played out. 'Formerly it was only to be Pitt and Fox, and the Cavendishes, Russells, etc. Now, it is plain that those persons cannot settle the state by their agreements or differences.'[1] For too long the Whigs had neglected the people out-of-doors, and although he explained that by 'the people' he meant 'the well-informed and weighty parts of the community', his purpose was to fit the mass of the population to the first part, at least, of his definition. More than any other politician of his generation Brougham worked to bring popular opinion to bear on national affairs and to provide the public with the means of understanding them.

Brougham's interest in raising the standards of education may have been stimulated by his Scotch upbringing, for since 1696 every parish in Scotland had been required by law to provide a school, the capital costs being defrayed by a rate levied on local heritors and tenants. Attendance at those schools was neither compulsory nor free, but many more chilren were given a rudimentary education north of the border than in England. In England the education of the poor, at the opening of the 19th century, was inadequately furnished by the Sunday schools and the charity schools, neither of which was interested in much more than training their charges to read the Bible, and by the private day schools, of scandalous reputation, known as dames' schools. The founding of Joseph Lancaster's Royal Free School in London marked a step forward. Lancaster's school was responsible for Brougham's first public appearance as an educational reformer. In 1808 a committee was formed to rescue Lancaster from debt. It called itself the Royal Lancasterian Association. After two years, William Allen, who with Joseph Fox took the lead in the committee, confessed that the effort to make the association solvent had failed. He turned to Brougham, his colleague in the anti-slavery campaign, for help. Brougham suggested the formation of a new committee of influential public figures to appeal to the country for funds, persuaded a number of his friends to lend their names to the venture and published an essay in the November issue of the *Edinburgh* recommending the extension of the Lancastrian monitorial system throughout the country. On 14 December he presided over a meeting at the Thatched House Tavern, in St James's, at which a committee of forty-seven men was appointed to raise funds for Lancaster's school in the Borough Road. The committee represented a broad spectrum of religious and political opinion, but its leading members were all friends of Brougham: the Duke of Bedford, who served as one of its presidents, Samuel Whitbread, Horner, Romilly, James Mill, Francis Place and, from the Clapham sect, William Wilberforce and Joseph Clarkson.

Relations between the new association and Lancaster were strained from the start and a running quarrel about whether the funds raised were Lancaster's personal property or moneys entrusted to the committee led to Lancaster's establishing a new school, independent of the association, at Tooting in 1813. A year later the association broke with Lancaster and changed its name to the British and Foreign School Society. Its rules and constitution were drawn up by Francis Place and Brougham was made a vice-president, a position he retained until his death. Its purpose was to help local communities to found schools by providing funds to cover the original capital costs. Although the society contained Tories and Anglicans, it insisted upon non-denominational religious instruction. Brougham told William Allen, a Quaker, that he would 'blow up the whole Lancastrian concern' if it became 'an instrument of bigotry and superstition'.[2] For that reason the society incurred the hostility of influential Tory organs such as the *Quarterly Review* and became associated, in the public mind, with Nonconformity. Brougham himself was careful never to be drawn into a religious quarrel with the society's rival, the National Society, founded by Churchmen in 1813 to counteract the sectarian tendency of Lancastrianism, but the split between the two bodies, however similar their educational objects, was the first formal expression of the denominational antagonisms which were to frustrate attempts to create a national system of education for the next sixty years.

Francis Place said of the founding members of the British and Foreign society that Brougham 'was one of the few who saw the whole scope and extent of what it may lead to'.[3] In 1815 fewer than half the children under the age of fourteen in England and Wales attended a school of any sort. Since a high proportion of them came from the upper and middle ranks of society and were enrolled at the grammar and public schools (the latter term had then a less precise meaning than it bears now), the number of working-class children receiving institutional instruction was very small. Brougham put the figure at 1 in 16, the lowest of any western European country. The two recently founded societies, relying as they did wholly on voluntary contributions, were impotent to repair the deficiency. In 1807 the House of Commons had shown itself to be in sympathy with the aims of the educational reformers: Whitbread's bill to establish a school in every English and Welsh parish had reached the House of Lords before being defeated. Armed with this precedent, Brougham told the House in 1816 that his object was to establish a system of schools with parliamentary sanction and parliamentary assistance. He knew, however, that the necessity of so fundamental a change in the nation's life had to be demonstrated. He therefore took a different course from Whitbread. Instead of bringing in a bill, he merely asked for a select committee to inquire into the state of education among the poor children of London.

The House of Commons accepted the proposition without opposition. Brougham was appointed chairman of the inquiry and was authorized to nominate his committee. Although prominent figures in the Lancastrian movement, men like Romilly, Horner and Wilberforce, naturally found their way on to the committee, Brougham took care to compose it of members drawn from all sections of the House. The committee was appointed on 21 May and immediately he had it sitting for three hours every day, examining witnesses and studying the replies to a questionnaire which he had posted to every master of a charity school, nearly ninety of them, in London. The committee amassed a store of information on the variety of schools in the capital, the curricula which they taught, the ways in which they were funded, the purposes to which their funds were put, and the number of children who were not receiving education. In addition, unsolicited testimony poured in from all over the country, the evidence from which pointed to one alarming conclusion: that everywhere charitable donations and endowments were being grossly misappropriated to almost every purpose other than the education of the poor. Grammar schools and public schools, intended by their founders to offer places to children of the poor, had become socially exclusive; endowments had been diverted entirely from their original educational purposes. By the end of the first week in June Brougham was able to present his first report to the House and to recommend, as a matter of urgency, the establishment of a roving commission to investigate charitable abuses throughout England and Wales. The fourth and last report of the 1816 session, given to the House on 20 June, stated that 120,000 children in London attended no school of any kind. Brougham estimated that a parliamentary grant of £18,000 would be sufficient to educate 30,000 of them.

The education committee was reappointed at the beginning of the 1817 session of parliament and again in 1818. During the second year little was achieved, chiefly because Brougham, after suffering a debilitating attack of pleurisy, was laid low by the mysterious melancholia which afflicted him in alternate years. In 1818, however, the committee was again driven hard by Brougham and by April he was confident that enough evidence of charitable abuse had come to light to warrant his bringing in a bill. Prepared with the assistance of Romilly and Thomas Babington, one of the original Saints, the bill had a distinct Benthamite flavour and provided a foretaste of the administrative revolution which was accomplished in the 1830s. Parliament was to appoint eight commissioners, separated into four boards of two members each, to travel around the country receiving evidence. They were to be paid and they were empowered to summon witnesses and to compel them to produce deeds and documents under the threat of penalty. Brougham would have liked the commission to investigate charities of all kinds, but he thought it prudent, as a first step, to limit the inquiry to educational foundations. He also exempted the two universities and three ancient schools, Westminster, Winchester and Charterhouse, from the inquiry.

The bill was greeted with such enthusiasm by the country that Brougham was able, when it reached the committee stage, to amend it to include all charities; but by the time it reached the House of Lords its opponents had worked on the prejudices of the Tory majority there. The cry went up that the proposals amounted to an invasion of private property and an unjustifiable interference in the management of charitable funds. Brougham had already answered those criticisms in the House of Commons. His bill interfered only with the *mismanagement* of funds; moreover, the money spent by trustees of charitable organizations was, in fact, public money, and the trustees were as accountable for its appropriation as any government officer. Brougham's defence of his bill would be commonplace today. It was not so in an age when the buying and selling of a parliamentary seat was considered a private transaction. The Lords ripped the heart out of the bill. The original bill named the commissioners; the Lords transferred the power of appointment to the Crown. They decided that there should be two boards only, each composed of three commissioners, thereby making it almost impossible for the whole of the country to be visited. Worst of all, they deprived the commissioners of the right to compel the production of evidence, prohibited them from inquiring into the general state of education, and exempted all public schools or foundations managed by visitors, governors or overseers from examination.

The remnant of the bill which came back to the House of Commons was reluctantly accepted by Brougham, not simply because half a loaf was better than none, but because he foresaw that it would work well upon public opinion to expose those schools which shrank from having their operations scrutinized. In the meantime he got on with publishing the three-volume report of the committee's findings and writing a pamphlet to explain to the public the iniquity of the Lords' actions. 'The charity abuses produce a vast effect every where,' he wrote to Lambton, a member of the committee, '& I think of publishing a letter on them to Romilly to blow up the coals.'[4] The pamphlet, entitled *A Letter to Sir Samuel Romilly, M.P., Upon the Abuse of Charities*, was issued in October.[5] Romilly, who read proofs of it, thought it too dry to excite public interest. He was mistaken. In less than a month it ran through eight editions. Brougham made particular play of the decision to strike out the clause enabling the commissioners to inquire into schools having visitors. Not only did they constitute a majority of schools, they were subject to the most lamentable abuses, not because the visitors were miscreants, but because they were too busy to take notice of what was happening or to compare the actual administration of schools nominally under their charge with the founders' intentions.

One instance of abuse instantly became infamous with the public. Pocklington school, in Yorkshire, with a large revenue, had fallen into decay. Only one boy was taught at it and the schoolroom had many years before been converted into a saw-pit. The master continued to draw his salary. Yet nothing was to be done, if the Lords had their way, because the school had a visitor, the Master of St John's College, Cambridge. Revelations of such wanton disregard of founders' intentions encouraged the public to believe that Brougham had reason to accuse the Crown of using its power of appointment to frustrate the spirit of the act which established the commission. Not a single member of the education committee had been appointed to the commission; Brougham was excluded from it; and the Crown (in practice, ministers) had gone so far as to appoint the bishops of Peterborough and St Asaph, one of whom had voted against even the Lords' emasculated version of the bill, while the other had retired from the chamber before the division.

> It might have been expected [Brougham wrote in the pamphlet] that either Mr Babington or myself, who had taken the principal part in the labours of the Committee, would have been placed upon the watch ... I was induced to tender myself, by the strong representations of my fellow labourers in the Committee. As the office conferred neither emolument, nor patronage, nor power; as it only gave the privilege of hard labour, of which the habits of my life and my zeal for the cause, made it very clear that I should cheerfully take advantage; I imagined that the most implacable species of malice ... could hardly impute any selfish views to the application ... I added that even if my temporary retirement from

Parliament were deemed an indispensable condition of the appointment, I still desired to have the option upon these terms.

At the beginning of the 1819 session of parliament Lord Castlereagh, the leader of the House of Commons, announced that the government was to bring in a bill to enlarge the powers of the commissioners and extend their range of inquiry. Gratified by another example of the force of aroused public anger, Brougham dropped his plans to have the education committee reappointed. When the government's measure was introduced in May it was discovered to reincorporate most of the provisions which the Lords had struck from his bill a year before. All charitable foundations were included, penalties were to be imposed upon offenders, and ten of the now twenty commissioners were to be paid an annual salary of £1,000 in addition to expenses.

Only in one respect did Brougham find the bill seriously at fault: the continued exemption of visited schools. His attempt to remedy this shortcoming failed, but his speech elicited a quite unexpected intervention in the debate by Robert Peel, then the darling of the die-hard Tories for his deeply Orange conduct as Irish secretary. Peel accused Brougham of packing the education committee with his friends, of extending his inquiries much farther than parliament had authorized, and of overriding oaths of secrecy sworn by trustees of public schools by publishing their founding statutes. Brougham was used to such misrepresentations. In the previous December the *Quarterly Review* had published a blast against the education committee and all its works. The article was written by Dr Monk (afterwards Bishop of Gloucester), but it was generally, and rightly, suspected of having had its most vitriolic passages inserted by Canning and Castlereagh, neither of whom had suffered themselves to speak against Brougham in the House. Peel's speech was little more than a pale rehearsal of Monk's ill-founded charges. It pricked Brougham into an immediate rejoinder. Most of his famous speeches were meticulously prepared; but he was also a master at *replying*, the most difficult and the most essential of parliamentary arts. On this occasion he spoke for two hours, entirely vindicating the work of the committee and fully exposing Peel's rashness and ignorance. On the question of the oaths he rounded on him with a ferocity that struck fear into the hearts of his opponents and hinted broadly that Peel, who had remained silent for three whole years while the committee was behaving in a way he now found shocking, had been put up to the job.

A few years later Brougham professed to feel regret at having laid so mercilessly into the 'low, miserable Spinning Jenny', as he called Peel: 'it was like having his hand seized while picking a pocket'.[6] At the time, the House of Commons, taken aback by Peel's shabby behaviour, was satisfied with the justice of Brougham's rebuke. Wilberforce spoke for all but the most benighted in praising him for the incalculable benefits which he had bestowed upon the country by letting air in upon a dank corner of the nation's life. The benefits were not immediately felt. Brougham's bill of 1820, which would have given England and Wales a parochial school system roughly parallel to the Scotch one, was abandoned in the face of the Dissenters' outcry against the provision which entrusted religious instruction to the Church of England. The day of a national school system was still far off. Brougham's notions themselves fell far short of what reformers fifty years later were to demand: education that was 'universal, compulsory, unsectarian and free'. Universality was the most that Brougham aimed at. Even so his path-clearing work richly deserved the tribute paid to him some years later by the Lancashire weaver, Samuel Bamford.

> Our educators are, after all, the best reformers, and are doing the best for their country, whether they intend so or not. In this respect, Lord Brougham is the greatest man we have. He led popular education from the dark and narrow crib where he found it, like a young colt, saddled and cruelly bitted by ignorance, for superstition to ride. He cut the straps from its sides and the bridle from its jaws, and sent it forth strong, beautiful, and free.[7]

By the time that those words were written, Brougham had accomplished his great work in adult education for the working man. The earlier achievements were no less praiseworthy. He had bludgeoned parliament, in paying salaries to the charity commissioners, to vote money for an educational purpose in England and Wales (Ireland already received a £40,000 annual grant) for the first time. The education committee's reports furnished the country, also for the first time, with a statistical framework for assessing the educational needs of the population. Nor was that all. In drawing fire upon the abuse of charitable endowments, he contributed to that awakening of the public conscience which produced, in time, the stringent criterion of administrative accountability which was one of the hallmarks of the

Victorian public ethos. The charity commission established in 1818 remained in existence until 1834 and during the course of its labours it pried into the affairs of 26,751 English charities.[8] And when at last the charitable trusts act was passed in 1853, Lord John Russell, the minister responsible for it, wrote to Brougham to congratulate him on 'the fruit of the tree which you planted thirty-seven years ago'.[9]

* * *

Lord Campbell once suggested that for so long as Brougham continued to sit for a nomination borough he remained shy of declaiming against the country's corrupt representative system. He took up parliamentary reform only when (to use a later term) he was unmuzzled by his election for Yorkshire.[10] Had Brougham been persuaded of the urgency of parliamentary reform, or its usefulness to the Whig party, scruples of the kind which Campbell suggested would scarcely have deterred him. It is true, however, that, eager to present himself as the 'man of the people', he was continually on the look-out for a popular constituency. He had failed at Liverpool in 1812 and at Westminster in 1814. When parliament was dissolved in 1818 he decided upon a far bolder course: to tilt against the near-sacrosanct electoral sway exercised by the Lowther family in Westmorland.

Rotten boroughs and unrepresented northern towns were not the only blots upon the English representative constitution. It was as deeply stained by the electoral power in the counties which both Whig and Tory landowners claimed of right. They called it the due influence of property and divided the county representation between themselves. To disturb this gentlemanly share of the spoils, as much social as political in its origins, was to unsettle the 'peace of the county'. So it was that most county seats went uncontested at elections. Nowhere was the right of property more arrogantly displayed, nor more jealously guarded, than in Westmorland, whose two parliamentary seats had been uncontested since 1774. Westmorland was the only county in England whose politics were controlled by a single landed family. At its head was the Earl of Lonsdale; in 1818 the two sitting members, until Brougham's audacious intervention confident of unopposed re-election, were the Earl's two sons, Viscount Lowther and Colonel Lowther, referred to by Brougham throughout the campaign as the 'two cubs'.

In those places where opinion counted the opposition expected to do well at the polls in 1818. As it proved, the unpopularity of the government, in a season of economic stagnation and popular discontent, produced a gain of about thirty seats for the Whigs. The elections did not take place until July, but Brougham began his canvass early in the new year, arranging to have himself invited by Westmorland freeholders to stand in their interest and establishing an amorphous association in London called The Friends of the Independence of Westmorland. Why did he undertake such a Sisyphean task? There were those who believed him to be settling an old score against Lonsdale, who in 1806 had turned aside Wilberforce's request that Brougham be brought into parliament via one of his pocket boroughs. Sydney Smith thought it sufficient to remark that Brougham's hatreds were 'not among the least durable of his feelings'.[11] Certainly Brougham felt no compulsion to treat the Lowthers gently. He had, for one thing, no class loyalty to inhibit him. His candidacy, announced far in advance of the poll and prosecuted with characteristic energy and thoroughness, cost the Earl of Lonsdale a deal of money. 'My satisfaction,' Brougham wrote to Creevey early on, 'is that he is now bleeding at every pore—all the houses open—all the agents running up bills—all the manors shot over by anybody who pleases.'[12]

Brougham contested Westmorland to make a splash and to strike a blow at the fetters which the influence of property placed upon the free expression of political choice. There is no need to go so far as Chester New and interpret his standing as 'a dramatic play in his movement for Parliamentary Reform'.[13] In June, at the height of the campaign, Brougham hotly repudiated the Benthamite plan of full reform in the House of Commons and he played a key role in persuading George Lamb, a regular Whig, to stand against and, as it happened, defeat the compromise Whig/radical candidate, John Hobhouse, at Westminster.[14] Hobhouse had delighted Francis Place and the Westminster radicals by the vehemence of his attacks on the boroughmongers; by opposing him Brougham set the seal upon his rupture with the radicals. He could nevertheless expect his speeches on the hustings and the sheer audacity of his challenge to the Lowthers to have a subtle effect. 'I should not wonder,' James Mackintosh wrote after reading accounts of Brougham's triumphal progress through Westmorland, 'if the absolute novelty of such proceedings should leave a deep and lasting impression in those lonely vales, which may be perhaps too strong for influence.'[15]

Brougham's purpose was not to crusade for parliamentary reform; it was to awaken the freeholders to exercise freely the franchise which was already theirs.

Brougham's courage is not in question. On 15 January, before he had formally entered the lists, the Earl of Darlington, who felt strongly 'the impropriety of countenancing in any way so direct an attack upon what has been so long considered an honourable and certain appendage (however I may disagree in that idea) to that family', informed him that to carry out his intention would be to forfeit his seat at Winchilsea.[16] Brougham had nearly all the Whigs against him. He told Creevey that the 'regular Coles' were 'astonished at this rebellion against legitimate authority'.[17] Tierney, with his usual timidity, did not 'exactly see the wisdom of the step' when Brougham had no clear prospect of victory before him.[18] Only the Earl of Thanet, the hereditary sheriff of Westmorland and the richest Whig landowner in the county, and John Lambton rallied to his standard. The Earl of Derby, the Duke of Devonshire and even Lord Grey turned down Thanet's appeals for assistance. Thanet was left to bear the expenses of the campaign, while Lambton accompanied Brougham on the hectic tours of Westmorland's towns and villages.

The campaign was a prototype of Gladstone's celebrated Midlothian crusades of 1879 and 1880. The gentry, the Church, the attorneys and the whole weight of government were against Brougham. So were Wordsworth and de Quincey, who lent their literary talents to the Lowthers and brought out pamphlets branding him as a vile demagogue and democrat. Everywhere Brougham went the Lowthers drew up troops, as much to taint him with rabble-rousing as to guard against any real threat of rioting. Brougham sent word to Lord Holland that even on a Sunday, one day when he was making his way across Westmorland to Lambton Castle, 'notwithstanding the holiness of the day, we were drawn & mobbed everywhere & had effigies of the Lowthers hanging etc.'.[19] Westmorland had never seen such crowds.

I have succeeded every where [Brougham wrote to Lambton as the first day of polling approached] in organising my forces & marshalling them under leaders, to *march* in bodies with music & colours— the lame following in carts etc. & those who have horses to ride. We have beds for them all in houses & barns etc. The multitude which is enormous, are to be camped. We have got the best arrangements for polling booths—*on sure & convenient ground*—& shall have the entire command of them. The enemy are having a mob of miners chiefly from Alston Moor, but we shall defeat them signally if they give battle.[20]

It was Liverpool all over again and Lambton, having his first experience of Brougham's whirlwind activity on the hustings, could scarcely believe the amount that one man, all the time heavily occupied in London with the education committee, was able to accomplish.

He worked like a horse. He was at once candidate, counsel, agent, canvasser, and orator, and changing his characters every hour,— and always cheerful and active. Really his energy of mind is beyond anything I could ever have conceived.[21]

Carried away by the tumult he was creating, Brougham was confident of success. 'The spirit of the freeholders, to be sure, is wonderful,' he told Creevey, 'and in the end we *must* beat the villains.'[22] The London newspapers, who reported the Westmorland election more closely than any other, made him the favourite. Long-toothed veterans of political warfare were less sanguine. Lord Rosslyn allowed that the zeal of the yeomanry was such that almost all the expense was confined to the Lowther side, but he was 'always afraid of money & power' and therefore sceptical of Brougham's high expectations.[23]

Brougham gave the Lowthers a real fright. The *Westmorland Gazette*, although de Quincey, its editor, was unable to get the first number out before the polling was over, was started in order to establish a Lowther-controlled, anti-Brougham organ in the county. In the end the Lowther money and the traditional pull of deferential ties proved too powerful to overcome. But Brougham ran the Tories close: his 889 votes fell only 168 short of Colonel Lowther's total. Two years later, at the elections caused by the death of George III, he contested Westmorland again, coming within 63 votes of the colonel and by the exertions which he forced upon the Lowthers proving, so James Losh believed, that he must triumph at a third try.[24] In 1826 he did stand once more and was once more beaten in a fierce campaign which cost the Lowthers at least £40,000.[25] Brougham was not cast down by his failures. He had demonstrated that the strength of the Tories, even in a county where Whig property commanded negligible influence, was far from invincible. He had raised the spirits of the freeholders of the northern counties and stamped himself as their champion. The fruit of the seeds which he sowed in Westmorland was harvested at the Yorkshire election of 1830.

* * *

The year 1819 opened with Brougham in low spirits. In November, Romilly, inconsolable at the death of his wife and deranged by his grief, had shut himself up in his room and, after five days of solitary brooding, cut his throat. Four years earlier Whitbread had done the same. And only a few months before Romilly's death, Francis Horner, no longer intimate with Brougham, but still his oldest friend, had died at Pisa. The departure of Whitbread and Horner made the death of Romilly all the more painful for Brougham. 'It is vain to regret or repine,' he wrote to Lord Grey, 'but I certainly never thought we should live to sustain a loss which might make even Whitbread's seem inconsiderable.'[26] Suicide, especially by the slitting of the throat, was a recurring event at Westminster in the early 19th century, and when Castlereagh had recourse to it in 1822 Brougham was led to strange musings, vengeful thoughts brought on by his apparent belief that Castlereagh's political friends were provoked to a charitable compassion they had not felt for Whitbread and Romilly. The coarse doggerel of Shelley* and the howls of the London mob who spat on Castlereagh's funeral carriage found in Brougham a muted echo.

> One can't help feeling a little for him [he wrote to Creevey], after being pitted against him for several years pretty regularly. It is like losing a connection suddenly. Also, he was a *gentleman*, and the only one amongst them. But there are material advantages; and among them I reckon not the least that our excellent friends that are gone, and for whom we felt so bitterly, are, as it were, revenged. I mean Whitbread and Romilly. I cannot describe to you how this idea has filled my mind these last 24 hours. No mortal will now presume to whisper a word against these great and good men—I mean in our time; for there never was any chance of their doing so in after time. All we wanted was a *gag* for the present, and God knows here we have it in absolute perfection. Hitherto we were indulged with the enemy's silence, but it was by a sort of forbearance; *now* we have it of right.[27]

---

* *So Castlereagh has slit his throat—the worst*
  Of it is, that his own was not the first.

The effect on Brougham of the deaths of Whitbread, Horner and Romilly is not to be measured. His closest allies on the left wing of the opposition had departed. With Horner and Whitbread his youth may be said to have slipped away from him. The future was drawing in. In the spring of 1819 he took to himself a wife. Brougham's contemporaries liked to remark that he was not a favourite with the ladies, for reasons which Harriet Martineau gave after observing him at dinner in 1834.

I remember—not a morsel of his dress being anything but black, from the ridge of his stock to the toes of his polished shoes. Not an inch of white was there to relieve the combined gloom of his dress and complexion. He was curiously afraid of my trumpet, and managed generally to make me hear without. He talked excessively fast, and ate fast and prodigiously, stretching out his long arm for any dish he had a mind to, and getting hold of the largest spoons which would dispatch the most work in the shortest time . . . I liked to watch him when he was conversing with gentlemen, and his mind and its manifestations really came out. This was never the case, as far as my observation went, when he talked with ladies. I believe I have never met with more than three men, in the whole course of my experience, who talked with women in a perfectly natural manner; that is, precisely as they talked with men; but the difference in Brougham's case was so great as to be disagreeable. He knew many cultivated and intellectual women; but this seemed to be of no effect. If not able to assume with them his ordinary manner towards silly women, he was awkward and at a loss. This was by no means agreeable, though the sin of his bad manners must be laid at the door of the vain women who discarded their ladyhood for his sake, went miles to see him, were early on platforms where he was to be, and admitted him to very broad flirtations. He had pretty nearly settled his own business, in regard to conversation with ladies, before two more years were over. His swearing became so incessant, and the occasional indecency of his talk so insufferable, that I have seen even coquettes and adorers turn pale, and the lady of the house tell her husband that she could not undergo another dinner-party with Lord Brougham for a guest.[28]

Miss Martineau, her vanity pricked by Brougham's indifference to her intellectual merits, angry, in addition, at his defaulting on a payment of £100 for four poor-law stories which she wrote for the

Society for the Diffusion of Useful Knowledge, was a hostile, and certainly priggish, witness. And although James Grant, a fellow lawyer with no axe to grind, said that Brougham had the least gallantry of all the public men of his acquaintance, his conventional understanding of such matters may be judged from his remark (although he was himself tinctured with liberalism) that 'the Liberals cannot stand a moment's comparison with the Tories, either for politeness to their fellow-men, or for gallantry to the fair sex'.[29]

Brougham's marriage appears, on the surface, not to have expressed any deep romantic attachment. For about a year he had been making himself agreeable to a Mrs Spalding, formerly Mary Ann Eden, the niece of the first Lord Auckland. At the same time he had been paying court to Georgiana Pigou, whose mother was a friend of Jeffrey and Sydney Smith. According to Smith, Georgiana turned Brougham down on two or three occasions, for although she was 'very much captivated by him', she was half-promised to a Mr Meynell (whom she married in August). Georgiana's virtues included a fortune of £20,000 in 'powder and cash'; Mrs Spalding's attractions were more modest, but they included a house in Hill Street, Mayfair, and an annual income of £1,500. Rejected by Miss Pigou, Brougham settled for the widow. 'I always told you that Brougham would marry the widow,' Smith wrote to Lady Holland, 'but you laughed me to scorn. I always told you he would not marry Miss Pigou, but you laughed me to scorn. A cool consciousness of being in the right supports me on these occasions.'[30] Smith had met Mrs Spalding for the first time at a dinner in January and he described her to Lady Grey as 'a showy, long, well-dressed, red and white widow who made some impression on me by her beauty'.[31] John Whishaw called her 'handsome and rather dashing'.[32] No one seems to have been struck by her conversation, but Smith, who reminded Lady Grey that fifteen years had passed since first she set eyes on Brougham's 'gristly face' and that their friend now required domestic comfort, found her to be 'a pretty good-natured woman' and was heartily glad that Brougham was 'wisely and comfortably settled'.[33]

Smith knew more of the match-making than anyone else—it was he who put it about that Mrs Spalding delayed the wedding until Peel's currency act of 1819, which returned Great Britain to a gold standard, enabled her to make a settled assessment of her financial position—but even he, like everyone else, was kept in the dark about the actual marriage. He had long since ceased to wonder at anything that

Brougham did: 'Brougham has hated always the broad Turnpike roads of life, and arrived at his Goals by crossing the Country over hedge and ditch.'[34] Brougham and Mrs Spalding were married in secret at Coldstream, just across the border in Scotland, for all the world as if they were eloping young lovers. The ceremony took place at Easter, but the world did not learn of it until July, when Brougham took his wife for the first time to the family home in Westmorland. Even while making the journey there, he wrote a letter to Whishaw without mentioning her.[35]

Once or twice a glimpse of Brougham's wife may be caught in contemporary correspondence, but she felt so ill at ease in the rarefied society in which her husband moved that she could seldom be brought to venture out without him. Once, in 1823, she appeared at Lord King's on her own, but only after apologizing beforehand on four full sides of notepaper, since, as she explained to Lady King, she well knew that she was asked only on account of Henry and trembled to incur the odium of going anywhere unaccompanied by him. Creevey, who arrived at Lord King's just as Mrs Brougham pulled up in her carriage, 'handed her out, dressed like an interesting villager, all in white, with a wreath of roses round her temples'; at dinner he sat next to her and found that 'her languishing was really beyond all bearing'.[36] Nor, by Creevey's account, were things much better when the Broughams entertained at Hill Street.

> Our dinner at Bruffam's yesterday was damnable in cookery, comfort and everything else . . . Mrs. Brougham sat like an overgrown doll at the top of the table in a bandeau of roses, her face in a perpetual simper without utterance. Bruffam, at the other end, was jawing about nothing from beginning to end, without attending to any one, and only caring about hearing himself talk.[37]

That was in 1825. Thereafter Mrs Brougham, who was evidently a neurotic hypochondriac, given to spells of depression so severe that she was commonly accounted mad, spent her life (she died in 1865) in the background, attending to the household accounts, but exercising no discernible influence on Brougham's public career.

* * *

When the House of Commons elected in 1818 assembled at the beginning of 1819, Brougham was back in his accustomed place on the opposition front bench, the Earl of Darlington having relented and allowed him to retain the representation of Winchilsea. Brougham did not learn of his patron's change of heart until after the elections were over, however, and in the Whigs' failure to find him a refuge should he be defeated at Westmorland he found fresh grounds for placing himself at odds with his party. Romilly, too, had been left to win at Westminster or else, and was saved only by his triumph there. Even more delinquent, in Brougham's view, was the treatment of James Scarlett, the barrister coming to pre-eminence on the northern circuit, whose claims on the party's gratitude, after standing unsuccessfully at Lewes in 1812 and 1816, were passed over in favour of a young, untried pet of the Whig clan. Once again Lord Holland was the recipient of Brougham's stern reproach.

I don't now write to complain on my own or Romilly's account. I certainly do think that what has been done amounts to a compleat dissolution of all party union. Every principle of a common interest or understanding has been grossly & childishly violated. In pursuit of the *newest*, the most untried man, the man who had the least claims on the party, Romilly, Scarlett & myself have been wholly overlooked. Scarlett's great sacrifices in every way—two contests & a third pending—ten years want of promotion in his profession—all overlooked, a lesson taught to all Whig lawyers that a man needs not be anything but new & untried, in order to be supported, & the loss sustained by the party of the man who in spite of party & court persecution has worked his way to the head of his profession, & would have come into Parlt. with all the weight of that high station.

Romilly had still higher claims to plead, & of my own, which are small enough, God knows, I say nothing, except that in 1812 I was more connected with the party and had gained (accidentally) a greater victory for it than I suppose the new favourite may win in several years to come, yet I was suffered to be three years out of Parlt without the offer of a seat on any terms. And now, when I had only this one chance of getting a seat should I be beat in West., I find the place occupied, and not only that, but the same sum that I was prepared to pay, raised in an instant for the new & untried supporter.

All this has quite made up my mind as to the futility of all party connexion. It means only a dupery of sixty or seventy people who don't reflect, for the benefit of two or three sly characters who go about *earwigging* the powerful ones for their own purposes.[38]

How Brougham's sham modesty and childish pouting tried the patience of his friends! Yet on this occasion his hectoring may have done good, for Scarlett, having sacrificed professional advancement by turning down repeated offers to come into parliament on the government interest, was returned, with the influence of Earl Fitz-william, at a by-election at Peterborough early in 1819.

The chief· event of political interest in 1819 was the 'Peterloo massacre' at Manchester on 16 August, when hussars broke up a mass outdoor meeting led by 'Orator' Hunt and in doing so killed eleven people and injured several hundred. Lord Liverpool's government bore no direct responsibility for the affray, since the yeomanry was called out by the local magistrates. Its error, as Brougham pointed out, was to prejudge the issue by resisting calls for an inquiry.[39] As Lord Eldon, the chancellor, put it, although the Manchester magistrates were very much blamed, they must be supported.[40] The instinct, in a crisis, to support the instruments of the law, occasionally lands Tories in difficulty. For what if the officers of the law have behaved injudiciously? Eldon himself half admitted that in suppressing a meeting gathered to petition the Crown for the redress of a grievance—in this instance the oligarchic nature of the electoral system—the Manchester magistrates were encroaching upon the constitution. In their defence it may be said that the meeting was the culmination of two years of increasingly strident radical agitation in the north, that the propertied classes were genuinely fearful of insurrection, and that local authorities had at their disposal no police force to control mass outdoor demonstrations.

Throughout the north feeling ran strong against the government. The Whigs had no difficulty in denouncing the insolence of the Manchester authorities and the cowardice of the Tory ministers. Seizing party advantage from the episode was more tricky. On the one side the radicals were pressing ahead with protest meetings in all the northern counties; on the other the government was preparing repressive legislation to present to a recalled parliament before Christmas. It was all very well for the Whigs to take up an independent position between what Lord Holland called 'two factions who from very opposite quarters are assailing the free constitution of the country'.[41] They were understandably eager to avoid leaguing themselves with the extreme followers of 'Orator' Hunt, who had alarmed the respectable classes with his veiled threats of being driven, in the last resort, to the use of physical force and who had deliberately provoked the Manchester authorities by arriving at St Peter's Fields waving a tricolour flag. But unless they took some sort of lead in the anti-government demonstrations they risked forcing moderate opinion, *faute de mieux*, into the radical camp.

Brougham's response to the crisis differed little from that of Lord Grey and most of the Whig party. His initial advice to the party, couched in the purest Whig language, was to do nothing.

> Nothing could be more unjustifiable than the conduct of the magistrates in employing the military as they did. Whether this will be the feeling of the country remains to be seen: if not, the consequences may prove most fatal to the freedom of the country: and this indeed is one of the most mischievous effects of the proceedings of the Radicals, that by abusing popular privileges they establish precedents for abridging them. My views of the state of the country are more and more gloomy. Everything is tending, and has been for some time tending, to a complete separation between the higher and lower orders of society; a state of things which can only end in the destruction of liberty, or in a convulsion which may too probably produce the same result. It has sometimes occurred to me that we ought to try once more whether, by placing ourselves on the middle ground, condemning the conduct of Hunt and his associates, but strenuously resisting the attempt that is making to attack through them the safeguards of the constitution, we could not rally to our standard all moderate and reasonable men (and a great portion of the property of the country), to whom the people might again be brought to look as their natural leaders and protectors. But as often as I cast my eye back on the events of the last thirty years, and consider the present state and condition of the country, that hope fails me. The result, therefore, of the consideration which hitherto I have been able to give to this subject is, that we must wait till the meeting of Parliament, unless sooner called forth by some strong manifestation of public feeling to take the part which, upon a full review of all the circumstances, our principles and our duty may dictate.[42]

Eventually the 'strong manifestation of public feeling' persuaded Brougham to follow Earl Fitzwilliam's lead in Yorkshire and organize meetings in Westmorland and Cumberland, where he succeeded in getting most of the principal landowners not of Lord Lonsdale's immediate connection to sign the requisition calling for an inquiry into the massacre.[43] The demand was not granted and, although the opposition voted almost to a man against the famous Six Acts which the government drew up to gag the popular press and stifle the agitation in the country, the Whigs' response to the whole episode revealed their want of imagination in diagnosing what was soon to become known as 'the condition of England'. Surgery was called for, but the Whigs looked to cure the patient with homeopathic doses of reform. So, in October, the plan of parliamentary reform which circulated among the leading members of the party called only for the addition of Manchester and a few Yorkshire towns to the representation. Brougham wished to strengthen it by adding Edinburgh, Glasgow and more Lancashire towns to the list and by including a proposal for triennial parliaments, but like his colleagues he recognized no immediate urgency to bring the plan forward. On no account, he wrote to John Allen, should the subject be mentioned in the pre-Christmas debates on the gagging acts. If it were, the party would be split both inside and outside parliament and the hand of the ministers strengthened. 'In the great interest of the present questions, we have a very fair excuse for delay. But no one is more convinced than myself, that Reform *must*, and that speedily, be taken up by us.'[44]

Whether Brougham meant what he said, the moment had passed. On 29 January George III died in his eighty-second year. For the next nine months all public questions were eclipsed by the extraordinarily fervent passions which George IV aroused in all classes of the nation by his decision to divorce his consort, Caroline, and strip her of the dignity and title of Queen.

7

The Queen's Attorney

'He who dares your Royal Highness to overlook the evidence of my innocence, and disregard the sentence of complete acquittal which it produced, or is wicked and false enough still to whisper suspicions in your ear, betrays his duty to you, Sir, to your daughter, and to your people.'[1] Princess Caroline issued the solemn warning to her husband, the Prince Regent, in 1813. The words may have been her own; the spirit that moved them was Brougham. In the year previous he had become her chief legal adviser. Brougham met the Princess for the first time in the latter part of 1809, when he turned up at one of her evening entertainments at Kensington Palace. There, once a week or so, Caroline played hostess to an unfashionable collection of savants and wits, men whose lowly ambitions placed them beyond the fear of incurring the Regent's displeasure. The poet, Samuel Rogers, and the politicians, George Canning and Lord Dudley, attended her, but rare indeed were such links of friendship with the great world, for she had long since been ostracized by the higher branches of society. Nor were her political alliances secure. Since being discarded by the Prince of Wales little more than a year after their marriage in 1795, and only a few months after the birth of the Princess Charlotte, Caroline had become a pawn in the party struggle. She had also, by the pathetic circumstances to which her husband had reduced her and by her artful exploitation of his cruelty, become the darling of the common people.

Caroline's sins were two. She did not all alone beweep her outcast state; by amusing herself with the less exalted friendships left to her, and by allowing the public to witness her amusements, she offended against the decorum of a cant-ridden court. Worse, by leading a life which, although chaste by her husband's standards, appeared to be unashamedly flirtatious, she defied the hypocritical canon that a man's peccadilloes were a woman's crimes. That Caroline, banished to a villa in Blackheath and separated from her daughter, fell in with a crowd of naval officers and befriended the poor (she grew and sold vegetables to raise money for the care of orphans), that she did not behave with customary royal dignity, meant nothing to the populace, who saw only that she was treated most unroyally by her husband and his advisers. It did, however, mean something to the politicians. Denied the prospect of office by George III, the Whigs had fallen back on that last recourse of oppositions, alliance with the heir to the throne. Unexpectedly placed in office in 1806, they consented to be the tools of the Prince's policy. They appointed a commission to inquire into his wife's conduct. Its object was to gratify the Prince's wish to be rid of her by discovering her to be an adulterer. The 'Delicate Investigation', as it was called, found in Caroline's behaviour much to its distaste, but it was unable to show that the orphan boy whom she had adopted and taken into her villa was her son. Deprived of evidence with which to convict, the Whig ministers did not exonerate: they advised the King that he had no grounds for refusing to receive his daughter-in-law, but recommended that he admonish her. Nor did they publish the evidence gathered by the commission. So the taint of suspicion was encouraged to linger, and as the years went by Caroline was treated with less and less charity. By 1809, the year in which Brougham made her acquaintance, visits to her daughter were restricted to two a month and correspondence between them had to be smuggled past the Prince's censoring eye.

For two years Brougham was no more than an occasional hanger-on of the Princess' circle. The political upheavals of 1812 altered his position. Cheated of office by their long-time ally, the Prince of Wales, the Whigs turned their wrath upon him, while Caroline, spurred by her husband's elevation to the rank of Regent, demanded to have her honour redeemed and her wrongs redressed. An avenging opposition might be of use to her; she, still warm in the affections of the people, might certainly be useful to the opposition. Brougham and Whitbread consented to act as her legal advisers. So the domestic quarrel of the royal couple became enmeshed in the politics of the Mountain. 'I really felt, as did Whitbread,' Brougham later recorded, 'that the conduct of the Prince had been such from the beginning towards his wife, and his later treatment of both mother and daughter so outrageous, as made it a duty to take their part; whilst his conduct towards the Whig party made this proceeding on our part quite justifiable, and not at all inconsistent with our party connection.'[2]

Brougham's chief interest was to enhance his popularity and prosper the Whig cause, but he was not talking mere cant when he said that, for Caroline's sake, he entirely disregarded the harm which he might do to his future advancement at the bar. If his gamble failed, if taking the part of Caroline and Charlotte did not bring him and the Whigs into office, then by making enemies of the Regent and his Tory ministers he risked being refused silk. That justice was on the side of the Princess Brougham had no doubt. That the affair could safely be left alone by the politicians he declared to be a misreading of the constitution. He had a short answer for those who pretended that parliament was incompetent to meddle in the private affairs of the royal family.

> The Crown has the disposal and superintendence of the family. Granted. But in what capacity? As father? No such thing . . . it is as *Crown*, and to the *exclusion* of the natural father . . . the Crown only exercises the superintendence as an act of state, and through responsible servants. Peace and war, treaties, &c., are matters left to the Crown, as better able to deal with them than the Legislature; so of every other branch of the executive. But do we say that these are not matters of state? No. The care of the family is better in the hands of the Crown. But has the state no interest in the exercise of such a trust? Who else, constitutionally speaking, has *any* interest? The idea of its being a family or domestic affair is completely negatived by the law itself, which (as declared by the judges in 1718) takes the care out of the hands of the father himself, and gives it to the King for the time being, who may be a distant relation. What, then, becomes the trash about interfering between father and daughter? Why, again, is the Princess to be treated as a state criminal? Why are we to have a Queen so brought up? Out of Turkey is there anything so barbarous?[3]

Brougham presented the argument, of enduring importance in a constitutional monarchy, more fully in an article in the *Edinburgh Review* published in the autumn of 1814. The gist of it he gave in his memoirs.

> Between the family of a sovereign and the children of a subject there is nothing in common. The members of a royal, as compared with those of a private, family, are by law debarred from feelings common to humanity, and from all free action. They cannot fall in love without the consent of the Crown; they may be over head and ears in that passion, but it must remain a dead letter to them unless

the sovereign in Council permits its indulgence. The King for a wife must choose some Protestant princess he has never seen; but this he must do for the sake of his people, and to secure a Protestant successor; and his heir comes into the world, not in the privacy of . the domestic household, but in the presence of a crowd of the great officers of state. All the tender feelings engendered in the private family, all the closest relations of parent and child, must be disregarded as if they had no existence. Such is the penalty of the exalted rank, and the sacrifice royalty must make in return for the very inadequate compensation of power and dignity.

The sovereign, as the executive branch of the Government, is also intrusted by the constitution with large discretionary powers in governing his family; but he is bound to exercise such powers not according to his own fancy, or for the gratification of his private feelings or individual caprices, but in such a manner as shall most conduce to the common weal. All the power he has, and every act he performs, is as *sovereign*, and not as a private person.[4]

Brougham's defeat at the 1812 elections left Whitbread the Princess's champion in parliament. Whitbread brought the scandalous treatment of his client continually before the House of Commons, but without the backing of the Whig leaders, who were reluctant to widen the breach opened between themselves and the Regent, he gained nothing practical for her. Brougham was careful to impress upon Caroline that the law gave her no claim to the supervision of her daughter. For support she must look elsewhere. 'Her Royal Highness will naturally regard the privations and hardships she now suffers as trials to which she is exposed, as her illustrious predecessor, Queen Elizabeth, formerly was, and will have the greatness of mind to disregard them, however painful at present, in the prospect of excelling even that renowned Princess, by reigning where *she* never did—in the hearts of a free people.'[5] Two actions inspired by Brougham and Whitbread placed Caroline's plight before the country. The first, to publish the evidence taken by the Delicate Investigation, may, by its revelations of her freedom from that reserve which sometimes passes for good manners, have dimmed her reputation in respectable society; the second, to publish in the press her letter of remonstrance to the Regent, was an undoubted success. The letter, from which the quotation with which this chapter began is taken, was written under the close direction of Brougham. It was sent to the Prince in January 1813, and appeared in the Whig *Morning Chronicle* a few weeks afterwards. It was designed to catch the sympathy of every mother and every friend to fair play in the country.

> Let me implore you to reflect on the situation in which I am placed: without the shadow of a charge against me; without even an accuser; after an inquiry that led to my ample vindication, yet treated as if I were still more culpable than the perjuries of my suborned traducers represented me, holding me up to the world as a mother who may not enjoy the society of her only child.[6]

Caroline warned the Prince—and the country—of the injury that was being done to Charlotte, the future sovereign: 'beyond a certain point the greatest natural endowments cannot struggle against the disadvantages of circumstances and situation'.

Brougham meant to embarrass the government as well as the Crown. For, in the days when a Whig ministry had carried out the Delicate Investigation, the Tory opposition, led by Spencer Perceval, had printed privately 2,000 copies of the report, only to burn them when they found themselves back in office. In the country the effect of both the letter and the published evidence was to inflame opinion. The Princess was showered with letters of sympathy and addresses of support got up by the counties. At first, Mackintosh recorded, men thought that Brougham had blundered: 'but it has since appeared that he was only wisely bold . . . All the world is with her, except the people of fashion at the west end of the town.'[7]

In the following year Brougham brought off another successful stroke. He dissuaded the young Princess, Charlotte, from carrying through her purpose to marry the Prince of Orange. Brougham's object was to keep Caroline, whose desire to take refuge abroad was strengthening, in England. He looked forward to Charlotte's accession to the throne. The Regent was grossly over-weight and his sensual indulgences placed a strain on his constitution. If he was not ill, neither was he in splendid health. If he were to die, he would be succeeded by Charlotte. What could be more natural than that the new sovereign should dismiss her late father's Tory accomplices, invite the Whig opposition to form a government, and insist that her friend and protector be placed at, or very nearly at, the head of it? These happy fancies were clouded by the apprehension that Caroline might take up residence abroad, where her indiscretions would very probably enable the Regent to begin divorce proceedings against her.

Rid of his 'greatest enemy' (the Prince once mistook the reference to Napoleon to mean his wife), he might remarry, sire a son, and so keep Charlotte from the throne. Brougham impressed upon Charlotte that her going to live in Holland would remove the only cause which kept her mother in England. The argument, Creevey said, 'had an effect upon the young one almost magical',[8] and she broke off her engagement.

Thereafter the game went badly for Brougham. London in the summer of 1814 took on a festive air as the Allied sovereigns from all over Europe made their progress to the Court of St James's to celebrate the defeat of Napoleon. But while society enjoyed its finest season for decades, Caroline was prevented by royal order from receiving, or being received by, any of the visiting dignitaries, even those of them who were her relatives. On 14 August, unmoved by the earnest pleadings of Brougham and Whitbread, she quit England for the continent. After a brief visit to her native Brunswick, she settled in Italy. 'She deserves death' was Brougham's comment, though he quickly added that she must not be abandoned 'in case P[rinney] gets the victory'.[9]

In November 1817 Brougham's scheme suffered an additional setback. Charlotte, who little more than a year earlier had married Prince Leopold of Saxe-Coburg, died of a haemorrhage after delivering a still-born son. Caroline, meanwhile, was gaining notoriety by the ostentatious display of her unorthodox intimacy with her 'chamberlain' (so she named him), the Italian, Bartolemmeo Pergami, a handsome, raffish soldier of undistinguished parentage. Once more her conduct was made the subject of official scrutiny, and the evidence collected by the Milan Commission was so damaging to her reputation that from the moment, early in 1819, when it was presented to the Regent, his mind was seized by the resolve to divorce her. By then, Brougham, watching helpless as events removed the imagined victory beyond his reach, was beginning to play his client false. In 1814, when it was suggested that Caroline accept an annual pension of £50,000 on condition that she remain permanently out of the country, he had persuaded her to reject the offer. It would, he told her, appear as an admission of guilt. In June 1819, nothing having occurred to change the argument, he undertook, without Caroline's knowledge, to put the very same proposition to the government. The Princess was to renounce the future title of Queen and pledge herself never to set foot in England again. Since Brougham breathed not a word of this startling change of tactics to Caroline—in his memoirs he explained his secrecy as the result of his wish not in any way to commit her![10]—she was unable to make the personal application to Lord Liverpool which he required before moving in the matter. The proposal therefore came to nothing and on 5 August Brougham learned of Caroline's intention to return to England. He informed Canning that he would attempt to forestall her by every means in his power,[11] and arranged to meet her at Lyons. What was in his mind we do not know, for, in an act of wanton discourtesy, he failed to keep the appointment, never, for the rest of his life, giving any reason other than the necessity of going the circuit. Caroline ceased to place confidence in his actions or his advice.

It is difficult to reach a satisfactory understanding of Brougham's vacillating behaviour during the twelve months which preceded Queen Caroline's trial by the House of Lords. On the face of it, Caroline's return to England held out promise for the Whigs by the political storm which it was certain to provoke and for Brougham personally by the spectacular trial which George's insistence upon a divorce would render unavoidable. Yet from the time that he failed to make the journey to Lyons Brougham appeared to be negotiating with the government terms of an arrangement which should keep her out of the country, and to Caroline herself his advice was at best equivocal. There are two plausible explanations, each little more than guesswork, of his behaviour. One is that he was willing to abandon Caroline, her honour and her dignity undefended, in order to curry favour with the government and extract some personal reward from it. The other is that he all along intended that Caroline should arrive in England, but that he wished to appear to have played the part of an honest patriot eager to avert a crisis. Wherever the truth may lie, his less than forthright manouevrings did his reputation no good.

> Brougham, it is said [John Croker wrote in his diary in April 1820], *grossly has sold* the Queen. There is no doubt that he has withdrawn himself a good deal from her, and I believe has been for some time in underground communication with Carlton House. Certainly none but madmen could think of making common cause with her a measure of party; but at the same time there will be something very revolting in Brougham's taking up the King's cudgels against her. Caring little as I do for her or B., I should still be sorry for the sake of public character.[12]

George III died on 29 January 1820. At once the new king, George IV, struck his wife's name from the liturgy of the Church of England, the last and meanest of his public insults to Caroline. He also requested his ministers to draw up a divorce bill. Lord Liverpool replied that his government was unwilling to comply; the King relented; but Brougham was told that if Caroline crossed the Channel, proceedings against her would immediately be started in parliament. Brougham, who two weeks earlier had pressed Caroline to proceed to the north of France, ready to come to England at a moment's notice, now let Canning know that the award of a silk gown might induce him to take the government's part. Lord Liverpool urged upon Lord Eldon, the lord chancellor, the importance of bowing to Brougham's demand: 'the character of the monarchy, and the reputation of a large part of the Royal Family, depend upon keeping this question out of *hostile discussion* in Parliament'.[13] Whether the offer was made is a matter of doubt. By April, at any rate, Brougham was changing his course again: on the 20th he was sworn in as the Queen's attorney-general in open court before Lord Eldon. However much Caroline had come to distrust Brougham, she was right to retain him. If it came to a trial, no other advocate in the country could be counted on to play with such skill upon her popularity in the country. No other advocate, in a cause in which legal considerations were bound to be outweighed by political ones, could strike such fear in the hearts of ministers.

Even now the well of Brougham's duplicity had not run dry. Four days after his formal appointment as the queen's attorney, the government, alarmed that he might now really mean to bring matters to a head, made its final offer. Its terms were those suggested by Brougham in the previous June, but once again he failed to communicate the offer to Caroline and once again he failed to meet her. Instead, he wrote to the Queen at Geneva, advising her to proceed to Calais. Delayed by illness, Caroline did not make her appearance on the French coast until late May. Then, at last, Brougham went to see her at St Omer. With him was Lord Hutchinson, an envoy of the government sent to conduct the last-minute negotiations. Only now, for the first time, was Caroline given the government's offer of a settlement. Probably the time for compromise had passed, for the Queen was now, as she had been for some months, under the influence of her companion, Alderman Wood, the London radical who was as eager as Brougham to use her against the Crown and the government. Even if the time had not passed, the conditions were unacceptable. The government would deny to Caroline what mattered most to her: the title and rank of Queen to enable her to carry herself with dignity in foreign courts. Alderman Wood, a true friend where Brougham was but a hired lawyer, impressed upon her that to surrender any of her rights was to confess her guilt. Having submitted to her own degradation, she could not expect the House of Commons to vote the £50,000 annual allowance with which the government sought to bribe her. Nor could she expect to retain the sympathy of the people. In short, to remain abroad was to court ruin.[14]

The day after Brougham's arrival at St Omer on 3 June, Caroline quit the town for the coast, where a boat was waiting to take her to England. Brougham sent a letter after her by courier.

> I entreat your Majesty once more to reflect calmly and patiently upon the step about to be taken, and to permit me to repeat my deliberate opinion. I do not advise your Majesty to entertain the proposition that has been made. But if another proposition were made instead of it, I should earnestly urge your Majesty to accept it—namely, that the annuity should be granted without any renunciation of rank or title or rights, and with a pledge on the part of the Government that your Majesty should be acknowledged and received abroad by all the diplomatic agents of the country according to your rank and station, but that your Majesty should not go to England. The reason why I should give this advice is, that I can see no real good to your Majesty in such an expedition, if your Majesty can obtain without going all that it is possible to wish. I give this advice, most sincerely convinced that it is calculated to save your Majesty an infinite deal of pain and anxiety, and also because I am sure it is for the interest of the country.[15]

Twelve months earlier there would have been point to such straightforward and sensible counsel. Coming when it did, it smacked of self-preserving. Within minutes of despatching the courier on a hopeless mission, Brougham wrote separate notes to Lord Hutchinson and Lord Liverpool. He assured them that he regretted the breakdown of the negotiations and that he had played his part 'in the spirit which has always regulated my conduct in this affair—that of preventing whatever tended only to annoy, and to force on discussions unnecessary in themselves and hurtful to the country'.[16]

Neither Brougham's friends nor the government believed him.

Creevey, writing a year later, remembered a conversation with Brougham in the spring of 1820.

> When I recall to mind how often, during our journey to Middleton at that time, he spoke of the Whig candidates for office with the most sovereign contempt—how he hinted at his own intercourse with the Crown and Ministers, and conveyed to me the impression that he thought himself more likely to be sent for to make a Ministry than anyone else—how clear it is that the accomplishment of this divorce was to be the ways and means by which his purposes were to be effected.[17]

The government chastised itself for being duped by Brougham. Canning, who never wavered in loyal friendship to Caroline, no matter what the risk to his ministerial future, had particular cause for self-reproach.

> Brougham has had his game too [he wrote to Hutchinson], and from a much earlier period, I suspect, than we apprehended. He dreaded compromise. He thought he saw how it might be effected. He barred that course by offering his own mediation. He thus got the thing into his own hands; and having got it there, he let it languish till success was hopeless. He *could not* go to Geneva, but he could go the circuit; and all this time, marvellous to think again!, Liverpool thought Brougham in earnest and plain dealing.[18]

*　　*　　*

On 6 June, seated in an open barouche with Alderman Wood at her side, Caroline made a royal progress through the streets of London to her companion's house in Mayfair. Everywhere the people of the capital turned out to cheer her. The omens were dark for George IV and the government. Five years of economic distress, years in which the government had done everything in its power to repress popular agitation, had left the unrepresented masses ready to vent their anger. Caroline was the instrument of their passion and the object of their generosity. Her sins, even perhaps her guilt—for the public knew enough of the Queen's life in Italy not to cherish sentimental notions of her blamelessness—were as nothing when set against the perfidy of her accuser. 'The zeal with which the lower orders supported her,' Lytton Bulwer wrote, 'was the zeal of Chivalry.'[19] Law was one thing; justice, as Brougham wrote, another.

It is one of the grossest and most unnatural of the outrages against all justice, to say nothing of charity, which despots and other slave-owners commit, that they visit on their hapless victims the failings which their oppressions burn as it were into the character—that they affect disgust and reprobation at what is their own handi-work—and assume from the vices they have themselves engendered a new right to torment whom they have degraded.[20]

George IV, too, was a victim. Led into undisciplined self-gratification by the very nature of a court upbringing, he was then compelled, in order to rid himself of huge debts, to marry a Protestant princess whom he had never set eyes on and whom, left to the devices of his own heart, he would not have given a second glance. Philanderer before his marriage, philanderer he remained. Hence another difficulty for ministers. In a divorce proceeding George IV would appear singularly miscast in the role of the injured party.

The government wished to draw back; the King was advised in the contrary direction by his vice-chancellor, Sir John Leach, the most unsafe counsellor in the land Brougham said, a fawning courtier who coveted the Great Seal and thought to get it by seeing every question in the light that his sovereign wished it to be seen. Fortified by Sir John's worthless promptings, George IV sent down to the two Houses of parliament the infamous green bag containing the evidence assembled by the Milan Commission and ordered the drawing up of a bill of pains and penalties against Her Majesty. Even so, ministers might have prevailed, for at the first opportunity Brougham announced in the House of Commons that if they were turned out for refusing to comply with the royal will, no member of the opposition would agree to form an administration in their place. On several occasions in his career Brougham astonished his colleagues by making unauthorized pledges on their behalf. Such was this one. Grey had remained studiously neutral on the question and Tierney had of late made it his constant object to persuade Leach (who would have liked nothing better than a Whig administration with himself on the Woolsack) that the opposition would be able to effect the divorce which the government shrank from proposing.[21] Lord Liverpool and his colleagues took no notice of Brougham's outburst. They clung to their places and, with deep misgivings, consented to bring in the bill.

Still Brougham's cunning had not exhausted itself. He could not bear to see Alderman Wood in possession of the Queen's confidence,

and in petty envy of a man whom no one could conceive to be his rival
he prepared, it appears, to throw the Queen over. He came down to
the House on the night of 7 June, if Creevey is to be believed, resolved
to renounce her, 'from motives either of personal ambition or
revenge', and was stopped in his course only by the firm part on the
Queen's behalf which Creevey, Bennet and other Mountaineers took
in that night's debates.[22] In his speech Brougham made a peevish and
baseless sneer at Alderman Wood's intelligence, suggesting that the
initials 'A.W.' stood for 'Absolute Wisdom'. The nickname stuck to
the unfortunate Wood for the rest of his life.

The impression that Brougham, at the last, was content to sacrifice
the Queen is strengthened by the part that he played in Wilberforce's
eleventh-hour effort to reach a settlement. Wilberforce's solution was
to have the House of Commons pass an address of thanks to the
Queen and take upon itself alone the responsibility for acquiescing in
the omission of her name from the liturgy. Caroline's yielding to the
wishes of the House could not then be construed as an admission of
guilt or a desire to avoid an inquiry. The address was voted on 23 June
and the next day it was presented to the Queen, who, as anyone might
have foreseen, rejected it—as anyone might have foreseen, that is, but
for Brougham's deceit. He and Denman declined to advise the Queen
what answer she should give to the House of Commons.

> This was, on every account, the necessary course to take, because, if
> she had been acting under our advice, it would have entirely
> destroyed the effect of her resolution; and we felt quite certain that
> if we advised her to comply with the desire of the Commons and to
> leave the country, we should have been proclaimed by her violent
> and secret advisers as the cause of her going; and it would have
> been affirmed that she was herself desirous of remaining and
> meeting the charges. Indeed, I doubt if we should have escaped the
> fury of the multitude.[23]

This was unexceptional prudence on the part of a solicitor towards his
client, but Brougham, knowing that he would not advise the Queen to
accept the address and knowing that without that advice she would
reject it, nevertheless wrote a letter to Wilberforce in which he
pledged himself that she would accept it.[24] Caroline's refusal distressed Wilberforce deeply; his charity was rewarded by accusations
that he had trifled with the House of Commons. Since no public
interest would be served by producing Brougham's letter, he spared

his old friend and bore in silence the unjust obloquy of his enemies. In his diary he wrote words which a less gentle man might have sent to Brougham.

> What a lesson it is to a man not to set his heart on low popularity, when after forty years' disinterested public service I am believed to be a perfect rascal! Oh what a comfort it is to have to fly for refuge to a God of unchangeable truth and love.[25]

*   *   *

Brougham never cared for Caroline's company. Although he praised her some years later as 'a Princess of singular accomplishments', quick of apprehension, ready of wit, charitable by instinct and free of all haughtiness and pride,[26] all the time that he was her counsel he referred to her as 'that old Bore'. Creevey thought it was 'not going too far to say that he absolutely *hated* her'.[27] Once the hope of compromise had faded, he nevertheless fought the battle for Caroline with unflinching spirit. There is no need to give much attention to his avowal that neither he nor the junior counsel for the defence would, upon oath as jurymen, have found the least ground for the charges against her.[28] What Brougham meant to do was to demonstrate to a rapt nation his powers as an advocate and to give the government a fright.

On 4 July the secret committee of the Lords appointed to examine the evidence in the green bag reported that the charges against the Queen were sufficiently grave to be made the subject of a solemn inquiry. On the following day a bill of pains and penalties, founded on that report, was introduced in the House of Lords by the prime minister. The bill contained three main sections. The preamble outlined the evidence of the Milan Commission with which the government sought to prove that Caroline had 'with a most unbecoming and degrading intimacy' entered into 'a licentious, disgraceful and adulterous intercourse' with Pergami. There followed two clauses, the one depriving Caroline of her title as Queen, the other annulling her marriage to the King. The bill was given its first reading and on 10 July the trial—in strict parliamentary language the second reading of the bill—was set for 17 August.

During the interval thus provided Brougham went the northern circuit in the company of two of the junior counsel retained by Caroline, John Williams and Nicholas Tindal (afterwards Lord Chief

Justice of Common Pleas). By virtue of his position as the Queen's attorney, Brougham was for the first time a leader, a leader, moreover, whose name just then filled the hearts and minds of the people. He made, Denman said, 'a wonderful harvest at York',[29] and at Newcastle, where he pleaded a minor cause for his friend, Lord Lambton, ladies secured their seats at seven o'clock in the morning, for all the world, *The Times* reported, as if it had been a trial for murder.[30]

Brougham returned to London a few days before the debate in the Lords began. The frenzied excitement which had gripped the capital all summer rose to its peak. As the first day of the trial approached, the press of people grew more alarming, the jostling more ugly. Mobs filled the streets, cheering the Queen and her advisers, hissing at her enemies. From the river shouts of 'The Queen! The Queen!' rang out until late in the evening. Castlereagh, who lived next door to Brandenburg House, St James's, where the Queen took up residence for the duration of the trial, removed all his belongings from his house and had it shuttered. When, on the morning of 17 August, peers arrived at Westminster to take their places—some of them in temporary galleries built to accommodate the overflow—they were left in no doubt of the public's mood.

What has, reasonably, always been called the Queen's trial was, really, an examination before the Lords, with the calling of witnesses by the Crown's legal officers, acting as the prosecution, and by the Queen's counsel, acting as the defence, of the truth of the accusations contained in the bill of pains and penalties. Such a bill, like a bill of attainder, although the latter alone was able to prescribe punishment by death, enables parliament to punish a subject without having to meet the rigorous standards in proving guilt required in a court of law. The action is a political action. Members are called upon to exercise their political, not their legal, judgement. They may find against a person whom they believe to have committed no crime or for a person whom they believe to be guilty. Hence Brougham had two purposes in conducting the Queen's defence: to destroy the credibility of the Italian witnesses called by the prosecution, but also, of far greater importance, to appeal to the Lords' concern to safeguard the monarchy and preserve the peace of the kingdom.

In his opening speech Brougham struck a pugnacious note. He issued a stern warning, offensive to many members of the bar, that the Crown could not sustain a vote in its favour.

I put out of view the question of recrimination . . . I dismiss for the present all other questions respecting the conduct or connexions of any parties previous to marriage. These I say not one word about; they are dangerous and tremendous questions, the consequences of discussing which, at the present moment, I will not even trust myself to describe. At present I hold them to be needless to the safety of my client; but when the necessity arises, an advocate knows but one duty, and, cost what it may, he must discharge it. Be the consequences what they may, to any other persons, powers, principalities, dominions or nations, an advocate is bound to do his duty; and I shall not fail to exert every means to put a stop to this Bill.

Only four days before, Caroline, pacing the floor of Brandenburg House and repeating over and over the phrase, 'If my head is upon Temple Bar, it will be Brougham's doing', had debated with Denman, her solicitor-general, whether she ought to dismiss her attorney. Brougham's words now, which she listened to from the chair provided for her within the bar of the House, must have convinced her that if she was not safe in his hands there was no safety for her. Brougham's warning was taken in the clubs to refer to the King's dalliances with Lady Jersey and others. It went much deeper, deeper than even Caroline knew. What Brougham was holding in reserve, 'for the present', was the revelation of the King's secret and illegal marriage to the Roman Catholic Mrs Fitzherbert in the days of his youth before Caroline had been forced upon him. Only a handful of peers, at most, knew of this dark secret, so that when on 19 August, after both sides had made their opening statements, Lord Grey moved that it was not necessary to proceed with the bill, his motion was defeated by 179 votes to 64.

The examination of witnesses which followed lasted until 7 September. It would be tedious to follow its course in detail. What posterity remembers is the celebrated speech with which Brougham opened the case for the defence, a speech which Charles Greville declared to be 'the most magnificent display of argument and oratory that has been heard for years'[31] and which Denman had foremost in mind when he wrote that Brougham won an immortal victory 'by the adamantine shield of his prodigious eloquence'.[32] In the course of the speech,[33] begun on 3 October and occupying two whole days, Brougham reminded their lordships that they were sitting, not as a court of justice, but as the assembled representatives of the nation.

They were under no charge to bring the matter to any issue. They might dismiss it and have done with it—'and, gracious God!, what was there in the case to induce the Peers of England to pursue a Queen to destruction! . . . what was there in that to induce them to run counter to a sentiment almost universal?'. The peroration, which Brougham rewrote seventeen times,[34] and which it is difficult to believe was not the source of the passage with which Macaulay brought his renowned reform speech of 1831 to a close, had one of the most brilliant successes in the history of parliament.

> My Lords, I pray your lordships to pause. You are standing upon the brink of a precipice. It will go forth your judgment, if it goes against the Queen. But it will be the only judgment you ever will pronounce, which will fail in its object, and return upon those who give it. Save the country, my Lords, from the horrors of this catastrophe, save yourselves from this peril, rescue that country, of which you are the ornaments, but in which you could flourish no longer, when severed from the people, than the blossom when cut off from the root and the stem of the tree. Save that country, that you may continue to adorn it—save the Crown, which is in jeopardy—the Aristocracy which is shaken—the Altar itself, which never more can stand secure amongst the shocks that shall rend its kindred throne. You have said, my Lords, you have willed—the Church and the King have willed—that the Queen should be deprived of its solemn service. She has indeed, instead of that solemnity, the heartfelt prayers of the people. She wants no prayers of mine. But I do here pour forth my own supplications at the Throne of Mercy, that that mercy may be poured down upon the people, in a larger measure than the merits of its rulers may deserve, and that your hearts may be turned to justice.

Lord Erskine rushed from the House in tears and Lord Minto took up his pen to inform Mrs Brougham that her son had 'just concluded a speech which has delighted and *astonished* the most sanguine of his friends, who, you may believe, were prepared to expect as much from him as man is capable of'.[35]

The chancellor, Lord Eldon, who presided over the trial, was not so easily moved. He rebuked Brougham for straying beyond the boundaries of the constitution. The censure came at the end of his summation, just before the division, and was the government's final appeal for votes.

One word more, my lords, and I have done. As to what has passed, or is passing out of doors, I will take no notice of it, for I am not supposed to hear it, or to know anything about it; only this I will say, that, whatever has happened, or whatever may happen, I will perform my duty here. But, in the course of this solemn inquiry, your lordships have heard from the bar of this House, what I was very sorry to hear, and what I believe was never before addressed to a court of justice. Something like a threat was held out to your lordships, that if you passed judgment against the Queen, you would never have the power of passing another judgment . . . such an address of such a nature, such an address of intimidation, to any court of justice, was never before this hour considered to be consistent with the duty of an advocate . . . I know the people of this country. I am sure that, if your lordships do your duty to them, by preserving their liberties, and the constitution which has been handed down to you from your ancestors, the time is not far distant when they will do their duty to you; when they will acknowledge that those who are invested with the great judicial functions of the state, ought firmly to meet all reproaches . . . to court no popularity; to do their duty; and to leave the consequences to the wisdom and justice of God.[36]

There was the voice of immovable Toryism, soon to be silenced by the clamour for parliamentary reform. Eldon could no more comprehend the nascent power of vulgar opinion than Brougham could refrain from courting it. Constitutionally speaking, he was in error. He was not presiding, except by analogy, over a court of law, nor was Brougham acting as an advocate. The government might have proceeded against Caroline by impeachment, but it had chosen to introduce a bill of pains and penalties. Brougham was entirely justified in asking the Lords to take a broad view of the question before them. His appeal was the first of many occasions in the 19th century when the upper House was warned that to place itself in opposition to the feeling of the country was to imperil its existence. The argument displeased Lord Eldon because it suggested that the House of Lords was not, or could not much longer afford to be, the counterpoise to democracy. Whatever the strength of Brougham's argument in the particular case at hand, there was no impertinence to his reminding the peers of their first duty as legislators, the duty to secure the commonwealth.

The bill was read a third time on 10 November. It received a majority of nine votes, a margin so slim that without the votes of members holding office under the Crown it would not have passed at all. The government, knowing it was beaten, announced the next day that it would not send the bill to the lower House. Brougham, after all, had not yet attacked the King directly. And even though ministers did not know that he had a witness to prove the King's marriage to Mrs Fitzherbert, by an invalid ceremony certainly (not only had George married a Roman Catholic, he had done so without the sovereign's consent), but none the less one which entailed the forfeiture of the Crown, they were not prepared to stand against his power to prolong the controversy in violent debates in the House of Commons.

The trial brought Caroline but a half-vindication, little peace of mind and no restoration to a respected place in English society. In the following July she beat her hands in vain against the doors of Westminster Abbey, closed to her on the occasion of George IV's coronation. It was a sweltering day and she returned to her home fatigued and feverish, her health gone forever. On 5 August she died. As her funeral procession made its way from Brandenburg House, soldiers fired on the carriages—one of the bullets struck Brougham's—to turn them out of Piccadilly. Brougham accompanied the funeral cortège to Harwich, where a multitude gathered to watch the crimson coffin, bearing the legend 'the injured Queen of England', lowered on to the vessel which was to carry Caroline's remains to their resting place in Brunswick.

Brougham's object in the Queen's great matter, to convulse the political world and dislodge the Tories, eluded him. Lord Liverpool remained prime minster for another six-and-a-half years. On the other hand, Brougham and his junior counsel had given sore offence in high places. Denman scored one of the most wounding hits when he applied to Leach the famous description of Iago.

> Some busy and insinuating rogue,
> Some cogging, cozening slave to get some office,
> Must have devised this slander.

Nothing, however, exceeded the savagery of Brougham's borrowing from Milton to brand the King a coward. In a dramatic intervention during the cross-examination of one of the government's witnesses, he suddenly asked the Lords who was their client or employer.

I cannot fix him with any character. If I am told who he is, I may then be able to trace his lineaments, and at length to bring out the mighty secret who and what he is from his own mouth—if he have one. I know, my lords, that the rule of law is close on the subject of the professional confidence of agents. I do not deny it. But here there is no party. Prove to me who the party is, and I will not disturb the professional confidence of his agent. And who is the party? I know nothing about this shrouded, this mysterious being—this retiring phantom—this uncertain shape—

> *If shape it might be called that shape has none*
> *Distinguishable in member, joint, or limb;*
> *Or substance might be called that shadow seemed,*
> *For each seemed either . . .*
> *What seemed his head*
> *The likeness of a kingly crown had on.*[37]

To compare George IV to the prince of darkness and to prick his vanity at its most vulnerable point—his physical grossness—was to make a lasting enemy. George IV was not the man to forgive such an insult and Brougham was to pay a price for his brutality.

For a summer Brougham had blazed in popular glory; his speeches rang through the nation; on the circuit crowds thronged to catch a glimpse of him; the freedom of countless corporations arrived in gold boxes and the 'Brougham's Head' became a common sign over public houses. Yet in his hour of triumph there was nothing to gladden the true radical's heart. For a friend of the people like Hazlitt, it was even a melancholy event.

The Queen's trial gave a deathblow to the hopes of all reflecting persons with respect to the springs and issues of public spirit and opinion. It was the only question I ever knew that excited a thoroughly popular feeling. It struck its roots into the heart of the nation; it took possession of every house or cottage in the kingdom . . . Truth has no echo, but folly and impostures have a thousand reverberations in the hollowness of the human heart. At the very moment when all England went mad about the poor Queen, a man of the name of Bruce was sent to Botany Bay for having spoken to another who was convicted of sedition, and no notice of it was taken . . . What was it then in the Queen's cause that stirred this mighty 'coil and pudder' in the breast? Was it the love of truth, of justice, of liberty? No such thing! Her case was at best doubtful, and she had only suffered the loss of privileges peculiar to herself. But she was a queen, she was a woman, and *a thorn in the King's side*. There was the cant of loyalty, the cant of gallantry, and the cant of freedom, mixed altogether in delightful and inextricable confusion . . . Though a daughter of the Duke of Brunswick, though a granddaughter of George III, yet, because she was separated from her husband, she must be hand-in-glove with the people—the wretched, helpless, doating, credulous, meddlesome people, who are always ready to lick the hands not just then raised to shed their blood or rivet on their chains.[38]

Yet how difficult it is to trace the chain of associations which our memory forges. It may be that the springs of sympathy which Brougham had tapped stood him and the country in good stead when he came to address the deeper questions of education, law reform and the abolition of slavery. There can be little doubt that his personal stature in the country, which dated in its fulness from the summer of 1820, was of golden worth to the Whig party ten years later when the crisis of parliamentary reform came upon the nation.

8

'A Most Powerful Man'

The death of Queen Caroline had one direct consequence for Brougham. So long as he had been her attorney he was entitled to wear a silk gown and a long-bottomed wig. On her death he returned to bombazine and a common tie. To Brougham himself the loss of rank was immaterial. The Queen's business had raised him to such eminence that a revolution in his legal practice was accomplished. He, who had practically abandoned the circuit for several years and so entirely neglected his House of Lords business that rumours circulated of his quitting the bar altogether, now found his parliamentary reputation merged in the forensic. The public, knowing nothing of Brougham's 'wrigglings and windings and infinite eel-motions'[1] as the Queen's adviser, esteemed the lion who had opposed the throne. 'When he next appeared on the Northern Circuit the attorneys crowded round him with briefs, that they might be privileged to converse with Queen Caroline's illustrious advocate. During one whole round of the assizes . . . crowds came from distant parts to see and listen to him, and the Civil Court and the Crown Court were respectively overflowing or deserted as he appeared in the one or in the other.'[2] His practice increased fivefold and, although 'Bear' Ellice, his Whig colleague in parliament, may have exaggerated when he said in 1825 that he was commanding at least 200 guineas a day at the Durham and Newcastle assizes,[3] his earnings in no single year fell below £7,000. The average was probably in excess of £8,000, a handsome sum for those days, even though his great rival, Sir James Scarlett, was reported one year to have earned £18,500.[4]

Brougham, Scarlett and Sir Frederick Pollock outshone all the rest of the advocates on the northern circuit in the 1820s. The three figured in a trial scene in Samuel Warren's novel, *Ten Thousand a Year*, as Mr Quicksilver, Mr Subtle and Mr Sterling, names aptly chosen, for Scarlett was the very exemplar of *nisi prius* tact and Pollock a conscientious and thoroughly informed plodder. (Perhaps Lord Melbourne read the novel, for in 1840, when it was coming out in serial form, he remarked of the French prime minister, Auguste Thiers, that he was 'a strange, quicksilver man' who 'puts me in mind of Brougham'.)⁵ Brougham was generally held to be the inferior of both Scarlett and Pollock as an advocate, possessing neither their profound legal knowledge nor their mastery of courtroom etiquette. The Duke of Wellington said of Scarlett that when he addressed a jury there were thirteen jurymen,⁶ and when Brougham and Scarlett found themselves on opposite sides in a case it was usually Scarlett who came out the victor. Sydney Smith spent three weeks at the York assizes in 1821 and wrote to Lady Grey of the great rivalry between them.

> Brougham was much employed and constantly opposed to Scarlett ... The prudence of Scarlett in conducting a cause Brougham can never attain, his knowledge and acuteness he will never surpass, but he excells him in force, and in Wit and humor. In singleness of heart and suavity of disposition, I will make no comparison.⁷

Pollock told an amusing tale of two Yorkshire jurymen who were discussing the merits of Brougham and Scarlett. Brougham, said the first, was the cleverer; indeed, agreed the second man, but Scarlett was such a lucky one, for he was always on the right side.⁸ How this came about was once explained by Chief Justice Tindal. At a supper of barristers on the northern circuit he complimented Scarlett on his genius in inventing a machine by which, though it was dexterously kept out of sight, he could make a judge's head nod in approbation of whatever he said. He then went on to speak of another gentleman who had 'for years been devoting his illustrious talents to surpass Mr Scarlett' and who had, after much labour, perfected his own machine. 'But you have observed that the motion he produces is of a different character. It is parallel to the horizon.' Brougham joined heartily in the laughter which the joke occasioned, 'his good nature', according to Scarlett, who recounted the story, 'being not less remarkable than his talents'.⁹

When Scarlett was appointed attorney-general in Canning's government of 1827, Brougham and Pollock were left to dispute the honours of the northern circuit. Thomas Macaulay had recently joined the circuit and he sent to his father, Brougham's ally in the campaign against slavery, an account of his early impressions.

Perhaps you will be pleased to hear that Brougham has been rising through the whole of this struggle. At York Pollock decidedly took the lead. At Durham Brougham overtook him, passed him at Newcastle, and got immensely ahead of him at Carlisle and Appleby, which, to be sure, are the places where his own connections lie.[10]

Brougham, Macaulay reported, was improving in industry and prudence, learning his story more thoroughly, and telling it more clearly. Continued improvement must take him to the very summit of his profession. His temper, however, remained ungoverned. He squabbled with Pollock, yawned while he was speaking, and said bitter things, in one case remarking that he was not surprised Pollock should grossly overestimate the value of some lead mines: 'it was no wonder that a person who found it so easy to get gold for his lead should appreciate that heavy metal so highly'.

It was not, however, on account of Brougham's waspishness that his professional colleagues withheld from him their unqualified praise. It was, rather, that he never came to distinguish, or, if he did, he thought the distinction unimportant, between parliamentary and *nisi prius* oratory. The House of Commons seldom wearies of the man whose trite commonplaces of a spuriously philosophical nature mark him out as a statesman. The press gallery is ever thankful for an adroitly turned phrase. In the House most members have already decided the issue before a debate takes place. At the bar the advocate's sole purpose is to impress upon a jury his interpretation of the facts. Ridicule and contempt, sarcasm and invective, so also the enunciation of eternal principles of human justice, are apt to distract an audience which cares only to be kept to the issue which it must try. James Grant, who considered Brougham to be 'the greatest man, taken all in all, which this country has in modern times produced',[11] described Brougham's courtroom manner in a long passage which merits quotation.

He was retained in almost all important cases. It was only in these, indeed, that he appeared to advantage. No two men could be more unlike each other than was Henry Brougham in a case of limited interest and in one of commanding importance. I know some barristers of great distinction and of first-rate talent, that can throw their whole soul into matters of the most trifling kind ... Mr Brougham was not a man of this kind. There was in all such cases a coldness in his manner and a languor in his eye which plainly showed, notwithstanding that he would now and then make an effort to rouse himself, that his spirit was not in the task . . . How striking the contrast when he appeared in an important case, especially if it were one involving any great principle of civil or religious liberty! On such occasions Brougham far exceeded, in the talent and energy he displayed, any man who has practised at the bar for the last quarter of a century. He usually rose in a calm and collected manner, enunciated a few sentences in a subdued tone, expressive of the sense he entertained of the importance of the task he had undertaken, and solicited the indulgence of the jury, while he trespassed on their attention for a short time. He then proceeded, in slow accents and in measured sentences, to develop the generalities of the case, gradually rising in animation of manner and increasing in the loudness of his voice and the rapidity of his utterance, until he arrived at the most important parts of his subject. The first indication he usually gave of having reached those points in his speech to which he meant to apply all the energies of his mind, was that of pulling his gown further up on his shoulders, and putting his tall gaunt figure into as erect and commanding a posture as he could assume without endangering his equilibrium. Then came his vehement gesticulation—the rapid movement of his right arm, with an occasional wafture of the left hand, and the turning and twisting of his body into every variety of form. His eye, which before was destitute of fire, and his features, which were composed and placid as those of a marble statue, were now pressed as auxiliaries into the service of his client. His eye flashed with the fire of one whose bosom heaved with tumultuous emotions, and the whole expression of his face was that of a man whose mind was worked up to the utmost intensity of feeling. And this really was the case with Brougham wherever the interests of his client were identified with some great principle. His principles, unlike those of barristers in general, were really a part of his nature. In vindicating, or asserting them, therefore, in the person of his client, he was, in point of fact, repelling some outrage which had been offered to himself.

To have seen him in some of these moods was truly a spectacle worthy of the name. It was only on such occasions that any accurate estimate could be formed of the vast resources of his mind. He then poured from his lips strains of the loftiest order of eloquence. Idea followed idea, principle succeeded principle, illustration accompanied illustration, with a rapidity which was astonishing. One moment he was strictly argumentative—the next declamatory. Now he stated in winning language and in an engaging manner, whatever was in favour of his client—then he inveighed in the fiercest strains, and in tones which resounded through the place in which he spoke, against that client's opponent. In such moments there would have been something absolutely withering to him against whom his denunciations were directed in the very countenance of the orator, even had he not uttered a word. His brow was knit. There was a piercing stare and wildness in his eye; and his sallow complexion and haggard features altogether presented an aspect which it was frightful to behold. The jury on such occasions often forgot the purpose for which they had been called into court; they forgot the case in the advocate . . . And yet, notwithstanding the vehemence of his manner, and the intensity of the passion into which he worked himself, his speeches, though he sometimes purposely wandered from the principal point before the court, were as well arranged, and every sentence was as correctly constructed—that is to say, according to the massy and involved style which he always preferred—as they could have been had he been speaking in the calmest and most collected manner. He seldom displayed much legal knowledge . . . He disdained, indeed, when he threw his whole soul into his speeches, to be fettered by what he considered, in such a case, the trammels of law or logic. Hence he could not so well be said to have gained the great triumphs he so often achieved at the bar by convincing, as by confounding, the jury . . . Mr Brougham may be said to have taken the jury on such occasions by storm. He *compelled* them to surrender to him . . . It is in this way alone that the fact is to be accounted for, that he often extorted from a jury a verdict in favour of his client, when it was equally notorious to the bench and to every professional gentleman in court, that all the law and the argument were on the opposite side.[12]

Brougham's unorthodox style was displayed in a cause arising from the death of Queen Caroline. That event was marked, in the customary manner, by the tolling of church bells throughout the kingdom. Durham Cathedral alone withheld its respect and a Mr Williams chastised the Durham clergy for its negligence in an article published in the *Durham Chronicle*. Williams remarked upon the Durham chapter's disregard of Christ's commandment of love as an example of the hypocrisy of the Church. 'It is such conduct which renders the very name of our established clergy odious till it stinks in the nostrils.' A criminal information for libel was filed against Williams and the case was heard at the Durham summer assizes of 1822. Scarlett led for the prosecution, Brougham for the defence. The night before the trial, a barrister came across Brougham pacing backwards and forwards along the bank of the Wear; as he approached, Brougham threw his arms in the air and shouted, 'Avaunt! depart! I am distilling venom for the Durham clergy!'[13]

The next day he delivered a speech which Lord John Russell praised for carrying satire and sarcasm to the heights of the sublime and which even the fastidiously critical Campbell declared 'worthy to be bound up in a collection of English oratory with Erskine's and Burke's'.[14] For a time Brougham condescended to treat the specific libel at hand, and any impartial observer was bound to admit that he showed by numerous precedents, drawn from the clergy and the most venerated of English poets, that the perpetrators of remarks more savage and more derogatory to individuals than Williams' had regularly gone unpunished. Brougham knew from his vast experience of libel actions, however, that the strong arm of censorship was not to be bent by such trifles; in the battle for civil liberty the sword of toleration had to be unsheathed. He threw away his scabbard with a flourish. He reminded the court that of all ecclesiastical hierarchies in the world the English had the most need of encouraging unreserved inquiry into its affairs. The English Church was the very child of revolution, the creature of free discussion, the most reformed of the reformed churches of Europe. If there was one corner of Protestant Europe where men ought not to be rigorously judged in ecclesiastical controversy, it was Great Britain, where the people lived under three orders—one where prelacy was instituted by law and practised by the people, one where it was instituted by law and hated by the people, and one where it was not even instituted by law. George IV was just then making a tour of Presbyterian Scotland.

> There he will see much loyalty, great learning, some splendour, the remains of an ancient monarchy and of the institutions which made it flourish; but one thing which the sovereign will not see. Strange as it may seem, and to many who hear me incredible, from one end of the country to the other he will see no such thing as a Bishop; not

such a thing is there to be found from the Tweed to John o'Groat's House. Not such a thing as a mitre; no, nor so much as a Minor Canon, or even a Rural Dean; and in all the land not one single Curate, so entirely rude and barbarous are they in Scotland. In such utter darkness do they sit, that they support no cathedrals, pay no pluralities, suffer no non-residence, nay, the poor benighted creatures are ignorant even of tithes. Not a sheaf, or a lamb, or a pig, or as much as a plough-penny do those hapless mortals render from year's end to year's end! Piteous as their lot is, what makes it infinitely more touching, is to witness the return of good for evil in the demeanour of those wretched people under all this cruel neglect of their spiritual concerns. They are, notwithstanding, actually the most loyal, contented, moral, and religious nation in the world! Let us hope (many, indeed, there are, not far off, who will with unfeigned devotion pray) that his majesty may return safe from the dangers of his excursion in such a country; an excursion most perilous to a certain portion of the church, should his royal mind be infected with the taste for cheap establishments, a working clergy, and a pious congregation.

Brougham then turned his fire on the Durham establishment, one of the richest and politically one of the most powerful in the country.

But if, in any part of the country, a more than ordinary latitude should be allowed to such controversy, surely it is in this bishopric, where in the nineteenth century we live under a palatine prince, the Lord of Durham; where the endowment of the church—I may not call it enormous, but I may be allowed to term splendid; where the establishment, I dare not say is grinding to the people, but rather a vast blessing, only it is prodigiously large; it is a blessing showered down so profusely as to be quite overpowering; it lays the inhabitants under a load of obligation overwhelming by its weight. It is in Durham, where the church enjoys such splendour and power, and the clergy swarm in every corner, an' it were the patrimony of St Peter; it is here where all manner of conflicts are at every moment inevitable between the people and the priests, that I feel myself warranted, as an advocate for that clergy, for the protection of their very existence, to challenge and provoke the most unreserved discussion both of their title and of their actings under it. In the present age they must be the most shallow, the most blind of mortals, who do not at once perceive that if that title is protected only by the strong arm of the law, putting down inquiry into its foundations and their conduct, it becomes not worth the parchment on which it is engrossed, or the wax that dangles to it for a seal. I have hitherto assumed that there is nothing impure in the practice under this system; I have taken it for granted that all of them does every one act which they ought to do, and which the law presumes they perform; that no one unworthy member up to this hour has ever belonged to it; that no individual has stepped beyond the bounds of his sacred functions, or given secular offence to any human being; I am taking it for granted that they all act the part of the good shepherd, making their flock their first care—that they indeed occasionally think of shearing, in order to prevent the too full growth of the fleece proving an incumbrance, or to eradicate disease. If, however, those operations prove so constant that the flock actually live under the knife; if the shepherds are so numerous, and employ so large a troop of the watchful and eager animals that attend them—some of them too with the cross of the fox, or even the wolf, in their composition—can it be wondered at if the poor flock thus fleeced, and hunted, and barked at, and snapped at, and from time to time worried, should now and then bleat, dream of preferring the rot to the shears, and draw disadvantageous comparisons between the wolf without, and the shepherd within the fold? At any rate, to chide and punish them for merely crying out is the height of cruelty and injustice. It is, moreover, the most contemptible folly to think of retaining their power, places, privileges, and enormous riches, by complaining of attacks upon their conduct; and to use their influence and wealth in prosecuting those who expose the pastors that are guilty of a dereliction of their duty.

It was casually, but wrongly, assumed that the prosecution of Williams had been instigated by Henry Phillpotts, the high Churchman who gained notoriety in 1831 when, shortly after his elevation to the bishopric of Exeter, he ranted so shrilly against the reform bill that his palace, under siege from the mob, had to be defended by coastguards. Phillpotts was a truculent Tory polemicist who, even in an age not distinguished by the spirituality of the episcopacy, displayed an exceptional and, some thought, unseemly absorption in secular politics. He owed his first preferment to the accident that his wife was the niece of Lord Eldon and he repaid his patron with repeated defences of the Tory ministry, none more disasteful than his spirited vindication of the Peterloo massacre in a pamphlet of 1819. Shortly before the Williams trial opened, Phillpotts had calumniated the defendant as 'a miserable mercenary who eats the bread of prostitution and panders to the low appetites of those who cannot, or who dare not, cater for their own malignity'.[15] The language was coarse and Brougham, at the end of his speech, replied in kind, comparing Phillpotts to 'the insect nestled in filth and brought into life by corruption' which 'though its flight be lowly and its sting puny, can buzz and storm, and irritate the skin and offend the nostril, and altogether give nearly as much annoyance as the wasp, whom it aspires to emulate'. No jury should give such 'reverend slanderers' shelter from just exposure.

> If all existing institutions and all public functionaries must hence-forth be sacred from question among the people; if at length the free press of this country, and with it the freedom itself, is to be destroyed—at least let not this heavy blow fall from your hands. Leave it to some profligate tyrant; leave it to a mercenary and effeminate parliament—a hireling army, degraded by the lash, and the appointed instrument of enslaving its fellow-citizens; leave it to a pampered House of Lords—a venal House of Commons—some vulgar minion, servant of all work to an insolent and rapacious Court—some unprincipled soldier, unknown, thank God, in our times, combining the talents of a usurper with the fame of a captain; leave to such desperate hands and such fit tools so horrid a work! But you, an English jury, parent of the press yet supported by it, and doomed to perish the instant its health and strength are gone; lift not you against it an unnatural hand—prove to the country that her rights are safe in your keeping; but maintain, above all things, the stability of her institutions by well guarding their cornerstone.

Perhaps the jury found Brougham's language extravagant, for they gave Scarlett the verdict. It was often so, but then it was also so that Scarlett appeared regularly for the Crown, Brougham for the defence. In the end Brougham's ridicule of the clergy gained its reward, for when, the next term, he moved a rule to show cause why judgement should not be arrested, no one came forth on the Crown side and Williams escaped punishment.

Soon after losing silk Brougham applied to Lord Eldon to have it restored to him by a patent of precedence. The chancellor, unwilling to incur the King's displeasure, refused to grant it, and although the snub harmed Brougham not a whit, it inflicted injury on all those barristers who, being his senior in years of practice, were prevented by professional etiquette from appearing as junior counsel under a leader who was a stuff gownsman. A dozen or so of them were thrown out of work because Eldon made himself 'the instrument of the King's caprice and revenge'.[16] By 1823 the business of the northern circuit was severely hampered (Scarlett was the only silk left practising on it) and Brougham renewed his application. Eldon did not bother to reply. Not until 1827, when Lord Lyndhurst accepted the Great Seal in Canning's government, was Brougham rewarded with the official rank which his continual appearances as a leader had long since rendered almost a necessity. In the interval he had his revenge. During the debate on the address to the throne at the beginning of the 1825 session of parliament, he asked the pro-Catholic members of Lord Liverpool's cabinet, in which Catholic emancipation was treated as an 'open question', why they did not press their arguments on their colleagues. They might, at least, have no fears of losing the lord chancellor's services.

Do they think he would resign his office? Prince Hohenloe is nothing to the man who could effect such a miracle. A more chimerical apprehension never entered the brain of a distempered poet. Anything but that. Many things may surprise me, but nothing would so much surprise me as that the noble and learned individual to whom I allude should quit his hold of office while life remains . . . Indeed, Sir, I cannot refrain from saying that I think the right hon. gentlemen opposite greatly underestimate the steadiness of mind of the noble and learned individual in question. I think they greatly underrate the firmness and courage with which he bears, and will continue to bear, the burthens of his high and important station. In these qualities the noble and learned lord has never been excelled—has never, perhaps, been paralleled. Nothing can equal the forbearance which he has manifested . . . Let him be tried. In his generous mind, expanded as it has been by his long official character, there is no propensity so strong as a love of the service of his country. He is no doubt convinced that the higher an office, the more unjustifiable it is to abandon it . . . His present station the noble and learned lord holds as an estate for life . . . I do intreat, that the perseverance of this eminent person may be put to the test . . . I am quite sure of the result. The Catholic question would be carried, but the noble and learned lord would retain his place. He would behave with the fortitude which has distinguished him in the other instances in which he has been defeated; and the country would not be deprived, for a single hour, of the inestimable benefit of his services.[17]

'No young lady,' Eldon wrote to his daughter, 'was ever so unforgiving for being refused a silk gown.'[18]

* * *

Brougham's wigging of Eldon had a purpose deeper than personal revenge. For some time it had been his object to drive a wedge between the 'liberal' and 'ultra' wings of the Tory party and bring about a ruling alliance of moderate men of the centre. Governments in the post-Waterloo years were sorely pressed, for just at the time that their responsibilities for social and economic legislation were being extended, their power to command a majority of the House of Commons was being weakened by the declining patronage of the Crown without being adequately reinforced by the bonds of party loyalty. To speak, as some do, of party as meaningless in these years is to belittle the emotional and intellectual prejudices which inclined one man to Whiggery and another to Toryism. For nearly half of the House of Commons the description of pre-1832 parties as nothing more than 'groupings of "friends" around leading aristocratic patrons, held together by the hope and expectation of "place" '[19] is unduly severe. On the other hand, the modern party system was still embryonic. Between 1780 and 1830, in a House of 658 members which never saw an opposition more than 250-strong, four governments were driven from office by forfeiting the confidence of the House.[20] It was the conventional wisdom of the day that an opposition of 175 members, well managed and supported by public opinion, could defeat any government. Brougham had demonstrated as much in 1812 over the orders-in-council and in 1816 over the income tax. Thomas Grenville was not being foolish when, in 1820, he expressed his concern that the opposition was continuing 'to muster in their original force of 160 upon their great questions'.[21]

The opposition muster, to be effective, needed to locate an issue on which it could combine with the independent country gentlemen, members who in the ordinary course of events were content to uphold the King's ministers. In the troubled post-war years an opportunity was always likely to present itself. So, in 1820, the government, resented by a large part of the population for its repression of civil liberties and shaken by the force of public anger at its treatment of the Queen, was looking to strengthen itself by bringing in one or two leading Whigs and breaking up the formidable body of the opposition. Chief among the Whigs rumoured to be in Lord Liverpool's sights were Brougham, Tierney and Lord Lansdowne.[22] That Brougham should join a government impregnated with the high Toryism of Eldon, Sidmouth, Vansittart and Bathurst was fanciful. In the aftermath of the Queen's trial, with the prospect of a brilliant and lucrative career at the bar before him, he was not likely to be tempted into even a Whig cabinet by anything less than one of the highest offices of state. There was no cause why he should have dissembled to his brother, to whom he confided in November 1820 that it was his fixed intention not to take office. 'My course is clear; I will not lose my influence in the country, so capable of being turned to the best purposes. This I should lose by taking such a place as Solicitor-General, and I can make as much money as I have occasion for, without place.'[23]

Brougham's broad parliamentary strategy in the last years of the Liverpool administration was to shed his radical leanings of the previous ten years and to concentrate upon those large questions which occupied the centre of the political stage—the conduct of foreign affairs, Catholic emancipation, and the state of the agricultural interest. Creevey cursed him for his moderation,[24] but Brougham, rightly, saw that the future of liberalism rested on the ability of the Whigs to woo the squirearchy away from Toryism, thereby isolating the ultras and undermining the sole ground of the moderate Tories' tolerance of them, namely office, while at the same time encouraging the co-operation of those moderates with the regular Whigs and giving the latter their only reasonable hope of executive influence. For, once the excitement of the divorce crisis had passed, the Whigs were exposed in their feebleness. Tierney, his reputation ruined by a grossly misjudged motion on the state of the nation in 1819 and his supremacy in financial debates undermined by Ricardo's expertise, had become a cipher in politics. By the spring of 1821 he had virtually abandoned all pretence to leadership. For the next six years, although Brougham unofficially filled the vacuum created by Tierney's decline, the Whigs scarcely behaved as a united opposition at all. To bring down Toryism it was necessary to look elsewhere.

Brougham cared nothing for the back-bench squires. 'I warn you,' he once wrote to Lambton, 'that you will soon grow into a regular country gentleman, which is one degree above a parson.'[25] But since ministries rose and fell on the votes of the independent country gentlemen, Brougham was happy to play suitor to them. He devoted himself in 1821 and 1822 to pleading the case of the farmers in distress. The exceptionally wet harvest of 1821 left corn so blighted that in parts of the country it was scarcely edible. At the same time, the sharp fall in the price fetched by sheep and cattle, especially in the western counties, left farmers unable to pay their rents. In 1821 Brougham's assistance enabled a motion to abolish the tax on horses used for agricultural purposes to be carried against the government; and on every opportunity which that session's debates offered, he stood forth as the farmer's friend, a task made easier by the circumstance that neither he nor any other of the Whig leaders had as yet taken up the nascent radical cry for free trade and cheap bread. Brougham's remedy, retrenchment and economy, found favour with the country gentlemen, whom Charles Arbuthnot, secretary to the treasury, reported to be 'all very much for taking off taxes & putting an end to the sinking fund, which would in fact be destroying the credit of the country'.[26] But when Brougham put the question to the test, at the beginning of 1822, the government let it be known that it would resign if beaten and his motion was lost by a majority of 108. Whig hopes of stirring the country gentlemen faded. By the beginning of 1824, as the economy improved, Charles Wynn was able to report that the government was vastly popular 'and all the country gentlemen disposed to support us warmly'.[27] 'You know,' Brougham wrote ruefully to Grey, 'when stocks are above 90, and corn bears a fair price, reasoning to the country, at least to the land and trade, is labour lost.'[28]

In August 1822, the political world was shaken and the future course of party politics thrown into confusion by Castlereagh's suicide. Castlereagh had been an adroit manager of the House of Commons and his death raised faint Whig hopes that the government would be unable to carry on. Brougham and Grey, although they thought it barely possible that George IV would actually send for the Whigs, busied themselves with preparing the party for the responsibility of office and settling the terms on which it should be accepted.

The first requirement, Brougham wrote to John Allen, was to gag Tierney, who, if not given a good scold, would 'assuredly convey to the King thro' that friend of his [the Tory, Charles Long] a very clear opinion that the opposition are wholly out of the question, that we can't conduct the Govt. in the H. of C. &c. &c'. Brougham was never faint-hearted.

Now a greater folly & one more wide of the fact, & one more offensive to all those whom it so absolutely undervalues, can't be imagined. We can do just as we please in the H. of C., almost, out of place, *but in office, compleatly*. I'll answer for this with my head. There might be some little puzzle about a leader, tho' I can see no reason on earth agt. Tierney himself being it, on as easy terms as he chuses, even if he were little more than nominally so. He would have plenty of official supporters, an excellent Atty. Gen., for Scarlett would be perfectly listened to (& most deservedly) when in office, a Solicitor Gen. if possible still better—I mean, of course, Denman, and he might rely upon me in all weathers. As I should be in no office (for I could not afford to quit the Law), I must be the better able to prevent mischief with the Mountain & should, generally, have the more influence with the House. If any man doubts our being able to carry on the Govt. triumphantly in the H. of C., he deserves to be well flogged.[29]

If negotiations were started, Brougham continued, the Whigs must state clearly their essential measures: putting down the Orange faction in Ireland, strict non-interference in the affairs of European nations, remission of bad taxes like those on houses and windows, repeal of legislation gagging the press, abolition of flogging in the army and parliamentary reform. In the previous April Lord John Russell's motion for a substantial widening of the franchise had received the support of 164 members, the highest number since 1785. Now Brougham argued that reform must be made a *sine qua non* of the Whigs' coming in. Lord Grey had advanced to or (remembering his youth) retaken the same ground. 'I could have no share in any Government,' he told Brougham, 'that was not founded on a change of system, both at home and abroad', adding that 'the *something* I should do on Parliamentary reform would be a good deal, and I think it would be necessary to take our stand upon it'.[30] As it turned out, Castlereagh's death did not herald a Whig spring. New life was breathed into the Tory government by the return of Canning (who had resigned in 1820 out of loyalty to Queen Caroline) and the promotion to leading posts of Peel, Frederick Robinson and William Huskisson. The mere possibility of office, nevertheless, had concentrated Whig minds wonderfully. In the correspondence of the party leaders in the autumn of 1822 can be seen the germ of that commitment to reform with which the Whigs, in 1830, came at last into power.

The great stumbling-block of 1830—what was to be done with Brougham—was also foreshadowed in 1822. No party, as Lord Holland pointed out a few years later, could be conducted with satisfaction to itself or benefit to the country unless it was led in the House of Commons by a figure of authority. Brougham stood head and shoulders above any other candidate and his repeated assertions that he would not accept any cabinet position worried Grey. Grey may have had doubts about Brougham's fitness for the lead; but he could not risk leaving him to behave like a gadfly on the back benches, starting his own schemes and disavowing responsibility for government measures which displeased him. He therefore promised him more than he wished or, probably, intended to offer him when the time came. The lead, he told him, must 'really and effectively, if not nominally be in your hands . . . and your saying you will take no office is, in my opinion, tantamount to saying no Whig administration can be formed'.[31] Grey's opinion was echoed in almost every quarter of the party. Lord John Russell remarked that there was only one man 'capable of standing up manfully and constantly against Canning' and James Abercromby, a rising Whig backbencher, assured Brougham that if he wished to be leader he would be elected by a unanimous vote.[32] Brougham was thus encouraged to believe that the leadership was his for the asking, whenever he should find himself able to sacrifice his career at the bar for it. He was not to forget the pledges of support when, eight years later, the party passed him over.

*　　*　　*

Brougham had established himself as the keystone of the Whig arch. His public fame eclipsed that of all his rivals. In 1825 the University of Glasgow elected him, in preference to Sir Walter Scott, to succeed Sir James Mackintosh as rector. On the day before his inauguration Edinburgh presented him with the freedom of the city and held a great public dinner in his honour. It was attended by 850 guests, more, Cockburn believed, than had ever gathered for a public political dinner in Scotland before and more, Brougham said, than he had ever addressed under one roof.[33] Cockburn was disappointed by Brougham's speech: it was jocular, sarcastic, declamatory and egotistical, displaying the variety of his oratorical powers, but heedless of Scotland's needs and interests. 'All, except the judicious, seemed perfectly pleased.'[34] At a similar dinner in his honour at Glasgow eighteen months earlier Brougham had been impressed by the 'improvement in public feeling and principle' among the Scots, especially as it manifested itself in an earnest determination to abolish slavery.[35] One of the reasons why the friends of improvement kept faith in Brougham was his unbroken attachment to the cause of human freedom. (It is worth recording an amusing instance, instructive of human folly, of a material loss suffered by Brougham on account of his principles. Sometime in the 1820s he received a visit from an unknown admirer who called to say that he had bequeathed to Brougham, in gratitude for his public service, an estate in Durham and a plantation in Barbados. He then asked him to take part against abolition! Brougham sent him away with copies of the Anti-Slavery Society's annual reports, hoping to change the mind of his benefactor. He heard no more from him and when, some years afterwards, the gentleman died, it was found that he had struck Brougham from his will.)[36]

For ten years or so after the outlawing of the slave trade in 1807, the abolitionists had been principally occupied in monitoring the success of the measure. The difficulty of enforcing the law had led to the passing of Brougham's bill of 1811 which made slave-trading a crime punishable by transportation. Even that punishment proved to be imperfect as a deterrent, and in 1824 parliament made the offence a capital one, a decision which seems to have achieved its object, since by 1837 there was no evidence that, except in Mauritius, British subjects were still engaged in the trade. Long before then, towards the beginning of George IV's reign as king, Wilberforce and his colleagues were coming to realize that attention must be shifted away from the slave trade to the institution of slavery itself. The time had arrived to mount a fresh campaign in parliament and the country. Wilberforce, his health too poor to allow him to continue as the active leader of the movement, chose as his successor Thomas Fowell Buxton, a young man unknown to the abolitionists before his appearance at a meeting of the African Institution in 1818, when he castigated the Institution for its blindness towards the real evil, the condition of the slaves in the West Indies. It was no slight to Brougham that Wilberforce passed him over. Buxton was an untried member of parliament, but he had made a mark for himself as a prison reformer and, what counted, was in a position to give his mind and his time wholly to the slavery question.

In 1823, largely at Zachary Macaulay's bidding, the Institution was changed into the Anti-Slavery Society and two years later it established its own journal, the *Anti-Slavery Reporter*. Brougham was persuaded from the outset to join in the new campaign and to write on its behalf in the *Edinburgh Review*. He also sided with Macaulay, against Wilberforce and Thomas Babington, in urging that women be drawn into the struggle, and it was by his influence that Lady Jersey, the lioness of fashionable society in the capital and for some years a particular friend of Brougham, became a kind of unofficial patron of the movement.

Two principal arguments were used against the abolitionists by their opponents. The first was that without the steady stock of fresh workers formerly supplied by the slave trade, the planters would be compelled to ameliorate the slaves' working conditions and educate them for the eventual day of emancipation. The second was that to interfere in the domestic laws of the colonies was an infringement upon the right of British colonial subjects to regulate their internal affairs. Neither argument withstood for long the leavening agency of facts upon public opinion. By the time of the 1830 elections abolition had become a vote-winning cry in most of the constituencies where the discussion of political questions carried weight. The Whigs came into office knowing that it was an issue impossible to shirk. That the battle was won in so short a time, and the influence of the powerful West Indian lobby in the House of Commons so swiftly and fatally eroded, was the work, above all, of two men, of Zachary Macaulay, who would not let his countrymen's consciences rest until the full horror of life on Mauritius had roused them to compassionate anger, and of Brougham, whose memorable speech on the trial and death of the missionary, John Smith, struck the first deadly blow at the shameless corruption and cruelty which stained every aspect of Caribbean society.

Smith was an Independent minister sent out to Demerara by the London Missionary Society in 1816. Seven years after his arrival there, the colonial office issued instructions to the Demerara government that the lash was no longer to be used in the colony. The local officials suppressed the instruction, but the slaves heard of it and an insurrection broke out among them. Smith was charged with helping to foment it and, despite lack of evidence, the authorities decided to prosecute. Inadmissible evidence was used to convict him. He was sentenced to death and placed in a small, fetid dungeon, where his health gave out before the day on which he was to have been executed.

On 1 June 1824 Brougham brought forward a motion of censure on the Demerara government and the court which had convicted Smith. In a long and masterly exposition of the case,[37] he showed that the authorities had behaved throughout with an insolent disregard of human courtesy and the law. Despite a blameless record in teaching the slaves, Smith, who was not a young man and who was suffering from severe illness, was dragged from his house without being allowed to put on proper clothing; his papers were seized without warrant; he was held for weeks in an airless cell until his trial. The trial itself was a mockery of justice. Smith was tried before a court martial, a thing unconstitutional in itself, and was therefore deprived of the advantages of a civil trial—delay, scrutiny of evidence, and professional representation. Leading questions were not struck. Hearsay evidence was admitted. False confessions implicating him were wrung from frightened slaves. The president of the court was the wealthiest slave-trader on the island. Above all, the death penalty was illegally prescribed for the plainly non-capital crime of misprision with which Smith had been charged.

The final part of Brougham's speech was directed at the Christian community in Great Britain, especially the Dissenters, who were naturally drawn by their own persecuted condition to sympathize with other victims of illiberal authority. Brougham dwelt upon the insult to all Christians implied in the contention of the Demerara government that Smith had taught seditious principles from the Bible. Not only was the notion insulting and absurd, but it struck at the root of the emancipationists' gradualist strategy. If teaching the slaves Christian ethics were henceforth to be regarded as a crime, then the evil of the trial went beyond the injustice done to Smith. It went beyond even the injury done to English law. It declared that the slaves were unteachable wretches to be kept down forever.

The debate on Brougham's motion was spread over ten nights. It was closed by him in a memorable speech which, though its cadences may be too rich for modern ears, was then held up as one of the masterpieces of denunciatory eloquence. Brougham stopped short of demanding immediate emancipation; but in the code language of the day he threatened the slave-owners with abolition by asserting the absolute sovereignty of the imperial parliament over the affairs of the colony.

Sir, it behoves this House to give a memorable lesson to the men who have so demeaned themselves. Speeches in a debate will be of little avail. Arguments on either side neutralize each other. Plain speaking on the one part, met by ambiguous expressions—half censure, half acquittal, betraying the wish to give up, but with an attempt at an equivocal defence—will carry out to the West Indies a motley aspect . . . Upon this occasion, most eminently, a discussion is nothing, unless followed up by a vote to promulgate with authority what is admitted to be universally felt. That vote is called for, in tenderness to the West Indians themselves—in fairness to those other colonies which have not shared the guilt of Demerara. Out of a just regard to the interests of the West Indian body, who, I rejoice to say, have kept aloof from this question, as if desirous to escape the shame when they bore no part in the crime, this lesson must now be taught by the voice of Parliament—that the mother country will at length make her authority respected; that the rights of property are sacred, but the rules of justice paramount and inviolable; that the claims of the Slave owner are admitted, but the dominion of Parliament indisputable; that we are sovereign alike over the White and the Black; and though we may for a season, and out of regard for the interests of both, suffer men to hold property in their fellow-creatures, we never, for even an instant of time, forget that they are men, and the fellow-subjects of their masters; that, if those masters shall still hold the same perverse course—if, taught by no experience, warned by no auguries, scared by no menaces from Parliament, or from the Crown administering those powers which Parliament invoked it to put forth—but, blind alike to the duties, the interests, and the perils of their situation, they rush headlong through infamy to destruction; breaking promise after promise made to delude us; leaving pledge after pledge unredeemed, extorted by the pressure of the passing occasion; or only, by laws passed to be a dead letter, for ever giving an elusory performance as adds mockery to breach of faith; yet a little delay; yet a little longer of this unbearable trifling with the commands of the parent state, and she will stretch out her arm, in mercy, not in anger, to those deluded men themselves; exert her undeniable authority; vindicate the just rights, and restore the tarnished honour of the English name.[38]

Brougham's motion was met by Canning, pusillanimously, not with a direct negative, but with a motion to read the previous question. Supported by his chief acolytes, Palmerston, Lamb and Grant, Canning carried the day for the government. The margin, however, was encouragingly narrow, 193 votes to 146, and in the country the case became a rallying cry for the friends of liberty. Brougham's statement that the warning he sounded rang the knell of the system was, however immodest, not unjustified.[39] As Trevelyan wrote, the trial and death of Smith 'was fatal to Slavery in the West Indies in the same degree as the execution of John Brown was its deathblow in the United States',[40] and it was Brougham who brought the full circumstances of the event into the purifying air of public debate.

* * *

Lord John Russell wrote in his recollections that Brougham's speech 'combined the closest and most pressing logic with the most eloquent denunciations of oppression and the most powerful appeal to justice'. It contributed, he said, 'in a very marked degree, to the extinction of slavery through the dominions of the Crown of England'. Russell rated the speech below Brougham's opening for the defence in the Queen's trial (the most wonderful effort of oratory he ever heard), but he placed it with the berating of the Durham clergy, the 1823 attack on the conduct of the continental powers towards Spain, the review of the criminal law in 1828 and the appeal to the Lords not to reject parliamentary reform in 1831, as one of those commanding performances which, even in the very years which were the most brilliant period of parliamentary oratory in his lifetime, raised Brougham to a height above his contemporaries.[41]

Elaborate sarcasm and uninhibited invective were the hallmarks of Brougham's parliamentary style. In one of the Runnymede letters, written in 1836, Disraeli addressed him as the man whose scathing voice had 'passed like lightning in that great Assembly where Canning grew pale before your terrible denunciation, and where even Peel still remembers your awful reply'.[42] During Canning's heyday, from

1822 to 1827, debates were regularly prolonged because Canning would not speak before Brougham and Brougham would not pass up the opportunity of replying to Canning. Canning's cousin, the Canon of Windsor, once suggested that he quote a passage from Clarendon's *History of the Rebellion* which bore on the matter at hand. The passage was found and it proved to be extraordinarily apposite, until, a few lines on, Clarendon's observations turned to the opposite tendency. The canon thought the quotation still worth hazarding. 'No,' Canning answered, 'I dare not. Brougham will find me out. Nothing ever escapes him.'[43] In the last two years of the decade, the Duke of Wellington was known to order his cabinet ministers in the Commons to stand up to Brougham and on no account to let Peel speak before him.[44] Not until Brougham had gone to the House of Lords did Peel rise to pre-eminence as a debater. Brougham, Peel said, was 'the most *powerful* man' he ever knew in the House,[45] and where Peel entered with misgivings, lesser mortals feared almost to tread. 'How does the House seem?' Sir William Scott, a Tory backbencher, would ask. 'Is Brougham there? Does he look savage?'[46] Brougham, Russell remembered, struck down an adversary, piling up his sarcasms and overwhelming him with refutation, until his victim was left 'an object of ridicule or of pity, crushed beneath the weight of accumulated epithets and a burning mass of invective'.[47]

Oratory is not given to a man. Knowledge, industry, ambition and ardour all contributed to Brougham's eloquence, were indeed its elements. He had, too, a powerful voice, loud and unmitigated in its vehemence, sometimes, Hazlitt said, approaching to a scream.[48] Seldom, however, did the sheer strength of his voice or the regardless warmth of his conviction carry Brougham away. He made a study of the great Presbyterian preachers of his youth, noting especially the attention they compelled by a sudden dropping of the voice and storing in his memory the image of arms raised high above their heads during the blessing. It was this gesture which he made famous. He used it, apparently without comic effect, in the peroration to the Lords on behalf of Queen Caroline. He used it again, at the end of another long speech, when he implored the Lords to bow to the reform tide. Even Cockburn conceded that Brougham was a master of oratorical action: the tall, erect posture, the angular, expressive face, the nervous twitching of the nose, the solemn projection of the right arm, the opening and shutting of the long, claw-like fingers, combined to produce, not a spectacle of the grotesque, but a manner natural, simple and elegant.[49] Brougham possessed, too, the eye of the ancient mariner to fix his audience. It was, Benjamin Haydon said, when he came to paint his portrait, as fine an eye as he ever saw. 'It is a clear grey, the light vibrating at the bottom of the iris, and the cornea shining, silvery and tense', an eye, in short, 'like a lion's, watching for prey'.[50]

'I don't at all object to what you say of sarcasm, which has often been commended,' Brougham wrote late in life to William Forsyth. 'But my forte always was argumentative declamation.'[51] The flights of oratory are remembered; it requires to read Brougham's long speeches through to admire their architecture. Figures, metaphors, sentimental allusions were sparingly introduced, in emulation of what Brougham called the chaste style of the ancients. Cockburn was forever disparaging Brougham's knowledge of the classics, accusing him, for instance, of affecting a familarity with Grecian eloquence and composition in his rectorial address at Glasgow because, knowing the value of the ancients, he wished to hide his deficiency.[52] Lord Grenville, however, after reading the address a number of times, thought it impossible to express more accurately or forcibly the differences between Greek and Roman oratory.[53] The study of the ancients, especially Demosthenes, occupied many hours of Brougham's time. He committed them to memory and translated them, for it was his belief that no man could excel as a speaker until he had mastered the art of written composition. Eloquence, Macaulay once said, is to be compared to fresco painting, the result of long study and meditation, but at the moment of execution thrown off with the greatest rapidity.[54] Brougham read Swift, Addison and Bolingbroke over and over. From them he acquired his diction. He wrote out his speeches a number of times, thereby enabling him to master what, in praising Canning's speeches, he called 'the last attainment of rhetorical art, of weaving the extemporary up with the prepared passages, and delivering the whole so as to make the transition from the previous composition to the inspiration of the moment wholly imperceptible, even to the most experienced eye'.[55] It is true that two of the greatest parliamentary speakers in Brougham's lifetime, Charles James Fox and Thomas Macaulay, never prepared their speeches in writing; but Macaulay had a memory which served him as a notebook, and Fox, for all the lightning blaze of his speeches, was not given to close reasoning upon facts. Brougham's genius was to bring facts and general principles, rational argument and impassioned pleading, into harmonious conjunction. Most wonderful of all, Gladstone thought, was his management of the sentences. 'He never loses the thread,' Gladstone wrote, 'and yet he habitually twists it into a thousand varieties of intricate form.'[56]

In all this studied 'Scotch eloquence' Hazlitt, who never exhibited the power of sustained argument, found little to admire.[57] Brougham's store of knowledge he allowed to be inexhaustible. 'Scarce a ship clears out its cargo at Liverpool or Hull, but he has notice of the bill of lading . . . he is at home in the crooked mazes of rotten boroughs, is not baffled by Scotch law, and can follow the meaning of one of Mr Canning's speeches.' But what was the worth of all this lavish detail, this relentless building up of the argument, this 'ticketed and labelled eloquence, registered in numbers'? Men were not to be *calculated* into contempt; their hearts were not moved when they could not carry in their heads all that Brougham could. So much may be said of any clever and insistent man in the English House of Commons. Hazlitt struck a truer note, touching the individual genius of Brougham more nearly, when he found fault with his loftiness.

> Mr Brougham has one considerable advantage in debate: he is overcome by no false modesty, no deference to others. But then, by a natural consequence or parity of reasoning, he has little sympathy with other people, and is liable to be mistaken in the effect his arguments will have upon them . . . It is not that he thinks too much of himself, too little of his cause: but he is absorbed in the pursuit of truth as an abstract inquiry, he is led away by the headstrong and overmastering activity of his own mind.

Brougham spoke as if from Mount Olympus. He overawed men. Consequently they feared him. It was a mournful day for him and his admirers when, to save the cause of reform, he fell headlong into the House of Lords.

9
The Schoolmaster Abroad

The rapprochement between moderate Whigs and liberal Tories, needing time to effect its purpose, did not issue in coalition until Canning formed his government in 1827. In the middle years of the 1820s Lord Liverpool contrived to hold the two mutually distrustful wings of his government together. The opposition, officially leaderless in the House of Commons, lost its appetite for the nightly party battle. 'Every thing goes on *sub silencio*,' Mrs Arbuthnot wrote in her journal; 'the estimates are all voted & they seem to have nothing to do, except on the nights when Ireland has been the subject.'[1] These were the years in which Brougham was establishing his ascendancy in the House. They were also the years when he was occupied in the most enduring of his life's works, carrying the lamp of learning into dark places where its light had not previously shone. Only one phrase uttered by Brougham has passed into the national memory. 'There have been periods when the country heard with dismay that the soldier was abroad,' he told the House of Commons when the Duke of Wellington became prime minister in 1828. 'That is not the case now. Let the soldier be ever so much abroad, in the present age he can do nothing. There is another person abroad . . . The schoolmaster is abroad, and I trust to the schoolmaster armed with his primer more than I do to the soldier in full military array for upholding and extending the liberties of the country.'[2]

Brougham's rectorial address at Glasgow in 1825 provided him with an opportunity to preach the gospel of universal enlightenment.[3] He spoke, he said, in a place 'consecrated by the pious wisdom of ancient times to the instruction of but a select portion of the community', but at a time when knowledge was ceasing to be a privilege of the well-born. Those who were fortunate to receive the education of a gentleman incurred an obligation to use it for the betterment of mankind. A man like James Watt, drawn from the lower ranks of Scotch society and achieving eminence by his own perseverance, had shown that the sublime truths of science were accessible to everyone and that the highest intellectual cultivation was compatible with the daily toil of a working man's life. Nor was there any danger to the state, except what was apprehended by tyrants and persecutors, in the widest possible dissemination of knowledge. 'Real knowledge never promoted either turbulence or unbelief; but its progress is the forerunner of liberality and enlightened toleration.' Brougham's creed was steeped in the secular humanitarianism of the 18th century.

> Assuming [he told the undergraduates of Glasgow] the improve-
> ment of his own mind and the lot of his fellow-creatures to be the
> great end of every man's existence, who is removed above the care
> of providing for his sustenance, and to be the indispensable duty of
> every man, as far as his own immediate wants leave him any
> portion of time unemployed, our attention is naturally directed to
> the means by which so great and urgent a work may best be formed.

The means, so far as Brougham had a hand in furnishing them, were the Mechanics' Institutes, the Society for the Diffusion of Useful Knowledge and the University of London.

The founder of the movement to establish Mechanics' Institutes was George Birkbeck, Professor of Medicine at Anderson College, Glasgow. In 1800 he delivered a course of lectures to mechanical labourers on natural philosophy and its practical applications. Those lectures constituted a revolution in higher education: no one before had thought it worthwhile to initiate working men into the mysteries of the higher sciences. Despite opposition from the professional classes of Glasgow, they were an undoubted success, and by the time that Birkbeck quitted Scotland for London a few years later his class was attended by about 700 men. The class was continued by Dr Ure, who added a library, to be run by the men themselves, and persuaded the Gas Light Company of the city to light the reading room two nights a week. The library committee came eventually into conflict with the institute's governors, seceded from the class, and formed a separate group. It was this breakaway organization which, when its enrolment reached 1,000 in 1823, was officially named the Glasgow Mechanics' Institute. A similar institute was started in Edinburgh in 1821, under the direction of Francis Horner's younger brother, Leonard, who added mathematics, architecture and veterinary surgery to the basic Glasgow curriculum of chemistry and mechanics.

Brougham took no part in the founding or the running of the Scotch institutes. Nor was he a founder of the London institute, which was proposed in 1823 by Thomas Hodgskin, the political economist whom Marx acknowledged as the inventor of the theory of surplus capital. A meeting to launch the London institute was held in November 1823, with Birkbeck in the chair. Brougham did not attend the meeting, but he sent a letter backing the venture and enclosed a liberal donation. The meeting elected Birkbeck president and in the following March the first lectures were delivered in a chapel on Monkwell Street, Clerkenwell. Over the next few months Brougham somehow found the time to attend lectures so regularly that the *Mechanics' Magazine* praised him for the encouragement which his example gave to others. By July 1825 the institute had received enough money in subscriptions, much of it collected from the trade unions by Francis Place and much coming from the pockets of Birkbeck and Sir Francis Burdett, to move into a permanent home, consisting of a lecture room, a library and several apparatus rooms, in Southampton Buildings, Chancery Lane.

In October 1824 Brougham contributed an article to the *Edinburgh Review* which was published separately as *Practical Observations Upon the Education of the People* in 1825.[4] Its purpose was to advertise the new London institute and to encourage the spread of similar institutes throughout the country. When the article first appeared, more than half a dozen northern towns had followed the example set by Glasgow and Edinburgh, so that Brougham was able to write confidently of the movement's future. 'To the Upper Classes of society . . . I would say, that the question no longer is, whether or not the people shall be instructed—for that has been determined long ago, and the decision is irreversible—but whether they shall be well or ill taught—half informed or as thoroughly as their circumstances permit and their wants require.' In a passage permeated by Malthusianism, the doctrine which Brougham and the Benthamites found entirely convincing and which underlay their unqualified approval of the controversial Whig Poor Law of 1834, he appealed to the rich for funds:

> Every person who has been accustomed to subscribe for the support of what are commonly called charities, should ask himself this question. 'However humane the motive, am I doing any real good by so expending my money? or am I not doing more harm than good?' . . . But in order to enable him to answer the question, he must reflect, that no proposition is more undeniably true than this, that the existence of a known and regular provision for the

poor, whether in the ordinary form of pensions, doles, gratuities, clothing, firing, &c., or in the shape of maintenance for poor children, in whole, or only in part, as clothing, has the inevitable tendency to bring forward not only as many objects as the provision will maintain, but a far greater number. The immediate consequence of such provisions is to promote idleness and poverty beyond what the funds can relieve: the continued and known existence of the provisions trains up a race of paupers; and a provision for children, especially, promotes improvident marriages, and increases the population by the addition of paupers. It is therefore a sacred duty which every one owes to the community, to refrain from giving contributions to begin such funds.

Great though the pamphlet's influence undoubtedly was (it went through twenty editions in six months), Brougham's most valuable contribution to the movement was the exertion he made in corresponding with the leading friends of education in remote towns of the kingdom. Throughout 1825 and 1826 his pen was rarely idle, as he sent messages of encouragement, distributed advice and collected information to pass on to his correspondents. To everyone engaged in setting up institutes, Brougham urged that working men themselves be given a majority of places on the management committee and that religion and politics be kept out of all formal discussion, principles which were adopted by almost all of the eighty institutes which were operating by the end of 1825. Brougham filled no official position at the London or any of the provincial institutes, but he was everywhere treated as their chief patron. His name gave lustre to the movement. His pamphlet served as its Bible. His portrait hung on institutes' walls. And year after year he travelled hundreds of miles to deliver the main address at anniversary meetings, never failing to be present at least at the London one, where the committee, indulging his taste for negus, annually provided six bottles of sherry and six bottles of port.

In the *Practical Observations* Brougham made the quite obvious point that the chief obstacles to the working man who wished to instruct himself were want of time and want of money. To overcome the first he had only to discipline himself to attend a Mechanics' Institute in the evenings. To overcome the second he needed the help of others. Comparatively high wages for labour and a heavy tax on paper meant that books cost twice as much in London as they did in Paris. Partly for that reason, partly to supply the lack of lecturers, Brougham organized what he called the system of Anonymous Lecturing.[5] During the summer of 1825 courses of lectures were written by experts and copies distributed to institutes throughout the country. They were then read by anyone with a clear voice. Brougham did not write any of the original lectures himself (later he prepared a course in political economy and several in the sciences), but the scheme was the germ which grew into one of the most successful of his educational enterprises, the Society for the Diffusion of Useful Knowledge.

It was not then easy for a labourer to lay his hands on a good book. Mudie's circulating library did not become a flourishing business until the 1840s and the first public libraries act was not passed until 1850. Moreover, although the practice of selling books in weekly or monthly numbers, the only method by which a weekly wage-earner could acquire a private library, was already well established, few serious books appeared on the market in that form. Especially wanting were books on politics and history, branches of learning which Brougham did not doubt fell under the head of 'useful' knowledge.

It is highly useful to the community that the true principles of the constitution, ecclesiastical and civil, should be well understood by every man who lives under it. The great interests of civil and religious liberty are mightily promoted by such wholesome instruction . . . The peace of the country and the stability of the Government, could not be more effectually secured than by the universal diffusion of this kind of knowledge . . . Assuredly, a country which tolerates every kind, even the most unmeasured, of daily and weekly discussion in the newspapers, can have nothing to dread from the diffusion of political doctrines in a form less desultory, and more likely to be both well weighed at the time, and preserved for repeated perusal. It cannot be denied that the habit of cursory reading . . . is unfavourable to the acquisition of solid and permanent information.[6]

Brougham was not first in the field. In 1819 Charles Knight, the son of a Windsor bookseller, published in the *Windsor Express* a paper entitled 'Cheap Publications' to plead the urgency of combating the flood of seditious and anti-religious broadsheets and pamphlets. A year later he started *The Plain Englishman*, a monthly devoted to the dissemination of useful knowledge. *The Plain Englishman* lasted until the completion of the third volume in December 1822. 'No publisher,' Knight wrote in explaining its demise, 'had discovered that it was to his interest that the profit of the middle-man should be small, so that a book should be vended at the cheapest rate. The very notion of cheap books stank in the nostrils.'[7] Knight was not beaten. In 1825 he devised the scheme of a National Library, to comprise about one hundred volumes treating science, art, history and literature. John Murray, the publisher of the *Quarterly Review*, agreed to back the venture, but before a volume had appeared Knight had been overtaken.

In April 1825 Brougham invited Birkbeck, George Grote (the Benthamite radical and, later, historian of ancient Greece) and William Tooke (brother of the economist, Horne Tooke) to form with him a committee to prepare and publish cheap books. Eighteen months later, in November 1826, the Society for the Diffusion of Useful Knowledge was born. Brougham became chairman of the governing committee and membership was offered to anyone who paid an annual subscription of one pound. A prospectus was privately circulated and the *Edinburgh Review* carried an advertisement announcing the society's intention to produce a Library of Useful Knowledge consisting of treatises of 32 octavo pages, containing as many words as were ordinarily to be found on 100 octavo pages, at a maximum price of sixpence per treatise. Brougham was assisted in launching the SDUK by Matthew Hill, a Dissenter and son of a rural schoolmaster, who had risen without friends in high places to become a barrister and member of parliament for Hull. Much of Hill's work at the bar was in causes heard before the Court of Exchequer involving the defence of civil liberties. In parliament, where he spoke seldom, he made something of a name for himself by his earnest campaign against the various duties on paper and newspaper publications which were known as 'taxes on knowledge'. He was the type of those provincial zealots for improvement who helped to sustain Brougham's immense reputation and popularity, especially in the northern counties, to a degree which the Westminster politicians never fully understood. He became a kind of factotum to Brougham and was repaid by the generosity of Brougham's friendship.

In the autumn of 1826, when he joined the committee of the SDUK, Hill mentioned the rival scheme projected by Knight to Brougham, who at once instructed him to bring Knight to London. By his own account, Knight was not jealous of his own project, but pleased rather to discover in the SDUK an opening for its nurture. He instantly went up to London to meet Brougham.

I had never come across the renowned orator in private life, or had seen him under an every-day character. There was an image in my mind of the Queen's Attorney-General, as I had often beheld him in the House of Lords ... equivocating witnesses crouching beneath his withering scorn; mighty peers shrinking from his bold sarcasm; the whole assembly visibly agitated at times by the splendour of his eloquence. The Henry Brougham I had gazed upon was, in my eyes, a man stern and repellent; not to be approached with any attempt at familiarity; whose opinions must be received with the most respectful deference; whose mental superiority would be somewhat overwhelming. The Henry Brougham into whose chambers in Lincoln's Inn I was ushered on a November night was sitting amidst his briefs, evidently delighted to be interrupted for some thoughts more attractive ... he went at once to the subject upon which I came. The rapid conception of the features of my plan; the few brief questions as to my wishes; the manifestation of a warm interest in my views without the slightest attempt to be patronizing, were most gratifying to me. The image of the great orator of 1820 altogether vanished when I listened to the unpretentious and often playful words of one of the best table-talkers of 1826,—it vanished even as the full-bottomed wig of that time seemed to have belonged to some other head than the close-cropped one upon which I looked. The foremost advocate of popular education made no harangues about its advantages. He did not indoctrinate me, as I have been bored by many an educationist before and since, with flourishes upon a subject which he gave Mr Hill and myself full credit for comprehending. M. Charles Dupin said to Mackintosh, after a night in the House of Commons—'I heard not one word about the blessings of Liberty'. 'No, no', replied Mackintosh, 'we take all that for granted.' So did Henry Brougham take for granted that he and I were in accord upon the subject of the Diffusion of Knowledge ... From that hour I felt more confidence in talking with perfect freedom to him who worthily filled so large a space in the world's eyes, than to many a man of commonplaces.[8]

The easy cordiality struck at that first meeting grew into a lasting friendship and fruitful working partnership. Some years later, when

Brougham was lord chancellor and Knight was editor of the SDUK's *Penny Magazine* and *Penny Cyclopedia*, the two men spent a week together at Brougham Hall, where Matthew Hill was also, and Knight's letter to his wife provides a rare description of Brougham's manner of life there.

> Our course of life is this. We rise at seven. Hill and I walk, if it is fine, for an hour. Then come the letters and papers. At a quarter to ten we breakfast. At the head of the table sits the Chancellor's mother—the most interesting old lady I ever saw in my life. Heavens, what he must owe to the care of that mother! Mr William Brougham is of the party. At eleven we go up to the library—the Chancellor and we two together—and there we discuss some point of national importance, with all sorts of documents before us, for three or four hours. We then start off for a drive amongst the Lakes—still we three—where the Chancellor delights to point out the beauties of the scenery, or tell us some local anecdote—ever and anon coming back to our morning's labours upon Education, Poor Laws, Taxes, Tithes, &c. &c. At half-past six or seven we dine—have a cheerful and animated talk for two or three hours— then the drawing-room and tea—and bed at eleven. I am quite sure this will have a lasting effect upon my temper and modes of thought. It is impossible to be in company with Lord Brougham for a short time, and not feel wiser;—but to meet him in his daily life— to witness his regulated industry, to enjoy his constant good humour, to partake his high hopes for the improvement of his fellow creatures, and to have one's own powers constantly called out by his wonderful talents, without being in the slightest degree under constraint—all this constitutes a rare enjoyment, and furnishes a powerful incentive to deserve the friendship of such a man.[9]

Knight was not immediately drawn into the SDUK, apparently because, despite the favourable impression which Brougham made upon him, he wished to publish his own series independently. John Murray, however, took fright at the magnitude of Knight's proposed Library and the competition from the SDUK and withdrew his support. In July 1827 Knight was appointed to supervise the SDUK's publications. By then the enterprise had been launched with resounding success by Brougham's introductory treatise, the *Discourse on the Objects, Pleasures and Advantages of Science*. Henry Crabb Robinson judged it to be 'remarkable only as coming from the busiest man living',[10] and it is true that Brougham lacked thorough grounding in the physical sciences. He had, however, a keen amateur knowledge and mathematics had been since his early youth his favourite intellectual diversion. In an essay whose purpose was to attract lay readers fearful of weights and measures and formulas, up-to-date scholarship was not wanted. What gave the treatise life was the author's manifest delight in the discoveries of science and the sincerity of his conviction that understanding them was within the compass of ordinary men. It touched rapidly on the many branches of the subject and its critics called it superficial. Knight's judgement was finer. It was, he wrote, the work of a full man, 'who had not laboriously elaborated this fascinating treatise out of books recently studied or hastily referred to, but had poured it forth out of the accumulated wealth of his rich treasury of knowledge'.[11]

The *Discourse* ran through eight editions in its first year and sold 39,000 copies. Brougham's only other known scientific writing for the SDUK, a paper on hydrostatics, was less successful. He made the fundamental error of confusing the weight and pressure of water, and when the error was detected the SDUK had to withdraw the edition and issue a revised one. Why Brougham did not give the subject to an expert is not known. Of course, his self-confidence was unbounded and his quickness of mind legendary. Lord Holland, who once had occasion to draw an analogy between real tennis and politics (remarking, during the struggle with the Lords over the great reform bill, that the King must give the Whigs a *bisque*, or privilege to call a point at any part of the match), apologized for using a metaphor which Brougham would not understand. 'I daresay, however, you will contrive before the sun sets to comprehend the whole craft and progress of tennis, chases and all . . . It is difficult to find an unknown tongue that you cannot talk at twenty-four hours' notice.'[12] So prodigious a facility of mind had its snares. Brougham's reliance on his own resources led him into indiscretions. Earlier in his career, when the *Edinburgh Review* was just starting, he had written an abrasive article dismissing Thomas Young's new theory of light, despite the fact that Young, having discovered the principle of interference, was able to confirm Huygens' hypothesis that light travelled in waves and so finally, after a century, overthrow Newton's particulate, or corpuscular, theory. The article, published anonymously, greatly damaged Young's reputation, yet seems never to have given Brougham a moment's embarrassment. At least, so far as is known, he never displayed the courtesy of apologizing to Young. No one was injured by the paper on hydrostatics, but Brougham's spectacular blunder left the SDUK committee feeling somewhat shamefaced.

The instant success of the Library of Useful Knowledge (the first annual report of the society boasted that each of the bi-monthly treatises so far published had sold nearly 20,000 copies) encouraged the SDUK to extend its operations. In November 1827 Knight proposed a rational and useful almanac to drive Old Moore's sham article out of the field. 'It is now the middle of November,' said Brougham. 'Can you have your almanac out before the end of the year?' Yes, replied Knight, if given help with with scientific matters. 'Then tell Mr Coates [the society's secretary] to call a meeting of the General Committee at my chambers, at half-past eight tomorrow morning. You shall have help enough. Go to work, and never fear.'[13] The meeting took place, Brougham's energy 'swept away every doubt', and *The British Almanac* appeared on the first day of the new year. It sold 10,000 copies in the first week and the Duke of Wellington ordered it to be used in government offices.[14]

In response to criticism that the Library of Useful Knowledge was too abstract and too didactic (Brougham boasted to John Allen early on that nothing 'attractive or popular' had been published[15]), the committee decided, in May 1828, to bring out a Library of Entertaining Knowledge to treat the same subjects in a lighter vein. It ran from 1831 to 1836 and attracted such distinguished contributors as Thomas Arnold and the scholar-bishops, Richard Whately and Connop Thirlwall. There followed a series on farming topics, a quarterly journal of education (the first of its kind), an edition of maps, and a gallery of portraits sold at one-third the normal price.

The SDUK was most famous, of course, as the publisher of the *Penny Magazine* and the *Penny Cyclopedia*, both begun in 1832 despite some Whiggish misgivings, not shared by Brougham, that weekly penny sheets were beneath the society's dignity. The *Magazine* was the child of a conversation between Knight and Hill, who talked one morning on Hampstead Heath about unstamped weekly publications and agreed that they all 'in some degree came under the character of contraband newspapers, and were nearly all dangerous in principle and coarse in language'.[16] Knight was appointed its editor and he also undertook the financial risk of publication. Its spirit approached more nearly to entertaining than useful knowledge. Knight described the magazine as 'the small optic-glass called the *finder*, which is placed by the side of a large telescope, to enable the observer to discover the star which is afterwards to be carefully examined by the more perfect instrument'.[17] It was necessary to tread warily on the safe side of the indefinite line between newspaper reporting, which was subject to the stamp duty, and essay-writing. After the first two numbers had appeared, the solicitor of stamps declared himself satisfied that the magazine was not liable to tax. The early sales were unprecedented. The magazine gained a circulation of 200,000, more than three times that of the *Saturday Magazine* published by the Society for the Promotion of Christian Knowledge and more than ten times that of the *Poor Man's Guardian*.[18] The *Penny Cyclopedia*, issued in monthly parts, never achieved so high a sale, its circulation dropping from an initial 75,000 to 20,000 in 1844, when its twenty-seventh and last volume was completed. By then the SDUK was in severe financial difficulty. In 1842 Brougham had decided to prepare a Biographical Dictionary, an expensive undertaking which he knew would require great exertion to carry out. The entire funds of the SDUK were devoted to the project (so that in 1845 the *Penny Magazine* ceased publication), but they proved to be inadequate. The first volume alone lost £5,000 and in 1846 the society, mired in debt, dissolved itself.

Although Knight bore the burden of the SDUK's labours, Brougham's sympathies were too vitally joined to the business for him to leave others to accomplish their work in peace. That he presided over the committee's meetings, that he pestered his friends for suggestions and books, was a matter of course. He was, after all, the progenitor and chairman of the society. But he was not capable of limiting himself to official duties. When John Allen resisted his appeal to write a history of parliament for the society, Brougham sought (in vain, as it turned out) to lure him with the promise that if Allen provided the materials, he would apply the polish.

> If you find it an annoyance to write (which I often do, & should always do so as to prevent me soon from ever thinking of it if I did not make a point of *resisting* the feeling & forcing myself to go on) you may *Benthamise*, & I undertake to furnish you a good Dumont.[19]

Beyond that, Brougham meddled, partly because his infinite curiosity and rampant self-esteem made him a born meddler, partly because he could not bear to have a word go out in the society's name which did not have his approval. The society, he told Creevey, would publish any work of a useful tendency and sound principles. 'Of course we avoid direct part in Church and State, but we *openly profess* to preach peace, liberty and absolute toleration, and I take care, as the works pass through my hands, to keep out all that is against these principles, and to put in *authoritatively* what is wanting upon them.[20] Even a writer of Leigh Hunt's stature was not exempt from his interference. 'Almost all that the Socy. publishes passes thro' my hands in one stage or another,' Brougham warned him, 'and I use some freedom in cutting out as well as in suggesting alterations & additions (the latter to inculcate good feelings). This seems to be incumbent upon me, *as our names are given*, and I am sure *you* will hold yourself safe in my hands.'[21]

Brougham's motives were unobjectionable, or at least understandable. His practices were occasionally unscrupulous. Harriet Martineau accepted Brougham's invitation to write a life of the prison reformer, John Howard, for the society. She submitted her manuscript, but was not paid, and when she asked for payment her letter was not answered. The life was never printed, and several years later the script was returned so grimy and mutilated that it was evident its contents had been quarried. The episode was one of several which earned Brougham Miss Martineau's contempt. That the most successful popular writer of the day on political and economic subjects, one, too, thoroughly moderate in her politics and Malthusian in her economics, was unable to work in harness with the SDUK was unfortunate for the society, but inevitable. Miss Martineau held unbendingly to the view that a writer can do good only if every word that he publishes is his own. It was an attitude which Brougham, a journalist from his youth, failed to comprehend. When, some years later, Harriet refused a government pension in order to preserve her independence, Brougham declared to a large company that, as for Harriet Martineau, he hated her. 'I hate her! I hate a woman who has opinions. She has refused a pension—making herself out to be better than other people.'[22] A just pride in her own literary property led Miss Martineau to the conclusion that 'all connexion with the Diffusion Society, and Lord Brougham, and the Whig government, was so much mere detriment to my usefulness and my influence'.[23] Brougham tore his hair and ranted that he would not 'be driven out of the field by a little deaf woman at Norwich'; Miss Martineau, who went about making fun of 'Lord Brougham and his teaching and preaching clique',[24] took revenge by making a villain of him in her *History of the Peace.*

* * *

At the beginning of the 19th century London was the only major European capital without a university, a deficiency made all the more injurious to the country by the fact that the two ancient universities at Oxford and Cambridge, the only ones in England, were religiously and socially exclusive. Undergraduates had to swear to the thirty-nine articles of the Church (to matriculate at Oxford and to receive a degree from Cambridge) and be able to pay £250 to £300 a year in fees and battels. The sons of the middling ranks of society and all those Jews, Dissenters and Roman Catholics who were unable to bear the expense of study on the continent were thus denied a university education. Dissenting academies, it is true, had in the 18th century been established in provincial centres such as Manchester and Liverpool; but by the 1820s they had narrowed into little more than sectarian theological seminaries. For some time Dissenters had discussed among themselves the need for a university of their own. Nothing was accomplished, however, until the poet, Thomas Campbell, whose *Pleasures of Hope*, published in 1799, had made him one of the literary lions of London, returned from Germany in 1820 enthusiastic to establish in London a university to rival the great Teutonic centres of learning which he had just visited. When Brougham suggested, in his *Practical Observations*, that universities open to all classes and all creeds should be started in England, he must have known that Campbell had been airing the idea in literary circles for four years. For what it was worth the honour of being the first man to propose a university for London probably belonged to Campbell, who was vexed that at the laying of the foundation stone in 1827 Lord Broughton gave all the credit to Brougham. Campbell protested that Brougham had stolen his idea and he declared him to be the 'greatest, brightest, *meanest* of mankind'.[25] The accusation was silly. There was little merit in simply desiring a university. Brougham, more than any other man, gave substance to the desire. 'London University,' *Fraser's Magazine* wrote, 'rose like an exhalation at his bidding.'[26]

On 30 January 1825 Brougham gave a small dinner to Campbell, James Mill and the radical member of parliament, Joseph Hume. Its purpose was to plan the foundation of the new university. Its outcome was a letter written by Campbell and addressed to Brougham, published in *The Times*, recommending a London university in the arts and sciences for 'the youth of our middling rich people'.[27] A series of meetings and dinners followed, mostly at Brougham's chambers, to discuss details of the project and arrange a canvass of probable sympathizers for subscriptions. Francis Cox, the Baptist clergyman from Hackney who wrote for the *Baptist Magazine* and had served for a time as general secretary to the dissenting ministers of south London and Westminster, was brought into the discussions. By April agreement was reached by the Dissenters' Provisional Committee, established to promote a university, and the circle attached to Brougham and Campbell to co-operate in founding a secular university free from every kind of religious test and teaching. Brougham had learned from the hostile reaction to his parish school bill of 1820 that to gain wide support for education which included religious teaching was impossible. Either the Dissenters or the Established Church were certain to find any method of introducing it weighted against them. Brougham was fortunate to find a moderate ally in Cox, for in those days of fierce sectarian pride there were as many Dissenters bleating righteously in the dissidence of their dissent as there were Anglicans rejoicing heartily in the strength of their salvation. It was fortunate, too, that rich men like the Quaker banker, Joseph Gurney, and the Jewish bullion broker, Sir Isaac Goldsmid, were ardent promoters of the university. Without the intellectual and financial support of such men it is doubtful that it would have been founded.

Secure in the knowledge that a new university would not want for friends, Brougham pushed forward with characteristic speed. Whether Francis Place was right to say that he rode roughshod over Campbell in order to extract maximum publicity for himself we may doubt;[28] more probably, Campbell simply discovered, as others did before and after him, that when Brougham was wedded to a cause there was no one to match his industry and resource. On 26 May he introduced a bill in the House of Commons to obtain a parliamentary charter for the university. 'This must be opposed and rejected,' Peel wrote to the Dean of Christ Church, Oxford,[29] and Brougham, acknowledging that even if the bill got through the Commons the Lords would throw it out, withdrew it. Since the government had already refused to grant a royal charter, the new university was denied the right to grant degrees. Undeterred, Brougham and his colleagues called a public meeting for 1 July at which, with the Lord Mayor of London in the chair, it was resolved to call the new institution the London University and to offer shares to the public at £100 each. By the end of August 1,500 shares had been placed 'in good hands' and Brougham, having made preliminary arrangements for the purchase of some waste land in Gower Street, began to look for an architect.[30]

A few months later the university was formally founded. Its first council was elected in December and the deeds of settlement approved in the following February. The two outstanding matters not yet resolved, the curriculum and the appointment of professors, were the province of the education committee, in which the lead was taken by Brougham and Sir James Mackintosh. The university was divided into two faculties, one of arts and law, the other of medicine, on which Brougham, remembering the fame which Edinburgh and Glasgow had won by their medical schools, laid great stress. Indeed, for all that Campbell was inspired by German scholarship, the Scotch influence was paramount in the shaping of the new university. Campbell himself was born in Glasgow and educated at the university there, where he succeeded Brougham as rector in 1826. Cox, though born in England, was a graduate of Edinburgh, and the rest of the inner band of founders, Mackintosh, James Mill, Birkbeck and Hume among them, were all, except for Zachary Macaulay (who was also on the committee of the SDUK), Scots. In the public mind the new university was distinguished from the ancient universities chiefly by its irreligion, but its singularity was also marked in other ways. Following the Scotch tradition, it opened its doors to men who wished to attend a single course of lectures. Like the Scotch universities, it was non-tutorial and non-residential. Later generations of London students had reason to be thankful that Brougham and his associates, in taking Scotland for their model, imparted to London's university an invigorating and adult atmosphere free from the cloying paternalism of its older and more celebrated English rivals.

Brougham, suffering from nervous exhaustion, was too ill to assist at the inaugural lecture in October 1828, but he received reports of the great success which attended it. The medical course opened with fifty-four students, the law course with ninety. Four years later the figures for the arts and law faculty were 148, for the medical school, 283. The university's total enrolment was thus more than that of its Anglican rival, King's College, which opened its doors in 1829. Just as the *Edinburgh Review* had provoked the Church-and-King party to found the *Quarterly Review*, so what may be loosely described as the Evangelical and Tory interest raised up King's as an antidote to the 'godless college' on Gower Street. Only one Evangelical, Zachary Macaulay, and one Tory, Lord Dudley (and he of Canningite inclinations), sat on the university's first council. The rest either withheld their approval or publicly declared their opposition. Zachary Macaulay was taken to task by his fellow-Saint, Henry Drummond: 'Three great principles have been warring against each other for these thirty years past—the Spirit of Despotism, the Spirit of Infidelity, and the Spirit of Popery; each pretending that if it could gain the mastery, it would bid the troubled sea of the nations be still; of this spirit of infidelity, all science, education, march of mind, intellect, and all the other cant, which is not founded upon the Scriptures, are part and parcel.'[31]

At first Brougham took delight in his opponents' disquiet. 'I wish you would speak or write to your friends,' he wrote to Lambton in 1825, when he was busy drumming up subscriptions. 'It is of immense consequence to give this finishing blow to the High Church Bigots & they are roaring out with fury at us already.'[32] Three years later, however, his influence persuaded the council to allow the three Anglican professors on the university's staff to deliver lectures on Christianity and Church history at a place near the university. From the beginning, he adopted a friendly attitude towards King's College. In a letter to Denman written in the summer of 1828 he gave his reasons for believing the rival college to be 'a *great* good, if not an unmixed one'.[33] Not only did it provide London with two universities, but, being the child of the ruling powers, it established a formidable precedent to stop the outcry against placing universities in large towns such as Manchester, Liverpool and Birmingham. Moreover, whatever the government might at any time choose to do for King's, it could not avoid doing also for London University. No countenance should be given to the storm being raised against King's by Joseph Hume and the radicals: 'K.C. cannot *hurt us* now and must further our common object.' A few weeks later the council met to consider what public stance it should adopt towards King's. Brougham, who was too ill to attend, wrote a letter to the secretary explaining the necessity of doing and saying nothing. 'The rivalry of the two seminaries will be salutary to both and useful to the community, nor can any true friend to either regard the other with any unfriendly feeling.'[34] His magnanimity had its reward in 1836, when his creation was renamed University College and affiliated to King's in the chartered, degree-granting institution which took the name of the University of London.

*   *   *

To do good is to invite censure. Brougham's effort to raise men made him the butt of endless raillery and abuse. Thomas Peacock's *Crotchet Castle*, published in 1831, was a playful treatment of the passion which men brought to the debate over the march of intellect.

'God bless my soul, sir!' exclaimed the Reverend Doctor Folliott, bursting, one fine May morning, into the breakfast-room at Crotchet Castle, 'I am out of all patience with this march of mind. Here has my house been nearly burned down, by my cook taking it into her head to study hydrostatics, in a sixpenny tract, published by the Steam Intellect Society, and written by a learned friend who is for doing all the world's business as well as his own, and is equally well qualified to handle every branch of human knowledge. I have a great abomination of this learned friend; as author, lawyer, and politician, he is *triformis*, like Hecate: and in every one of his three forms he is *bifrons*, like Janus; the true Mr Facing-both-ways of Vanity Fair. My cook must read his rubbish in bed; and as might naturally be expected, she dropped suddenly fast asleep, over-turned the candle, and set the curtains in a blaze. Luckily, the footman went into the room at the moment, in time to tear down the curtains and throw them into the chimney, and a pitcher of water on her night-cap extinguished her wick: she is a greasy subject, and would have burned like a short mould.'

Reproached for making light of science, Dr Folliot held his ground.

'Yes, sir, such science as the learned friend deals in: everything for everybody, science for all, schools for all, rhetoric for all, law for all, physic for all, words for all, and sense for none. I say, sir, law for lawyers, and cookery for cooks: and I wish the learned friend, for all his life, a cook that will pass her time in studying his works; then every dinner he sits down to at home, he will sit on the stool of repentance.'

So thorough an enemy of Benthamite utilitarianism as Carlyle applauded an age in which knowledge and education were 'opening the eyes of the humblest';[35] but orthodox representatives of the establishment recoiled from the spectacle. Lord Lowther wrote to his father during the struggle over the great reform bill that meddling 'politicians' who wished to bring everyone down to their level were about to inflict a Mechanics' Institute upon Whitehaven. 'The over-education produces the greatest mass of *floating discontent* that pervades this country and France. Men are raised beyond their station in society, and blame the government for not finding ample provision for them.'[36] The *Quarterly Review*, even while it ridiculed Brougham for so misreading human nature as to believe working men would find the time for instruction, thought it prudent to damn the Mechanics' Institutes by assailing their patron.

It is his singular infelicity to prejudice every cause which he undertakes to advance:—with all the zeal, industry and perti-nacity,—all the power of labour, endurance and privation, mental and bodily,—all the self-confidence and versatility which Sallust attributes to his hero, and far more than all his talent, information and eloquence, he is yet confessedly the most unfit of all dis-tinguished public men of the present day to lead a party, or to conduct the struggle for any great and opposed measure. His weapons are commiseration of besotted ignorance, sarcasm of interested motives, assumption of measureless superiority.[37]

Dr Arnold, liberal in politics and Christian in his pedagogy, sought to persuade the SDUK to add 'the slightest touches of Christian principle and Christian hope' to its publications. In the purely scientific treatises there was, perhaps, a 'show of reason' in excluding religion, but in the *Penny Magazine* it would be 'a sort of living salt to the whole'. 'In a paper intended to improve its readers *morally*, to make men better and happier, as well as better informed, surely neutrality with regard to Christianity is, virtually, hostility.'[38] When his entreaties effected no change in the SDUK's policy, Arnold started his own weekly newspaper, the *Englishman's Register*.

Dr Arnold's 'Broad Church' latitudinarianism stood at one extremity of the early Victorian religious spectrum, John Henry Newman's Anglo-Catholic Tractarianism at the other. Newman's assault on the march of intellect (Lord Eldon called it 'the rogues' march'),[39] decked out with all the subtlety of his feline prose, was occasioned by Peel's address at the opening of the Tamworth Reading Room in 1841, a speech which Newman described as 'pure

Broughamism'. It drew forth from Newman the series of letters, signed 'Catholicus', which were published under the title, *The Tamworth Reading Room*. Brougham, he contended, had fallen victim to one of the chief errors of the day, the notion 'that our true excellence comes not from within, but from without, not wrought out through personal struggles and sufferings, but following upon a passive exposure to influences over which we have no control'. He offered useful occupation and rational recreation as the fruits of knowledge. 'Can the 19th century produce no more robust and creative philosophy than this?' Man was not a reasoning animal, but a seeing, feeling, acting animal.

> Taking human nature as it is actually found, and assuming that there is an art to life, to say that it consists, or in any essential manner is placed, in the cultivation of knowledge—that the mind is changed by a discovery, or saved by a diversion, or amused into immortality—that grief, anger, cowardice, self-conceit, pride, or passion, can be subdued by an examination of shells or grasses, or inhaling gases, or chipping of rocks, or observing of barometers, or calculating the longitude, is the veriest pretence which sophist or mountebank ever professed to a gaping auditory. If virtue be a mastery over the mind, if its end be action, if its perfection be inward order, harmony, and peace, we must seek it in graver and holier places than libraries and reading rooms.

Like many a mystic before him and after, Newman poured scorn on the stumbling attempts of men who sought, by tentative steps, to stem the sources of human unhappiness. 'Many a man will live and die upon a dogma,' he wrote; 'no one will be a martyr for a conclusion.' He did not ask himself, in his flight to the mediaeval embrace of the Roman Church, whether knowledge could bestow liberty and power and pleasure. That he was fighting a lost cause troubled him without deflecting him from his path. 'The ascendancy of faith may be impracticable, but the reign of knowledge is impossible. The problem for statesmen of this age is how to educate the masses—and literature and science cannot give the solution.'

Slings from the godly were blunt instruments against the armour of the Enlightenment. The arrows shot from radical bows had more power to wound. When, in 1897, Hilaire Belloc sneered at 'all that social work of which Lord Brougham was the leader in the earlier part of the century—the attempt to create small capitalists by thrift, and to secure their position by technical knowledge',[40] he echoed Cobbett's complaint that 'Brougham and Birkbeck, and the rest of the Malthusian crew, are constantly at work preaching *content to the hungry and naked*'.[41] As a counterblast to the SDUK Cobbett started his famous *Twopenny Trash* in 1830, issuing it monthly to escape the fourpenny stamp on newspapers. SDUK treatises such as Knight's *The Results of Machinery*, which appealed to workers to stop their machine-breaking in the autumn and winter of 1830–31, and his *Capital and Labour*, which counselled thrift and industry and a proper respect for the just rights of property and the freedom of capital, gave substance to the radicals' accusation that the lectures at the Mechanics' Institutes and the tracts issued by the SDUK were baits flung out to working-men by their middle-class, Whig oppressors. Brougham became staple fare for radical caricaturists like Robert Seymour, whose *Patent Penny Knowledge Mill*[42] depicted a machine cranked by Brougham and Lord Althorp while Lord John Russell emptied into it a tankard of 'Whig liberalism'.

Against the Tories Brougham preached the benefits of education to civil society. No argument, no speech, no treatise, no diffusion of knowledge, he argued in his SDUK treatise, *Discourse on the Objects, Pleasures and Advantages of Political Science*,[43] could make a well-governed people feel themselves ill-governed, or a contented people feel discontented. On the other hand it could—and here he gave a handle to the radicals—save them from the errors and false doctrines of demagogues and agitators.

> The necessity of some considerable degree of restraint to the well-being of society—the impossibility of the supreme power being left in the hands of the whole people—the fatal effects of disregarding the rights of property, the great corner-stone of all civil society—the interest which all classes down to the humblest have in the protection afforded by the law to the accumulation of capital—the evils of resistance to established government unless in extreme and therefore very rare cases—the particular interest which the whole people, low, as well as high, must ever have in general obedience to the supreme power in the state—the almost uniform necessity of making all changes, even the most salutary, in any established institution, gradually and temperately—all these are the very first lessons which every political teacher must inculcate if he be fit for his office, and commonly honest.

Just as important was the dissemination of the true principles governing the relations of capital and labour: that the repugnance on the part of labourers to change their residence and their habit of raising large families produced that unlimited supply of labour which was the main cause of the depression of the working classes. Unlimited provision for the poor was no solution.

> The outcry raised in favour of unlimited provision for the poor, and against the reasonable, indeed the necessary rule which would confine each man to living upon the produce of his own industry, or the income of his own property, never could arise, at least never could have any success, but among the most ignorant of mankind. So, the strange delusions propagated by some wild visionaries, and by some ill-disposed men, that labour alone gives a right to enjoyment, and that the existence of accumulated capital is a grievance and an abuse, could not have the least success with men who had been taught to reflect that the accumulation of capital is the necessary consequence of the existence of property and its secure possession, and that no classes have a stronger interest in the protection of capital than the labourers whom it must necessarily always be employed in supporting.

The important thing, Brougham told Peel some years later, was to imbue the higher classes and the more respectable class of tradesmen and artisans with 'right notions', since 'by degree these get to the one below & so downwards'.[44] Such, Brougham believed, had been the method of the *philosophes* of the *ancien régime*, and like his intellectual hero, Voltaire, he let slip no occasion to propagate his creed. 'My original lectures,' he confessed to John Allen, referring to the anonymous lectures written for the Mechanics' Institutes, 'took every opportunity of introducing *good matter* of a general kind, and I stept aside from Cavendish's discovery to praise the Whig families & to lecture the enemy, & from Napier's logarithms to lecture of feudal nobility & so forth . . . In all this I don't conceal that my object is at least partly political. I hold certain principles & I am above all things anxious that they should prevail.'[45]

All this Whiggery was reflected, too, in London University, to which a great proportion of the subscriptions came from the landed chieftains of the Whig party. Sydney Smith was pleased to see Lord Grey presiding at the first annual general meeting of the 'Democratical College': 'he would do it in the very best manner the thing could be done'.[46] The Greys and the Bedfords were essential to Brougham's purpose. They were also his friends. Perhaps there is something disquieting in Brougham's conviction that right notions existed to be taught. Yet who has ever done anything for the world without the impulse of a strong moral purpose? To wish men to think as he thought was better than to dread, as less charitable men around him dreaded, that they should think at all. Whatever Brougham's motives, the circulation figures achieved by the SDUK were impressive. The boast made in the Society's final *Address*, issued in 1846, that the public was 'supplied with *cheap* AND *good* literature to an extent which the most sanguine friend of human improvement could not, in 1826, have hoped to have witnessed in twenty years', was justified.[47] Let us suppose, with Brougham's enemies, that he went to bed at nights pleased to reflect that he was making yet another name for himself and that he was the object of an emancipated people's gratitude. Ambitious men must serve some cause and some causes serve ambition better than others. Brougham was fond of saying that he desired for his tombstone no other epitaph than that he was the founder of the universal education. What other politician of his stature, what other aspirant to high office, half a century before Forster's education act, would have hitched his posthumous wagon to so faint-beckoning a star?

10

Canning and Coalition

In a rhapsodic passage in his *England and the English*, Lytton Bulwer wrote that the death of Lord Byron in 1824 marked the point at which the English people, having run a career of dreams and extravagance, turned back to the prudent and the practical. Politics once more absorbed the attention of men who, having been captivated by the poets and the refiners, grew to identify their feelings and causes with statesmen and economists. 'Thus, first Canning, and then Brougham, may be said, for a certain time, to have represented, more than any other individuals, the common Intellectual Spirit; and the interest usually devoted to the imaginative, was transferred to the real.'[1] The remark bears resemblance to John Stuart Mill's more suggestive judgement that the two seminal minds of their age were Bentham and Coleridge, the one representative of the progressive spirit, the other of the conservative. Brougham and Canning were not opposites. For all Canning's veneration of the existing constitution and Brougham's hankering after radicalism, both men gravitated naturally towards the political centre. They wished, in different ways, to give practical expression to that movement of public opinion which Peel, using what he called 'an odious but intelligible phrase', described in 1820 as more *liberal* than the policy of the government.[2] So far as the course of politics hangs on the actions of individuals, it hung, in the 1820s, chiefly on the actions of Brougham and Canning, each of whom had the power and the latent temper to shake the fragile foundations of his party. So far as it is determined by the force of great public questions, it was determined, in the 1820s, by the swelling current of Irish nationalism. Roman Catholic emancipation was, to borrow a phrase from Thomas Jefferson, like a fire-bell in the night, sounding the knell, if it were granted, of old Toryism, if withheld, of the union between Great Britain and Ireland. Brougham and Canning were emancipationists, but neither was ready to sacrifice his prospects by uncompromising fidelity to the cause. Great was the interest, therefore, to see whether together they might bring the issue to its resolution.

In 1822 Canning's intended departure for India, as governor-general, had been stopped by Castlereagh's suicide. At that moment of anxiety for the government, Brougham's view of Canning was ambivalent. Canning would be mad, he said, to surrender the wealth and splendour of India to rejoin Lord Liverpool's cabinet: the 'vile creatures' of the old guard would turn him out within a year.[3] On the other hand, those Whigs who dreamed of catching Canning were also mad. 'As he at present stands (his peculiar ground being that of champion agt. all reform, all improvements of every sort) he is more opposed to us than almost any body.'[4] Once Canning had become foreign secretary and Tory leader in the House of Commons, Brougham's line changed. Canning's return, accompanied by the promotion of Peel, William Huskisson and Frederick Robinson (the future Viscount Goderich) to important positions in the government, brought the liberal element in the cabinet more into balance with the ultras. The stability of the government was thereby rendered more precarious. Lord Grey's enmity towards Canning was immovable, but the prospect of Tory disunion stirred the enthusiasm of those Whigs, especially Lord Lansdowne and Brougham, the one prepared to stifle his Whig pride, the other with none to stifle, who looked to achieve their political objects, especially Catholic emancipation, by a junction with the forward-looking Tories. Canning was to be taken up, flattered into liberalism, in order to widen the rift between the liberal and ultra wings of the government. 'My solution,' Brougham told Lansdowne on the eve of the 1823 session of parliament, 'is "abstinence" from needless attack for a while.'[5]

Had Brougham's colleagues not come to expect almost anything from him, they might, therefore, have been startled to observe him, not long into the new session, engaged in an altercation with Canning. During a debate on the Roman Catholic question, Brougham rose to taunt the new foreign minister with having preferred 'hard labour in England to honourable exile in India', a pleasing enough jibe at Canning's awkward position as a pro-Catholic in the old firm of Eldon and Co., but at once made ugly by the accusation that in taking office, and implicitly abandoning the just claims of the Irish Catholics, Canning had exhibited 'the most incredible specimen of monstrous truckling for the purpose of obtaining office that the whole history of political tergiversation could furnish'.[6] Canning leapt to his feet. 'I rise to say that that is false.' Called upon to retract his words, he refused. Nor would Brougham recant, so that it appeared that nothing could prevent seconds being named and pistols drawn, a prospect amusing enough since Brougham and Canning were the two pre-eminent outsiders in the aristocratic world of early 19th-century politics. In the end tempers were soothed and the near-combatants brought to agree, however ludicrously, that Brougham's words had been intended to touch Canning's official, not his personal, character. Brougham's language was offensive and provocative, but the House, its traditions breached by the lie direct, was, as Creevey reported, '*decidedly* against Canning'.[7] Lady Holland, while she agreed that Canning had done himself incalculable mischief, feared as much for Brougham. 'B. has acquired great control over the House by his judgement & temper. If he can hold this hitherto even temper, he will be the greatest man there; but he has always erred in the moment of victory, become intoxicated & offensive.'[8]*

The row with Canning, like a summer squall, rose from seemingly nowhere and quickly subsided. The patient approving with which Brougham meant to beguile Canning had been disclosed at the start of the session when, having intended to move a hostile amendment to the government's address to the throne, he changed his mind on listening to Canning's warm espousal of the Spanish liberals in their struggle against Ferdinand VII and his despotic friends in the Holy Alliance. On Canning's insistence (although Castlereagh had taken the same line in a private instruction), the Duke of Wellington, Great

* Three years later Brougham again narrowly missed being called out, in a curious episode which provides a sidelight on the contemporary practice of anonymous reviewing. Albany Fonblanque, who in 1830 took over control of the *Examiner* from Leigh Hunt, was a friend of Bentham and the Mills and with them a founder of the radical *Westminster Review*. In 1826 he reviewed Thomas Moore's *Life of Sheridan* in the *Westminster* and for some unfavourable comments was taken to task in the *Edinburgh*. Fonblanque wrote to Brougham, owning to the authorship of the *Westminster* article and demanding to know whether Brougham had written the reply. Brougham refused to divulge the information (he *had* written it) and denied Fonblanque's right to ask the question. An acrimonious correspondence followed, in which Brougham charged Fonblanque with intending to insult him and Fonblanque declared himself ready 'to give satisfaction'. Seconds were named and arrangements made before Lord Dudley, a mutual friend, stopped the nonsense. Little time passed before Fonblanque was assuring his acquaintances that he and Brougham had forgotten the affair. Dudley's summary of the dispute was that 'when the case is like the present, that of an anonymous writer animadverting, however severely, upon another, merely with a view to what he has written, and without the slightest reference, directly or by innuendo, to any particular person, I do not think that the party aggrieved can be allowed to individualize himself, and to call upon whomever his suspicions may happen to light upon, to declare whether or not he is the man who has transgressed the limits of propriety in a controversy with an unknown antagonist'. (E. Barrington de Fonblanque, *The Life and Letters of Albany Fonblanque*, London, 1874, 14–18).

Britain's representative at the 1822 congress of Verona, had informed the European powers that the English government would stand aside from any military intervention in the internal affairs of another country, specifically from a French-led invasion of Spain to defend the monarchy against the constitutionalists. The cause of Spanish liberty had long been trumpeted by Brougham, and Canning's evident resolve to disentangle Great Britain from the congress system and its repressive purposes caused him to forgo his planned assault on the government and aim his fire directly at the northern autocracies instead. In one of his finest *ex tempore* displays,[9] he rounded on Russia, 'a power that is only half civilised . . . still quite as much Asiatic as European, whose principles of policy, foreign and domestic, are completely despotic, and whose practices are almost altogether Oriental and barbarous!'. The Russian minister had recently complained of blood's having been shed in the royal palace at Madrid, when all the world knew that Alexander I had entered the church on his coronation day 'preceded by the assassins of his grandfather, surrounded by the assassins of his father, and followed by his own'. 'If I had been one of the counsellors of the Emperor of Russia,' Brougham declared, 'the last subject I would have advised my master to touch upon, would have been that of "bloodshed in the Royal Palace".'

Canning had to go softly in weaning his ultra colleagues away from their attachment to the enemies of liberal nationalism. Brougham sounded the notes the Tory minister was unable to play. 'No news, except universal praise of Brougham and some lurking fears of hollow professions from the ministers,' Henry Fox wrote after the debate. 'Canning is never direct and open in his way of proceeding, and there is such a variety of plots and counterplots that it is difficult to know his real drift.'[10] Brougham and Lansdowne made it their purpose to keep Canning up to the mark. Brougham was so eager to make himself friendly to the new foreign secretary that a few weeks later he set aside his customary zeal for retrenchment and told the government that its proposed increase in the size of the Navy from 21,000 to 25,000 was too little and that it would receive the support of the House if it went further. Why, asked a lady friend of Creevey, did Brougham make such love to Canning? Was it catalepsy?[11]

Great Britain was unable to prevent the French army from crossing the Spanish border; but when Canning, overcoming opposition from Lord Eldon and others in the cabinet, recognized the independence of the South American colonies which had rebelled against Spanish rule, Brougham and the opposition were delighted. Canning's famous speech of 1826, in which he said that to mitigate French influence in Spain he had called the New World into existence to redress the balance of the Old, was heard in silence on his own back benches and loudly cheered by the Whigs. Brougham, as had by then become almost habitual, paid Canning a handsome compliment, remarking that his liberal sentiments reflected the highest honour on his character. All this praising and wooing of Canning, this sweetness of temper, was so remarkable that Lord John Russell had difficulty in taking it seriously. 'Brougham is not so brilliant as usual,' he commented in 1826, 'very moderate and conciliatory. But a man who pounces and claws like an eagle cannot coo as a dove.'[12]

Brougham and Canning did not, of course, see eye to eye. Canning took little interest in popular education; he opposed Brougham's motion of censure on the Demerara authorities for their treatment of the missionary, John Smith, in a speech so 'heathenly and planterly and almost slave-trading' that Brougham later declared him to be 'our very worst adversary on all that related to West Indian affairs';[13] and he was adamant against any tinkering with the electoral system. Indeed, had the Whigs and Brougham cared deeply about parliamentary reform, had they made even their temperate fondness for it part of their public persona, Brougham's nuzzling up to Canning would have been impossible. It was the Irish issue which formed the bond between them. In 1823 Tierney hinted broadly at the possibility of Catholic emancipation's being carried by the Whigs and Canning acting in concert, and a year later he went out of his way to deny that the opposition would make parliamentary reform a condition of taking office.[14] In Ireland the emancipation issue was gaining heat from the oratory of Daniel O'Connell, whose eloquence convinced the Irish peasantry of his inability to temporize with the imperial government at Westminster. The Catholic Association, brought back to life by O'Connell in 1823, raised for the first time since the Union of 1801 the prospect of a mass movement's acquiring sufficient strength to overthrow the Protestant ascendancy in Ireland. The Association, for all that its stated object was simply Catholic emancipation, threatened the very existence of the Union. By 1825 there was not a politician in England who did not understand that the empire had a crisis on its hands.

When parliament assembled at the beginning of 1825 Brougham

opened for the opposition—he was now its *de facto* leader in the House of Commons—with a speech praising ministers for the steps they had taken towards freer trade. Most of their actions, he went on, had first been proposed by him, a species of self-congratulation which drew from Canning one of his better hits. Since Brougham had at one time or another proposed almost every imaginable sort of innovation, it was difficult for ministers to suggest anything without seeming to borrow from him.

> In the reign of Queen Anne there was a sage and grave critic of the name of Dennis who, in his old age, got it into his head that he wrote all the good plays that were acted at that time. At last a tragedy came forth with a most imposing storm of hail and thunder. At the first peal, 'That's my thunder' said Dennis. So, with the honourable and learned gentleman there is no noise or stir for the good of mankind . . . but he instantly claims it for his thunder.[15]

The marrow of Brougham's speech, however, was the urgency of conceding Catholic emancipation in order to arrest the growth of Irish nationalism, and when, a week later, the government brought in its bill to suppress the Catholic Association he tore its arguments to shreds. The Association, said ministers, collected 'rent' and in doing so usurped the authority of the exchequer. But so did the Methodists collect 'rent'. The Association, said ministers, initiated prosecutions and interfered with the administration of justice. But in Ireland there was no justice. It was a fact, acknowledged even by Lord Redesdale, the former Irish lord chancellor, that a Roman Catholic defendant stood almost no chance of a fair trial. The object of the Association was just. If ministers wished to dissolve the Association, they could easily do so by granting its demand. 'My speech,' Brougham later wrote, 'was considered very successful; and certainly, considering that during the whole continuance of this long debate I had been very hard worked—every day in court, and most part of every night in chambers—I had every reason to be satisfied . . . About four in the morning we divided, and were beaten by nearly two to one.'[16]

For all the uncompromising air of that speech, Catholic emancipation showed Brougham in the character of a trimmer. In official English circles it was taken for granted that emancipation, if it had to come, must be hedged round by safeguards, the two most frequently projected in 1825 being the disfranchising of the 40s. freeholders, a device to prevent the Catholic peasantry from swamping the Protestant voters at elections, and the payment of the Roman Catholic clergy by the state, a device to tie them to the English connection and, by giving them their own 'establishment', disarm them from attack on the Church of Ireland. In March 1825, when Burdett's emancipation bill, unsullied by those two 'wings' as they were called, passed in the House of Commons by a majority of 21 votes, rumour spread that the government would concede the struggle if the safeguards were attached to it. Alarmed by the rumour, Lord Lambton announced that no bill which disfranchised electors would have his support, a declaration of purity which, if sworn by the opposition as a whole, would put paid to an alliance with Canning. Brougham rounded on Lambton so severely that Lambton declared that he would not be browbeaten into another course though he might lose the dearest friendship in the world. So, as Lambton's biographer put it, was made 'the little rift in the lute which afterwards widened until harmony was lost in discord'.[17]

Brougham was also brought up short by Lord Grey in a correspondence which revealed a difference of opinion far more important to his future than his quarrel with Lambton. At the end of 1825 Brougham wrote to Grey that for the moment it was prudent to let the Irish question lie fallow: Burdett and most of the Whigs, Tierney and Althorp excepted, were preaching patience to the Irish. Grey's reply was sharp.

As to what you say about Ireland, I can only repeat my former opinion, that it is best for us not to advise at all. But if I were bound to give an opinion, it would be with Tierney and Althorpe [sic]. It may be very convenient to *us* to have no Catholic question, but is it equally good for the Irish? Have they ever got anything except what has been extorted in the hour of distress? Is it not, then, *their* interest to keep alive and inflame a spirit of discontent for that season? If they are quiet, will their adversaries be so? The contrary is pretty evident from what is now going on with a view to the approaching elections, unless these distresses produce a change of conduct. Whether the Catholic Association is acting in the best way for their own purposes, is another question; but if I were an Irish Catholic, I should consider myself as in a state of war with the English Government, and think only of the means of reducing to submission an enemy whom I could never hope to gain by conciliation. But this advice I should be very sorry to give to the Irish Catholics;

and as I could honestly give no other with a view to *their* interests, I should certainly remain silent.[18]

Brougham was an emancipationist, but he always treated the Irish question as a pawn in the party game. In 1810, when the Whigs had hopes of office, he had sternly advised Grey not to throw away everything for the sake of making Catholic relief a condition of coming in. Now he was disturbed lest Whig intransigence lock Canning within the Tory fortress. Grey, as he told Brougham in 1824, believed that Canning would never do anything on the Catholic issue 'but by accident or compulsion'.[19] Brougham believed that he could be prised away from Toryism. The ground between the two men was, or so it seemed, narrow. But when, early in 1827, Lord Liverpool suffered a stroke and resigned the premiership, it proved to be unbridgeable.

* * *

Lord Liverpool suffered his stroke on 17 February. It was some weeks before it was evident that he would not recover, and while men speculated on the future the Whig rulers took counsel together. Their discussions fixed on one supreme question: what to do about Catholic emancipation. Liverpool's administration had preserved its semblance of unity by treating the issue, in the language of the day, as an 'open question'. The government took no official line and each minister was free to speak and vote, as we should say today, according to his 'conscience'. It was an admirable device for mixing the oil of Eldon with the vinegar of Canning; but it brought no succour to the Irish, for it was, in truth, the easiest and least honourable means of doing nothing. At a number of meetings held early in March, by which time it was becoming obvious that George IV would have to send for Canning to succeed Liverpool, the Whigs came to an agreement that they would offer unqualified opposition to any new government formed on the basis of leaving Catholic emancipation an 'open question'. Brougham lent himself whole-heartedly to the agreement. The time had come, he told John Allen, for the Whigs to shake off their stupor and stand forth as a united party of principle.

Assuming that Canning plays the shabby game of place hunting and consents to a divided & neutralised govt. our course is plain. We have done quite enough, God wot, to show our disinterested feelings & our candour. We have supported him & his part of the Govt, when we could have turned them out, or left them to the mercy of their colleagues of the ultra persuasion (which would possibly have hanged them). Are we to go on making fools of ourselves & of the country? We surely have a right now to act once more as a party, and in reorganising, or rather forming on new principles adapted to the times & circumstances, an efficient party, we shall do our duty & regain the respect & influence we have lost.[20]

It was settled that Brougham should move an address to the Crown advising in the strongest language against the perpetuation of a divided administration. Brougham was playing a double game. There is little doubt that he inspired the leader in *The Times* of 27 February which looked forward to an alliance between Lansdowne and Canning, the former 'stipulating only for the ministerial support of the Catholic question, and not rendering the admission of many of his friends a *sine qua non*'.[21] Yet secretly Brougham and Lansdowne were assuring Canning that he would receive Whig support even if he did not make Catholic relief a test of office.[22]

In mid-March Brougham quit London to join the northern circuit, happy in the knowledge that the King would not send for a new prime minister for some weeks. Before leaving he instructed his Whig colleague, Sir Robert Wilson, to assure Canning, whenever the assurance should be appropriate, of his certain support and of his entire lack of interest in office for himself. He was not long away from Westminster before he began to fret. What if Canning, suspicious of the fragility of Whig support, should take fright and turn outright Tory to preserve his place? 'Is it possible Canning can dream of safety for six weeks if he thinks of taking office with the Ultras and no arrangement?' he wrote nervously to Wilson from York. 'Or is it possible he could doubt of our entire and cordial support if he holds out? For my own part I will only say that I am ready to back him in whatever way he himself would deem most effectual. It is our duty and we shall all be found at our posts.'[23]

Brougham was still in the north when the King asked Canning to form a government on 10 April. Canning first attempted to continue the existing Tory ministry in its integrity. Neither Peel nor the Duke of Wellington would serve under him and their example was followed by four other 'Protestant' members of Liverpool's cabinet. Canning then opened negotiations with Lansdowne, having obtained the King's consent to them, according to Greville, by playing what may be called his 'Brougham card'.

> Brougham wrote to Canning and made him an unqualified offer of support, and when the King asked Canning how he was to obtain support enough to carry on the Government, he pulled this letter out of his pocket, gave it him, and said, 'Sir, your Father broke the domination of the Whigs; I hope Y.M. will not endure that of the Tories'. 'No,' said the King; 'I'll be damned if I do'; and he made him Minister. This Canning told Melbourne himself.[24]

Brougham came quickly up to London, determined that the negotiations should not fail. 'A greater or more ruinous error never was yet committed, or one more fatal to the Catholic question,' he wrote to Lord Althorp, who inclined towards Grey's position, 'than by holding out on subordinate points and punctilios of honour, to throw open again the Cabinet to the ultra-Tories.'[25] Feeling in the Whig camp was running high in favour of coalition. 'It is right I should state to you,' Sir James Macdonald, the Whig member for Calne, had written to Lansdowne on 14 April, the day before Brougham's return, 'that, with the exception of some crotchets of Lord Grey's, which vary every hour, there seems to exist hardly any difference among those called the Opposition, of the necessity of your doing more than giving your support to a Government that should be formed *without any restrictions* on the Catholic question. Duncannon [the whip], backed by Lord Sefton and some of the most unlikely men, are of opinion that nineteen in twenty so think.' The Irish members, he added, 'would be in perfect despair if, when all that is Orange and illiberal is arrayed against Canning, a distrust of the man were to limit your powerful aid to a mere support'.[26] Lansdowne, whom Brougham described as 'as thoroughly honest and humble as a man can be',[27] could not bring himself to sell Whiggery's proud name so cheaply. On 20 April negotiations with Canning were broken off, wrecked on what Brougham would have called the punctilio of standing out, against the King's insistence that to preserve some balance in an overwhelmingly 'Catholic' government the Irish lord-lieutenant and secretary should both be 'Protestants', in favour of all the offices in the Irish executive being filled by pro-Catholics.

Lansdowne left London for the country believing that the business was over. He underestimated Brougham, who now took command of

C. H. Lear's drawing of Brougham in 1857,
when he was aged seventy-nine.

Last two pages from a letter written, in his notoriously illegible hand, by Brougham to John Allen in 1835, after he had been omitted from Lord Melbourne's cabinet: '. . . and most of them as individuals my hearty pity—if not contempt. My principles will require the one—& justice towards myself the other course. That any thing short of the absolute necessity of the case could ever have made me enter the same cabinet with them—you must thus plainly see to have been impossible. I don't envy them what Ld Holland calls their "*triumphant* return" to office (power they will have none). But they will as soon

[manuscript letter in cursive, signed H. B.]

as they are strong enough to stand alone have some questions to answer respecting me, & if I dont put these, others will. No man can be expected so far to forget what he owes to himself as to be quiet a moment longer than the necessity of repelling the common enemy requires. They (the ministers) are now too weak to make any shake a safe thing. I hope they will soon be strong enough to bear it, and then we shall ascertain how far all parties—& the country indeed—are to be made playthings to amuse Lord Grey's children.'

TO THE TEMPLE OF FAME.

Mr. Punch (with the Greatest Respect). "AFTER YOU, MY LORD!"

A *Punch* cartoon of 23 October, 1857, makes gentle fun of
Brougham's supposedly insatiable ambition. In 1857 Brougham
took the lead in founding the National Association for the
Promotion of Social Sciences.

events. 'My support in the House of Commons,' Brougham told Campbell, 'is of much more importance than Lansdowne's in the House of Lords.'[28] Wilson and Brougham, the latter described by Mrs Michael Angelo Taylor as being 'in a state of insanity' over Lansdowne's timidity,[29] hastily rounded up about thirty or forty sympathizers at Brooks's Club, where Brougham harangued them on the folly of deserting Canning. As Chester New put it, 'Brougham's remarkable gift for anger was exceeded only by his gift for conveying anger to others',[30] and the meeting was a noisy affair. Brougham offended the sensibilities of those Whigs, like Lord Essex, who deplored the settling of matters of high politics, not at Lansdowne House or Devonshire House or Burlington House, but 'at a club'.[31] The meeting, however, achieved Brougham's purpose. It sent a delegation to remonstrate with Lansdowne and to urge him to renew the negotiations. The following day Brougham wrote in high spirits to Creevey.

> As I am sure by instinct that you are with the true and faithful servants of the Lord in this time of our trial, and not with the vain and foolish Malignants, I write to say that the negociation was off last night, and we had a row at Brooks's (which I own I created) and the negociation is on again to-day, with a fair prospect of success. These difficulties come from some of our friends being still in the year 1780 . . . My principle is—*anything* to lock the door for ever on Eldon and Co.[32]

When Creevey replied that he was in favour of supporting, but not joining, Canning, and that he had 'an instinctive horror of the very name of coalition',[33] Brougham upbraided him for being 'a rural politician'. 'How *can* you . . . possibly think that the Ministry—or any Ministry—can stand on volunteer and candid support? My only principle is:—"Lock the door on Eldon and Co."; and this can only be done by joining C.'[34] That was the prevailing sentiment at the Brooks's Club meeting and those who had attended it fired off letters to Canning and Lansdowne. Sir Francis Burdett's remonstrance to Lansdowne might have been written by Brougham himself.

> A greedy, bigoted, narrow-minded faction has like a nightmare oppressed the country ever since the commencement of the reign of George III to the present time, and so exhausted it, or possessed themselves of its strength, that it had lost the power, and almost the

will, to shake it off. This their strength, however, probably produced their overthrow, for presuming too far, thinking they could
not be got rid of, when no one else could, they unseated themselves;
having done so, are we to endeavour to set them up again?[35]

The sentiment spread far beyond the walls of Brooks's. The Duke of
Devonshire, who conducted the renewed negotiations with Canning
until Lansdowne returned to town on the 25th, was sickened by 'the
absurd way in which our wretched whigs always cut their own
throats',[36] and Cockburn reported that in Edinburgh 'the decided
opinion of the wise' was that the Whigs had a duty 'to take office and
do what good they can, though with the minimum of power'.[37]

Arrangements were concluded by Lansdowne and Canning when
they met again on 27 April. Most of the Whig opposition was willing,
with varying degrees of enthusiasm, to follow Brougham in accepting
almost any terms in order to block the return to office of the ultra
Tories. Canning got by far the better of the horse-trading. He relented
on the Irish executive to the extent of appointing William Lamb, a
pro-Catholic, secretary, but everywhere else he got his own way. Only
three Whigs were given cabinet places—Lansdowne as home secretary, Tierney as master of the mint, and Lord Carlisle as privy
seal—and they were not to take them up until near the close of the
current parliamentary session. They took office, too, at a price.
Catholic emancipation was to remain an 'open question', while
ministers were to unite in opposition to parliamentary reform and the
repeal of the Test and Corporation Acts (ancient statutes which laid
upon Dissenters civil disabilities akin to, but less severe than, those
imposed upon Roman Catholics). Grey and his small band of
supporters, including the Duke of Bedford, Lord Rosslyn, Edward
Ellice and Lord John Russell, watched in dismay the bulk of the
opposition cross the floor of the Commons. 'I see our friends have at
last taken their places in the tail of this new Comet,' Ellice wrote to
Grey,[38] while Russell complained of Lansdowne's 'negligent and
unnecessary sacrifice of our importance as a party'.[39] Towards
Lansdowne, Russell's father, the Duke of Bedford, was more charit-
ably condescending. 'I do not blame Lansdowne,' he wrote to Lord
John, 'because I am sure he has acted from motives of the highest
honour, but I do very sincerely pity him . . . He has been the victim
and dupe of the two greatest rogues (politically speaking) in the
kingdom . . . I consider the hope of carrying the Catholic question

now at an end.'[40] In the House of Lords Grey delivered an anti-coalition speech so venomous that Canning said he contemplated taking a peerage in order to answer it.[41]

There was justice, from their point of view, in the anger which Grey and the 'Malignants', as the coalition Whigs took to calling them, bore Brougham. Brougham's discovering in Canning the saviour of the country from Toryism was dislocating. For twenty years he had vied with Grey to find language sufficient to describe the perfidy which would cling to men of liberal sentiments who made common cause with the arch-defender of the unreformed constitution; as recently as 1825 they had concurred in dismissing as impossible rumours that Lansdowne and Canning were to join forces.[42] Brougham, it is true, had lately made it his purpose to praise Canning in order to disrupt the Tory party, but it was reasonable for Grey to expect that the outcome of the strategy, if it were successful, would be a government with the power to implement Whig policy. Was it not Brougham, after all, who, when the possibility of a Whig government had flitted across the political stage in 1822, had urged the necessity of the Whigs' taking a forward line on subjects of domestic policy, not excluding parliamentary reform? What was Grey, then, to make of the alliance which Brougham, more than anyone else, had now brought into existence? Catholic emancipation remained at the idle mercy of a divided administration and parliamentary reform was proscribed. It was, in Grey's view, the humiliation of a great party in the state, proud of its antecedents as the defender of the rights of the people and the champion of political and civil liberty, to lend its name and a few of its eminent persons to so illiberal a cause as Canning's patchwork government. However much Grey's critics made of his personal distaste for Canning, his course was determined by his jealous regard for the integrity of Whiggery. Grey acted in the tradition of the Rockingham Whigs who, in the latter part of the 18th century, had boldly adopted the policy of 'forcing the closet', of taking office only if the sovereign accepted *their* men and *their* measures. Brougham scorned the high road which Grey travelled.

I differ with the great men of 1784, who preferred saving their party & personal honour on a punctilio with the King & Pitt & Lord Shelburne, to doing their duty, & the day after joined their enemy Lord North. I equally, or almost so, differ with the great men of 1809 & 11 & 12 in their cursed punctilios with the Regent & Moira

. . . Don't let us again ride the same fiery *Grey* charger (called Hotspur). By the popularity of individuals, their useful measures of reform & retrenchment & improving the people, and their liberal policy at home & abroad, we have regained nearly all the ground lost [in 1809–12], but *hope* is wanting to give us weight in the country. I admit things are on a new foot, & the old party arrangements, become nearly useless, are remodelled. The advantage is the same, don't lets quarrel about names & associations.

The temptation to shut our eyes & pocket all we can is very strong at present. A year hence after so long a cooperation with our new & *excellent allies*—I will so call them for I know it to be their due—the power we shall have will be tenfold, & the king will not then be able to try tricks with us. Do not all minor considers, yield to this?[43]

Canning died less than four months after taking office as prime minister. Had he lived Brougham might have been proved right in the long run. From its unpromising beginnings the Whig/Canningite experiment might have grown into a strong and enduring agency for liberal policy. As it was, the Whigs got nothing for their pains in 1827. While Brougham went about boasting of his influence on the government, Grey and his friends pointed to the series of 'Protestant' appointments which Canning's government inflicted on Ireland. That government, formed in the middle of a parliamentary session and ended so abruptly by Canning's death in August, had not the time to yield the legislative fruit which Brougham expected to harvest. But from the beginning the two partners in the experiment lived uneasily with one another, and when the Whigs threatened to bolt on Lord John Rusell's motion to disfranchise the corrupt borough of Penryn and transfer its representation to Manchester, Canning gave a hint of his rigidity by warning them 'that he was clinging to the tree [i.e. the King], but that they were only hanging to his feet'.[44]

Brougham's personal relations with Canning quickly soured. He had hoped to be given the office of attorney-general,[45] and when the offer was not made he discredited himself by telling the world that he had turned it down, a silly lie, since everyone knew that the King's animosity towards him put the appointment out of the question. Brougham's pesterings on his own behalf (for he was bitter at his exclusion) and on behalf of his Whig friends (for they constantly pressed Canning to provide places for more of them) eventually drove Canning to exclaim, 'Damn him, he shall have my place!'.[46] Brougham's influence over Canning, had the latter lived, is unlikely to have been commanding. He promoted junction with Canning on two principal grounds, that it would advance the Catholic cause and that it would be the death-blow to ultra-Toryism. On both tests events showed Grey's judgement to have been the finer. In 1828 the old Tories clambered back into office under the Duke of Wellington, and Catholic emancipation, when it came in 1829, was the concession wrung fom the Duke's 'Protestant' government by exhibition of the Catholic Association's power to render the existing system of exclusion unworkable.

*   *   *

Years afterwards Brougham wrote that his quarrel with Grey in 1827 was the only serious difference the two men had in the course of a long and unusually intimate friendship and that the coolness it produced did not last. 'Grey, with his usual fairness and candour, gave me credit for the perfectly unselfish motives which had actuated me; and not very long after the Canning Government was formed, we were as firm friends as ever.'[47] The assertion was false on two counts. In 1834 the two men had an even more painful falling out than they had in 1827; and Brougham exaggerated the degree to which his friendship with Grey, after 1827, recovered its former confidential ground.

Brougham vexed everyone by bragging that his zeal for the success of Canning's government was entirely disinterested. 'I wish,' Creevey wrote to Lord Sefton, 'you could see the veins of Lord Grey's forehead swell and hear his snorting at Brougham's demand for justice to his *pure disinterested motives*.'[48] Having betrayed his resentment at not being made attorney-general, Brougham merely appeared ridiculous when he represented his refusal to become Chief Baron of the Court of Exchequer as virtuous self-denial. It is true that he turned down a secure income of £7,000 for life, but no one, including himself, doubted for a moment that Canning's object was to remove him from the House of Commons. Since April Brougham had perched ominously on what was called the 'Hill Fort', on the third bench behind ministers, where, as he grandly recalled, 'Pitt used to sit while supporting the Addington ministry'. Canning, who had not forgotten what Pitt did to Addington, attempted to bribe Brougham by pointing out that the office of Chief Baron was halfway house to becoming lord chancellor. 'Yes,' Brougham replied. 'But you deprive me of the horses to take me on.'[49]

When Canning died the Earl of Goderich, a fellow liberal Tory, succeeded him. One of the new prime minister's first acts was to appoint John Herries, a dismal economist and a narrow-minded 'Protestant', chancellor of the exchequer. The appointment was an affront to the Whig partners in the coalition and Lansdowne, Carlisle and Tierney were on the verge of resigning if Herries were confirmed in office. They might have done so, had they understood what was from the beginning evident to Lord Grey, that the Tory 'Protestants' in Goderich's government looked upon the continuance of the coalition as the best means of postponing Catholic emancipation. Lord Bexley used the argument to encourage Herries to be resolute in overcoming the difficulty of conciliating Lansdowne and the waverers. 'As long as they act with you the Whig party will be too much divided to be formidable, and we have the best chance possible (though certainly a doubtful one) of the Catholic question being kept quiet for some time.'[50] Brougham, although he owned that he 'abhorred' Herries, became almost frantic to prevent the break-up of the government.

> What nicety-mongers, what refiners . . . are we at the mercy of? The king has every wish to keep well with us . . . our moderate Tory Colleagues, with whom I correspond, as Dudley & Palmerston & I believe Huskisson are quite *fond* of us. In God's name let us not throw away our true & honest game. *I* am in fact the only one of the whole party who am excluded by the King's prejudices, but I therefore am the more anxious to keep all right. *My* reward is to be the vast improvements in the Law . . . which I am sure I can carry next session in the present happy junction of affairs, & for the prospect of which & for the good of our party I have refused the most brilliant & secure emolument in my profession, too—but out of the H. of Coms. & therefore I thought forbidden to me in C.'s precarious health, a presentiment too soon realised.[51]

One of the objections to Herries was that he lay under the imputation of having made his fortune illicitly in the money market. Brougham allowed that it would not do to have 'this *stockjobber* crammed down our throats' unless he cleared himself,[52] but he ignored the political objection to Herries and let Goderich know, without consulting Lansdowne, that the Whigs would in the end swallow him. It was secretiveness of that kind that John Arthur Roebuck, the Benthamite radical who came to know Brougham well in the 1830s, had in mind when he described him as 'self-willed and self-confiding'.[53] Lansdowne, who had once before, in April, had to endure Brougham's preemptive meddling, reproached him for his want of candour.

> I have as sincere a deference for your judgment as that of any man, but I think it right you should know that in the last discussions respecting an appointment which I had *first* been led to consider as *most objectionable*, by a statement of yours which had been communicated to me, I was met by the observation I could not deny, that *you* were well known to be quite ready to acquiesce in it; precisely as in the first negotiation with Canning, in attempting to obtain some security, not for personal objects of my own, but for the public, as far as Ireland was concerned, I was met by the statement, pretty well founded, that my Whig friends in St James's Street were ready to join Government on any terms.
>
> These circumstances increase the embarrassment of a position otherwise difficult enough. I am willing to hope for the public what has been recently done may be for the best. For my personal credit and character I must take my chance for the present, and take care of it myself for the future. I have no right to expect that it should be the concern of others.[54]

Brougham's advice prevailed; the Whig ministers bowed to Herries' appointment. Goderich's government, however, never recovered from its acrimonious beginnings. Squabbles over patronage marked the whole of its existence and when the King refused to accept Lord Althorp as chairman of the Commons' finance committee or Lord Holland as foreign secretary the coalition fell apart. In January, grateful to give up a position which his gifts ill fitted him to fill, Goderich resigned in tears, and the two wings of the Tory party made their peace and joined together to serve under the Duke of Wellington.

That Brougham should have cared so distractedly for the coalition is difficult to explain. The answer cannot be his hopes for law reform, although he spent much time in the autumn of 1827 preparing the mighty speech which he delivered on the subject early in 1828. Did he expect eventually to claw his way to the leadership of the coalition? There are no clues to answer the question. Did he simply pale at the thought that a coalition which was so largely his creation should, by failing, expose him to the taunt of misjudgement? Even he would not have been so indiscreet as to disclose such a motive. No doubt it fed his vanity to pretend that he had the ear of the King, and that, despite describing his position on the Hill Fort as 'awkward and anomalous',[55] he was privy enough to cabinet intentions to invite his Whig friends 'pray . . . for a moment to consider what kinds of reforms you will have carried next session'.[56] Yet the most probable explanation is that he had simply worked himself into a froth of anti-Toryism. Lord Eldon and his gang had been ejected. They must not be allowed to return. The failure of Lord Grey and his circle to seize upon the exclusion of the ultras as the one, over-riding political object of the day lowered them, Brougham told John Allen, in his respect.

> If the king would take some of them in, their chief objection would be removed. They can't be in office and they don't like to lose the importance, which I fully admit, leaders of the opposition always have far more than followers of a ministry. But who is entitled to act on this selfish view? I wish to know whether any one man in either house gives up more of that kind of gratification than I do, or at least did in becoming a private under Canning. It makes perhaps some little difference now, but I had no idea of Canning's dying when I did so. What is the compensation? The inestimable benefit of keeping out the Ultras and getting for the country, if not the best possible Govt., at least the best the King & country are ready to take. I say country as well as King. You are woefully mistaken if you think a true Whig govt. would stand long. My belief is that time may come, but it has not yet arrived, and if the King had sent for me, I should have said 'Send for Goderich & don't tell you saw me'.
>
> As for the Whigs having 'got a few baubles' that is a way of speaking . . . Rely on it the King will become more favourable & the country will come round. At any rate we are better than with the ultras, and may I never *again* be in an opposition such as the men you speak of made me pass my best years in, & would do so tomorrow if they could, viz, constant abuse of each other & as constant a refusal to make head against the enemy, except on some infinitely small matter once a year.[57]

Allen might well have concluded, incoherent and self-regarding as Brougham's ravings had become, that he meant to be rid of the Whig connection for ever. Yet Brougham's ardour for the coalition did not blind him to the importance of retaining Grey's friendship and confidence. It led him, however, to take a false step. When Canning died he wrote to Grey that he hoped the principal obstacle in the way of Grey's supporting the coalition was now removed. It was an insulting suggestion, entirely casting aside Grey's objections to what from the beginning he had looked upon as a misalliance deeply dishonouring to the traditions and purposes of the Whig party. Grey sent him a frosty reply.

> The recollections of the last session are indeed most painful, and the more so as the causes of them are, I fear, not likely soon to be removed. The difference of opinion which then produced the dissolution of the party in the support of which my whole public life had been spent, could not fail to extend itself to the consequences of that unfortunate event; and it is a matter rather of regret than of surprise that our views of what the present state of affairs may require each of us to do should not agree. But I will not enter into any discussion, which would be useless, as affording little probability of bringing us nearer together.

Grey did not deny that from long experience and observation of Canning's conduct he had formed a rooted distrust of him.

> But the impossibility, in which I found myself, of supporting the new Government, did not arise so much from personal objections to him as from those which I felt to the principle on which the Administration was formed. Those objections are rather increased than diminished by all I hear of the manner in which the vacancies [presumably a reference to Herries] occasioned by Canning's death are likely to be supplied . . . I must remain, therefore, in the same position, supporting such measures as are consistent with my principles, and opposing, without any inducement to forbearance, whatever may appear to militate against them.[58]

Grey passed both Brougham's letter and his own reply to Lord Rosslyn, himself as deeply opposed to the junction with Canning as Grey. Rosslyn sought to prevent a breach between two of his oldest friends by urging Grey to consider that Brougham's motive in writing to him as he had done was to mend broken fences.[59]

No doubt Brougham would have liked to keep all his friendships in repair; once rebuffed, however, he turned to abusing Grey in violent language. 'Ld. G. is a goose,' he wrote to John Allen, '& does nothing but blubber & take physic.'[60] He attempted, and the attempt merely made him appear foolish, to detach Rosslyn from Grey by holding out the prospect of a seat in the cabinet. Grey and Rosslyn made capital fun of Brougham's supposing that government appointments were his province. 'I must revert to the persuasion,' Rosslyn wrote, 'that Brougham has made this proposal ... without any authority or encouragement from Ministers; but it is beyond me to form even a conjecture with respect to his motives.'[61] Brougham hinted that the Whigs' scheme of bringing Lord Holland into the cabinet (Goderich had done no more than allow the possibility some time in the future) depended on Rosslyn, since Holland, he said, would not come in without him. Such brazen dissembling was more than Rosslyn could bear in silence.

> I did not receive your letter of Friday till last night [he wrote to Brougham], and I must confess that it greatly surprised me ... I have no hesitation in replying to it with perfect frankness. I have had no reason to believe that it has ever been in the contemplation of ministers to offer me the Ordnance, and I have heard from various quarters that the same high authority which has excluded you from the great offices in your own profession to which your talents and influence entitled you to aspire, is no less adverse to the admission of Lord Holland into the Cabinet. But be that as it may, I cannot bring myself to believe that his acceptance of office, if it were offered to him, could in any way be influenced by the decision of so inconsiderable a person as myself, more especially as we have had no communication upon politics, and I know that everything I have said or done since the formation of Canning's Government has met with his disapprobation.

Rosslyn would not abandon Lord Grey. 'The very circumstance that he appears to have been thrown over by many of his friends, is with me an additional motive for adhering to him.' Brougham and the coalition Whigs had, by their pusillanimous behaviour, gravely damaged the cause of Catholic emancipation.

> I perhaps attach more importance than you are supposed to do to the success of the Irish question; but, believing as I do that the peace and security of the empire do mainly depend upon it, it gives me very painful forebodings to observe that in every single instance the patronage of Government has been exerted in a manner to support and encourage the declared enemies of that cause, and to

indicate either the indifference, or, as I believe, the weakness, of its friends.[62]

Brougham also invented the story that Grey and Rosslyn were leaguing themselves with Lord Bathurst and the ultra Tories in a sort of systematic opposition to the government. 'Can any man in his senses comprehend Ld Grey being hand in glove with the Bathursts etc.,' he asked Allen, 'a set he could not go one step with in office, unless he or they gave up all their principles?'[63] Parliament had not met since Canning's death, so that no opportunity for such an opposition to express itself had arisen. Once again Rosslyn was moved to defend himself and Grey against a baseless charge. 'You are entirely mistaken with respect to Grey and me,' he lectured Brougham; 'we are engaged with no Opposition or other political party, but disposed to persist in supporting the principles upon which we have been acting for so many years, and pursuing steadily, as we have done, the great objects to which every personal consideration has been sacrificed.'[64]

By December Brougham's stock with the old Whigs was depleted. As Goderich's ministry fell apart, and his Whig colleagues, unable to secure for their friends the places to which they believed their cooperation entitled them, came to feel that they had been duped by Canning and the King, Brougham lashed out in angry frustration at all sides.

Brougham was evidently in the state you described him in town [Ellice wrote to Grey on 16 December]. Abusing the objects of the favour & the patronage of the ministry, but still having no patience with those who ventured to find the most fault with the Government. I told his Brother, as all parties feared & hated him, it would end in a general league to proscribe him—that he would then lose his temper, talk a little too much . . . and get shot in some personal squabble. And if his disappointments, & the failure of all his intrigues & calculations, have a little time to work upon his Temper, nothing can contain it.[65]

Grey's creed, Creevey reported, was that 'Brougham must *blow up*, that he is in so many people's power with his lies of different kinds, that one fine day they will be out'.[66] Rosslyn had come to the same sorry conclusion. 'I lean rather to the opinion that his uneasiness and dissatisfaction with himself and discontent with his own situation does amount nearly to madness.'[67] Brougham raged at seeing Stephen Lushington, an anti-slavery colleague and a founder member of the SDUK, passed over for a legal promotion and Grey thought that this proof of his inability to influence the government in its disposal of patronage explained what he, too, had come to call Brougham's 'madness'.[68] Even Lord Holland, one of the few Whigs to retain hopes of Brougham's becoming leader of the party, acknowledged, as the Duke of Bedford informed Grey, that he was 'wholly devoid of *truth*'. 'Ld Hd says he is firmly persuaded that he is mad, which is the only way he can account for his Conduct. I don't know whether I ought to say I fear, but I believe it is so.'[69] From the autumn of 1827 onwards, there were always to be people, friends and foes alike, ready to pronounce Brougham 'mad'.

By the time that the Duke of Wellington formed his government in the last week of January 1828, Grey had ceased to write to Brougham. A coda to their quarrel, however, had still to be played. Since October Brougham had been spreading the tale that Grey, in casual gossip at the Doncaster race meeting, had said to the Marquess of Cleveland, Brougham's borough patron, that the substance of his opposition to Canning's government was that it was too favourable to the people. Brougham gave the story to Lansdowne on 22 October.

> I know not if Lord Holland has written to you the fact (on the authority of Lord Darlington [Cleveland's son], far too accurate to leave any hope of its being untrue) that Lord Grey's ground of difference resolves itself into the Government being popular and consulting public opinion instead of the feelings of the aristocracy, which he thinks requires support and is resolved to stand by as against the Government . . . It is really as if he had taken up his own party expression of 'his order', and was determined to make it his creed merely because it was attacked. I never have felt in my life more pain than in making the avowal which such conduct wrings from me, viz., that I no longer feel anxious as before about the line he takes.[70]

The first Grey heard of it was in February. He wrote at once to Cleveland asking for a contradiction. Cleveland, to refresh his memory, applied to Brougham. What, he asked, had been the gist of the conversation with Grey which he had reported to Brougham? Brougham gave Cleveland the version he had given Lansdowne, adding that 'respecting Lord Grey (in case you see him again on this matter) . . . he is mistaken, or rather I believe greatly & wilfully misinformed by some designing people, if he thinks I have ever taken any part against him'.[71] Cleveland sent Brougham's letter to Grey, who was unmollified by it and again asked Cleveland for an 'unequivocal' denial of the reported conversation. As for Brougham's statement that he had been a constant defender of his old leader, 'I do not think,' Grey wrote, 'it necessary to advert'. To Grey it was manifest that Brougham had been spreading the slander to 'prejudice' him.[72] Cleveland wrote by return of post to deny explicitly that he had repeated the conversation in the offensive manner which had reached Grey's ears. Grey was content with Cleveland's denial, but he had still to receive a satisfactory statement from Brougham. 'As matters now stand,' he told Cleveland, 'I must admit that all confidential intercourse between Mr Brougham and me is suspended.'[73]

There is no telling who had the truth in this dispute. From what we know of Grey's lofty regard for 'his order', as he habitually put it, and his contempt for Canning's 'speechifying' and running after popular approval, it would be rash to assume Brougham's dishonesty. Privately he maintained that what Grey considered ill-treatment was 'being taken at his word'.[74] He refused to make the unqualified contradiction which Grey required. 'Does Ld G desire me,' he asked Cleveland, 'to say not only that I never imputed to him anything of the kind, but that his informant grossly & wilfully invented words for me without a colour of foundation? I really cannot say so, for I am quite persuaded that a very honest mistake may have been the cause of the misunderstanding.'[75] Creevey, who saw much of the correspondence Cleveland had with both Grey and Brougham, thought that no one who had not seen it could conceive of Brougham's 'low, lying, dirty shuffling villainy'.

> He attempts to make out that the words are vague and may not warrant the construction put upon them, and the Lord knows what besides. He goes into fresh lies as to his uniform support of Grey's character, and how he silenced *three* London channels of abuse of him, and was only too late by half an hour in not stopping the hostile article in the *Edinburgh Review*, and concludes with a warning against michievous tale-bearers, who, for their own purposes, would make mischief between Grey and him.[76]

Creevey's testimony was not third-party. For some time the intimacy which he and Brougham had first shared in Edinburgh twenty-five years before had been evaporating. In the autumn of 1827 it disappeared altogether. Brougham and Creevey had over the years delighted to sprinkle their correspondence with irreverent nicknames for the good and the great—'Mrs Cole' for Tierney, 'the Beau' for Wellington, 'Mouldy' for Vansittart, 'the Stale' or 'Snoutch' for Lord Grenville. Brougham's turn now came. Creevey, thick with Grey and the 'Malignants', fixed upon him the name of 'Arch-Fiend'.

Grey, like Creevey, bristled at Brougham's recourse to an 'honest mistake' as the cause of their quarrel, since he knew that Brougham had his letter of August in which his objections to Canning's government were clearly stated. Nevertheless, since Brougham went halfway to meeting him by declaring that he had intended nothing to his 'prejudice', the matter, Grey told Cleveland, was closed.

> This declaration relieves me from all further difficulty; & though, after what happened last year, I find myself under the necessity of standing aloof from any political connection, there can no longer be any obstacle, on my part, to our being again, in every other respect, on the same terms as before this unfortunate misunderstanding.[77]

For long years afterwards the recollection, perhaps guilty, of the events of 1827 had power to disturb Brougham's peace of mind. In 1852, when Lord Grey had long lain buried and Brougham had ceased to have any intimate bond with the Whig party, he was still exercised to justify his actions. In a letter to Grey's son he maintained that the coalition with Canning had *alone* broken the Tory party and, after a short interval, brought the Whigs into office in 1830. Moreover, Lord Grey—'I could prove it to you'—had come very near to supporting the coalition.[78] If Brougham was seeking absolution, he did not receive it. General Grey reminded him, with some justice, that it was Wellington's *volte face* in introducing Catholic emancipation that brought down Toryism. And his father's sorrow at the conduct of the coalition Whigs was not in question.

> I know, on the contrary, that he was deeply hurt at their defection . . . & that in acting as they did, they violated all his notions of what became a great Party in accepting office. This, he always thought, they could only do honourably *as a Party*, & with full power to carry their principles into effect. Surely such were not the conditions under which the Whigs joined Mr Canning, who was even *insulting*

in the manner in which he proclaimed that his govt. was formed on the principles of Lord Liverpool's, & that his opinions on the principal questions which had so long divided parties had undergone no change.[79]

11

Pride and Fall

On a famous night in the House of Commons in November 1830, after the House had voted to bring down the Duke of Wellington's Tory government, but before Lord Grey had fulfilled King William IV's commission to form a Whig one, Brougham, himself at the very centre of speculation about the new ministry, rose to say that he intended, whatever administration might be formed, to press forward, independent of party, the parliamentary reform motion he had tabled before the House. The tone which he adopted startled his audience. He spoke as if he expected to be heard, not as a mere Whig, not as a mere party leader, hardly even as a mere politician. Political trafficking, his tone suggested, might safely be left to lesser men like Lord Grey and Lord Althorp, each of whom on the same night announced that he had no reform plan to propose. Brougham spoke from a high vantage point. He was the newly elected member for Yorkshire. More than that, he was the member for all those people who cared about the abolition of slavery, the extension of education, the reform of the law—all the great subjects with which, acting nearly alone, he had invested the Whig party. That section of the public whose voice had been so loudly heard at the late elections knew, when it looked to the Whigs to take up the torch of reform, whom it had to thank for the revival of its aspirations. By his immense correspondence with the leaders of liberal opinion in the provinces, Brougham had identified himself with their causes. In their eyes he stood remote from the contentions of party, divested of the very character of a partisan. James Losh, the Tyneside coal-owner and barrister who for thirty years took a leading part in almost every reform movement, moral and physical, in the north-east, and who came to know Brougham well through his work in education, could never be brought to believe rumours drifting up from London that Brougham would sacrifice principles to personal interest. So, in 1828, he scorned reports that Brougham was making terms with Wellington's government. 'That this extraordinary man is ambitious it would be absurd to deny, but his ambition is of a kind not to be satisfied by the exchange of character and the power of diffusing useful knowledge and guiding public opinion, for the mere possession of high rank and the patronage and emoluments of office.'[1] Losh's admiration of Brougham was unqualified. He knew that Brougham's enemies said that he began many things and finished nothing, but the truth was that he neither began nor finished. Destined by Providence to rouse and direct the energies of an improving nation, he availed himself of the feelings and wants of his fellow men: 'he points their feelings to proper objects and shows them how their wants may be supplied'.[2]

How different was Brougham's reputation at Westminster! How impossible was it for those colleagues who had suffered the shifts and turns of his restless ambition, the contorted self-pleadings of his invincible pride, to grasp, let alone comprehend, the favour which the public, as it had not done since the days of Chatham, so expectantly bestowed upon him! Since 1827 the divergence between the public's trust in him and the party's distrust of him had widened into a chasm. Down to 1827 men at Westminster asked of Brougham, 'What will he become?'; after 1827 they asked, 'What is to become of him?' When, in February 1827, the Whigs put Brougham forward to address the Crown for an undivided administration, they acknowledged that, for all his shortcomings, he was yet their unrivalled leader in the House of Commons. Three years later, scarcely a dissenting murmur was heard when they gave the palm to Lord Althorp.

On 2 January 1828 Charles Greville recorded his impressions of a visit to Lord Cowper's Hertfordshire seat of Panshanger. Brougham was also a guest there and for two days he captivated Greville, who had rarely come across such facility in conversation, such varied and extensive information in one mind, such powers of sarcasm unblemished by ill-humour, or such childish gaiety and animal spirits. No man had ever impressed him with such an idea of his superiority over all others. As another of Lord Cowper's guests, the poet Rogers, remarked on the morning of Brougham's departure, 'this morning Solon, Lycurgus, Demosthenes, Archimedes, Sir Isaac Newton, Lord Chesterfield, and a great many more went away in one post chaise'. Yet even with the experience of Brougham's brilliance fresh in his memory, Greville drew a moral lesson from the political fate which, even then it was clear, awaited him.

After all, Brougham is only a living and very remarkable instance of the inefficacy of the most splendid talents, unless they are accompanied with other qualities, which scarcely admit of definition, but which must serve the same purpose that ballast does for a ship. Brougham has prospered to a certain degree; he has a great reputation and he makes a considerable income at the Bar; but as an advocate he is left behind by men of far inferior capacity, and whose names are hardly known beyond the precincts of their Courts or the boundaries of their Circuits. As a Statesman he is not considered eligible for the highest offices, and however he may be admired or feared as an Orator or Debater, he neither commands respect by his character nor inspires confidence by his genius, and in this contrast between his pretensions and his situation more humble abilities may find room for consolation and cease to contemplate with envy his immense superiority. To suppose that his ambition can be satisfied in the possession of natural and acquired powers far greater than the majority of mankind would be contrary to all experience. Such men consider their acquirements as means for the attainment of greater ends, and the disappointments which they frequently meet with in the pursuit of their objects of ambition more than counteract all the feelings of pride and satisfaction which conscious superiority is calculated to inspire. The life of a politician is probably one of deep mortification, for the race is not always to the swift nor the battle to the strong, and few things can be more galling than to see men far inferior to ourselves enabled by fortune and circumstances to attain what we toil after in vain, and to learn from our own experience how many things there are in this life of greater practical utility than splendid abilities and unwearied industry.[3]

When the 1828 parliamentary session began only a handful of men believed that the institution of party, even in the rudimentary forms which it then took, still existed. The Duke of Wellington had offended the ultra Tories by reconciling himself with the Canningites at the expense of die-hards like Bexley, Westmorland and Eldon, none of whom was invited to join his government. Within months the Canningite ministers made their exit from the cabinet, leaving Toryism splintered into three mutually unforgiving, if not exactly warring, camps. Whiggery, too, was in disarray. Brougham railed at 'Lord Grey & his little knot who have inflicted Wellington on us';[4] Grey retreated with his conscience to his Northumberland lair; and the Lansdowne faction, their leader discredited and disillusioned, waited upon events. 'I think the best, the wisest and the thing most useful for the country, which we can do,' Althorp told Lord John Russell, 'is to be very quiet and to allow ourselves to be absorbed to the general Whig party. I am for this, because I consider it the best chance of again restoring Party feelings and replacing everything in the position in which it was before the Insurrection at Brooks's and Lord Lansdowne's weakness did the great injury of destroying Party in the Country.'[5]

Brougham began the 1828 session by speaking in the debate on the address to the throne as if he were a party leader. He described himself as standing at the head of two hundred members of the House of Commons, a foolish assertion belied by the failure of a party dinner which he gave not long afterwards. Creevey was delighted to see Brougham's pretensions pricked.

> Dined at Lord Grey's last night . . . Grey and my lady [i.e. Lady Grey] were both very much amused at my making Lord Durham [Lambton had been made Earl of Durham in 1827] tell who dined at Brougham's *Cabinet dinner* last Sunday. Durham was one, and Sefton and the Duke of Leinster, Lord Stuart (Sir Charles that was), old Essex and four Scotch barristers. So much for a Cabinet dinner by a person who says he is at the head of 200 gentlemen of the House of Commons, and who could only muster *one* member of that body (Sefton) on this great occasion.[6]

That Brougham meant to bid for the leadership may, perhaps, be inferred from his prudence in rejecting Francis Place's suggestion that he make a grand speech on the state of the nation. Place had in mind a rallying-call to reformers. Brougham would rehearse the evils of the national debt and exorbitant taxation, chastise ministers for their indifference to falling trade and persistent unemployment, and announce his intention to make war against the standing army, the game laws, the excise duties 'and so on to the end of the chapter'. His parliamentary friends, Brougham told Place, would not approve the speech, and to make it without consulting them would be a gross breach of decorum.[7] Yet his major effort of the session, delivered in the first week of February, lay outside the conventional boundaries of party debate. It was the celebrated review of the shortcomings of the English law which stamped Brougham as Bacon's successor. The speech, which has remained the longest one ever made in the House of Commons, was, Roebuck wrote, one which displayed Brougham's power to give assistance to the Whigs, rather than derive it from them. 'Mr Brougham was at once separated from and made superior to all who stood beside him in the ranks of opposition . . . They were striving, men believed, for mere party objects—he it was supposed for his country.'[8]

The middle years of the 19th century were an age of reform as much in the operation of the law and the courts as in anything else. The intellectual foundations of that reform were laid by Bentham. 'The age of Law Reform and the age of Jeremy Bentham,' Brougham wrote in 1838, 'are one and the same.' Others before him, like Justinian and Napoleon, had codified the law; others, too, like Montesquieu and Locke, had exhibited its defects; but Bentham was the first man to examine defects over the whole range of the law and at the same time to propose general principles upon which laws should be constructed. None before him had treated the study of law as a science. That, as Brougham justly affirmed, was Bentham's pre-eminent distinction, as proud a title to fame as any philosopher ever possessed.[9] Bentham let dry air in upon the mouldy recesses of the English law; official men began to scrub the growth away. Peel, at the home office in the mid-1820s, first revealed his administrative gifts in humanizing the criminal law. In 1827 appeared the *Jurist*, the child of the Benthamites, Henry Bickersteth and Joseph Parkes, and the first English journal devoted to the science of jurisprudence.

Bentham looked chiefly to Brougham to embody his ideas in legislation. It is difficult to believe that had Brougham been made Master of the Rolls his inventive mind and imperturbable self-assurance would not have made of him, as of Lord Denning in our day, a radically 'creative' judge. Yet, curiously, he had imbibed Bentham's doctrine that the whole field of law should be turned into one shining edifice of statute law in order to free it from the choking tanglewood of common, or judge-made, law. In the autumn of 1827 he and Bentham worked together preparing the materials for his great speech. After it was made Bentham expressed his disappointment with it. Brougham's mountain, he said, had brought forth a mouse. Posterity has dissented from Bentham's judgement. The speech, Sir William Holdsworth wrote in his monumental *History of English Law*, was 'the most learned and thorough criticism of the many defects of the common law that has ever been made since the Commonwealth period'; it led, Atlay said in his *Victorian Chancellors*, 'to a greater number of beneficial and useful reforms than any other, ancient or modern'.[10] Bentham may have been irked by Brougham's discourtesy in not mentioning in his speech the debt he owed to his master. Brougham said nothing of the eternal truths of jurisprudence, nor anything of the merit of Bentham's universal touchstone, the principle of utility. He left alone the tortuous workings of the Court of Chancery: Romilly and others had already exposed the evils that had attended Lord Eldon's long presidency there. He ignored the criminal law: in Peel its reform had already found a champion. 'The evils, inconsistencies, and absurdities of the system of civil procedure was therefore singled out as the principal object of attack,' Brougham afterwards explained, 'the rather because, in Mr Bentham's writings, the other branches of the mighty subject had been more copiously handled.'[11] Equity and the criminal law, moreover, touched a small portion of the population. It was the operation of the civil law that denied the people of England what Brougham pleaded for, 'the pure, prompt and cheap administration of justice'.

The two great defects in the law, then as always, were the delays which caused hardship and distress and the high cost of litigation which made the courts an instrument of redress for the rich and an instrument of oppression for the poor. It would be tedious to follow Brougham's recital of those defects in detail. His object was to 'abolish all obsolete proceedings which serve only as a trap to the unwary, or tools in the hands of litigious and dishonest parties'. He called for an end to the requirement that fees be paid in advance to the Court of Common Pleas and for an end to the court's monopoly of advocates, which excluded many barristers from using the court and thus contributed to the pile of arrears in King's Bench; for an end to a similar monopoly of attorneys in the Court of Exchequer; for a drastic simplification, and hence cheapening, of the procedure for dealing with wills and land tenure; for the abolition of the costly process of fines and recoveries; for borrowing from the French and the Danes the admirable practice of arbitration before causes were brought to trial; for the admission of declaratory judgement; on and on, through more than sixty 'capital defects', for a host of improvements, drab enough taken individually, but together certain to make the law more readily accessible to the people.

Cheapness and speed were not Brougham's only objects. Justice needed also to be just. Brougham dealt at length with the slipshod justice meted out to the colonies when appeals were heard before the Privy Council, a long-standing grievance which he repaired in 1833 when he established the Judicial Committee of the Privy Council. At home, two aspects of the law, the treatment afforded debtors and the venerated institution of the justice of the peace, came in for scathing criticism. The arrest of debtors by *mesne* process, which assumed the defendant guilty and placed him in prison or compelled him to find bail, favoured the rich man and often punished the innocent. 'Perhaps no man ever holds up his head, or is the same man again, after having once been in prison, unless for a political offence.' There should, therefore, be no arrest or imprisonment for debt except when the accused was charged with fraud, gross extravagance or the refusal to yield up property to his creditors.

The long section which Brougham devoted to the justices of the peace touched most nearly the sensitivity of his audience. Trial by a justice of the peace was, next to trial by jury, probably the most revered legal institution in the land. It enshrined two qualities esteemed by the English, the charity of local action against the impersonal authority of the central state and the common sense of the amateur against the expertise of the trained professional. 'I approach this jurisdiction with fear and trembling,' Brougham began, 'when I reflect on what Mr Windham was accustomed to say, that he dreaded to talk of the game laws in a House composed of sportsmen; and so too, I dread to talk of the quorum in an assembly of magistrates.' Casting his qualms aside, he went on to declare that there was 'not a worse constituted tribunal on the face of the earth, not even that of the Turkish Cadi, than that at which summary convictions of the Game Laws constantly take place—I mean a bench or brace of sporting Justices'. In the previous seven years more than 1,800 boys, many of them mere children, had been committed for poaching in the Warwick district alone. They entered the prison gate hardly as thieves; they came out fit, not perhaps for treason, but certainly for stratagems and spoils. And who sent them there? Men of property, appointed by the lord-lieutenant of the county, a man intimate with his neighbours who was unable to make his selection free of the judgement-impairing ties of friendship. Those local magistrates had the power to license inns, commit for offences against the game laws, punish for non-payment of tithes, sentence offenders to long terms of imprisonment and transportation, and in all those matters, so long as they did not state their reasons, they could not be appealed against to any higher power. Yet it was through the magistracy, more than any other agency except the tax-collector, that ordinary people came into contact with the government. Three reforms were necessary: justices of the peace must be appointed, not by the lords-lieutenant alone, but actually, rather than theoretically, in partnership with the lord chancellor; their decisions must be liable to reversal by a higher court; and they must be paid. 'Cheap justice, Sir, is a very good thing; but costly justice is much better than cheap injustice. If I saw clearly the means by which the Magistrates could be paid, and by which, therefore, a more correct discharge of the magisterial duties might be insured, I would certainly prefer paying them.'

The peroration was in Brougham's grand manner.

> It was the boast of Augustus . . . that he found Rome of brick, and left it of marble; a praise not unworthy a great prince, and to which the present reign also has its claims. But how much nobler will be the Sovereign's boast, when he shall have it to say, that he found law dear, and left it cheap; found it a sealed book—left it a living letter; found it the patrimony of the rich—left it the inheritance of the poor; found it the two-edged sword of craft and oppression— left it the staff of honesty and the shield of innocence.

There Brougham might have sat down. Instead, he ended with one of those whimpers of self-pleading which all his life he found it difficult to suppress.

> To me much reflecting on these things, it has always seemed a worthier honour to be the instrument of making you bestir your-selves in this high matter, than to enjoy all that office can bestow . . . And as for the power supposed to follow it—I have lived near half a century, and I have learned that power and place may be severed. But one power I do prize; that of being the advocate of my countrymen here, and their fellow-labourers elsewhere, in those things which concern the best interests of mankind. That power, I know full well, no government can give—no change take away!

Brougham had begun to speak at five o'clock. When he finished it was past eleven. He had consumed a hatful of oranges. Scarlett sneered at the length and superficiality of the speech, but through it all the House had remained nearly full, even during the dinner-hour. Scarlett was envious, Croker believed, because he feared that Brougham would run away with all the honour of amendments which had been in common discussion at Westminster Hall for years.[12] Scarlett had reason to feel envy. He possessed neither the power in the country, nor the voice in the House of Commons, to carry the discussion out of Westminster Hall and place it before the nation. That was Brougham's achievement. The government at once appointed two commissions of inquiry, one into the procedure of the common law courts, the other into the law affecting real property. In the course of the next ten years nearly all of the changes Brougham asked for were effected, many of them by his own hand, either by bills which he introduced into parliament or by his revision of the Judges' Rules. Even Campbell, censorious of Brougham as an advocate, was moved, when he came to review Brougham's career, to write that without his exertion in 1828 'the optimism of our legal procedure might have long continued to be preached up, and Fines and Recoveries might still have been regarded with veneration'.[13]

Soon after making the speech Brougham went north to join the circuit. The labours of the previous eighteen months, during which he had had only a fortnight's rest at Brougham Hall, told on his constitution. For most of the spring and summer of 1828 he was reduced in strength and haggard in appearance, too ill even to attend the opening of London University in October. He continued, nevertheless, to attend meetings of the Anti-Slavery Society and to supervize the work of the SDUK. In August John Allen advised him not to over-tax his resources. Brougham answered that circuit laywers had no choice. 'No one can tell you, save they who belong to it, how ill adapted our profession is to taking any care of health, unless it just happens to suit the arrangements. These are inexorable and above all, they allow no respite except for a few weeks in autumn. Now fain would most of us (who are in business) sacrifice a part, aye & the greater part of our gains to have more time for relaxation, & other pursuits! But it is impossible—it would be sacrificing not the bulk, but the whole.'[14]

*　　*　　*

The most important political event of 1828 was Daniel O'Connell's election to a seat in the imperial parliament at the Clare by-election in July. By defeating Vesey Fitzgerald, who had just taken up his post at the board of trade and had therefore been required, as the law then was, to submit himself for re-election, O'Connell demonstrated the power of the Catholic Association to persuade the southern Irish electorate to throw out even a popular, emancipationist member of parliament in order to compel the government to redress its grievances. Fitzgerald's defeat meant that in future no Irish member could be appointed to the government with any assurance of his being re-elected. It raised also the prospect of a host of Irish Catholics, like O'Connell, being returned at the next general election but prevented from taking their seats by their inability to swear the Protestant oath. Should matters come to that pass, to continue to defy Irish Catholic opinion would be to risk provoking armed rebellion. Where reason had failed, force prevailed. In 1829, Wellington and Peel turned round on their former opinions, bore the reproaches of their embittered Protestant supporters and, by dint of Whig votes, carried Catholic emancipation through parliament and into law.

Lord Grey, delighted that his most cherished political object had been won, saw no cause to abandon what he called his 'friendly neutrality' towards Wellington's government. Grey's impracticability, as Brougham put it, prevented the organization of a direct and powerful opposition.[15] Catholic emancipation nevertheless marked a turning-point in English politics. By driving an immovable wedge between Wellington and the ultras, it fatally weakened the parliamentary strength of Toryism. And by removing from the political debate the question which had most pointedly distinguished the Whigs from the Tories, it encouraged the former to look for a new flag to fly. By the spring of 1830 the opposition, aware that the tide in its affairs was coming to the flood, was preparing to get its crew into line and to nail its colours to the mast of parliamentary reform.

Early in 1830 Brougham's connection with the Marquess of Cleveland came to an end. In an abrupt change of position, Cleveland announced at the beginning of the parliamentary session that he intended to give his decided support to the Duke of Wellington; in the House of Commons the address to the throne was moved by his son, Lord Darlington. Cleveland had never interfered in Brougham's political conduct, but Brougham felt the awkwardness of their altered relationship. He informed the Whig leaders of his predicament and at the bidding of Lord Holland and others, who feared that he might follow his patron into the Tory ranks, the Duke of Devonshire was called upon 'to be the means of saving the political reputation of the greatest man in the House of Commons'.[16] Devonshire brought Brougham in for Knaresborough, a nomination borough vacated by George Tierney's death in January, and Brougham resigned the representation of Winchilsea. Cleveland expressed his sorrow at the decision, but apart from his wounded suggestion that Brougham had wished to place himself under a younger and more consequential patron, the parting was amicable.

The first signs of renewed Whig unity came early in March at a meeting of forty members of the House of Commons who agreed to act together to force a reduction in taxation on the government. The real significance of the meeting was that Lord Althorp consented to act as the group's leader. Althorp, who had told Grey in 1827 that Brougham alone was competent to lead, was reluctant to accept the responsibility thrust upon him and he did so only after reflecting that the great body of the opposition would not follow Brougham.[17] From that moment Althorp was effectively the Whig leader in the lower House. In his early days he had been an unremarkable, pleasure-seeking county member, until the premature death of his wife led him to abandon society and retire from fox-hunting because he thought it wrong, after such a loss, that a man should be so happy as the sport would make him. After 1815 he gave himself earnestly to politics. He was a timid and halting speaker and never rose in the chamber, he said, without throat and lips as dry as those of a man about to be hanged.[18] But many a poor and infrequent speaker has been an able leader of the House of Commons. Althorp was conscientious and incorruptible. His followers liked him for sharing their ignorance of the higher flights of economics and political philosophy. His mind, it was said, was like a reserve fund, not invested in showy securities, but always of staple value. He became for a time, as a cabinet colleague later put it, the tortoise on which the world reposed. When, after 1830, he complained that he disliked the burden of leadership and that he rose every morning hoping to hear that the government was out, men knew that he was speaking true. He had, Macaulay said, the temper of Lord North and the principles of Romilly. 'I doubt whether any person has ever lived in England who, with no eloquence, no brilliant talents, no profound information, with nothing in short but plain good sense and an excellent heart, possessed so much influence both in and out of Parliament.'[19] Althorp was, in short, the perfect foil to Brougham, whom Hazlitt described as 'too improvident for a leader, too petulant for a partisan' and, from his habit of acting without consulting his colleagues, too deficient in 'the principle of co-operation'.[20] Althorp had stuck by Grey in 1827 and he was rewarded with Grey's confidence. Yet there is rarely a tangible point to explain why one man fails to inspire the trust that is freely reposed in another.

Brougham's behaviour in 1827 was not the cause of his exclusion; it was the symptom of a deeper cause, the workings of which Sir James Mackintosh once sought to describe to Thomas Moore by reference to the French notion of *caractère*.

He expressed his inability to distinguish that particular quality of mind, which confers the superiority over others, which is always the result of *caractère*. *Caractère* does not seem necessarily to involve a superiority of understanding; neither is it absolutely courage. Men have been known to possess it, who were not personally brave. Whatever it is, or whatever confers it, it raises the man who is gifted with it, by an irresistible necessity, to dominion and sovereignty over those who have it not. We see its effects on all assemblies of man. It designates a man for command with almost as much certainty as birth in some countries. All feel its dominion; all, however unwillingly, pay homage to it. Equals meet, but the equality lasts no longer than till the man 'de caractère' makes his appearance.[21]

Brougham acquiesced in Althorp's elevation without demur; he had no choice. The appointment signified little so long as George IV remained on the throne, since the King's hostility to the Whigs remained implacable. On 5 June, however, George died. The tolling of his funeral bells sounded like a reveille to the opposition. On Brougham the accession of William IV had a dramatic effect. For a year he had been reluctant to fire into ministers with his usual gusto. Had Wellington followed the advice of his friends and succeeded in bringing Grey into his government, Brougham would very probably have tagged along. The Duke, however, mistakenly supposed that he could patch up his quarrel with the ultras. No offer was made to Grey and Brougham. Brougham saw that his chance lay, not with the Tory ministers, but with the new sovereign. He unmuzzled himself. On 30 June he compared Wellington to Polignac, the French minister whose reactionary policy was breeding the discontent that was to issue in the July revolution, and implied that the Duke intended to rule by royal favour and military power, supported by—Brougham pointed his long arm at the treasury bench—'his flatterers, those mean, fawning parasites'.[22] Two days later William Huskisson, Canning's successor as leader of the liberal Tories, described him as being in 'a state of excitement bordering on insanity'.[23]

The accession of William IV entailed, as the law then stood, the dissolution of parliament. For some time the campaign to abolish slavery in the colonies had been gaining strength in the north and there the Whigs looked forward to reaping electoral benefit from emancipationist opinion. On 13 July, as the old parliament approached its demise, Brougham gave notice that he intended to bring forward the question of colonial slavery and asked the House of Commons to resolve to consider the matter at the earliest possible moment in the next session. The motion was defeated by 29 votes, but Brougham went farther than he had gone previously in recommending a swift abolition. The imperial parliament had the right to determine the issue. It had the right to encroach upon what was called private property, since no man was justified in having property in his fellow-creatures. 'Let the Planters beware—let their Assemblies beware—let the Government at home beware—let the Parliament beware! The same country is once more awake—awake to the condition of Negro Slavery; the same indignation kindles in the bosom of the same people; the same cloud is gathering that annihilated the Slave Trade.'[24]

On no one did Brougham's eloquence work to more effect than on the Dissenters of the north and it was one of the most influential of them, Edward Baines of Leeds, the editor of the *Leeds Mercury*, who secured him the nomination to stand at the elections as a candidate for Yorkshire. In 1830, for only the fourth time in a century-and-a-half, the Yorkshire electors were treated to the spectacle of a contest. Each of the three previous contests had coincided with public clamour on a great national question: the excise tax in 1734, the Spanish war and Walpole's unpopularity in 1741, and the slave-trade issue in 1807. So it was in 1830, when, in addition to the anti-slavery agitation, the demand for parliamentary reform was reviving in the industrial counties of the north. Yorkshire elections were the most expensive in the land. In 1807 Lord Harewood and Lord Fitzwilliam each spent £100,000 on their sons' candidacies; in 1826, when there was no contest, John Marshall spent £30,000 to get himself elected. Brougham was able to accept the invitation to stand only because he was assured that he would have to bear none of the expense, eloquent testimony of his promoters' eagerness to secure his candidacy. Their motive was not simply admiration of Brougham. In Yorkshire the influence of the landed aristocracy had long been overwhelming, partly from the local custom by which tenants farmed their land on six-month leases; but that landed ascendancy was not always proof against the votes of the weavers and clothiers, many of them Dissenters, who were concentrated in the West Riding and who, in combination with the 40s. freeholders, could occasionally spring an electoral surprise.

In 1784 the support of the West Riding had gained the representation of one of Yorkshire's four seats for William Wilberforce, then only twenty-four and, as the son of a Hull merchant, not calculated to appeal to the great county families who were accustomed to send to Westminster unassuming, game-preserving squires. Brougham was even more unpalatable to them, for he was not a Yorkshireman and none but a native had sat for the county since the mid-17th century. Had the choice of Whig candidates remained in the hands of the leading Whig families he would not have been selected. He was chosen only because Baines, working on behalf of the West Riding Dissenters and manufacturers, stole a march on the gentry, who were bickering among themselves about the choice of a second Whig candidate to stand with Lord Morpeth. On 17 July Baines praised Brougham to the skies in an article which advised the electors to adopt Brougham and pay his expenses.

> The honourable and learned member for Knaresborough stands without a rival among the public men of the present day in their claims upon the gratitude of their country and of mankind. He has no competitor in the House of Commons, either in eloquence, in statesmanlike talent and information, or in the good he has effected for his country and for the human race . . . There is no great cause involving the public interests, the rights of man, the reform of abuses, the redress of wrongs, the improvement of the law and of the Government in all its departments, which has not found a ready and effective support in the mighty eloquence of Mr Brougham.[25]

A week later West Riding Whigs turned up in force at the selection meeting and after a lengthy and disputatious discussion in which most of the country gentlemen opposed the candidacy of a 'foreigner' they succeeded in having Brougham adopted.[26]

When he was younger and more ambitious, Brougham told the Duke of Devonshire, the nomination would have given him great pleasure. Now he looked upon it more as a bystander 'and only like it because it bears a strong testimony to our opinions and principles, and because it gives me (whether I accept or refuse) a great weight and power to promote those principles in Parliament and the country'.[27] But he knew that to be brought in from outside at no expense to himself was an honour unmatched, perhaps, in English history, one at any rate so unheard of that he was 'beyond measure astonished' by it.[28] His selection owed something to his campaign against the orders-in-council, still remembered by merchants in many parts of Yorkshire, something to the popularity he had acquired by the Queen's business, and something to the part he had played in the anti-slavery campaign. After consulting persons of position in the county about the probability of a successful contest, he accepted the nomination.

Parliament was prorogued on 24 July. The election took place during the York assizes, where Brougham had an unusually large number of briefs. He was obliged to work every night preparing his causes and appear in court every morning at half-past nine as if no such thing as an election were pending. Then, throwing off his wig and gown, he was hurried into a carriage and driven furiously around the various towns within twenty or thirty miles of York. At each town he made a speech—Denman wrote to his wife that Brougham was addressing 70,000 electors a day[29]—before returning to York after midnight. 'It was,' Brougham wrote, 'by much the hardest work I ever went through; but good health, temperance, and the stake I was playing for, carried me through. I not only survived, but during the whole of this laborious time, I never in my life felt better, or more capable of even further exertion, had such been called for.'[30]

On 6 August he was returned. Although he trailed just behind his Whig ally, Lord Morpeth, the glory of the fray was his. That evening he took part in an ancient ceremony which always closed a Yorkshire election. He buckled on a sword, placed a cocked hat on his head, fastened a pair of long spurs to his legs and mounted a charger to ride round the castle yard at York and then through the streets of the town. Although he was not a horseman, he remained in the saddle. In old age he remembered the occasion with pride.

> I may say, without hyperbole, that when, as knight of the shire, I was begirt with the sword, it was the proudest moment of my life. My return to Parliament by the greatest and most wealthy constituency in England was the highest compliment ever paid to a public man. I felt that I had earned it by the good I had done—that I had gained it by no base or unworthy acts.[31]

Campbell wrote that Brougham's triumph, the 'spontaneous declaration' of the most intelligent constituency in the kingdom that he was the fittest man to guide the destinies of the country, was the more gratifying for having been gained unsolicited, without hint of bribery and without tricks of demagoguery.[32] Althorp congratulated him on deserving 'the greatest reward that ever was bestowed upon a public man, and the greatest that can be'.[33] Brougham himself, assured of victory after the first day's polling, was able, at the last moment, to have his own view of the election inserted in the July number of the *Edinburgh Review*: 'Of all the portentous signs of the times for the present ministry, the most appalling is the nearly unanimous choice of Mr Brougham to be member for Yorkshire. This is assuredly the most extraordinary event in the history of party politics.'[34]

*   *   *

For many years afterwards Brougham would speak of 'my old Yorkshire constituents', as if the connection had been a long one. It lasted not quite four months, until the day when he consented to become lord chancellor in Grey's government. In his victory speech to the Yorkshire electors Brougham made a ringing declaration of independence.

> I am now possessed of a power (having such a constituency to support me) that will enable me to compel the execution of measures which I have only hitherto been ventilating. Nothing on earth shall ever tempt me to accept place. I have more pride in representing Yorkshire than I could derive from any office the King can bestow, because I have more effectual means of being useful to my fellow-citizens, and of gaining for myself an honest fame.[35]

The abolition of slavery took pride of place among the measures ventilated. Not far behind came parliamentary reform. William Ord, the Whig member of parliament for Newcastle, had the hostility of Yorkshire's landed grandees in mind when he called Brougham 'the member for Yorkshire, or rather one should say the member for Leeds, Huddersfield, and Sheffield',[36] but Brougham was also the representative of the towns in another sense. In speech after speech he had made himself the spokesman for all those manufacturing towns of the north, in Yorkshire, Lancashire and the Midlands, whose wealth and population remained unrepresented at Westminster. Brougham pledged himself to triennial parliaments, the transfer of seats to the large towns and the extension of the suffrage to inhabitant urban householders. At Leeds, at the end of September, speaking at a dinner to honour him and Morpeth, he made a second declaration of independence, one which made his parliamentary colleagues' blood run cold. 'I will leave in no man's hand,' he promised, 'now that I am member for Yorkshire, the great cause of parliamentary reform.'[37]

The Whigs became anxious lest Brougham was putting himself forward as the leader of the opposition, for they believed that the opposition motion on the regency in July, the last important party division of the old parliament, had been decisively beaten (by 247 votes to 93) because of his part in it. 'At the present moment,' Althorp had said after the vote, 'all our people hate him so cordially that it is only necessary for him to say or do any thing for them to dislike it.'[38] Brougham had taken the initiative, in pamphlets and articles for the *Edinburgh*, in arguing strenuously for the overthrow of Wellington's government. The elections had brought a gain of about thirty seats to the Whigs and Brougham was busy negotiating a junction with the ex-Canningites to defeat ministers in the new parliament. Lord Grey's son, Viscount Howick, was astonished that he seemed to pay no regard to his entire want of a following in the House of Commons, and expected him to prove troublesome when parliament assembled. 'His return for Yorkshire seems to have increased his before intolerable vanity to the highest pitch and I should not be the least surprised if he should insist on managing everything in spite of his total want of discretion.'[39] Durham thought that the Whigs' alarm was misplaced. He told Grey that Brougham had no intention to make himself leader, only an intense ambition to throw out the Tories.[40] Grey and his circle were not easily persuaded of Brougham's docility. Two days after the new parliament opened, Ellice reported that he saw '*on all sides* great jealousy of B's assumption of the office of Leader, great distrust of his prudence or intentions, & much apprehension of his committing some fault which will strengthen ministers by throwing back the old Tories into their Ranks'.[41]

Brougham's reform plan, which he unfolded at meetings with leading Whigs in October, had three components: enfranchising the great towns, extending the vote to copyholders, leaseholders and borough householders, and limiting most of the small and close boroughs to one, not two, members. Though it fell short of what Grey's government was eventually to introduce in 1831, it was a marked advance on anything previously proposed by a leading politician of one of the major parties. Brougham said that it was the most any person, out of office, could hope to force on the government. The Whigs, who wished to proceed cautiously now that the anti-Wellington elements in the House of Common were drawing closer together, were happy to use him. Sir James Graham, a leading ex-Canningite, candidly confessed to him that 'the public will be satisfied with *less* from you than from any other member of the house of commons, when you declare that you bring forward *all* which you can hope to carry with a due regard to the circumstances of the present time'.[42] The Whigs did not want the sections of the opposition, so disparate in their antecedents and opinions, so little genuinely united except by the desire to bring down the Tory government, to fall out among themselves over details of a proposed reform. Brougham therefore found himself faced with the first challenge to his boast that he cared only to be the faithful representative of Yorkshire. The Whigs asked him to table, not a specific reform proposal, but simply a notice of his intention in general terms. He demurred; Lord Durham, whom even Brougham could scarcely accuse of being a trimmer, pleaded for the Whigs; he yielded. He gave notice on 16 November that he would ask the House for a committee to inquire into the state of the representation.

Before that day arrived Wellington's government had come to its end. On 2 November the Duke, oblivious of the unrest in the country and the near-riotous excitement in favour of reform, made his historic declaration, heroic or merely short-sighted, that the English constitution was virtually incapable of improvement. If he meant, at the last hour, to rally the ultra malcontents to his standard, he failed. On 15 November they combined with the Whigs and Canningites to defeat his government on a relatively minor division pertaining to the civil list. Brougham's reform motion was down for the following evening. Rather than face it, Wellington resigned. William IV sent for Lord Grey and asked him to form a government. Alexander Somerville, the Scotch labourer who wrote an *Autobiography of a Working Man*, recalled that November day when he and his mates, quarrying on the Lothian coast, heard a small boy approach, waving a newspaper and shouting 'The Tories driven from power at last!'. 'Those of us who knew least of politics knew enough to understand the importance of this announcement. We took off our hats and caps, and loud above the north wind, and the roaring sea, shouted "Henry Brougham for ever!". At that time we knew little of Earl Grey.'[43]

The changed political circumstances placed Brougham's reform motion in a new light. It was no longer a stick with which to beat the Tories. Lord Grey was making a reform government. Brougham could therefore safely abandon his motion. Such was the Whigs' reasoning. Brougham agreed to postpone his motion, but he was adamant that he would not allow it to be made 'the stepping stone of a party'. He went to the House on the evening of 16 November and issued a warning in a low, hollow voice which Campbell could still hear twenty-five years afterwards, full of suppressed wrath and purposed vengeance. 'As no change that may take place in the Administration can by any possibility affect me, I beg to be understood that in putting off the motion, I will put it off until the 25th of this month and no longer. I will then, and at no more distant period, bring forward the question of parliamentary Reform, whatever may be the condition of circumstances and whosoever may be his Majesty's ministers.'[44] Casting a glance of defiance behind him, he strode off to the members' bar. That evening the Duke of Bedford found him in an agitated humour at Holland House. 'Angry at having been persuaded to put off his motion—too absurd!' the Duke wrote to Lord John Russell. 'Lord Holland thinks he ought to resign his reform measure into the hands of the new Ministers. The lawyer thinks differently.'[45] The next day Brougham declared, in the King's Bench robing room, that he would accept no place in any government. He then went down to the House, where a motion to postpone the hearings before the election committee (which decided appeals against members alleged to have been returned by bribery or corruption) was being debated. He demanded to know why there should be an interruption of the hearings merely because place-hunters were making their arrangements.

What do we want with the presence of Ministers on election petitions? What do we want with them? We can do as well (I speak it with all possible respect of any future Ministry); but I say we can do as well without them as with them. I have nothing to do with them except in the respect I bear them, and except as a member of this House. I state this for the information of those who may feel any interest in the matter.[46]

Lord Grey had partly himself to blame for Brougham's surliness. That morning (the House of Commons who heard Brougham's harangue did not know it) he had insulted him by offering him the post of attorney-general. It was one thing for the party to have decided that Brougham was ineligible for the leadership. It was quite another to imagine that he could be fobbed off with a minor legal appointment that did not even carry with it a seat in the cabinet. Disraeli repeated the colourful tale that Brougham 'took the offer of the Attorney-Generalship, and held it up to the scorn of the assembled Commons of England, and tore it, and trampled upon it, and spat upon it in their sympathising sight'.[47] If Brougham tore up Grey's note he did not do so in front of the House. He was, however, indignant. Everyone knew that had Althorp refused the lead in the Commons, Grey must have offered it to Brougham. Althorp, indeed, felt obliged, as he told Lord John Russell, to sacrifice himself in order to rescue Grey from his difficulty.[48] For ten years Brougham had protested that he could not afford to give up his career at the bar for a cabinet position. No doubt he meant it. But to be offered the attorney-generalship! Brougham coveted the Rolls, but neither the King nor Grey was willing to leave him in the Commons, with a secure income for life, independent of government and poised to wreck any ministry he chose. Very well, Brougham told Grey, if not the Rolls, then nothing. He would remain in the House of Commons as an independent member.

By 19 November, two days after Brougham had turned down the attorney-generalship, Lord Grey faced a crisis. If Brougham could not be accommodated a Whig government was impossible. His exclusion would provoke an outcry in the country and he would be able to speak in the Commons as the voice of the people against the Whigs. The King came to Grey's aid: he consented to Brougham's being offered the Great Seal. The day before Brougham had written to the Duke of Devonshire that only the lord chancellorship would tempt him to abandon Yorkshire.[49] 'Do not be tempted,' his mother wrote anxiously to him, 'to leave the House of Commons. As member for Yorkshire, backed by all you have done for the country, you are more powerful than any official that ever existed, however high in station or in rank. Throw not away the great position you have raised yourself to—a position greater than any that could be bestowed by king or minister.'[50] Brougham would rather almost anything than displease his mother. Stiffened by her advice, he called on Grey on the morning of 19 November. Grey offered him the Great Seal and assured him that the attempt to make a government was over if he stood apart from it. Brougham refused the offer, but he agreed to see Althorp before making the refusal absolute.

He then went to the House of Lords, where he was arguing an appeal, and sent for Althorp and Lord Sefton to meet him there. They arrived in the company of Duncannon, the whip, and Brougham's brother, James. Brougham found them in the consultation room and stated his objections to the Great Seal. It would remove him from the Commons, where he was powerful, and bring to an end a lucrative career at the bar. The expense of living in the style required of a peer was beyond his means, not perhaps while he enjoyed the chancellor's salary of £10,000, but certainly afterwards when he came to depend on his modest income from rent and the £4,000 pension given to ex-chancellors. The discussion ended with Althorp's saying that he had no answer to Brougham's objections. The others then left, thinking the game was up. Althorp stayed behind.

> Well [he said to Brougham], I have not a word to say against your reasons and your feelings, and therefore there is an end of the matter; and you take upon yourself the responsibility of keeping our party for another twenty-five years out of power, and the loss of all the great questions which will follow, instead of their being carried.[51]

Brougham countered by saying that he was willing to devote himself to the party out of office. Althorp continued.

> That is a totally different thing from official support, because every now and then there comes a question on which you really differ, and have not the excuse of supporting the Government against your opinion, which you consent to waive in order not to break up the Ministry. However, there is no use in arguing the matter. Grey is determined, and will let the King know today, when he goes by appointment at two o'clock, that there are such difficulties in the way that the Government cannot be formed; and you take upon yourself to let our friends all know that *you* are the cause, and the only cause, of the attempt failing.

Brougham then asked for an hour more to consider. He sent for his brother and Lord Denman, and when he heard them speak exactly as Althorp had, saw that he stood alone, unsupported by any of his friends, not even by Sefton and Denman, on whose judgement and goodwill he had become used to rely, he relented. He sent word to

Lord Grey that he had surrendered to the remonstrances of others.

Reform had been taken out of Brougham's hands and he had been consigned to the relative obscurity of the upper House. 'Nobody cares a damn for the House of Lords,' Wellington had said in 1818; 'the House of Commons is everything in England and the House of Lords nothing.'[52] Great was the surprise and greater still the joy, Greville recorded, at 'a charm having been found potent enough to lay the unquiet spirit, a bait rich enough to tempt his restless ambition'.[53] If Whigs crowed that tune, they were unkindly false. It was precisely *not* his ambition which Brougham served in quitting the House of Commons. Having made his name as a radical, he could not use the House of Lords to advance himself. If he were to speak for the people, the place to do it was the House of Commons. 'All men feel,' Greville wrote, 'that he is emasuclated and drops on the Woolsack as on his political deathbed; once in the H. of Lords, there is an end to him, and he may rant, storm, and thunder without hurting anybody.'[54] 'You are all under great obligations to me,' the King said to Lord Holland. 'I have settled Brougham. He will not be dangerous any more.'[55]

No man in modern times has been lord chancellor and subsequently filled any other political office. Sefton tried to console Brougham with the witticism that the fall on to the Woolsack was one of the softest, but Brougham knew the hurt that it did him. He gave up to party what he had intended for mankind. The ambition which Brougham served, at that high moment in the history of Whiggery, belonged not to himself, but to others. No one has seen fit to belittle the sacrifice which he made, nor the language in which he described it in his memoirs.

The step, however, was taken; and the only justification of it in common prudence was, that the party would have been next thing to ruined had I refused. But the folly of the step, as a selfish one, was abundantly evident. I took a peerage and £4000 a-year for life, without the chance of making my income greater, however inadequate I might find it. I had been accustomed to spend a great deal more, without any rank to support; and I gave up an income of more than double, and which the first change at the bar would raise to above £10,000 a-year. I also gave up a profession of which I had become extremely fond; and I gave up the finest position in the world for an ambitious man like me—a man who loved real power, cared little for any labour, however hard, and less for any rank, however high. But I made this sacrifice, for which the gratitude of the party at first knew no bounds, and afterwards was reduced to less than nothing.[56]

Whether, having lain down like a lamb, Brougham would rise up again in the shape of a lion, remained to be seen. Lord Holland, for one, doubted that he had been metamorphosed. At Lansdowne House, where the Whigs met to approve Brougham's admission to the cabinet, he was heard to murmur, 'Then we shall never have another comfortable moment in this room'.[57]

12

The Woolsack: I

The advent of the Whigs was greeted with satisfaction by all those persons whose lives had been spent in hitherto futile denigration of Tory wickedness. Even Henry Cockburn, long in tooth, hailed the innocent brightness of a new-born day.

> Grey permitted to close the end of his days by realising, in power, all the splendid visions of his youth! Toryism, with its narrownesses and abuses, prostrate! Whiggism no longer the watchword of a faction but expanded into the public creed! Government by patronage superseded by the necessity of governing by right measures. The last links of the Scotch feudal chain dropping off under the hammers that one may distinctly hear erecting the first Hustings our country ever saw! . . . Our sons may see the fulfilment of these glorious things. Happy are we who have been permitted to scent 'the morning air'.[1]

'Ultra Tories and High Churchmen have had their revenge upon us,' Peel wrote to a friend, 'and the natural consequence of inflicting that Revenge—the triumph of a radical press—the downfall of the aristocracy—and the administration of the Church Patronage by Lord Brougham and Lord Holland.'[2] Strange that the aristocracy should tremble, for the cabinet which Lord Grey gathered around him owned more land than any of its predecessors and all but two of its members were either peers or heirs to a peerage. The sight of Brougham and Francis Jeffrey (appointed lord advocate for Scotland) in such exalted company amused Sydney Smith. 'How very singular! The Review began in high places (garrets) and ends in them.'[3]

What most excited men's curiosity or horror was the spectacle of 'godless' Brougham occupying the highest dignity in the government—the Evil, Cockburn chortled, the head of the Church![4] Anxious defenders of the Church misread Brougham's mind. Like a true

Whig, he held that an established religion, whatever the truth of its creed, was in a general way morally wholesome and that, as establishments went, the English Church was the most tolerant and the most learned.[5] He scorned to burden himself with tedious inquiries into the sectarian prejudices of small parishes awaiting the appointment of a new curate. Within days of taking the Great Seal he charmed the archbishop of Canterbury by offering to present the livings in his care (all Crown livings under the value of £20 annually) to any clergymen whom the primate would recommend;[6] true to his word, he had, at the end of the first year in office, surrendered two-thirds of his patronage to the bishops. 'The Chancellor's wise and munificent arrangement of his minor patronage,' the bishop of Durham wrote, 'did much to conciliate the Church and also went far to set us right in the minds of men who look with a just confidence to his opinions.'[7] In the summer of 1831 Brougham made a well-tempered speech against a bill to commute tithes and in favour of the archbishop's tithe composition bill. The speech was noticeably deferential towards the bishops and it strongly upheld the sanctity of Church property. 'It seems,' a Whig colleague remarked, 'that all great men getting into power see the necessity of doing homage to the Church.'[8]

Brougham received the Great Seal from the King at St James's Palace on 22 November and later that day took his seat on the Woolsack, where, Lord Ellenborough remarked, he endeavoured to look as demure as possible.[9] That was Brougham's last day as a commoner (his patent of nobility was not yet completed). His sadness at leaving behind for ever the arena of his greatest triumphs may be measured by his resolution never again to set foot inside the House of Commons, even as a visitor in the peers' gallery. It might, too, be inferred from his habit of continuing to sign his letters with the commoner's plain 'Henry Brougham' or 'HB' that Brougham cared little for pearls and coronets, were it not that on 23 November it was announced that he had taken the title Baron Brougham and Vaux, a form usually adopted when an individual united two titles of the same grade. The announcement was greeted with great mirth and Brougham was able to satisfy no one that he came by the ancient title of Vaux (pronounced *vox*) by an obscure descent through the female line. The wits made capital fun of his pretension. He ought, they said, to have chosen 'Vaux et praeterea nihil' and they renamed Lincoln's Inn, where he had his chambers, after the pleasure garden, Vauxhall. Brougham's assumption of a subsidiary title, Atlay wrote, 'was an act of vanity which first gave the world at large an inkling of the latent vein of eccentricity in his character'.[10]

In the early days of the new government's existence Brougham attracted more notice than Lord Grey or any other minister. When he first took his seat in Chancery in the robes of his new office, the court and gallery were crammed with more spectators—ministers, foreign ambassadors, royal dukes and peers of both parties—than the oldest lawyers could remember for any similar occasion. The next day he delivered his maiden speech in the House of Lords. Thomas Whishaw, the 'Pope' of Holland House and one of Brougham's earliest London acquaintances, contrasted the cold reception given to it with the cheers which Brougham had habitually received in the lower House.[11] Maiden speeches are usually dull affairs. Brougham's gained interest by his reply to a spiteful accusation against him which John Croker had found the courage to make in the House of Commons only after Brougham had been removed from the scene. With distilled ungenerosity Croker had railed at him for having paraded his political virtue as the representative of Yorkshire all the while that he was engaged in a shuffling intrigue for place. For once Brougham was able to defend himself with a clear conscience.

> Up to that time when I am reported to have stated my intention of not severing myself from the representation of Yorkshire . . . I no more contemplated the possibility of my being prevailed upon to quit the station I held for that I now occupy, than I, at the present moment, fancy I shall ever go back to that House from which the favour of his Majesty has raised me.[12]

He accepted his new office, he declared, because he decided that he could do more good for the country as lord chancellor than as the member for Yorkshire.

Brougham had had little experience of civil law courts. His practical knowledge of equity was confined to what he had gained incidentally in the two courts of appeal where he had occasionally taken briefs, the High Court of Delegates and the Cockpit. Many a lord chancellor has come to the Woolsack similarly unprepared and by study and attention learned to adjudicate tolerably well. A good lawyer's head and the quickness of mind to unravel the technicalities of a case and grasp the gist of the precedents which bear on it readily repair the deficiencies of an original ignorance. Brougham possessed both, and although Greville was right to say that he had neither the habits nor the turn of mind compatible with profound law-learning, he exaggerated when he said that the bar universally condemned him as a bad chancellor.[13] Denis le Marchant, Brougham's secretary, and alive to his shortcomings, said that by constant application he made himself extensively acquainted with cases and that the most eminent Chancery advocates found his judgements more valuable as precedents than those handed down by Lord Lyndhurst.[14] Lyndhurst, for all his reputation as the finest judge of his era, grappled with no difficulties he was not certain to surmount; Brougham, on the other hand, cut through the web of sophistry and technicality that surrounded the law. The famous *mot* of the wag who lamented that Brougham did not know a little law, for then he would have known a little of everything, was, as Bagehot said, the remark of someone who assuredly knew only one thing. Sir Frederick Pollock thought Brougham's judgements 'remarkably good', informed by a greater general knowledge than was possessed by any other contemporary chancellor.[15]

Much of the criticism of Brougham in Chancery stemmed, not from his judgements, but from the manner in which he conducted himself. Now he chatted too much to counsel (although even Lord Ellenborough, his severest critic, acknowledged that his doing so often brought them to the true points),[16] now he was ostentatious in ignoring them and seeming to be inattentive. He signed papers, corrected proofs for the SDUK or wrote letters, all without pretending, as Eldon had done, that he was making notes of the court's proceedings. Once, when Brougham was scratching away with his pen, Sir Edward Sugden, a rising Tory who had clashed with him in the Commons, stopped in the middle of a sentence. 'Go on, Sir Edward,' Brougham drawled; 'I am listening to you.' And when Sugden remarked that he evidently was not listening, Brougham replied, 'I am signing papers of mere form. You may as well say that I am not to blow my nose or take snuff while you speak.'[17] There were occasions when Brougham's half-mocking, half-serious drolleries bordered on indecency. One morning, as the court rose, he was presented with a petition from a Mr Parkin, editor of *The Christian Corrector*, who faced financial ruin from his inability to answer a bill filed against him in Chancery. Religious scruple prevented him from swearing the oath. Was he a Quaker or a Moravian, Brougham asked, and when Parkin replied that he was neither recommended that he become one or the other, since for each of them relief from the oath was provided. Brougham then continued.

> I will put a case to you, as I, in many instances, have done before, and beg of you seriously to think upon it by Monday. If you were called upon to give evidence in the case of a murder; yea, suppose you could prove the innocence of a man about to be tried for such a crime, how would you feel if you refused to give your testimony? I have no difficulty in saying, that it would, in such cases, be your duty to obey the laws of man, though, in your opinion, in violation of the laws of God, who would excuse you, as all the blame would be chargeable upon human legislation.[18]

Accusations that Brougham turned the Court of Chancery into a bear garden were founded on the malice of political opponents, although his blustering, sarcastic manner provoked many a raucous debate, marred by personal recriminations, in the House of Lords. Abstemious by long habit, he was frequently charged with being tipsy, on one occasion in a newspaper report of a speech he had made in the Lords after having taken nothing since breakfast but beef tea.[19] Brougham gave a handle to his critics by his dress. He took to wearing tartan trousers. He declined into slovenliness. Lord Sefton could scarcely mention his name without remarking how inconceivable the state of his filth was and Greville, after a dinner at Holland House in 1832, described him as 'looking like an Old Clothesman and dirty as the ground'.[20] Vanity and egotism landed Brougham in scrapes which demeaned the dignity of his high office. Most notorious was a rumpus at the Horse Guards only a few months after he had been sworn in. On days when the Queen had her drawing room, carriages other than those of the archbishop of Canterbury and the speaker of the House of Commons were forbidden to pass through the Horse Guards. Brougham, ignorant of the rule, drove his carriage to the gate. The sentry stopped it, explained to the coachman that he must turn back, and held the reins of the horse while an officer of the guard was fetched. After a few words of explanation the officer turned away and the sentry released the horse, whereupon the carriage hurtled through the gateway. Both Greville and Creevey believed that Brougham had deliberately ignored the officer's instruction. Creevey heard from Sefton that he had found the slight of being placed below the speaker of the House of Commons more than blood and flesh could bear and had ordered the driver of his carriage forward.[21] In the

House of Lords Brougham defended himself by saying that his coachman did not hear his order to turn back. It was a lame excuse, made worse by the statement that no one thought less of the state and pomp of office than he did. 'I am sorry to say,' Lord Ellenborough wrote in his diary, 'the Chancellor is the most important liar I ever knew.'[22]

Brougham's antics brought down ridicule on his head, but his deeds in Chancery gained credit for the government. Hardly had he been fitted in his new robes than he announced bills for the reform of Chancery and the bankruptcy laws. His legislative reforms were accomplished mainly in the sessions of 1832 and 1833. What impressed the public during his first year in office was the speed with which he resolved suits in Chancery. For years, as Sydney Smith put it, Lord Eldon and the Court of Chancery had sat heavy on mankind. Eldon arrived in London as a penniless young man. By intensity of application he raised himself to the top of his profession. As a judge he was thorough in examination and lucid and impartial in judgement. No political opponent ever withheld from him esteem for his judicial learning. The trouble was that he took such pains to hand down definitive judgements, was so careful to leave no argument untested, that by the end of his long career arrears piled so high that suitors despaired of ever gaining redress. Brougham set out to repair the injury, and although his boast at the end of the court's sitting in 1831 that there were no more arrears was not quite accurate, for there were some in the vice-chancellor's business, he had heard and given judgement upon every appeal within his immediate province, a feat unremembered by any man living and one for which Lord Holland thought him 'justly elated'.[23] The officers of the court and the members of the bar were less pleased, since Brougham, displaying his legendary appetite for work, had disregarded vacations and sat longer into the night than any previous chancellor. At this period he was in close confederacy with Thomas Barnes, the editor of the *Times*, and along with the rest of Brougham's bodyguard in the press Barnes kept the chancellor's good works constantly before the public. It is a rare day when admiration of a lord chancellor runs so strong that his exploits in Chancery afford plausible ground for a party appeal to public sympathy. Yet it was so with Brougham. In October 1831, three days after the Lords had thrown out the government's parliamentary reform bill, Sydney Smith addressed a public meeting at Taunton. The peace of the country was endangered by serious rioting. To reassure his audience that the government would not lose faith with the people and that the opposition to the Lords would be overcome, he reminded them that the cabinet contained Lord Brougham.

> Look at the gigantic Brougham, sworn in at 12 o'clock, and before 6 has a Bill on the table, abolishing the abuses of a Court which has been the curse of the people of England for centuries. For twenty-five long years did Lord Eldon sit in that Court, surrounded with misery and sorrow, which he never held up a finger to alleviate. The widow and the orphan cried to him, as vainly as the Town crier cries when he offers a small reward for a full purse; the bankrupt of the Court became the lunatic of the Court; estates mouldered away, and mansions fell down; but the fees came in, and all was well. But in an instant the iron mace of Brougham shivered to atoms this house of fraud and of delay; and this is the man who will help to govern you; who bottoms his reputation on doing good to you; who knows, that to reform abuses is the safest basis of fame and the surest instrument of power . . . Look to Brougham, and turn you to that side where he waves his long and lean finger; and mark well that face which nature has marked so forcibly—which dissolves pensions—turns jobbers into honest men—scares away the plunderer of the public—and is a terror to him who doeth evil to the people.[24]

*   *   *

At the end of 1831 Brougham had been occupied, with only two days' holiday at Christmas and Easter, every day from six or seven o'clock in the morning until after midnight. Yet he was frequently heard to describe the Great Seal as a mere bauble. The office of lord chancellor, he declared, was so modest in its demands that he knew not what he would do once he had cleared the slate of arrears. Were it possible, he would throw his patent of peerage into the fireplace. Of course, Brougham could play the mountebank; but he had always been discontented with the life of the bar, or had, at any rate, to guard himself against becoming bored by it, and never before had he been required to spend part of every day in court and then go on to the Lords to hear yet more appeals. The drudgery of the law failed to entertain his essentially speculative mind. Nor was conveyancy his strong point, so that the drafting of bills wearied him. 'He must,'

Greville wrote, 'inwardly chafe at being removed from his natural element and proper sphere of action, and he must burn with vexation at seeing Peel riot and revel in his unopposed power, like Hector when Achilles would not fight, though this Achilles can never fight again.'[25]

For the first year-and-a-half of its existence Lord Grey's government was preoccupied with the great reform bill. For Brougham it was galling to have the question of parliamentary reform placed in other hands. He was excluded from the committee (Lord Durham, Sir James Graham, Lord John Russell and Viscount Duncannon) which laboured throughout December and January to prepare a draft bill for the cabinet, because Grey feared that he would be too disputatious, too fond of his own plan to yield gracefully to other men's suggestions, and too closely allied to Barnes and the *Times* to keep the committee's discussions secret. Barnes relied on Brougham and Brougham's brother, William, for inside political information and when, early in the new year, a series of sharp attacks on Grey appeared in the *Times*, it was natural for the Whigs to accuse Brougham of having inspired them.

The charge against Grey was nepotism. It was well-founded. Grey had provided places for a number of his relatives in the government, including his son-in-law, Lord Durham, and his brother-in-law, Edward Ellice. Brougham had never disguised his contempt for the self-preserving Whig 'family compact'. His Scotch upbringing, his long association with Bentham and James Mill, and his faith in the improving power of education made him as devoted to the principle of 'careers open to talent' as any French *philosophe* or English radical. Barnes, however, required no prompting from Brougham. In 1815 he had described the Whigs as 'dull and pompous Aristocrats, who assuming a popular title for private purposes' were 'bolstered up with heaps of wealth and stiffened into one compact mass by family alliances'.[26] Brougham's share in the *Times*' campaign against Grey is impossible to determine. His conversations with Barnes took place over the breakfast table, not through the post. He may have done nothing to inspire the attacks. What angered the Whigs was that he did nothing to stop them. Lord Sefton called him to task. It was notorious, he told him, that for two months the *Times* had been writing down Grey and producing panegyrics of the chancellor. Since it was well known that his brother wrote frequently for the paper, he could rid himself of suspicion only by summoning Barnes and insisting that he alter his course. If Creevey's report of the conversation is accurate, Brougham cut a sorry figure in the exchange.

> Sefton says nothing could equal the artificial rage into which Vaux flung himself. He swore like a trooper that he had no influence over the *Times*—that he had never once seen Barnes the editor since he had been in office, and that William had never written a line for it . . . This storm being over, Sefton collected from him distinctly that he had seen Barnes *perhaps* once or twice, and that brother William might *perhaps*—tho' quite unknown to him—have written an article or two in this paper. In short, as our Earl [Sefton] observed, never culprit was more clearly proved guilty than he was out of his own mouth, and it ended by his affecting to doubt which would be the best channel for getting at Barnes . . . but at all events he pledged himself to Sefton *that it should be done.*[27]

No one was more angry at the *Times*, nor more convinced of Brougham's duplicity, than Lord Durham, who complained so noisily that Brougham felt obliged to write to Lord Grey to explain himself. The letter was foolish. Brougham defended himself by avowing that he had no influence with Barnes, yet in the same breath said that he had sent his brother to remonstrate with him.

> Lambton's extreme absurdity really reduces me to a most humiliating pass—namely to write & ask you whether you believed it possible that I could have the most remote concern in these newspaper attacks on you!! I suppose if there is one man in the world more entirely incapable than another of such monstrous folly as well as spite & treachery it is myself and I really must do you the justice to say it never could have entered your mind to suppose such a thing possible. I was as much provoked I believe with the insidious remarks as yourself—indeed I think I was a great deal more so, having first heard of them from yourself. Now having said so, I really must say once for all that I trust you will find some opportunity of making L. sensible how impossible it is for me to submit to such vile suspicions & *to be answerable . . . I have not the most remote* influence in the quarter referred to, and as soon as I heard of the thing, I asked my brother to see the person supposed to be concerned & express how amazed I was at such a way of praising me at the expense of those I most loved & respected . . .
>
> I again repeat that I am sure you are quite as incapable of

harbouring such suspicions as I of deserving them. But once for all I must add that I have not the most remote influence in the world *over any such quarter* as the one alluded to, and what is more, that I do not desire to have any from what I now see & hear.[28]

Grey was not prepared to put his government and the reform bill at risk by a quarrel with Brougham. At the very height of the storm Brougham passed a convivial evening at Lady Grey's 'in his accustomed overflowing glee'.[29] Grey contented himself, in his reply to Brougham's letter, with saying that, although he did not suspect Brougham, he could not help noticing the correspondence, in general, between statements in the *Times* and language that Brougham had been heard to speak. 'You have somewhere a most injudicious friend and I a most unprovoked and malicious enemy.'[30]

Brougham was licking his wounds. The reform question had been taken out of his hands and he found himself being overtaken by Durham as the leader of that section of the Whigs which had earlier been called the Mountain. Brougham's sudden prominence as a radical parliamentary reformer in the summer and autumn of 1830 had, at any rate, been fortuitous, the accident of his standing for Yorkshire, where in the 1780s Christopher Wyvill and Sir George Savile had begun the modern reform movement. The scheme of reform which he proposed in November went further than any previous Whig plan. But although it was bold in its extension of the vote, it was timid in its reallocation of seats. For that reason it was impossible. It paid scant attention to the very abuse in the electoral system which most seized the public mind, the endless number of rotten boroughs which remained represented in parliament while all those sturdy towns whose manufactures sustained imperial trade went unrepresented. The fall of the Tories and the advent of the Whigs sent popular expectations soaring. Half-measures which might have satisfied the country six months earlier would no longer do. Hence the Whig bill, to the utter astonishment and dismay of the Tory opposition, contained two schedules, the famous schedules A and B, the first to disfranchise entirely sixty ancient boroughs, the second to take away one member from forty-seven more. Brougham attempted to preserve the nomination boroughs doomed by schedule A. He was defeated by the united action of the rest of the cabinet. His influence on the shape of the bill was, indeed, negligible. There is no evidence to support his statement that, when the secret ballot included by the committee in its original draft was removed by the cabinet, he succeeded in having the householder qualification lowered from £20 to £10.[31] Certainly he was in favour of the wider qualification; his plan had gone much further in enlarging the electorate. But the compromise which the cabinet settled upon—a £10 franchise in exchange for retaining open balloting—was not of his making. It had been the object of the drafting committee when it proposed a secret ballot and a £20 qualification in the first place.

That Brougham should have been solicitous of the nomination boroughs, the most infamous blot on the electoral system, when all the rest of a cabinet composed of landed grandees was persuaded of the necessity of being rid of them, is a curiosity. He had sat in parliament, it is true, as the member for two boroughs, Camelford and Winchilsea, included in schedule A and he defended the pocket boroughs on the well-trod ground that they provided an avenue into parliament for young men of talent without wealth or connections. Grey was sufficiently alarmed by his obstinacy to fear that he might use the issue to 'throw us over with the King',[32] but Sir James Graham foresaw no danger. Brougham, he believed, was peeved at being isolated from the framing of the bill and was merely 'disposed to carp'.[33] Against the argument that there was no rational basis on which certain nomination boroughs could be protected while others were cut down Brougham was powerless. At the cabinet meeting held to approve the bill he did not even bother to raise the subject. The country knew nothing of his reservations and for that his colleagues had reason to be thankful. In the months that followed his influence with the public was of inestimable worth to the government. '*You* are aware,' he wrote to James Losh, 'that I am a VERY MODERATE reformer and far far less than the Bill would have satisfied *me*. But now I am quite convinced that the fate of this country depends on its passing. Pass it will and must, either this year or next.'[34]

As soon as the bill was introduced Brougham worked behind the scenes to stir public support for it. At his suggestion the Lord Mayor of London, Sir John Key, called a meeting in the city known as a 'Common Hall', where speeches and resolutions in favour of the bill were applauded without dissent. Reports of the meeting were then drawn up by Le Marchant, and sent to Grey and the King. 'As his lordship guessed,' Le Marchant wrote, 'London set the tone of the great towns and he soon saw the country was entirely with him.'[35] There was never much doubt that the country, despite the disappointment in extreme radical circles at the omission of the secret ballot and the failure to extend the vote to all householders, would rally to the bill. The difficulty lay in parliament, where the government was heavily outnumbered in the House of Lords and had only a small and uncertain majority in the Commons.

The second reading of the bill passed the Commons by 302 votes to 301 on 22 March. The large towns of the north were illuminated in celebration; Tory opponents of the reform were burned in effigy; and more than half the counties of England carried resolutions in support of ministers. Inside parliament the Tory opposition did not abandon hope. On 19 April it succeeded in inflicting defeat on the government on General Gascoyne's amendment that the number of constituencies in England and Wales should not be reduced. Grey and his advisers decided that the vote signified a rejection of the bill. Ministers had either to resign or request a dissolution. For two months William IV had refused to promise Grey a dissolution. Now, when the moment arrived, he behaved, as Grey said, like an angel. Within twenty-four hours the opposition set in motion a plan of obstruction. In the upper House Lord Wharncliffe put down a motion for 23 April to address the Crown with a request not to dissolve. The mere passing of such a resolution could not, of course, restrict the Crown in the exercise of its prerogative. Grey feared, nevertheless, the consequences of an openly displayed breach between the two Houses of parliament and between the Lords and the Crown. He wished to prevent 'his order' from behaving rashly. Only one sure means was available: to have the King prorogue parliament in person.

In ordinary circumstances a prorogation is performed by lords commissioners of the Crown. They, however, unlike the sovereign, may be kept waiting while the lords finish their business, in this instance while they dealt with Wharncliffe's motion. To thwart the opposition, the cabinet decided on the morning of 22 April that Grey and Brougham should go at once to the King and ask him to prorogue parliament that afternoon in person. When the Duke of Richmond protested against such haste, and suggested that the whole matter of a dissolution needed to be reconsidered, Brougham asked him if he had ever seen a council of war held on the field before going into action. 'By God! never' the Duke replied and the issue was settled. Brougham and Grey went to the King and informed him of the opposition's mischief. 'He fired up at this—hating dissolution, perhaps, as much as ever, but hating far more the interference with, or attempt to delay, the exercise of the prerogative.'[36] It was then one o'clock, only an hour before the Lords were to begin the day's proceedings. The King protested that it would take several hours to make the necessary preparations for the ceremony: the escort of troops would have to be ordered. Brougham explained that he had taken the liberty of ordering them for half-past one—'a strong measure' said William, who afterwards would remind Brougham of his 'high treason'.[37] Whether the King also said that if the stage coach could not be got ready in time he would go in a hackney coach, the remark displays the generous spirit with which he placed himself at the government's service. 'I am always,' he told Grey, 'at single anchor'.[38]

Brougham then went away to robe himself in the gold gown required for the occasion. He arrived at the Lords just after two o'clock. Since the King was not to appear until three, it was necessary to prevent, by whatever means, a division on Wharncliffe's motion for an hour. After prayers Brougham left the Woolsack in order to be ready to meet the King outside the chamber. Lord Shaftesbury was voted into the chair *pro tempore*. Wharncliffe rose to move the address, whereupon, as Brougham wrote, there began a scene 'never exceeded in violence and uproar by any bear-garden exhibition'. Those who were present told Greville that it resembled nothing more than accounts of the Tennis Court Oath in Paris in 1789: 'the whole scene was as much like the preparatory days of a revolution as can well be imagined'.[39] The Duke of Richmond tried to stall Wharncliffe on a point of order, requesting that the Lords should take their appointed places, for, he said, he observed a junior baron (Lord Lyndhurst) sitting on the Dukes' bench. At this Lyndhurst stood up and shook his fist at Richmond, while Lord Londonderry, screaming to be heard above the din, accused Richmond of resorting to a wretched shift and was stopped from flying at him by four or five persons who held him back by his coat-tails. Wharncliffe at last began to read the words of his motion when Brougham came skipping back into the House, shouting that it was an unheard-of doctrine that the Crown ought not to dissolve at the very moment when the House of Commons had just refused to vote supplies. He lied and the Lords knew it. All the Commons had done was to postpone the report of the ordnance estimates already voted. The chancellor was loudly hooted, but he kept speaking amid the tumult until the guns which heralded the royal arrival were heard, when he was dragged from the chamber by the Usher of the Black Rod to receive the King. What, William asked, was all the uproar? 'If it please your Majesty,' Brougham replied, 'it is the Lords debating.'[40] The King entered the chamber, which fell into silence and heard him announce, dwelling upon the adjective, that he had come to prorogue parliament with a view to its *immediate* dissolution.

*   *   *

As a peer Brougham was prevented from playing a public part in the elections which followed, but if Lord John Russell's memory was correct he was the begetter of the famous slogan which was shouted from every hustings—'the Bill, the whole Bill, and nothing but the Bill'.[41] The elections gave the government an unassailable majority in the House of Commons. There the reform bill, reintroduced in slightly revised form, received a majority of more than 100 on its third reading in the last week of September. The Lords were thus given their first opportunity to speak on the measure. Their debate on the second reading of the bill, a debate which lasted for five nights, surpassed anything that had gone before in the House of Commons. Grey, recovering his youthful spirit, came to the aid of his recovered youthful opinions in two speeches which carried old-timers back to the days of Pitt and Fox. Brougham, on the last night, delivered a speech which Greville said eclipsed all his previous exploits and which Grey called superhuman.[42] 'Lord Brougham's display,' Lord Holland wrote the day after, 'was almost preternatural and miraculous. His voice, delivery, and action, perfect; the variety and versatility of his genius, his general knowledge and particular information, his readiness of retort and reply, and the soundness of his philosophical views delighted and astonished the house, though interest or prejudice were too strong to allow any marks of conviction to appear in their votes.'[43]

Brougham rose at nine o'clock in a House so full that the thermometer recorded a temperature of 85 degrees. He spoke until after midnight—the longest speech ever made in the House of Lords—and without a single note went through all the speeches delivered by the bill's opponents during the five nights' debate, analyzing them one after another and, as Campbell wrote, 'with a little aid from perversion, giving them all a seemingly triumphant answer'.[44] To come to the yellowed pages of a speech armed with the knowledge of its prodigious contemporary effect is to invite disappointment; the columns of Hansard are filled with withered blooms. But Brougham's speech retains its glory. It is impossible not to be stirred by his passion, to feel the lash of his contempt for the *soi-disant* friends of reform in principle who would not suffer the bill to go into committee, to admire the ease with which sarcasm and invective were mixed with the elucidation of the bill's merits, and, at the last, to be held by the sustained peroration in which, in accents as noble and sentiments as proud as Macaulay's, he pleaded with the aristocracy of England to ignore the Jeremiahs who foresaw ruin in yielding to popular clamour and to stand by its ancient ties with the people.

If there is a mob, there is the people also. I speak now of the middle classes—of those hundreds of thousands of respectable persons— the most numerous and by far the most wealthy order in the community, for if all your Lordships' castles, manors, rights of warren and rights of chase, with all your broad acres, were brought to the hammer, and sold at fifty years' purchase, the price would fly up and kick the beam when counterpoised by the vast and solid riches of those middle classes, who are also the genuine depositories of sober, rational, intelligent, and honest English feeling. Unable though they may be to round a period, or point an epigram, they are solid right-judging men, and, above all, not given to change. If they have a fault, it is that error on the right side, a suspicion of State quacks—a dogged love of existing institutions—a perfect contempt of all political nostrums. They will neither be led astray by false reasoning, nor deluded by impudent flattery; but so neither will they be scared by classical quotations, or brow-beaten by fine sentences; and as for an epigram, they care as little for it as they do for a cannon-ball. Grave, intelligent, rational, fond of thinking for themselves, they consider a subject long before they make up their minds on it; and the opinions they are thus slow to form, they are not swift to abandon. It is an egregious folly to fancy that the popular clamour for Reform, or whatever name you please to give it, could have been silenced by a mere change of Ministers. The body of the people, such as I have distinguished and described them, had weighed the matter well, and they looked to the Government and to the Parliament for an effectual Reform . . . Rouse not, I beseech you, a peace-loving, but a resolute people; alienate not from your body the affection of a whole empire. As your friend, as the friend of my order, as the friend of my country, as the faithful servant of my Sovereign, I counsel you to assist with your uttermost efforts in preserving the peace, and upholding and perpetuating the Constitution. Therefore, I pray and I exhort you not to reject this measure. By all you hold most dear—by all the ties that bind every one of us to our common order and our common country, I solemnly adjure you—I warn you—I implore you—yea, on my bended knees, I supplicate you—Reject not this Bill![45]

Brougham finished on his knees, his arms outstretched above his head. He had been sustained by drinking three tumblers of unwatered negus, so that it was with difficulty that he raised himself back on to the Woolsack. 'His fun,' Edward Littleton wrote, 'never deserts him even in the most serious occupation. After testing his negus, he had put it down on the bench behind him next Lord Bathurst, when, thinking it in danger, he stopped in the middle of a sentence and removed it to the table in front of him, amidst some laughter.'[46] Brougham remained on the Woolsack until the House came to divide at six o'clock in the morning, by which time, having continued to drink, he was barely able to put the question.[47] Even so he was dissuaded from proceeding in three hours' time to the appeal cases before the House only by the exhausted clerks. He put the cases off until noon and, after hearing them, went directly to a cabinet, where he appeared 'as marvellously lively, vigorous, and vehement' as he had been the evening before.[48] Crowds gathered to cheer him, late that afternoon, on his way home and when he reached Charing Cross, where the largest multitude was assembled, the horses were taken out of his carriage and he was drawn the rest of the way to his house in Hill Street by the people.

The eloquence of Brougham and Grey won them plaudits, not votes. By the unexpectedly large majority of 46 the Lords rejected the second reading of the bill. The dismissal of Lord Howe, the Queen's chamberlain, for voting against the bill reassured reformers of the Crown's continuing favour; and in the Commons a vote of confidence in ministers succeeded without difficulty against the shrunken Tory benches there. But the reform battle had entered a new phase, destined to be prolonged. The future of the bill hung on the answer to one of three questions. Would the King consent to, or a Whig cabinet containing some of the oldest and proudest names the aristocracy of England boasted dare to insist upon, a creation of peers large enough to overcome the opposition in the upper House? If not, would the

Tory peers imperil the place of the Lords in the constitution by resisting to the last the expressed wish of the elected representatives of the people? Or, to avert either extremity, would a compromise be reached between the two parties acceptable to both Houses? Despite the rioting which followed the Lords' rejection of the bill, some Tories were encouraged by one or two by-election results, the near-defeat of a reformer at Dorsetshire and the victory of an anti-reformer at Liverpool, to believe that reaction was setting in, a reaction which, given time, would enable a Tory government to take office with the authority to resolve the crisis by a watered-down reform bill.

For the rest of the year ministers were occupied in arguing the ticklish question of peer-creation among themselves and negotiating a compromise settlement with the small band of Tory peers known as the 'Waverers'. The cabinet separated itself into two factions, one for going boldly ahead with the bill in its integrity, the other for back-stepping. The moderate party included three ex-Canningites, Melbourne, Palmerston and Stanley, and one former ultra Tory, the Duke of Richmond. The root-and-branchers included Brougham. In August he had written to James Losh of his alarm at the supineness of some anti-reformers. 'The Reform feeling is not dead, but sleeps, and the thoughtless men who would throw out the bill on the supposition of its being altered will find to their cost, but to the grievous cost of the country and the Monarchy also, that the feeling is indeed *altered*, but only to become far more universal and ungovernable.'[49] A month later, concerned at the dawdling pace of the bill's progress through the Commons, he warned Lord John Russell that every day's delay injured the government in the country and encouraged the anti-reformers to stop the bill altogether. If the anti-reformers did succeed, it was important for the Whigs not to act defensively, but to be 'loud on the *grievance*—that puts the saddle on the right horse'.[50] The bill's failure in the House of Lords in October stiffened Brougham's resolve. From that moment until the day that the bill finally reached the statute book he did the Whig government and the cause of reform signal service. He lent no succour to the negotiations with the Waverers and he steadfastly urged the necessity and policy of a large addition to the peerage.

That Brougham should take up arms against the trimmers and the faint-hearted, when at the beginning of the year his had been the most conservative voice in the cabinet, asks for explanation. In part it was simply in his nature, once he found himself in a scrap, to fight to the finish. He was kept up to the mark by Benthamites like James Mill, who fed him reports of the latent insurrectionary temper of the country, and by provincial liberals, like Losh, who believed that the feeling for reform, whatever the Tories might argue, was simply 'hushed in grim repose'.[51] There was, too, his personal standing in the country to consider. He was, Macaulay said in November, next to the King the most popular man in England. 'There is no other man whose entrance into any town in the kingdom would be so certain to be [met] with huzzaing and taking off of horses.'[52] Pride in his reputation and the consciousness that he was called upon to speak for the people at a critical moment in the nation's history wedded Brougham to unadulterated reform. How much, Lord Holland mused as the year 1831 came to its close, depended on three men—William IV, Lord Grey and Lord Brougham![53]

Relations between Grey and Brougham were once again uneasy. In July Brougham had refused to make a speech when his health was toasted by the Lord Mayor of London at a Mansion House banquet, simply because he was piqued at Grey's having been called upon, instead of himself, to return thanks for his Majesty's ministers.[54] A month later, when Grey voted against the motion of the attorney-general, Brougham's old friend, Thomas Denman, to institute proceedings against persons charged with bribery at the Dublin elections, Brougham became 'almost frantic on the subject' and in his rage let phrases escape from his lips which indicated, Holland reported, 'not only some dislike of Grey but regret at having accepted the seals and even an inclination to throw them up'.[55] By the end of November Grey had become deeply suspicious of Brougham's motives, imagining him to be looking for an excuse to resign and having some desperate game in view.[56]

The background to Whig discussions in November and December of 1831 was largely filled by the activities of those political unions which, on the model of the first of them, Thomas Attwood's Birmingham Union, had sprung up in almost every borough of consequence in the country. Trade unions, too, were expanding. Trade unionism had no place in the Whig creed. Thomas Arnold called them 'a fearful engine of mischief' and it was a Whig commonplace that their object of securing higher wages and steadier employment was visionary. 'The inequality with which wealth is distributed forces itself on everybody's notice,' wrote Macaulay. 'The reasons which irrefragably prove this inequality to be necessary to the well-being of all classes are not equally obvious.'[57] Brougham disliked unionism as much as any of his colleagues. He supported Lord Melbourne's severe punishment of union members, most famously the Tolpuddle 'martyrs' of 1834, who swore secret oaths. But like Melbourne and Holland, he believed that the shortest answer to the unions was an unwavering prosecution of parliamentary reform in order to remove the middle classes' inclination to join them. Holland had a long conversation with Brougham in mid-November and found him to be 'in high health, spirits, and good humour, vehement for an early meeting of Parliament and the immediate introduction of an unaltered bill'.

He, the Chancellor, saw the King twice today, and in two conversations impressed on his Majesty forcibly the alarming state of the Country, the probable necessity of calling parliament soon, and the extension of unions and of intense feeling in the country on the subject of reform. He denied that such feelings were confined to the lower orders. He drew a clear distinction between the middling classes and the mere rabble, and between the determined reformers which composed the last and the lovers of plunder which had no doubt too much preponderance in the latter. He stated yet more forcibly the utter impossibility of keeping down the plunderers in a community like ours, if the middle classes were adverse to Government and disposed to be the allies of the mob or even neutral and indifferent in the hour of tumult and confusion.[58]

The last session of parliament had continued long after its normal term and Grey was reluctant to subject members to the additional inconvenience of returning to town before Christmas. He suspected that Brougham was pressing for an early recall of parliament in the hope that the cabinet would decide against him and provide him with an excuse to resign the Great Seal. Lord Holland assured Grey that it could not be so, for if that were Brougham's intention he would not have wasted so much time persuading his colleagues of the necessity of an early parliament.[59] Brougham's purpose was to get the reform bill reintroduced in its integrity before the talks with the Waverers could bear fruit. Backed by Melbourne and Holland, he got his way. Grey informed the King on 19 November that, against his judgement, he had felt bound to acquiesce in the view of the majority of the cabinet, 'which was founded (excepting the opinion of the Chancellor, who argued the necessity of an early meeting on the question of

Reform, independently of every other consideration), on the present state of the country, and the danger of depriving ourselves of the power for so long a time, of applying to Parliament for its authority in support of any measures which might be required in ... circumstances which might arise dangerous to the public peace'.[60]

Grey continued to complain of the decision and was 'manifestly chagrined at the Chancellor'.[61] He was not alone. The moderates in the cabinet were angry that the reform bill was to be reintroduced before the channels of compromise had been properly explored. They saw no outcome to that manner of proceeding other than a collision between Lords and Commons. They were angry, too, at Brougham's influence with Barnes, who was using the *Times* to stir up enthusiasm for a swift recall of parliament. 'It is evident,' Lord Palmerston wrote to Melbourne, 'that Brougham has pledged himself in conversation with Barnes and others that Parliament *should* meet before Christmas, and is determined from vanity to redeem his pledge, in order to show his ascendancy in the Cabinet.'[62] 'There is something at work here which we in the country cannot comprehend,' George Lamb, Melbourne's brother, wrote. 'In such cases Charles IV of Spain used to say there was a woman in them. I say there is Brougham.'[63]

The House of Commons reassembled on 6 December. Two weeks later it gave the reform bill its second reading. The country was quieted. At the first cabinet after Christmas, Grey acknowledged with admirable candour that, contrary to his apprehensions, the meeting of parliament had been most beneficial.[64]

* * *

Having secured his immediate object, Brougham went north, as he always did, to spend Christmas with his mother and family. Brougham Hall was undergoing rebuilding. Parts of it were open to the December winds and freshly plastered walls were still damp. Brougham, who was fatigued by twelve months' uninterrupted labour, had been home only a few days when he was seized in the night with violent vomiting and diarrhoea. He was found in the morning so weak that there were fears for his safety. He rallied, however, and by late January was back in town. James Losh, probably rightly, attributed the illness to a nervous disorder which sapped the digestive powers.[65] Nothing else is likely to explain its persistence. In April Lady Holland, now like Lord Holland almost permanently confined to a wheelchair and surrounded by what her husband called her 'host of leeches', reported that Brougham was still low. 'But he does all his duties perfectly; so it is only his private friends who have reason to complain from his want of former gaiety, tho' today he is however full of stories & fun.'[66] The same ailment afflicted Brougham in 1836, when it caused him to miss most of the session. He then sent advice to a fellow-sufferer, Macvey Napier, Jeffrey's successor as editor of the *Edinburgh Review*.

> I am truly concerned to find you have had a relapse. The care to be taken against *cold* is one of the very first of all considerations with a convalescent. You should wrap yourself up even in getting out and into a coach, and have a fur foot-basket, with a flat pan or tin of hot water under your feet while lecturing. I sat in Court and House of Lords all the winter of 1831 and 1832 in that way, and never caught cold, though in a very weak state. This attack is in some respects worse, the debility being greater; but I think I shall get round sooner, because it has come on quicker. The colchicum [meadow-saffron whose corn and seeds yield a drug used to treat gout and rheumatism] agrees with me, and I have been better within the last two or three days, though at first I suffered a good deal. These stomach ailments, whether connected with gout or not, are tedious beyond endurance. Unless I make a much more rapid progress than is very likely, I don't see the possibility of my being in town at the first part of the Session.[67]

The great question facing the cabinet at the beginning of 1832 was how to carry the reform bill through the House of Lords. In November Brougham had given his opinion that, while there might be no harm in listening to the Waverers' suggestions and accepting minor amendments, it would be foolhardy to 'sacrifice a tittle of our principle or a grain of the Confidence we had gained in the House of Commons and Country by any thing like negotiation'.[68] In short, he opted for a creation of peers. In this view he was supported by Durham and Holland. Grey, however, thought that the number of new peerages required—at least forty and more probably sixty—rendered that solution impossible. By the end of 1831 the idea of a compromise with the Waverers had faded and Grey was forced to reconsider. Brougham was too ill to attend the cabinet of 1 January, when the matter was fully debated, but in two letters which were read to the meeting he strongly urged the policy of creating peers and creating them, moreover, before the crisis of the second reading should be reached.[69] Suppose, Brougham argued, that the House of Lords was left unaltered. The Lords might then accept the reform bill in principle on the second reading, but savage it by amendment after amendment in committee. The government would then find itself beaten since no single amendment could be made to appear sufficiently damaging to justify the dangerous precedent of a large creation of peers. If ten or twelve peers were created immediately, the country and the Tory opposition would learn that the King was in earnest in supporting ministers and their bill.

Grey accepted Brougham's advice. He received the King's written permission to use his discretion in making whatever addition to the peerage was necessary. He made no immediate creations, however, and affairs ambled towards the event that Brougham had prophesied. The Lords gave the bill its second reading in mid-April and three weeks later tore the heart out of it in committee by passing Lord Lyndhurst's amendment requiring a postponement of the clause disfranchising the boroughs listed in schedule A. On 7 April the King had pledged himself once more, as he had in January, to allow ministers to act 'up to the full exigency of the case'. The majority in favour of Lyndhurst's amendment was 35. Immediately after the House rose, in the early morning of 8 May, the cabinet gathered in the chancellor's private room and agreed to ask for the King's permission to nominate fifty or sixty new peers. Brougham and Grey went to Windsor that afternoon to see the King, who told them that he must have the night to consider his answer.

> Grey and I then set out, and on our way home had a wretched dinner at Hounslow, where we ate mutton-chops, and I insisted upon a broiled kidney being added to the poor repast. He laughed at me for being so easy and indifferent; and said 'he cared not for kidneys'. Nevertheless he ate them when they came. And we were in all the print-shops in a few days.[70]

The next day Grey received the King's refusal and the government resigned. There is no reason to doubt that the relief which ministers expressed at going out after months of uncertainty was genuine. Brougham, still debilitated by his winter illness, had replied to Lyndhurst's wrecking amendment in the Lords with unwonted calm and 'without that peremptory and fearless repudiation of the motion, as utterly inimical to the principle of reform and fatal to the bill, which seemed necessary to expose the plot'.[71] When the note came to him from Grey announcing that the King had accepted their resignations, he was sitting with Le Marchant and Lord Sefton. Creevey, whose information came from Sefton, probably exaggerated when he wrote that Brougham 'sprung from his chair and, rubbing his hands, declared that it was the happiest moment of his life'.[72] Le Marchant's account was more sober.

> I was sitting at 10 minutes to 10 in Berkeley Square when a note was delivered to the Chancellor. He read it out.
> 'Our resignations are accepted.' (Grey)
> His countenance did not change, nor did he give any sign of caring about the matter. Indeed he had for some time been prepared for it. He said that during the last 2 months the King had evidently thrown himself into other hands—his confidence in the Government was withdrawn.[73]

William IV was not a learned king. When Brougham delivered up the Great Seal he implored him to stay on as *his* chancellor, a touching request that harked back to the constitutional habits of the early days of George III. Brougham gently told him that he could not separate himself from Lord Grey. William discovered that ministers were his servants in theory only. He discovered also that the power of the Crown to make and unmake ministries was nearly exhausted. The fiasco of the Tory attempt to form a government lasted for six days. William recalled the Whigs and consented, at last in earnest, to the creation of as many peers as were necessary. The knowledge of the King's surrender was all that was needed to end the crisis. There was an element of logic to Wellington's argument that bowing to the threat of new peers was just as bad as actually creating them: 'it does by violence force a decision on this House'.[74] Enough Tory peers, however, saw the wisdom in preserving a Tory majority to fight another day. By seceding from the House they brought the reform struggle to its conclusion. Brougham urged the King to attend parliament and give the royal assent to the bill in person. Nothing, he said, after the display of public hostility to the King during the 'May Days' when the Tories were trying to form a government, could do more to attach the people to the monarchy and the constitution. Sir Herbert Taylor, replying for the King, said that Brougham's request did him credit. 'But this is a question of feeling—that which ought to actuate his conduct as a sovereign and a gentleman, not one of duty nor of ordinary usage or precedent—and he cannot bring himself to truckle to that mob which has grossly insulted him, instead of giving him the credit which he feels he deserved for having endeavoured to discharge his duty to the best of his judgment, and according to the dictates of his conscience.'[75] On 7 June, therefore, the reform act took its place on the statute books by commission.

* * *

In 1843 Brougham published in his *Political Philosophy* an opinion which provoked the Duke of Wellington to accuse Grey's government of having played a game of brag with the opposition. Brougham replied that at the time that was not what ministers thought they were doing. In his memoirs he repeated the opinion and added that Grey, after the dust of the battle had settled, had entirely concurred in it.

> Since 1832, I have often asked myself the question, whether, if no secession had taken place, and the Peers had persisted in opposing the Bill, we should have had recourse to that perilous creation. Above thirty years have rolled over my head since the crisis of 1832. I speak as calmly on this, as I now do upon any political matter whatsoever, and *I cannot answer the question in the affirmative*.[76]

13

The Woolsack: II

Samuel Romilly once wrote, when he was dreaming of the day that he might take his seat on the Woolsack, that no man in England was so well placed to influence the happiness of his fellow men as a lord chancellor.[1] He presided, as a judge, over a system founded on the common law which established precedents of enduring power for good or ill. And as a politician he had the authority, if he wished to exercise it, to compel the reform of the statute law both civil and criminal. In the past that authority had habitually been used to prevent reform. By their training and their long years of practice lawyers had, for the most part, come to the lord chancellorship imbued with an unshakable reverence for the law. Even chancellors of liberal temper and reforming intentions had found themselves so occupied by business, so involved in party intrigue and so distracted by the empty pageantry and solemn trifling of their office that, by the end of their tenure, they were happy simply to have fulfilled their duties without impropriety. There was, Romilly believed, only one remedy. A man must have established his principles, formed his intentions and settled his purpose before coming to his high dignity. If he left those things undone until after he took office, he would find neither the time nor the inclination to do them.

Brougham, like the generations of his predecessors on the Woolsack, was a lawyer. But it was his very weakness as a lawyer (not as an advocate), his relative ignorance of the law by comparison with the learning of men like Lord Eldon and Lord Lyndhurst and his impatience with its arcane mysteries, which helped him to be a reforming chancellor. He had sat too long at the feet of Bentham to venerate the archaic forms of the law. He cared less for the law than for the victims of it. His exhaustive speech of 1828 was testimony that he came to the Woolsack with a steadier resolve and a more prepared mind than any chancellor since Bacon. He was ambitious of lasting fame and his ambition came to the aid of his country. 'I am very glad that Brougham is Chancellor,' the Duke of Wellington said. 'He is the only man with courage and talent to reform that damned Court.'[2]

The Duke made his remark after coming up to town to hear the speech, delivered on 22 February 1831, in which Brougham introduced his proposed reforms of Chancery. Law reform was a subject calculated to incur the hostility, or at least leave undisturbed the lethargy, of the House of Lords. Fewer than three dozen peers were present to hear the speech, although the bar and throne were crowded with spectators. Brougham began by attempting to cajole the House, while at the same time impressing the public with the mighty works he was about to accomplish.

> I, a mere novice in the law of that Court, nevertheless begin with attempting what others, to the very close of their career, have not attempted—a change, an innovation; and to sum up all in one expression so hateful, so alien to long-established habits, so sore, so agonising to the experienced practitioner,—in one hateful word, the head and front of my offending—A CHANCERY REFORM. Reform, odious and reprobated in all places, is especially odious and especially reprobated there, when it appears as it were a monster, composed of two parts so utterly irreconcilable and incongruous as CHANCERY and REFORM.

He then continued for four hours to provide a perspicuous analysis of the labyrinthine ways of Chancery practice. The speech, a splendid reminder of his heroic effort of 1828, convinced those who heard it of the seriousness of his purpose. The Duke cheered loudly at the end of it and went away content in the understanding that reform was at last at hand.[3] Upon the public, who had not yet heard details of the cabinet's parliamentary reform bill, it made a deep impression. It gave the first turn to public feeling since the advent of the Whigs to office and was thus of essential service to the government. More than any other of his colleagues Brougham had the tact to carry the arguments of the executive into the hearts and minds of the people. Two years later, when he came to introduce his reform of the local courts, Lord Holland remarked that one of the several merits of his speech was 'the artful manner in which he identified both his bill and the Government with popular feelings at this critical period when it is so essential to reconcile the press and the publick to our administration'.[4]

Over the next few years many useful reforms were enacted: the abolition of countless sinecures and the better regulation of other

offices, the substitution of fixed salaries for fees (in the other Westminster courts as well as Chancery), the removal of the care of
lunatics from the chancellor's charge, and the establishment of
separate courts to deal with bankruptcies. Those reforms were not
paltry. They entailed the loss of much patronage and, in some
instances, income. Less had been accomplished during the whole of
the previous century. But Brougham shrank from putting his sword to
the most vexatious of Chancery procedures, the ancient system by
which every cause was referred to the masters in Chancery, who had
power to appeal over and over against every question, whether of fact
or of law, which had been decided by the equity judge. The procedure
caused many a suit to lie dormant in the masters' office or to pass back
and forth in a *perpetuum mobile* between master and judge, so that years
often passed before a dispute was determined. Yet to have proposed
its abolition in 1831 would, Campbell wrote, have been looked upon
'as preposterous as a bill to abolish the satellites of Jupiter'.[5] When, in
1852, the reform was at last accomplished by Lord Derby's government, the credit was due to Brougham, for having first aired the
subject and for continuing, in the twenty years after his stint on the
Woolsack had ended, to subject the law to vigorous scrutiny, chiefly
through the agency of the Law Amendment Society which he founded
in 1845.

To Brougham was due also the merit of establishing the Old Bailey
as the central criminal court. The Old Bailey had since the Middle
Ages sat throughout the year to try causes arising from offences
committed in the county of Middlesex and the City of London. The
spread of the metropolitan population into Surrey, Kent and Essex,
especially rapid during the latter part of the 18th century, had not
been accompanied by an extension of the Old Bailey's jurisdiction,
and the evil of leaving an area of such concentrated population to the
mercies of infrequent assizes had for some time drawn criticism. Yet
no remedy was applied until 1834, when Brougham established the
central criminal court, with ten sessions a year, to try defendants for
offences committed within twenty miles of St Paul's Cathedral. The
new tribunal, of which the chancellor himself and all the high-court
judges were members, served a population of about two-and-a-half
million.

The year preceding was the most contentious in Brougham's career
as a law reformer. In that year he presented to parliament a bill to
establish local courts for the recovery of small debts and a bill to

reorganize the judicial functions of the Privy Council. The first of those reforms had long been mooted and when Lord Redesdale had proposed it in 1824 even Eldon had admitted its utility. The Privy Council reform was a larger and a more revolutionary undertaking. Yet Brougham was beaten on the first and successful with the second.

Brougham's local courts bill provoked a scrap in the House of Lords that was one of the spectacles of the 1833 session. Pitted against him was Lord Lyndhurst, his predecessor on the Woolsack. Lyndhurst had been appointed Chief Baron of the Exchequer by Lord Grey, but he was not on that account inhibited from playing his part as one of the leaders of the Tory opposition in the upper House. In a few years' time Brougham and Lyndhurst, who shared a rich store of legal and political recollections, were to succumb to friendship, a friendship that gladdened the old age of each of them. In 1833 they were rivals for pre-eminence in the House of Lords, envious of each other's contrasting marks of superiority. Brougham was adored by the populace for the impetuosity with which he embraced popular causes; Lyndhurst was revered by the legal profession and his fellow peers for the measured dignity of his oratory and the close reasoning of his arguments. Lyndhurst fretted to see Brougham in his chancellor's wig, for it was well known that only political necessity had kept Grey from retaining him in his old office. Brougham had made more of a success in the upper House than sage heads had predicted. But he spoke too often, was sometimes too personal in his attacks, and employed too declamatory a style to accommodate himself to the grave expectations of a chamber which flattered itself as a modern Senate. The House never lost the feeling that Brougham was somehow an alien in its midst. Brougham contrived to give the most uncontroversial measures a party tinge; Lyndhurst, who spoke seldom and therefore, when he did, with the authority that derived from men's believing that a grave issue must be at stake, was able, by his dispassionate, analytical manner of address to shield the most partisan of motives in the armour of disinterest.

In 1833 a vociferous section of the Tory peerage was growing restless under the diffident leadership of Wellington and Peel, neither of whom saw virtue in leading a factious opposition to Lord Grey's reforming government. The Tory malcontents were impatient to assert the dignity and independence of their House, so recently humbled in the struggle over the parliamentary reform bill. Brougham's local courts bill gave Lyndhurst an opportunity to lead them into battle. Had Lyndhurst not exerted his powerful talents against the measure it would have passed quietly through the lobbies. Lyndhurst chose, instead, to place himself at the service of those London attornies whose petty grievance it was that the bill would take business out of their hands and give it to barristers in the provinces. He presented Brougham's bill as an encroachment upon the central administration of justice from which all the excellence of the English legal system flowed. The argument had no merit. The bill had one excellent object, to establish local courts where creditors could swiftly and cheaply recover debts of less than £20, debts which were too small to justify the expense and time required to recover them by litigation in the Westminster courts. It foreshadowed no intention, on Brougham's part or the government's, to dismantle the great law courts of the land. True, it added a little to the patronage at the government's disposal and Lyndhurst delighted the more violent Tories by playing on Brougham's supposed rapaciousness. Yet, for all that, the Lords drew back at Brougham's insistent hectoring. They were not, when the bill came to its second reading, seduced by the more subtle arts of Lord Lyndhurst. They followed Wellington's advice and allowed the bill to proceed, without a division, into committee.

Lyndhurst fumed. He would, he said, cease to come to the aid of his party if the party would not come to his support. He would, in future, cease even to attend the House. Impotent threats. But Lyndhurst's spirits revived when Brougham blundered into one of those errors of judgement which from time to time dismayed his colleagues. The bill was entirely Brougham's. He had not divulged its contents to the cabinet. He had introduced it as an individual member's bill. Yet one day in committee, in answer to a question from Lyndhurst, he let from his lips the falsehood that it was a government measure. At once the debate assumed a party aspect. The whips of both parties stirred themselves to collect proxies from every corner of the country and when the day for the third reading came on, Samuel Warren, a barrister and a Tory, went down to the House expecting to see 'a fair stand up fight between the big 'uns'. When he arrived he saw Brougham on the Woolsack, 'his features full of feverish anxiety, and his gestures of impatience—beckoning hurriedly now to this, and now to the other friend, as he observed the Opposition peers flowing into the House'.⁶ The antagonists spoke each for about two hours, Lyndhurst in calm tones warning the House that cheap justice was not necessarily sound justice. 'Carping, declamatory sneering' was Brougham's reply. Among those present the issue was drawn: 81 for and 81 against. Tory proxies carried the day.

Brougham was saddened to see a useful, practical reform sacrificed to Tory malignancy. The defeat occurred at the same time as the Tory peers were arraying themselves against the government's chief measure of the session, a bill to lighten the burden imposed upon the Catholic population of Ireland by the Irish Church. Brougham wrote in despondent mood to the King and received from Sir Herbert Taylor, the King's secretary, a kind reply.

> The King is not surprised that you should be tired and disgusted with the present course of things, and with holding office in such times, and with the annoyance of encountering almost daily the bitter hostility of the House of Lords; and he can easily conceive that you often heartily wish yourself out of so unpleasant and unprofitable a concern; but I need not say how strongly his Majesty feels that you can on no account be spared. Times may mend, and the best chance of their mending is afforded by the continual services of such men as yourself. If these should cease to put their shoulder to the wheel, the machine will stop.[7]

Defeat on the local courts bill, although vexing to Brougham, was overshadowed by his signal success in remodelling the appellate jurisdiction of the Privy Council.[8] The council heard appeals from ecclesiastical and colonial courts. Brougham's bill dealt chiefly with the latter jurisdiction. Appeals from colonial courts were heard in an *ad hoc* committee of the council and over the years, as the size of the empire increased, the system had fallen into disrepute. In his law reform speech of 1828 he had drawn attention to the most iniquitous defects of the system. Since every Privy Councillor was entitled to take part in the appeal hearings, lay members outvoted judges and lawyers. Once he had cleared the arrears in Chancery and removed bankruptcy suits from the chancellor's jurisdiction, Brougham himself took care to attend appeals heard by the Privy Council, but he was the first chancellor to do so and the only other regular professional judge to attend was the Master of the Rolls. Yet this unprofessional and uninformed committee, composed of members who happened to turn up on the day, was required to pass judgement on a host of complicated decisions which had been reached according to a wide variety of laws, including Muslim and Hindu law. The committee sat far less often than any other court—in the twelve years after 1815 an average of only nine days a year—because it had no regular bench and no regular bar. The result was that, despite a high proportion of causes in which the appeal was successful, few appeals were entered, since it was known that they would not be heard for years. To treat subjects of the Crown with such flagrant disregard amounted, as Brougham said, to an absolute denial of justice. His remedy was to recast the committee, to make it a properly constituted court which sat frequently throughout the year, with a permanent bench and a permanent bar, and to appoint to its bench judges of wide legal and general information who should make it their duty to acquaint themselves with the laws of the colonies.

From the moment that Brougham began to draft his bill in late 1832 he encountered the peevish opposition of Charles Greville, a clerk of the council, and James Stephen, who acted as standing counsel to the council. The chief elements of the bill were the exclusion from the judicial committee of all lay persons, including the lord president, and the appointment of four salaried judges to comprise the permanent bench under the lord chancellor. Greville, whose dislike of Brougham breathes through his diaries, and Stephen, who was nettled by Brougham's refusal to give him silk, worked upon Lord Lansdowne, the lord president of the council, to discredit the bill. Greville represented it as nothing more than a cover for Brougham's ambition, 'and one which Lord L[ansdowne] ought not to consent to, the object evidently being to make a Court of which Brougham shall be at the head, and to transfer to it much of the authority of the Crown, Parliament, and Privy Council; all from his ambitious and insatiable desire of personal aggrandisement'.[9] Stephen drew up a list of objections to the bill and sent them to Lansdowne, who asked Brougham to answer them. 'Ch[ancello]r. will be very angry,' Greville wrote, 'for he can't endure contradiction.'[10] Stephen put three chief objections to Lansdowne: the judicial committee had been established by order-in-council and to alter it by act of parliament was an injury to the royal prerogative; Brougham was attempting, by making the chancellor head of the court, to usurp the place of the lord president and gain permanent authority for himself; by removing the lay members from the committee, Brougham was transferring the powers of government to the new court. The first two objections were silly, but the third had a measure of logic, since governments had been accustomed to use the judicial committee to enforce imperial policy. In cabinet Brougham was persuaded to accept a compromise by which the lord president should continue to sit on the committee and the Crown should retain the power to appoint two councillors to it in addition to those councillors who, by virtue of their past or present experience as judges, were members by right. The concession was minor, insufficient to wreck his purpose, and the bill passed through both Houses of parliament— 'smuggled', the former vice-chancellor, Leach, commented sourly— without the 'slightest notice or remark'.[11]

The harvest of Brougham's labour was quickly reaped. The committee doubled the number of its sittings and doubled the number of appeals which it heard. 'In depriving the imperial government of any real share in the determination of Conciliar appeals,' the most recent student of the court's establishment has written, 'Brougham had made it plain that the jurisdiction exercised by the Judicial Committee now existed for the benefit of the suitor, not for the benefit of the Mother Country.'[12]

The new judicial committee was Brougham's finest and most enduring legislative achievement. It is a pity that Bentham did not live to see its enactment. Shortly before his death, in 1832, he published a crude attack on Brougham in a pamphlet entitled *Lord Brougham Displayed*. Bentham was disappointed by the bit-by-bit approach which Brougham had adopted in the reform of Chancery and the bankruptcy courts. He railed at him for having fallen prey to 'sinister influence, interest-begotten prejudice, and interest-begotten sympathy'. The language was immoderate and the charge itself ill-founded. Bentham, as James Mill once described him, was a 'one-eyed man'. He left out of his account the obstacles which a deliberative assembly places in the way of root-and-branch reform. Had he lived a year longer, he would have seen Brougham establish a commission to prepare statutes for the consolidation (bringing statutes together) and the codification (the orderly statement of the leading rules of law) of the criminal law, the very objects, that is, to which Bentham had devoted so much of his mind. The commission and its successor remained in existence until 1859 and, if they failed to remodel the law of England on the French example, they nevertheless initiated many a useful improvement of it. To achieve what Brougham achieved in the 1830s, against the lethargy of the House of Lords, was, as Arthur Turberville wrote, a high tribute both to his extraordinary gifts and to the urgency with which he brought them to bear on the subject. 'Though he failed in some of his attempts,' Turberville summed up, 'he accomplished so much either directly in his own time or indirectly by making the way clear for others, that the modern lawyer thinks of him as the man who brought order out of chaos.'[13]

* * *

While Brougham was pursuing his programme of law improvement, the Whig government which had come into office two-and-a-half years earlier was beginning to run into difficulties. At the elections held under the new rules laid down in the reform act, the Tory party, not unexpectedly, had suffered heavy losses. Supporters of the government filled three-quarters of the House of Commons. Their allegiance, however, was not of the stuff which modern governments have come to expect. What constituted the apparent Whig majority was an amalgam of conflicting interests. In addition to the true representatives of old Whiggery, who made up perhaps half of the pro-government 'party', there were the large body of Irish members ready to follow O'Connell in threatening the dissolution of the Union, a radical section displeased by the half-baked democracy of the reform act and waiting to ambush the government if it trimmed on other questions, and a small group of ultra Tories who had still to make their peace with Sir Robert Peel and the Duke of Wellington. To keep such troops marching in one direction was a test, not only of the skill, but of the resolve of the man placed in their command. Lord Grey was tired. The reform struggle had sapped his political will and exhausted his ambition. He looked forward to an early retirement. Grey was seventy. Brougham was in his early fifties, and the predictions that the House of Lords would swallow him into oblivion had been falsified. The publicity which attended the passing of the reform bill raised him to a pinnacle of fame nearly equal to that which he had occupied twelve years earlier during the royal divorce trial. 'For a brief space,' Campbell wrote, 'comprising the end of the year 1832 and the beginning of 1833, he enjoyed, I really believe, a greater supremacy and popularity than any of his predecessors, Cardinal Wolsey alone excepted. The nation was actually mad about the Reform Bill, and the merit of carrying it through the Lords was chiefly attributed to Lord Chancellor Brougham.'[14]

Much of that popularity derived from Brougham's influence with the press, especially the *Times*, whose daily flattering of the chancellor was irksome to his colleagues. When the newspapers were lauding Brougham's virtues as a law reformer, Edward Ellice comforted Lord Grey by reminding him that he, too, had friends. 'Altho' they have not puffed you to the same extent, which his satellites & companions, greater adepts from practice and experience in the art, & less scrupulous in the use of it, have . . . it has been because they were more restricted by good taste, & a sense of what was equally due to others of yr. Colleagues. You do not stand lower in the estimation of respectable people, & whose opinions are really valuable, for not employing trumpeters of all disabilities, & at all times, to sound your praises in the newspapers.'[15] Brougham's fussiness made him a difficult colleague. On one occasion, when he suggested that he should travel to America to study secondary punishments in penitentiaries there, Grey wrote wearily to Lord Melbourne that 'as Brougham seldom fails to carry a point on which he has set his mind, I suppose we must acquiesce in this mission . . . tho' I still retain all my doubts as to its real utility'.[16]

In 1833 the more radical followers of the government began to suspect Brougham of trimming on those issues by which he had been assisted in his rise to place. Slavery was abolished in 1833, but Brougham took little part in the cabinet discussions of the bill, other than to lend his weight to the provision which most angered the abolitionists, the substitution of a period of seven years' apprenticeship in freedom for outright, immediate emancipation. When the government took the first, tentative step towards establishing a system of state-assisted education by providing a parliamentary grant of £20,000 to be distributed among the various voluntary societies, Brougham supported the scheme, but he had retreated so far from the advanced position he had taken up in his own parish schools bill of 1820 that he now deprecated legislative interference with the voluntary system and opposed, what had once been his principal object, the levying of a compulsory rate for the support of primary education. He seemed ready, too, to abandon the Dissenters. In March 1834 Lord John Russell prepared a bill to redress a major grievance of the Dissenters by making it lawful for them to be married in a civil ceremony outside the Church of England. Brougham and Althorp succeeded in blocking the bill, just as they had blocked a proposal to establish a civil registration of births and deaths, on the ground that it would be too expensive. Denis le Marchant was astonished to discover that Brougham cared little about the matter and was unwilling even to discuss it.[17]

Years of near ceaseless work, accompanied by periods of ill health, may have robbed Brougham of energy and dimmed his enthusiasm. Greville observed him at Stoke Farm, the Buckinghamshire seat of Lord Sefton, in August 1833, and remarked that he was not so talkative as usual. 'His dignities, his labours, and the various cares of his situation have dashed his gaiety, and pressed down his once elastic spirits; however, he was not otherwise than chearful and lively.'[18] Indeed, his colleagues had many occasions to wish that he were less lively. Brougham diminished his standing within the Whig party by interfering too often in the departmental business of others, by persisting too long in his own opinions on small points, and by playing too independent a part in parliament without informing Grey or anyone else of his intentions. Week after week, at the end of 1832 and the beginning of 1833, he nagged at Grey to move Edward Stanley, the Irish secretary, to the colonial office, and would not let the matter drop despite the conviction of the entire cabinet that the time for the change, necessary as it certainly would become, was not ripe. Having failed to get Stanley transferred, he then meddled in the work of the Irish office by preparing his own draft of an Irish Church reform bill. And when the government's bill, later in the session, was in danger of being emasculated by the Lords, he overreached his authority by informing the King that the government would ask for a creation of peers to overcome the Lords' resistance. Grey rebuked him for his high-handedness. 'This, you may remember,' the prime minister wrote to him, 'the Cabinet had agreed in considering as out of the question, on the present occasion.'[19] Brougham offended, too, by taking credit for measures which were not his. At the close of the 1833 session he postponed the reading of several bills which had come up from the House of Commons, thereby incurring the anger of some Whigs, notably Thomas Kennedy, who saw his small debts legislation sacrificed. To the great displeasure of Lord Holland, habitually mild-tempered, he then 'redeemed his character by suddenly appropriating to himself the merit of a bill of Lord Althorp's on English Corporations, which he announced and in some measure described for the subsequent Session, and which was next day represented in many of the papers as a work of consummate wisdom, conceived and nurtured in his powerful and prolifick brain'.[20]

The year 1834 opened with Brougham downcast at the death, in the last week of December, of his brother, James. James had for some years acted as a kind of amanuensis to the chancellor, although no one was able to discover in him any talent to fit him for the role. His death saddled Brougham with the responsibility for large debts and for a time he seemed unable to attend to public duties with his characteristic zest. Late in March, Le Marchant noted the change that had come over him. 'Whether it is the death of his brother, or the apprehension of misfortunes arising out of that event, but he has been since his return [from Christmas at Westmorland] entirely of a different temperament. He has lost his accustomed energy and become irresolute and indifferent to politics. He rarely attends the Cabinet, and when he does it is usually at the close of the sitting when everything has been settled before his arrival. Lord Grey and Lord Althorp complain of this loudly.'[21] Brougham's explanation of his apparent listlessness was somewhat different. In a memorandum for the cabinet, written on the last day of April,[22] he complained of the vast quantity of work which he was compelled to undertake, work which he described, either disingenuously or under the influence of a temporary lassitude, as uncongenial to his real tastes. What, he asked his colleagues, if the government should be removed from office?

No one of its members has, perhaps, more reason personally to desire the ease which such an event would bestow on him than the writer of these pages. The labour which he undergoes and cannot escape, and which, since the 2d of November last, with the interruption of a fortnight far more painfully passed, must be continued three months longer; he feels it every hour more irksome, and looks forward to its becoming unbearable. When he says that, besides sitting daily in court seven hours, he is never in bed before two, and that he has since November written with his own hand above seventy long judgments, some of which took an hour, and some two, to read, and all of which would fill two very large printed volumes—he is far from desiring to boast of hard work; but he makes the statement as an irrefragable proof that he must have a singular taste to love such an existence. And to what does he prefer it? To a state which he has all his life deemed the perfection of happiness, and never enjoyed for a week—namely, being free from all care and all occupation, and at liberty to devote himself to his public and Parliamentary duty as an independent member of

Parliament, upon the side of the question most congenial to his habits.

The memorandum, a lengthy one, was written to encourage a dispirited and wrangling Whig cabinet. For some time William IV, the heady effect of his popularity as the reformers' king having passed away, had been reverting to his more natural Toryism. Lord Grey and Lord Althorp were candid in their desire to be released from office. Twice in the previous eighteen months, most recently in January, when the cabinet was divided in its attitude towards Portugal, Brougham had taken the lead in persuading Grey that his retirement would be fatal both to the ministry and to the prospects of the country, left as it would be to a minority Conservative government or a gravely weakened Whig one. Now, in the spring of 1834, the government was in peril of its existence. A most delicate and disruptive issue, the reform of the Irish Church, brought to the surface the latent antagonism in the cabinet between leftward-leaning ministers, led by Lord John Russell, and conservatively inclined ones, led by Edward Stanley, the future Earl of Derby. The division in the cabinet was an accurate reflection of the state of opinion in the country. On the one side stood the Irish followers of O'Connell, representatives of the Catholic peasantry, insistent in the demand that the Anglican Establishment in Ireland be uprooted, since it was both a moral outrage and a financial burden imposed upon the majority of the Irish population by a selfish imperial parliament for the gratification of the tiny Protestant minority. The Irish view commanded the sympathy of English radicals and progressive Whigs. On the other side stood those Tories who were determined that no capitulation to the Irish Catholics should impair the integrity of the Established Church, undermine the rights of property, or weaken the bonds of the imperial union with Ireland. Between the two extremes stood most of the Whig cabinet, willing to make concessions to the Irish, but wary of alienating Protestant opinion in England.

In his last act as Irish secretary, in the early months of 1833, Stanley had guided through the House of Commons a two-pronged strategy for Ireland. In order to put a stop to the outbreaks of violence there, violence directed chiefly against the collection of the tithe to support the Church, he introduced a harsh coercion bill. Its severe restrictions of Irish liberties persuaded Lord Durham to make his escape from a cabinet in whose ability to initiate radical reforms he had already lost faith. To balance the heavy dose of coercion, Stanley prepared a bill to diminish the weight of the Church in Ireland. The bill abolished ten of the twenty-two Irish bishoprics, got rid of the cess, a local tax equivalent to the English Church rate, and reduced the income of the primate of Ireland by one-third. The bill stopped short of addressing the critical matter of the tithe, but it went farther than the conservative element in the cabinet desired by including the proposition that 'surplus' revenues of the Church could be 'appropriated' by parliament to other purposes. That principle was laid down in Clause 147. It was the principle on which Lord Grey's government foundered.

In cabinet Lord John Russell fought for parliament's right to appropriate revenues of the Church to secular purposes. He lost the fight. Clause 147 merely said that the revenues could be used for religious and charitable purposes. Even so, when it came to be debated in 1833 the strength of the Tory resistance to its supposed interference with the rights of private property (the logical ground for calling it 'interference' was shaky, since the Church was parliament's creature) was such that it was obvious that it could not be carried through the House of Lords. To the delight of Stanley, Melbourne and, indeed, the majority of the cabinet, it was therefore agreed that the clause would be withdrawn. There the matter might have rested, but for Russell. He acquiesced in Stanley's bill, but he did not abandon his belief in the justice of 'lay appropriation'. Nor was he happy to see Stanley, his chief rival, men thought, for the future leadership of the Whig party, steal a march on him. When, therefore, an Irish tithe bill was brought before the cabinet in February 1834, he expressed his disquiet at its omitting any reference to the question of appropriation. From that moment Russell and Stanley were locked in a duel to determine the future course of Whig policy towards Ireland. Brougham's April memorandum was a piece of cautionary advice to Russell not to force the issue to the breaking-point.

Men were always quick to perceive behind every one of Brougham's actions a scheme to advance himself towards the premiership. Early in 1834 his proposal to separate the Great Seal from the political functions of the lord chancellor was interpreted in that light and scotched. Yet if Brougham were to rise to the top, the means would have to be something other than the Whig party. When he asked Russell in 1832 whether the party would have him as its leader, Russell had simply and truthfully answered him, 'Not at all'.[23]

The road to power, if it existed at all, would have to be opened up by the King, who hankered after a government of the centre composed of Whigs and moderate Tories (or Conservatives, as they were now coming to call themselves). Yet that Brougham, for all that the King continued to flatter him, should be placed at the head of such a coalition was improbable, since its formation would depend upon a final rupture in the Whig cabinet which would leave Stanley the leader of the anti-Russell Whigs. Brougham's immediate prospects, therefore, were limited to retaining the Woolsack and, as the means of doing that, keeping Lord Grey's government in office.

In his memorandum of 30 April Brougham warned his colleagues that if the ministry broke up the only alternative was the formation of a Conservative government, an outcome which would be attended with 'the most imminent hazard to the country'. It therefore became every member of the government 'on any question of individual conduct or feeling ... to submit to many things—to bear and forbear—to undertake tasks alien to his inclinations—to do all but abandon principles'.

> Friend to Reform and improvement as he is, and always has been, and even disappointed at some measures having been postponed so long, he infinitely prefers the disappointment, the sickness arising from hope deferred, to the perils of too rapid changes—to sweeping reforms.

The advice was pointed chiefly at Stanley and Russell, who cannot have forgotten Brougham's forbearance and submission in 1830. They believed, however, that lay appropriation raised a principle which could not be swept out of sight. On 6 May Russell rose in the House of Commons to declare, to the cheers of the Irish and the radicals, his implacable attachment to the principle, whereupon Stanley passed to Edward Ellice a note on which were scribbled the words that have since become famous, 'John Russell has upset the coach'. At the next day's meeting of the cabinet, Lord Grey announced that he would resign if the quarrel were not at once patched up. Brougham spoke next and observed, according to Lord Sefton, that he was placed in a different situation from Lord Grey's, 'that, while he considered his political life as closing, I considered my own as only just beginning—that I never felt younger or more vigorous—that, from the moment the present Government was broken up,. all my occupation and resources should be devoted to destroying *any other* one—that there was nothing I would not under-take to accomplish that object—that I would attend all political meetings out of Parliament, publick and private, and that from the present temper of the publick, which I well knew, I was as sure as I was of my existence that *no* Government but an ultra-Liberal one, both in Church and State affairs, would be endured for a week'. Having failed to restrain Russell, Brougham was making an appeal to Stanley. His object, he told Sefton, was to 'frighten the damned idiots Stanley and Co. from attempting by themselves, or by coalescing with Peel and Co., to set up a Church government; and I think I did so'.[24]

A couple of weeks later, when neither Stanley nor Russell were showing any spirit of accommodation, Brougham made a last effort to save the government. In a paper circulated to the cabinet he argued that Russell's declaration, being quite personal, was not binding on any other minister. How then could anyone think it dishonourable to remain in office, when that declaration produced no practical effect, called upon no one to pursue any course of action, and left every minister free to act as he pleased?[25] The question had only a temporary force. Had Stanley and his cohort, Sir James Graham, had nowhere to go, had they not been nurturing hopes of forming a centre party of their own, had they been convinced, that is, that their future careers were entwined in the future prosperity of the Whig party, they might have drawn back from the brink. Had Russell, for his part, not come to believe that the cause of justice to Ireland and the cause of Whiggery were inseparable, he too might have backed down. Brougham represented as tactics what Stanley and Russell recognized to be fundamental. Time would widen, not close, the rift. Neither Stanley nor Graham had any longer a home in the Whig party. On 27 May they resigned their offices, taking with them the ex-Tory, the Duke of Richmond, and the ex-Canningite, the Earl of Ripon. Brougham, blinded by anger and frustration, fixed his scorn on Russell. 'Henceforward,' he wrote to him, 'the name of Whig and driveller are synonymous.'[26]

*   *   *

Lord Grey, who would gladly have grasped the opportunity to retire to private life, was persuaded by the entreaties of the King and a vote of the House of Commons to remain at the head of the government. Remaking the cabinet was a messy affair, conducted amid unseemly displays of ministerial ill-temper. The press made much of Lord Durham's exclusion, but he had damaged himself by his highly coloured, public disclosure, after his resignation from the government in 1833, of the confidential cabinet discussions which had taken place during the struggle for the great reform bill. Thomas Raikes, the journalist and diarist, was wrong to assert that Durham was kept out by a 'manoeuvre' of Brougham, who worked to 'create unnecessary confusion' in order 'to ride the whirlwind and direct the storm'.[27] There was scarcely a minister who, having suffered Durham's tantrums in the cabinet before, was willing to remain if he were re-admitted to it. Brougham's behaviour in the crisis, nevertheless, displayed symptoms of that unsteadiness which had earned him the nickname, 'Old Wickedshifts'. Lord Holland described it in his diary.

The Chancellor was in a state of much agitation or, as the fashionable phrase now is, 'excitement', and as usual with him on such occasions vehement, indiscreet, unscrupulous in his assertions and overbearing in his manners, but full of eloquent invective, satirical wit, extraordinary knowledge, and singular resources, sometimes hyperbolical and sometimes scurrilous, in arguing the pretensions of those he favored or the disqualifications of those he disliked, but yet more anxious to have the fame of doing all than to do it, and willing therefore even when thwarted to adopt and father the appointment which had thwarted him as the offspring of his own designs.[28]

Brougham did more than make life difficult for Grey. He usurped the prime minister's functions by personally advising the King on the progress of the negotiations and assuring him that he would answer for their success. Midway through the negotiations Grey was at the point of throwing the game up.

I feel more and more doubtful as to the possibility of our going on [he wrote to Brougham]. The whole press and the high popular party against us on one side, the Tories on the other, and our friends, notwithstanding their parting solicitations to me to go on—instead of showing confidence and giving us support, even if in some instances they make think us wrong—full of complaint, and assisting the attacks of our enemies;—what have we to expect but that, on the very first occasion, we should be exposed to a new difficulty like that which has brought on the present crisis? We may stagger on for a while, but we must strike at last under circumstances much more disadvantageous both to ourselves and to the public.

I feel greatly inclined, therefore, to give the thing up at once, stating both to the King and the country that we were willing and desirous to do everything in our power to avert the consequences of a change, but that we have found it impossible to form an Administration sufficiently strong in public confidence to conduct the affairs of the country with advantage.[29]

Brougham played upon Grey's patriotism and persuaded him to persevere, but Grey came to rue the hour that he forsook his own instincts. The remodelled cabinet, its vacant places supplied by second-rate men, failed to rekindle enthusiasm in progressive quarters. A 'lath-and-plaster Cabinet' Thomas Barnes, editor of the *Times*, called it. And within a month Grey's forebodings were vindicated. The refloated government foundered, like many a government before and after, on the rock of Ireland, steered on to it, Grey and almost everyone else believed, by Brougham.

The new cabinet met for the first time on 8 June, when the session was well advanced and the government had still two important and controversial Irish bills to conduct through parliament. One was the tithe bill, which, in an attempt to remove the chief cause of agrarian disturbances in Ireland, proposed to commute the tithe (collected for the support of the Established clergy) into a land tax payable, not by the peasant farmers, but by the landlords, and to hand over the revenue to ecclesiastical commissioners to distribute among the clergy. The bill was vitiated, in Irish eyes, by its failure to make any concession to the Roman Catholics' argument that the Church of Ireland was over-funded. No surplus revenue was to be released to deal with Ireland's distressing social conditions. It was for that reason that Lord John Russell had made the declaration that drove the Stanleyites out of the Whig party. It was for that reason, also, that O'Connell denounced the bill outright. Despite a number of amendments introduced to propitiate the Irish members, the bill was certain to provoke heated and protracted debates in committee.

The government had also to consider its attitude towards the Irish coercion bill, introduced by Stanley in 1833 and due to expire after one year unless it were formally renewed by parliament. To the Irish its most obnoxious feature was the ban on public meetings, which they regarded as an unjust infringement upon their constitutional liberties. The English defence of the ban was that political agitation and rural outrage went hand in hand. In 1834 ministers cited the diminution of offences in proclaimed districts as evidence that the ban was effective. The question therefore became whether its success argued for its continuation or, since quieter times prevailed, its demise.

In the spring of 1834 the lord-lieutenant of Ireland, the Marquess of Wellesley, appeared to have no doubt of the answer. In a letter written to Lord Grey on 21 April he gave his unqualified opinion that the ban should be renewed. He repeated the advice in another letter to Grey of 11 June. Grey found the advice unexceptionable and assumed that the cabinet would accept it without argument. He put the matter out of his mind. Brougham saw the question in a different light. He fancied that by dropping the public meetings clause the government would both win fresh support among disaffected radicals in England and assuage Irish anger sufficiently to ease the burden of getting the tithe bill carried through parliament. He decided to take matters into his own hand, without consulting either the prime minister or Lord Melbourne, the home secretary. He suggested to Edward Littleton, Stanley's successor as Irish secretary, that he write to Wellesley to ask him to recommend that the offending clause be withdrawn. He had himself, as he told Littleton, already written to Wellesley in that vein. Littleton, whose official career was in its first week, did Brougham's bidding and the effect was to change the lord-lieutenant's mind. Wellesley wrote to Grey on 21 June, only days before the bill was to come before parliament, to say that he now believed that it would be wrong to continue the prohibition of public meetings. The prime minister, incensed by so sudden and inexplicable a turnabout, replied immediately to rebuke Wellesley for his inconsistency. He decided to regard the letter of 21 June as a piece of private correspondence and to act in the light of Wellesley's initial, more considered, advice.

Unknown to Grey, his policy was being undermined. When Littleton was informed of Wellesley's change of heart, he went to Lord Althorp to suggest a meeting with O'Connell, who might, if the new circumstances were intimated to him, be deterred from mounting a fresh campaign of agitation. Althorp, without seeking Grey's permission, authorized Littleton to talk to O'Connell, warning him, however, not to commit the government to any course of action, but simply to say that the issue was still unresolved. Althorp also told

Littleton that he would resign from the government if the cabinet insisted on retaining the ban, once again warning Littleton not to divulge the information to O'Connell. O'Connell was a wilier man than Littleton and in the course of their conversation he drew from him the statement that Wellesley had formally advised the prime minister not to renew the ban and that he and Lord Althorp concurred in the lord-lieutenant's opinion. Gulled by O'Connell's pledge of secrecy, Littleton then committed an additional blunder by neglecting to inform Althorp that he had exceeded the terms of his commission.

The cabinet met to consider the coercion bill on 29 June. Wellesley's letter of 21 June was laid before it and Grey and Melbourne spoke unreservedly against it. To Althorp's astonishment Brougham, without alluding to his part in the business, sided with them, and to his dismay he learned for the first time that Wellesley's latest letter contradicted his earlier advice. Finding himself stranded, he stood his ground, divided the cabinet against the clause, and was beaten. That night he sent a letter of resignation to Lord Grey, who replied in a long letter which gave release to his sorrow and his anger.

> Your letter, as you anticipated, has certainly distressed me to the greatest degree; I at present can see no way out of the difficulties but that of resigning the government. That I was induced to go on after the division that took place in the former Cabinet is now to me an object of increased regret; I could then have retired on grounds which nobody could have disapproved—I am now brought into a situation in which whatever care I take, I must be exposed to censure and reproach . . . I feel that I have great reason to complain that, after a measure had been agreed upon, and no doubt existed with respect to it, private communications are made to the Lord Lieutenant without my knowledge, which induce him to express an opinion inconsistent with that which his own views of the state of Ireland have suggested, and chiefly maintained on grounds from which I entirely dissent . . . A difference with you is that which affects me most, but I cannot ask you to violate a conscientious opinion, and you, I am sure, will feel that it is entirely impossible for me to acquiesce in a course from which my judgment entirely dissents.[30]

Grey did not resign, nor could Althorp bring himself to abandon him. On 1 July Grey introduced the coercion bill, the meetings clause intact, in the House of Lords. Like Althorp he was even at that late hour ignorant of Littleton's indiscreet confidences to O'Connell. On the following day O'Connell broke his promise of secrecy to Littleton and disclosed to the House of Commons that he had been duped. Althorp listened until O'Connell had finished, then turned to Lord John Russell, who was seated next to him. 'The pig's killed,' he said.[31] The government clung to office for six more days, until a motion to compel publication of the correspondence between Wellesley and ministers was debated in the House of Commons. The motion was defeated, but Althorp wrote to Grey that 'the debate which preceded the division placed us in so disgraceful a position that I cannot expose myself to being in the same position again'.[32] Althorp's determination settled Grey's course. On 8 July the King accepted both men's resignations.

Each of the actors in the farce, except Lord Grey himself, contributed to Grey's downfall. Littleton, indeed, laid the blame on Grey. The prime minister, he argued, had no right to act contrary to the advice of his lord-lieutenant. 'When a Lord-Lieutenant asks for unconstitutional powers,' he wrote to Wellesley on 23 June, 'they may properly be withheld by a Government at home. But when he declares that they can be dispensed with, no Government can require them from Parliament.'[33] After the event Littleton repeated the charge. 'Lord Grey is really greatly in fault in this business. I myself have scarcely erred more than the Minister who insisted on forcing on a Lord-Lieutenant an unconstitutional power he did not want.'[34] As a guide to practical action Littleton's argument had undoubted force; as a constitutional principle it was worthless. A prime minister is never compelled to follow the advice of a lord-lieutenant. Grey had reason to question Wellesley's motives in changing his opinion. It was Wellesley who erred in paying regard to suggestions from Littleton and Brougham. They were moved by considerations of political expediency in England; it was Wellesley's duty to judge the state of Ireland. He ought at least, on so grave a matter, to have informed Grey of the circumstances which prompted him to reverse his judgement. Althorp, too, acted with strange recklessness for a man with a high reputation for common sense and political sensitivity. To entrust a delicate commission to Littleton, an infirm and fledgling minister, was an error, and the error was made worse by his failure to inform Grey of it and his failure to get a report from Littleton. Littleton blamed Althorp for not keeping to his word and resigning when the cabinet voted to retain the meetings clause. Althorp answered that he would have done so, had Littleton told him of his indiscreet remarks to O'Connell.

Littleton's indiscretion was the root cause of the government's fatal embarrassment. Yet the most severe censure was reserved for Brougham. Grey's family, whom Greville saw regularly, were unsparing in their contempt for him, especially since, although they were convinced that he was the prime mover in the affair, his part in it had not been revealed to the public.[35] Creevey (he was not alone) suspected Brougham of plotting to overthrow Grey.

> I am all ashamed to say that I dined at Brougham's on Saturday, because I am as sure as I am of my existence that it was *he* who drove Lord Grey from the Government by his perfidious correspondence with Lord Wellesley respecting the Coercion Bill; and moreover I am equally certain that the driving Lord Grey from the Government has long been the object nearest Brougham's heart. How then can one dine at Brougham's one day with all the rubbish of Lord Grey's Government, with Beelzebub himself in roaring spirits (his servants in *silk* stockings and waiting in *gloves*), and then dine at Lord Grey's yesterday, with *him* quite knocked down and poor Lady Grey actually speechless—both feeling that he has been the victim of the basest perfidy? Poor Lady Grey! you must remember how often she told me at the formation of the Government, and with her uniform horror of Brougham, how completely she had got him in a cage by having him in the House of Lords. They were both quite sure he could do no harm, tho' they well knew his dispositions.[36]

Lord Sefton, too, who considered that Grey had been sacrificed by 'a low-lived crew, not worthy to wipe his shoes', believed 'that the Archfiend Brougham has been all along the mover of this plot for his own base and ambitious selfish purposes'.[37] Had Brougham, both in the cabinet and in parliament, given a straightforward account of his actions, some of the sting might have been removed from the arrows shot by his critics, although his reputation had already sunk so low that they would not have been disarmed. Instead, Brougham provided them with weapons by his declaration in the House of Lords that the resignation of Grey and Althorp had not dissolved the ministry and by his strange correspondence with the King, in which he extolled the virtue of the House of Lords and disparaged the House of Commons. But those were not, Lord Holland wrote, actions calculated to remove royal suspicions of Brougham's unfitness for the premiership. Holland found it impossible to imagine that Brougham had visions of replacing Grey.

> There were indeed in these notable performances, as well as in many other passages of the Chancellor's speeches and conduct at that time, no very covert threat of resorting to furious popular courses if driven by despair to adopt them, but there were also many assurances and declarations which, if divulged, would have shaken all reliance in the sincerity of such a course, and the King moreover was well aware that his position in the House of Lords was of itself an insurmountable bar to such a career and that the Commons were by no means so favorable as to give him in his situation of exclusion from its debates so unusual an advantage as an ascendancy over its decisions. Of this latter misfortune and the signal loss of his popularity in that house, some gleams must have flashed on his mind, however his vanity strove to fortify himself against them. His idle practice of signing Hry Brougham and his ill concealed jealousy of Lord Althorp afforded some proofs that he was not blind to the fact, and that circumstance among others leads me to acquit him of all those designs, of undermining Grey and placing himself in his post, which so many both in the palace and in the publick attribute to him and of which they considered his unjustifiable and restless conduct through these transactions a strong indication. That he was the original if not chief cause of Lord Wellesley's and Mr Littleton's disposition to wave the Clauses, and that he in a clandestine manner organized an intrigue to cajole or compel Lord Grey into a relinquishment of them there can be no doubt . . . All however must acquit him of any actual design of bringing in Tories or Radicals, and I believe it was as little his intention to worm out Lord Grey. Restlessness and a desire to curry favor with the Commons and the publick by appearing to force or cajole his Colleagues and especially Lord Grey into popular courses were, I believe, his chief motives in this most unnecessary, unlucky, and discreditable intrigue.[38]

Littleton shared the view of Lord Holland.

> After Lord Grey's retirement his resentment was strongly directed against Lord Brougham, whom he suspected of having originated

all the mischief by secret communication with Lord Wellesley . . . I had told Lord Grey of the exact nature of the communication I had with Brougham. But it seemed to strengthen rather than diminish his suspicion of Brougham's motives. It was impossible to have erred more widely. The Chancellor, entirely engrossed and fatigued with the business of his court and the House of Lords, was only anxious to find a way of smoothing a course for the great contested measure of the session, and of obtaining new allies for the Government. Beyond this he had not a motive. Every one knew that his ambition was unbounded, and it is possible that on Lord Grey's often repeated determination to retire he might have conceived the notion of succeeding him. But of his anxiety to uphold the fabric of Lord Grey's administration there was as little doubt in the minds of all who knew him as there was of his affection and regard for Lord Grey personally.[39]

Even Lady Grey came eventually to acquit, though not to absolve, him. 'I have a little changed my mind about this same Achitopel,' she wrote to Creevey in September. 'I begin to believe that he really did not *at that time* mean to turn Lord G. out. I believe so, because it was not essential to his interest to do so, not that I suspect him of any scruples. I am inclined to think his own version of it is true. He expected to bully Lord G. and to shorten the session. He afterwards got into a mess, and it cost him nothing to tell a thousand lies.'[40] One of Brougham's versions of events was that he wrote to Wellesley with the sole intention of shortening the session so that he might visit the Rhine. 'Now, from the creation of the world,' asked Creevey, 'was there ever such a defence—be it lie or be it true? And then the villain says it never entered his imagination that it would lead to the result it did.'[41]

Brougham's error, whether his motive was to suit his own convenience or to lighten the parliamentary load of the government, was to meddle in an affair for which he had no departmental responsibility without informing either Lord Grey or Lord Melbourne. Once the game was up he kept a self-regarding silence about his part in the drama and allowed others to shoulder the public disgrace. Worst of all was the graceless and brutal letter which he wrote to Lord Althorp on the day after the government's downfall. Impending dismissal from office drove from his heart every feeling of private charity, from his mind every remembrance of the selfless service which

Althorp, the least corruptible of men, had performed for the Whig party.

> Your step of resigning has I fear sealed the fate of this country. Rather than be plagued by two or three speeches addressed to a House of Commons which has more confidence in you than ever, you have done your best to dissolve the only Government the country will bear . . .
>
> I shall do all I can to ward off the calamity; but how can I if every one in the House of Commons is afraid to keep his ground? At least I am resolved that the country shall see who it has to thank for whatever is to happen.
>
> I really must say, I look upon all of you as answerable, and most deeply answerable, for the event.
>
> One thing of course you must make up your minds to. As you and your companions in desertion will most probably prevent a Liberal Government from being made, you are of course prepared to give your cordial support to a Tory one. Surely you don't mean we should have no Government.[42]

Althorp contented himself with a restrained reply.

> I admit that I am answerable as the proximate cause of the dissolution of the Administration, but the situation in which I was placed was not by any act of my own. I wish you would look a little at the share you have taken in the business. Without communication with one of your colleagues, with the view I know of facilitating business in Parliament, you desired Littleton to write to Lord Wellesley, and you wrote to him yourself . . . but you, having originally produced the difficulty by writing to Lord Wellesley, gave your decision directly against what you had advised Lord Wellesley to do . . .
>
> I am aware that the man who by his resignation produces the dissolution of an Administration takes a great load upon his shoulders, and more especially when there is so much difficulty in forming another; this load is increased greatly when he cannot explain the causes which compelled him to take such a step without involving others, whom for every reason he is determined not to involve.[43]

Brougham had done great deeds for the country and for the Whig party. Because of his powerful talents, allied to great causes, his

colleagues had learned to bear his vanity, his deceits and his pomposi-
ties. It was impossible that they should bear them for much longer.
Melbourne, not for the first time, gave his decided opinion that
Brougham was mad: 'he will one day, in sacrificing everything for his
own personal whim, be sacrified himself'.[44] When Melbourne made
the remark he had become prime minister and Brougham's fate lay in
his hands.

14

'A Grotesque Apocalypse'

Brougham was not in the running to replace Lord Grey. Amid all the private conversations, court communications, club discussions and ministerial manoeuvres which followed upon the announcement that Grey and Althorp had resigned their offices, there was, Lord Holland noted, 'no mention or thought of Brougham but such as marked curiosity, wonder, and even distrust—certainly not a word implying confidence or hope'.[1] The King wished to install a mixed government of Whigs and Tories and he was aided in his design by Althorp's statement in the House of Commons that the government was dissolved, when only he and Lord Grey, admittedly the leaders in the two Houses, had handed in their seals. To thwart the sovereign, Brougham acted with speed and daring. He informed him, in an unsolicited letter, that ministers were resolved to remain in office, that Althorp could be persuaded to return, and that, if Lord Melbourne were appointed in Grey's place, all would be well. William IV replied that he regarded the ministry as having 'fallen to pieces' and that he had invited Melbourne to form a coalition government.[2] Before receiving the King's reply, Brougham went to the House of Lords to announce that Althorp had misled parliament. So long as its supporters in the House of Commons did not waver, the Whig government could not be dislodged. 'I have as you see stood firm,' Brougham wrote to Wellesley, '& I am rallying the scattered troops.'[3] William IV complained of a 'disregard of the most constitutional views of the royal prerogative',[4] but Brougham's intervention stifled the royal will.

This speech [he later wrote] decided the affair, for the Commons and the country rallied round me . . . But the King never forgave it. I pardon him—the measure was a strong one, but it was necessary. The letter to himself prevented him from dismissing us, except at the peril of being opposed in and out of Parliament. My speech prevented any relaxation of support in Parliament. If I had deferred it, even for twenty-four hours, I should have given him time for intriguing with other parties, and accomplishing his favourite object of turning us off and taking in the Tories. Both steps were necessary, but that could not well make either step agreeable to him. He yielded a sullen compliance, wrote me a letter that he accepted Melbourne for Minister, and never more smiled on me while he lived.[5]

However immodest Brougham's version of events, it is not entirely to be discounted. It was only four months later that the King, disregarding the huge Whig majority in the House of Commons, availed himself of an unguarded phrase of Melbourne's to dismiss him and bring in the Tories.

Lord Althorp, who, had his resignation not been the proximate cause of Lord Grey's, might have been the King's choice as first minister, withdrew his resignation. Melbourne therefore took charge of an administration unchanged except for the departure of Grey. In 1830 Grey had wounded Brougham's pride by offering him the attorney-generalship. Brougham now, whether, as everyone believed, with conscious malice, got his tit-for-tat by offering *him* (without Melbourne's authority) the consoling compensation of the privy seal. Grey 'rather smiled at the proposition'; the Grey women would have murdered the chancellor if they could.[6] Melbourne, famous in Disraeli's phrase for lounging over the destinies of an empire, was considered to be lax in his morals, indifferent to religion and pliant in his politics. Greville thought him 'certainly a queer fellow to be Prime Minister' and him and Brougham 'two wild chaps' to have the future of the country in their hands.[7] Thomas Moore observed them early in August at Holland House in a scene 'that would rather have alarmed, I think, a Tory of the full dress school. There was the Chancellor in his black frock coat, black cravat; while upon the sofa lay stretched the Prime Minister, also in frock and boots, and with his legs cocked up on one of Lady Holland's fine chairs.'[8] Francis Place believed that Brougham was now the Whigs' master,[9] but Melbourne's insouciant manner concealed a firm political discretion. The transportation of the Tolpuddle martyrs was in keeping with his severe treatment of political and trade unions as home secretary in Grey's government. He remained prime minister (with a brief Tory interlude) until 1841. It was Brougham whose official career had all but run its course.

Grey quit public life with one great piece of legislative business unfinished. Perhaps no statute of the 19th century so sharply divided the English nation as the Whig poor law of 1834. For several decades the poor rate, levied on the landed class, had been rising steeply, a consequence, in large measure, of what was known after the Berkshire parish in which it was first applied as the 'Speenhamland system'. By that system (whose roots lay, in fact, in Elizabethan law) relief payments awarded by local magistrates to the unemployed were brought up to the level of wages prevailing in the neighbourhood. Benthamites, Malthusians and the landed ratepayers denounced with one voice a practice which, they alleged, encouraged idleness and discouraged thrift and which also, by enabling men and women to marry early and procreate freely, placed an unbearable burden of population upon the available wealth of the country. Seeming charity merely piled poverty upon poverty. The critics' solution was to exempt 'able-bodied' paupers from receiving parish relief and to give assistance only to those who were in workhouses. By what became celebrated as the 'less-eligibility' principle, idleness was to be made less desirable than employment. Brougham was a disciple of Malthus. In his *Practical Observations upon the Education of the People* he wrote that 'a known and regular provision for the poor . . . trains up a race of paupers'[10] and in his *Discourse on the Objects of Political Science* he argued that the 'main cause of the depression of the working classes' was their ignorance of the law of wages and hence their improvident marriages.[11]

In 1832 the government appointed a commission to inquire into the operation of the poor law. It was largely organized by Brougham and Althorp and its proceedings were dominated by the ardent Benthamite, Edwin Chadwick. The commission's report, published early in 1834, called for a thorough recasting of the poor law along lines advocated by Bentham in his *Constitutional Code*. The cabinet eagerly accepted the recommendation and drew up a bill to establish a central board to administer a new system incorporating workhouses and the less-eligibility principle. In other circumstances large sections of parliament might have decried the centralizing tendency of the bill as an illiberal intrusion upon the venerated autonomy of the local justices of the peace. Ministers, however, presented the measure as a species of agricultural relief and backbenchers tucked their constitutional scruples inside their wallets. The bill encountered little opposition in either House, but Brougham nevertheless prepared himself meticulously for its introduction in the Lords, where he took charge of the measure. On 21 July, in a four-hour speech which even Greville described as 'luminous',[12] he treated his audience to a magisterial exposition of the case for reform.[13]

He began by condemning the payment of 'wages' to the unemployed out of parish rates as a constant, wilful and deliberate sin against the fundamental rule of political economy that men should be paid according to their labour. 'Parish allowance is far worse than any dole of private charity, because it is more likely to be abused—because it is better known, more established—because it approaches in the mind of the poor to the idea of a right.' It destroyed the independent character of the English peasant.

> No longer is it thought a scandal upon the labourer to claim relief from the parish—no longer does it inflict a pang upon his mind to darken the overseer's door. No doubt he comes with a firm gait, with a manly air; but rather let us say, he comes with a sturdy gait and a masterful air. He presumes to domineer over the honest and hard-working ratepayer, and the servant of the ratepayer—the overseer—whom he insults and tramples upon. Secure, in the protection of the law, he demands his allowance not as a man, but as a master; his tone is imperative, for he knows he must be obeyed. Such a system deadens all sense of shame—all sense of real dignity; erases from the mind every feeling of honourable independence, and fits its victims only for acts of outrage or fraud.

To speak in those tones was to speak, not from experience of the lives led by the poor, but from knowledge gained from the library. Brougham paused in the middle of his argument to lavish praise upon Malthus, 'a most learned, a most able, a most virtuous individual', distinguished by talent, humanity and a sense of public duty as 'one of the most enlightened, learned, and pious ministers whom the Church of England ever numbered among her sons'. He did not lay blame upon his predecessors. 'My Lords, those who framed the statute of Elizabeth were not adepts in political science—they were not acquainted with the true principle of population—they could not foresee that a Malthus would arise to enlighten mankind.' But the results of their ignorance were everywhere to behold: improvident marriages, pauperism and field after field thrown out of cultivation. He left out of his account that the vast tracts of marginal land brought under the plough during the French wars could not be economically worked in peacetime. It was the poor laws that put the broad acres of England at risk and with them the safety of English institutions.

Brougham's poor law speech was the last of the great orations which he delivered as a minister. He never again spoke with the authority of office, nor was listened to with the attention given to a rising statesman. One passage will serve as a farewell example of the overblown, mock-heroic style of rhetoric which was even then passing from English parliamentary life and which had in Brougham one of its most practised exponents.

I will not say that as yet the system has so worked as to lay waste any considerable portion of territory. That it has a direct and necessary tendency to do so—that unless its progress be arrested, it must go on till it gain that point—that ere long we must reach the brink of the precipice towards which we are hurrying with accelerated rapidity—that the circumstance of one parish being thrown out of cultivation, inevitably and immediately tends to lay three or four others waste, and that this devastation, gathering strength as it proceeds, must needs cover the land—of these facts no man, who consults the body of evidence before your Lordships, can entertain the shadow of a doubt . . . This is the aspect of affairs, menacing the peace of society, undermining the safety of dominion, and assailing the security of property, which the system, as now administered, exhibits to the eye. In this it is that the schemes of man, as shortsighted as presumptuous, have ended, when he sought to reverse the primal curse, under which he eats his bread in sorrow and the sweat of his brow. Our Poor Law said, the sweat shall trickle down that brow no more; but the residue of the curse it has not reversed—for in sorrow he shall eat it still. The dispensation of wrath, which appointed toil for the penalty of transgression, was tempered with the mercy which sheds countless blessings upon industry—industry that sweetens the coarsest morsel, and softens the hardest pillow; but not under the Poor Law! Look to that volume, and you will find the pauper tormented with the worst ills of wealth—listless and unsettled—wearing away the hours, restless and half-awake, and sleepless all the night that closes his slumbering day—needy, yet pampered—ill-fed, yet irritable and nervous. Oh! monstrous progeny of this unnatural system, which has matured, in the squalid recesses of the workhouse, the worst ills that haunt the palace, and made the pauper the victim of those imaginary maladies which render wealthy idleness less happy than laborious poverty! Industry, the safeguard against impure desires—the true preventive of crimes; but not under the Poor Law! Look at that volume, the record of Idleness, and her sister Guilt, which now stalk over the land. Look at the calendar, which they have filled to overflowing, notwithstanding the improvement of our jurisprudence, and the progress of education. Industry, the corner-stone of property, which gives it all its value, and makes it the cement of society; but not under the Poor Law! For it is deprived of its rights and its reward, finds its place usurped by indolence, and sees wrong and violence wear the garb, and urging the claims of right; so that all property is shaken to pieces, and the times are fast approaching when it shall be no more! In this devastation but one exception remains, in those seats of industry, where the miracles of labour and of skill have established the great triumph of the arts, and shed unnumbered blessings on all round; those arts, whose lineage is high—for they are the offspring of science, whose progeny is flourishing—for they are the parents of wealth. They have, indeed, stayed for a season in the districts which they nourish and adorn, the progress of the overwhelming mischief: but long even they cannot arrest its devastation, and this last pillar cannot long remain, after all the rest of the edifice has been swept away! They cannot stay the wide-wasting ruin; but we can, and we must. It behoves us to make a stand before one common ruin involves all, and tread back our steps, that we may escape the destruction which is on the wing, and hovering around our door.

Three years after the passing of the new poor law, Brougham, who never once visited a workhouse, took pride in the good it had already done 'in bettering the condition of the poor, in elevating the poor man's character, in increasing the poor man's comforts, and, above all, in imparting to his character a higher tone of moral feeling and a greater portion of self-respect'.[14] In the southern half of the country, still largely immune to the cycle of industrial unemployment, his words made, perhaps, some sense. In the manufacturing districts of the north, where the outcry against the inhumane working of the new law was loud and raw, they were of the kind that was soon to open men's minds to Chartism. It was an outrage that factory operatives, laid off in the depressed circumstances of the latter 1830s, should be branded as moral cripples or near-criminals. The Whigs, and most of the Conservatives, were deaf to the cries of the hungry and the dispirited. But from the beginning a small band of Tories, heirs to the tradition of rural paternalism, had condemned the harsh illogic which underlay the Whig law. Impotent inside parliament, they had powerful allies outside, none more powerful than John Walter, the owner of the *Times*, and Thomas Barnes, his editor. Since 1830 the *Times* had stood by Grey's government. In particular, it had heaped praise upon the lord chancellor. The poor law opened a breach.

The *Times*' quarrel with Brougham was one of the talking-points of the year 1834. Anger at the new poor law contributed to it, but its origins were personal and it ended in an utter falling-out between Brougham and Barnes. Since the formation of the Whig government, Barnes had depended on Brougham, for the most part through Brougham's secretary, Le Marchant, for inside political information. He knew, of course, of Brougham's reputation for duplicity, but down to the spring of 1834 he had not been a victim of it. 'Were the noble and learned Lord himself to advise or undertake the formation of a Ministry,' he wrote in a leading article when Stanley resigned, 'there cannot be a shadow of a doubt that it would be one at which the cordial and enlightened friends of constitutional reform would have no cause to murmur.'[15] That was a pipe-dream. Barnes' real object was to see Lord Durham, whose standing with the radicals far surpassed Brougham's, reinstated in the cabinet. In a conversation with Le Marchant, Barnes stated his wish for a 'liberal and decided course being pursued', one which included Durham's restoration, and since Le Marchant did not demur, he assumed that Brougham was of a like mind.[16] When the new appointments were announced, and Durham's name was not among them, the *Times* dissociated Brougham from them. Brougham kept silent. If the *Times* went uncontradicted, he might, for a time at least, be shielded from the censure of Durham's followers. The government, however, was bound to remove misunderstanding from the public mind. Its organ, the *Globe*, corrected the report in the *Times*. 'We may specifically state, that . . . no member who has been in the cabinet with Lord Durham is disposed to act with him again, and we defy the best informed journal in existence to prove that in this respect Lord Brougham is of a different opinion from his colleagues.'[17]

Barnes was indignant to learn that the *Globe* spoke with unimpeachable authority. He complained to Le Marchant that he had been ill-used.

How could I imagine that I was not serving the cause of your friend by urging the appointment of such men? When you talked of the Chancellor standing down rather than a Liberal Government should not be formed, how could I suspect that in the formation of the Cabinet the Chancellor would yield . . .? You never gave me a hint about Lord Durham's temper and the insuperable dislike of other Ministers to such a colleague: and yet as I frankly told you I was in communication with Lord Durham, I surely ought to have had some intimation of the sentiments of the Chancellor and his friends.[18]

Le Marchant replied that the *Times* had lately become highly critical of the government, an unconvincing defence, since the close relationship between Brougham and the newspaper had never required Barnes to be the slavish admirer of every Whig act. At any rate, Barnes was sore, not so much because Brougham had taken a line which he disapproved, as because the chancellor had deceived him. 'I must say,' he wrote to Le Marchant, 'that I do not think I have always been treated by your *friend* with that frankness to which his long knowledge of my character ought to have ensured me. I have been ready always to comply with every request and even anticipate his requests: but it is not on that account—it is because *he* must know that I am incapable of betraying or injuring him, that I have been mortified by partial explanations and half confidences when I ought to have been altogether and unreservedly trusted.'[19] Barnes might have looked more dispassionately at his own position. He was just then engaged in the proud undertaking to free the *Times* of government influence. He won the battle in the end and his triumph was a milestone in the history of English press freedom. To seek independence of the government, while attempting to retain Brougham as a source of information, was, like many an editor since, asking to have his cake and eat it too.

What might have remained merely an unhappy episode in a private friendship erupted into a public war. Early in June, Lord Althorp, incensed at the *Times'* accelerating campaign against the new poor law, sent a short note to Brougham. 'My dear Brougham,' it ran. 'The subject I want to talk to you about is the state of the Press, & whether we should declare open war with the *Times*, or attempt to make peace.'[20] Brougham received the note while presiding in Chancery. He tore it up and threw the pieces into a waste-paper basket. They were retrieved by an officer of the court, who fitted the fragments together and sent the note to Barnes. Within hours Barnes demanded an explanation from Le Marchant. (Brougham, in his fury, was unable to discover the culprit and threatened to dismiss every officer of the court.) Le Marchant's reply to Barnes implied that the government expected the *Times* to behave as its poodle. Barnes agreed to abstain from personal attacks on ministers; he would not promise more. 'After all, our support is in a great measure indeed I may say altogether a matter depending on yourselves. If you bring forward beneficial measures and urge them on with the same persevering firmness with which you passed such unpopular measures as the Coercion Bill last Session and the Poor Bill now, we *must* support you.'[21]

One of the popular measures which Brougham was preparing was the abolition of the fourpenny stamp duty on newspapers, a measure which had long been on the radicals' agenda. The tax injured the popular press (like Brougham's own *Penny Cyclopaedia*) and left well-financed, middle-class papers like the *Times* in a favoured position as formers of public opinion. The issue set Brougham and Barnes against one another. Nor did the *Times* welcome the news that Brougham was founding a Society for the Diffusion of Political Knowledge and negotiating to take over Charles Knight's *Companion to the Newspaper*. By mid-July, when he had become the object, for the first time, of personal abuse in the *Times*, Brougham was taking pugnacious delight in helping to defeat the *Times* and the Tory opposition in their call for the production of the private correspondence between ministers and Lord Wellesley which had brought about the retirement of Lord Grey.

> You'll see the London press furious at me [he wrote to Wellesley], especially the Times . . . The key to it is, that they all wanted *dissolution* & revolution, or at least some confusion & some weak govt—at the mercy of *the Gentlemen of the Press*, and they accuse me, most justly, I am glad to say, of having defeated their prospects by standing firm. But my attacks in the Libel Commee. on their . . . monopoly, are also a cause of this spite. I succeeded, I believe, in putting an end to the Newspaper Stamps, which the great papers hold to be one of their great securities against competition. I have also fulfilled a threat I then held out of ending the violent & slanderous press by an association. For, joined by the most

respectable Merchants & Bankers . . . by Lawyers & by Literary men, I have commenced a Socy for diffusing *Political* Knowledge, & this the Times fancies will emancipate the '*courteous Readers*' & put them in the hands of Gentlemen.[22]

The letter is characteristic blustering of the kind that everyone who knew Brougham found amusing and irritating. It did not require Brougham's advocacy to gain a large majority against the publication of Wellesley's correspondence. Nor did he succeed in ending the stamp duty (two years later it was reduced to 1d.). And to find relish in deriding the 'gentlemen of the press' was, if nothing more, ill-mannered. No other politician of the day had exploited the press so assiduously as he, and the reward had been, as Le Marchant said, that the newspapers had served him in preference to any other public figure.[23]

Whatever Brougham's answer to Althorp's note, a decision was taken to make war on the *Times*. Barnes ceased to receive privileged information and the *Morning Chronicle* and the *Globe* suddenly became diligent in exposing errors printed in the newspaper. 'If the Government wish to cut the rope,' Barnes warned Le Marchant, 'well and good; we shall then know what course to take.'[24] Week after week for the remainder of the year the chancellor, as Greville put it, was flagellated until he was raw.[25] The opening lash was delivered on 19 July, two days after the last of three articles high in the praise of Brougham and the poor law had appeared in the *Chronicle* over the signature 'Vindex'. Whether Brougham wrote the articles, as everyone thought, matters little. He had overseen the transfer of the *Chronicle* to new proprietors and had appointed new editors. The politics that appeared in the paper had his blessing. The *Times*, with leaden sarcasm, affected to believe that he was not the author.

We cannot for a moment believe that such tawdry attempts at fine writing, such bull-frog efforts at energy of diction, can proceed from a man whose taste has been formed on the best models, and who has always shewn himself a master of language. The maudlin affectation of some passages and the fussy splutterings of others, indicate rather the manner of a waiting gentlewoman who has quarrelled with her master's valet.[26]

The *Times* now raised the cry that Brougham had deliberately sabotaged Grey's government; it falsely portrayed him as a persistent drunkard; and it took to gainsaying all its previous utterances by belittling his intelligence. 'Persons acquainted with the furniture of Lord Brougham's mind, know that it is like the specimens of an upholsterer's show-room—some piece of every set, but nothing in completeness and arrangement—a lumber of fineries, odds and ends, at once more and less than necessary to the fitting of any one mansion of the understanding.'[27] Brougham considered prosecuting for libel. In a public speech he boasted that he had 'allowed certain persons to go on', but 'the net is enclosed around them, and they shall soon be held up to ridicule and to scorn—ay, and to punishment'.[28] He was persuaded to abandon the project, but his threats were repeated often enough for men to believe it was his wish, if not his practical object, to close the paper. On 17 September the *Times* gave great amusement to Brougham's enemies.

> The public sees that the *Times* yet exists. Lord Brougham has *allowed* us *to go on* for another day, as he has *allowed* us *to go on* for some weeks past, and it is possible that we may appear to-morrow, but if not, let us be looked for in the Lord Chancellor's pocket . . . It is hard to be so cut off in the flower of one's days, and the full tide of prosperity, but relentless Brougham wills it so, and as he has *allowed* us to go on, so he must have the power to stop us.[29]

A more prudent man than Brougham might have followed Newman's dictum that a gentleman does not engage in newspaper controversy. Lord Grey reminded him that nothing answered the purpose of newspapers better than rejoinders from those whom they attacked. But Brougham was heedless of the advice and he carried the war into the Whig party itself by accusing Thomas Young, Lord Melbourne's secretary, of instigating the *Times*' crusade against him and stopping the *Globe* from coming to his defence. Melbourne contented himself with informing Brougham that he was not 'simpleton enough' to believe him. 'I did not know that it [the *Globe*] had preserved the silence you mention. I only know that if I were attacked I would rather have its silence than its defence.'[30]

For the chief law officer of the Crown to conduct a personal campaign against a newspaper was to abuse his high authority. To be bested in the fight was to make himself a figure of public fun. The public learned, what was fatal to Brougham's political standing, not to take him seriously. Scarcely a figure of importance in the Whig party did not now believe that he was mad, and the impression was deepened by his antics during the recess. In an attempt to regain popular favour, Brougham organized a progress of public meetings through the north of England and Scotland. The tour, unprecedented by a lord chancellor and never copied since, coincided with a public dinner in Lord Grey's honour at Edinburgh on 15 September. At first Grey was prevailed upon by his friends and family to decline the invitation. 'I hope the Edinburgh dinner will not take place when Brougham is there,' Sydney Smith wrote to Lady Grey; 'he will make it appear as if the dinner was for him.'[31] Brougham, who wished to demonstrate to the world that he and Grey remained close friends, pressed his ex-chief to reconsider. 'I have told them at Edinburgh that if the dinner takes place I will preside, as they desire it.'[32] The citizens of Edinburgh preferred to place Lord Rosebery in the chair and Grey, thinking it discourteous to the loyal Scotch electors to stay away, ended by accepting the invitation.

Brougham then set out on a flamboyant tour of the north that Disraeli called his 'vagrant and grotesque apocalypse'.[33] In three weeks of junketing and speech-making he covered himself in disgrace. He took the Great Seal with him (the King thought that to carry it north of the border without the sovereign's leave was little short of treason) and played games with it in the evening. At Rothiemurchus, the home of the dowager Duchess of Bedford, a party of English ladies hid it where it could not be found until the chancellor, becoming anxious, was led blindfold by a piano, played loudly when he was 'warm', to the tea-chest where it lay. At Edinburgh he turned up at the races in his full regalia of chancellor's wig and gown. All this was harmless mischief, no doubt, but it reached the ear of the King, who was not amused. Even less did he enjoy hearing that Brougham was announcing himself as the particularly intimate adviser of the monarch. At Inverness he told a large crowd that he would write to the King that night to tell him how deeply he was held in the affections of his people, an impertinence which Albany Fonblanque lampooned in the *Examiner*.

Brave news, indeed, for the King! . . . But here is encouragement to boroughs to entertain Lord Brougham; if they make much of him, he will tell the King what good people they are by the night's post. There is nothing in farce to exceed this, and we recommend the idea to Kenny or Buckstone. Reeve, so rich in Magog the Beadle, would be exquisitely droll in Magog the Chancellor, assuring the burgesses at a town-feast that he would write home to the King, and tell him what good fellows they are, their loyalty being measured by their feasting and cheering him, the said Magog. Upon every petty occasion, the promise or threat, 'I'll write to the King by this night's post', might be introduced with the broadest farcical effect. If Magog the Chancellor has an unaired night-cap at an inn, he should write to the King about it by that night's post, and inform him that he does not live in the heart of the chambermaid . . . Our farce-writers are dull dogs indeed, if they do not draw on the materials which our great law authority is so copiously affording. To borrow from the French while we have a Brougham, like a Matthews, 'at Home', were indeed inexcusable. 'The Chancellor at Inverness, or I'll write to the King!' would be a most taking title in the play-bills.[34]

'Good God, Gentlemen!' Disraeli asked the electors of High Wycombe after Melbourne's dismissal three months later, 'could this go on?'[35]

Brougham was pleased by the tour, which he described as 'very unexpectedly & not very agreeably turned into business instead of relaxation by the great kindness of the people wherever I went'.

Had I foreseen it, I should certainly not have stirred from my fireside, but finding I was in for it, I resolved to go thru' with it so as to do good to the Govt & the stability of the Country's institutions, & I really think I *preached the word* with some good fruits. The enthusiasm for Govt all over Scotland is at its acme.[36]

It is true that large crowds turned out to hear him, but his speeches brought him much discredit. They were riddled with inconsistencies, now calling for more reform, now for a breathing space from innovation, at one place extolling the House of Lords, at another vilifying it. Even when he preached the virtues of moderate Whig government he did so in a way that embarrassed his colleagues. At Inverness he remarked, reasonably enough, that after the legislative achievements of Grey's first three years—enfranchising the £10 householders, abolishing slavery, opening trade with China, reforming Chancery— the pace of reform had slackened. But he then went on to make an admission which the radicals, whose support was essential to the Whigs, seized upon: 'If we have done little last session, I fear we shall do less the next.'

315

Brougham arrived at Edinburgh a laughing-stock and before a vast assembly of fifteen hundred dinner guests, come to thank Lord Grey for his long services to the country, he made a woeful speech.[37] 'My fellow-citizens of Edinburgh,' he began, 'these hands are clean' (and those close to him observed that they were distinctly not).

> In taking office, and holding it, I have sacrificed no feeling of a public nature—I have deserted no friend—I have forfeited no pledge—I have done no job—I have promoted no unworthy man, to the best of my knowledge—I have stood in the way of no man's fair pretensions to promotion—I have not abused my patronage—I have not abused the ear of my master—and I have not deserted the people. I am one of those ministers, and my Noble Friend is another, who have never feared the people. I rejoice, and delight, and glory, in office and out of office, in every opportunity of meeting the people, to render an account to them of my stewardship.

The government, he said, would proceed steadily and unflinchingly to discharge its duty by promoting liberal opinions. It would not be hurried out of its course by zealots of the left.

> We shall go on, heedless of the attacks of those hasty spirits. They are men of great honesty, of much zeal, and of no reflection at all. They would travel towards their object, but they are in such a hurry to set out, and to get three minutes earlier than ourselves, that they will not wait to put the linch-pins into the wheel. They would go on a voyage of discovery to unknown regions, but will not tarry to look whether the compass is on board.

Brougham always denied that the passage was directed at Lord Durham, but it was impossible that men should not think it so. Durham had discredited himself with his former colleagues by his shameless dexterity in preaching up the reform act as *his* creation, while denouncing its failure (before it had scarcely been tried) to provide for household suffrage and a secret ballot. At the Grey dinner Durham spoke after Brougham. He denounced 'the clipping, and paring, and mutilating which must inevitably follow any attempt to conciliate enemies who are not to be conciliated'.[38] Durham was hot-tempered and thin-skinned; Brougham was indefatigable in self-defence. Three weeks later, in a speech delivered from the balcony of an inn at Salisbury, Brougham chided Durham directly. It was the first and last time that autumn that he did so, but the speech coincided with the appearance in the *Edinburgh Review* of a lengthy polemic against Durham and the radicals. The prose is unlike Brougham's. Probably he did not write it, but Durham, like many people, believed that he did. A long and warm friendship came to an end. 'All his expressions and actions were those of a private friend,' Durham wrote to Lord John Russell, 'all his actions, behind my back, those of a bitter enemy.'[39] Brougham's 'systematic treachery' he vowed never to forget.[40]

That Brougham had engaged in systematic treachery was nonsense. He was envious of Durham's high standing with the radicals and when he was moved to envy his vindictiveness could be terrible. But treachery was not needed to keep Durham out of place. 'Lambton, as it appears to me,' Ellice wrote to Grey, 'has entirely thrown away the only chance he had of admission into any reasonable Govt. I know of no person . . . who will subscribe to his *new articles* of Faith.'[41] Durham was the instigator of the fight and when Brougham discovered that ministers, following the line taken by the press, laid the blame on him, he was disgusted. He had reason to be angry, but he injured a strong case by the spitefulness with which he prosecuted it. His letter to the whip, Viscount Duncannon, was the outpouring of a mind stretched to the breaking-point.

It is a very unpleasant thing to find oneself living among people who are the *slaves of a couple of slanderous newspapers* and as many silly gossipping women. For what would you say if I were to advise you to take care of your character, for you are reported to have been picking people's pockets? Now in all you believe of me, because newspapers say it, you have exactly the same foundation—and no more. You actually at this moment think I have been attacking Durham—and you speak of the *contest* between Durham and me! Where? When? In what manner? You at this moment really believe I have been in conflict with him—and you believe it because you see it in papers! You don't judge for yourself. You don't trust your own senses—but because a newspaper says so, you *must* and you will believe it. What use is there in trying to open your eyes? None—you are a *man*—have been a minister—may be one again— and yet no silly woman of them all is more the dupe and the slave of gossip and of papers than you. Therefore I am doing a foolish and vain thing in trying to undeceive you. Yet I must, and as much on your account as my own, for really, *if I had* attacked Durham, God knows, after he had attacked me, there would have been no crime in it. But I now do most positively tell you—and remember I expect when I say this that *I shall be believed and not the papers*—that there never WAS ONE WORD *said by me even* on the subject of Durham or *on anything connected with him*—except what I said at Salisbury—and that was in these words—'I wish those who attack our measures would do so in Parliament if they happen to have seats in either House'. Now that was the whole I have ever uttered which could be said to have any relation to Durham, so help me God! And I desire to know by what right Lord Durham complains of that? *He* attacked me at Edinburgh when he knew I could not defend myself without annoying Lord Grey. He then attacked me at two different public *meetings by name*, and after those attacks, all I said was what I have quoted—and this is what you are pleased to call '*a contest with Durham*'.

The letter was written at the end of the year, when Melbourne had been dismissed by the King and a Tory government brought in to replace the Whigs. The newspapers and the club gossips made out that William IV had been driven to an extreme measure by his determination to be rid of Brougham for ever. Brougham hotly repudiated the charge.

I plainly see by what a frail tenure public men hold their character in this country, at least *among the upper classes*. No tradesman, no farmer, none of the middle classes would have been the dupe of a few newspaper paragraphs as you have been. You speak of me as a person whose character is gone—who has lost his place in public estimation—who may, if he pleases, regain his former place in 1829. Sir, I would have you know that I utterly deny this! I repel the insinuation with indignation! I lost my place in Parliament when, *to enable Lord Grey to make a ministry*, I consented most reluctantly, and I admit, most foolishly, to abandon my proper place—in the Commons! I have since then earned more gratitude of my countrymen than I ever did before. I fearlessly appeal to them . . . I would have you not suppose that the gossips of Brooks's whose effeminate minds can only see out of one newspaper into another, are the true judges of whether a person in my position has lost or has gained reputation in the country . . . The result of my experience of this last year has been a very thorough contempt for the understanding and firmness of my own rank in society—and a great increase of respect for the middle classes. With the latter I shall take my stand in the times that are coming.[42]

*   *   *

'Now for Lord Durham and our Brougham and Vaux,' Creevey wrote a month after the Edinburgh dinner. 'Now my own deliberate opinion is that Vaux is at last caught and will be ruined . . . His going to Scotland at all with the purpose he did—to rob Lord Grey of his fame—was an act of insanity, and the disease has increased since.'[43] The judgement was nearly universal. Sefton thought that 'his career latterly has really approached to insanity' and Melbourne 'admitted that he did not think him of sound mind certainly'.[44] Most men, when they described Brougham as 'mad', meant little more than that they found him unpredictable, devious, self-centred and therefore uncongenial. Henry Cockburn, who renewed his forty-year acquaintance with him in Edinburgh in 1834, located Brougham's weakness in the habit of bullying which men sometimes acquire when they feel themselves to be surrounded by inferior minds.

> I saw a good deal of Brougham during the few days he was here. He is in prodigious force—not in the least changed from his look, manner or style thirty years ago. The least amiable man, and I think not entertaining, but only because I cannot be entertained where there is a constant dread of some explosion; for what he says is in itself always powerful and curious. He is an instance of the blunders men commit about themselves. He thinks that his power lies in his formidableness—in the terror of people to incur his violence; but in truth that is his weakness. Could he retain the esteem of men half as well as he provokes their hostility he would be omnipotent. He has as yet always espoused right public causes, and always displayed talents of the highest order and the greatest variety, yet he has never had any moral influence, but is a mere intellectual machine. Nothing resembling the reverence and love in which Grey and Althorp are held ever came near to Brougham; nor would any charm have been connected with the name of Fox if his disposition had made him think the glory of intellectual force impaired by its union with sweet blood and a soft heart.[45]

Early in November 1834, Lord Althorp was removed to the House of Lords by the death of his father, Earl Spencer. The search for his successor as leader of the House of Commons gave William IV a pretext for turning the Whigs out and sending for the Tories. William acted abruptly and he learned his lesson a few months later when the Whig majority in the Commons bludgeoned the Tory government into resignation. Lord George Bentinck, one of the Stanleyite renegades from Whiggery, wrote that the King's grand object was to jettison Brougham, 'about whom I understand he had got to feel as some people do when a cat is in the room'.[46] It is true that the King recoiled from Brougham's 'itinerant speechifying'. Melbourne told Grey that the chancellor's recent conduct had created 'absolute disgust & alienation' in the royal mind.[47] But Brougham was not the sole, nor the most important, influence on the King. As Ellice said, he could have 'continued insane' or been removed singly.[48] The real cause was the King's fear for the safety of the Irish Church in Whig hands, especially if Lord John Russell were to succeed Althorp. Melbourne would have no one but Russell and the King would not have Russell. So Melbourne went out. Brougham wrote the King a letter in which he protested at the constitutional impropriety of overturning a government with a large majority in the House of Commons and received an 'extremely gracious reply'. 'I think,' he explained, in a mystifying remark to Wellesley, 'this has a view to my new position as our Opposition Chief.'[49]

Brougham took the government's dismissal in bad heart. He leaked the news to the press before Melbourne had time to inform the whole cabinet and he almost certainly inspired the *Times'* absurd phrase, 'The Queen has done it all'. While most of the ex-ministers were seen mingling at Brooks's over the next few days, Brougham prudently stayed away; he dared not appear even at Holland House. He offended the King by refusing to deliver up the Great Seal in person, preferring to hand it to the royal secretary in a bag, 'as a fishmonger might have sent a salmon for the king's dinner'.[50] Unlike his colleagues, who exchanged civilities with the incoming Tory ministers in the outer room at St James's, he 'stalked through looking as black as thunder and took no notice of anybody'.[51] Most extraordinary of all, he wrote to Lord Lyndhurst, who returned to the Woolsack, a letter offering to save the country money by taking the office of Chief Baron of the Exchequer for nothing and living on his chancellor's pension. This last act was derided as a shabby ruse to deprive James Scarlett, his old rival on the northern circuit, of a just reward for a long and eminent legal career. When it was rejected, Brougham took himself off to France. 'The Comet Brougham is gone to Paris. Why?' asked Samuel Rogers. 'But how can the orbit of such an eccentric planet be calculated? I hope the moon has nothing to do with it.'[52] For Brougham to quit Westminster during a high constitutional drama—Peel was hastening back from Italy to take charge of the Conservative government—was unexpected. His explanation to Lord Wellesley was characteristic.

> I came abroad to recreate my body & mind after 34 years of slavery with the Liberty & the *Liberales* of Paris . . . My stay at Paris would have been a week, but I heard that the good people—not of England, but of Brooks's—had laid me under an ostracism. In truth it really was such for a fortnight or 3 weeks, & . . . seeing the prevalence of this folly, I resolved to come & see some old & dear friends I have in the North of Italy & to examine minutely the State of things in the south of France—well knowing that the said *ostracism* would soon be over, & that it would then be in power to make them eat the *shells* of their own oysters.[53]

Brougham returned to London for the opening of the 1835 session of parliament. From the outset he laboured nightly to help defeat Peel's government. When it fell in March, Melbourne came back into office; Brougham did not. 'I will have nothing more to do with Brougham,' Melbourne had written to Grey in January. 'I need not state to you the reasons for this determination. They reduce themselves readily under two heads—viz. his whole character, and his whole conduct.'[54] Brougham's faults, as Lord John Russell listed them, were a recklessness of judgement, an omnivorous appetite for praise, a perpetual interference in matters not his concern, and a disregard for truth.[55] To those must be added what Melbourne considered to be conduct with the press unbecoming in a minister. Russell argued that Brougham should be retained in some capacity, perhaps as secretary of state, and Grey advised Melbourne not to reject 'the co-operation of a person like Brougham, who was intimately connected with you in office, who professes the same principles, and who, whatever may be the justice of the censure which he has so generously incurred, will, immediately after the meeting of Parliament, by his extraordinary activity and talents, again attract the attention, and not improbably conciliate the favour, of a great portion of the Public'.[56] Russell made the curious suggestion, years later, that Melbourne dropped Brougham because he feared he had not the strength to resist him.[57] It would be truer to say that to have included Brougham from fear of what he might otherwise do would have been weakness. The Whigs were short of debating ability in the Lords and their hold on popular affection was waning. Yet Melbourne risked making an enemy of the party's most redoubtable parliamentary speaker and one of the best-known politicians in the country. The very boldness of the decision was, as he ruthlessly stated some time later in the House of Lords, proof of its necessity. The occasion was an evening when Brougham had just made a stirring speech against the Whig government. 'My Lords,' Melbourne said when Brougham sat down, 'you have heard the eloquent speech of the noble and learned Lord—one of the most eloquent he ever delivered in this House—and I leave your Lordships to consider what *must be* the nature and strength of the objections which prevent any Government from availing themselves of the services of such a man.'[58]

Exclusion from a cabinet led by a man who had voted with the Tories for the repressive acts of 1817 to 1819 mortified Brougham. Whatever his shortcomings, he had for twenty-five years been a stalwart champion of his party. He complained to John Allen that he was given no explanation of the ban placed upon him. It was, rather, that he was unable to accept the explanation. Melbourne had put matters plainly to him.

> You must be perfectly aware that your character and conduct have since November last formed the principal and general topic of debate and discussion . . . It is a very disagreeable task to have to say to a statesman that his character is injured in the public estimation; it is still more unpleasant to add that you consider this his own fault; and it is idle to expect to be able to convince almost any man, and more particularly a man of very superior abilities and of unbounded confidence in those abilities, that this is the truth. I must, however, state plainly that your conduct was one of the principal causes of the dismissal of the late Ministry, and that it forms the most popular justification of that step.[59]

When Brougham demanded more specific charges, he got a stern reply.

> You are generally for specific charges—*ubi lapsus, quid feci*? Allow me to observe that there may be a course and series of very objectionable conduct, there may be a succession of acts which

destroy confidence and add offence to offence, and yet it may be very difficult to point out any great and marked delinquency. I will, however, tell you fairly that, in my opinion, you domineered too much, you interfered too much with other departments, you encroached upon the province of the Prime Minister, you worked, as I believe, with the press in a manner unbecoming the dignity of your station, and you formed political views of your own and pursued them by means which were unfair towards your colleagues. If a proof of this latter accusation were demanded, I should adduce your conduct in those unfortunate transactions which led to the resignation of Lord Grey last summer . . . If you suppose that my conduct has been influenced by any notion that you are so lowered and weakened as to be powerless, I can assure you that you are much mistaken. Nobody knows and appreciates your natural vigour more than I do. I know also that those who are weak for good are strong for mischief. You are strong for both, and I should both dread and lament to see those gigantic powers, which should be directed to the support of the State, exerted in a contrary and opposite direction . . .

I have written this with great pain. I owe it to myself and to you, to truth and fair dealing, to be explicit. I can only add that, whatever may be your determination, no political differences will make any change in the friendship and affection which I have always felt and still continue to feel for you.[60]

In the brief space of four years Brougham had fallen from a height of popularity rare in the English party system to a depth from which he was never, politically speaking, to recover. In all of English history was there ever a more rapid demise not inspired by criminality or high impolicy? 'What an issue for Brougham!' Cockburn wrote. 'When he began his Chancellorship it was usual to compare him to Bacon, little anticipating that the comparison was to be truest in his decline.'[61] Not one of Brougham's friends in politics thought him ill used. They were left to sorrow at the spectacle of uncommon talents rendered unserviceable by common delinquencies.

One cannot but feel pain at Ld Brougham being so completely out on the shelf [Lady Holland wrote to her son]; but it was impossible to do otherwise. The King would not have acquiesced; & the whole country would have supported His Majesty in his refusal, for it is but too true that every man's hand is up against him. There are few to whom he has not broken his promise, & then quarrelled with them. In short, the total want of *truth* has been his ruin. Sir Samuel Romilly above 20 years ago foretold, in spite of all his personal affection & high opinion of his great powers, that he would fail from that defect. He inspires no man with confidence.[62]

15

A Political Ishmael

Lord Melbourne placed the Great Seal in commission. Brougham was therefore allowed to hope that it might one day be restored to him. For the remainder of the year he gave no public indication of resentment at the Whig government. Indeed, the Whigs had reason to be grateful for the energy with which, almost single-handed, he defended the government's chief measure of the session, the bill to open membership of the English municipal corporations to popular election. The bill signalled the demise of the oligarchic corporations, most of them Tory, which had controlled local government for generations. Had it not been for Brougham, who fought Lord Lynd-hurst 'like a tiger in a jungle, dealing out death wherever he fixed his prodigious claws',[1] the Tory majority in the House of Lords would have utterly destroyed the bill. Ministers nevertheless set little store by Brougham's outward show of good faith. He had made it his rule never to be seen with them at private gatherings and he openly avowed to Lord Althorp that he lay in ambush ready to expose their perfidy.

> I wait till this Session is over, and the work done; I also wait until I show that I have in no one *tittle* let my private quarrel interfere with my public duty. Really, after all I have done these seven months, no one can complain of me on that score. I go on day after day defending them—their only speaker. I never even have had one civil word from one of them—not only not one acknowledgement in speeches, while they loudly praise any man who makes even a decent speech on the enemy's side. But I don't value their praise.[2]

At the end of the year Melbourne gave the Great Seal to Lord Cottenham. Lord John Russell, the new Whig leader in the House of Commons, pleaded for Brougham to be offered the Rolls, but Melbourne told him that it would be indelicate even to suggest the appointment to the King. Brougham could no longer disguise to himself the truth that he was banished from Whig counsels for so long as Melbourne remained the party's chief, and the sentence was made all the harsher by Melbourne's meanness in allowing him to learn of it from the newspapers. Campbell was no less than just when he wrote that on this occasion, 'considering his distinguished reputation, considering what he had done for the Liberal cause, considering his relations with the Melbourne government', Brougham was 'atrociously ill-used'.[3] The new lord chancellor was sworn in on 16 January 1836, and on that day Brougham wrote to Lord Althorp.

> I must be a stock or a stone not to be sensible that my treatment affords an instance almost unparalleled of gross injustice. Whether the ministers have acted from fear of one or two newspapers, or of a set of jobbing members of Brooks's calling themselves the Whig party, or from all these fears combined, is quite immaterial . . . As for the party, my sacrifices to it have been constant, long, and ungrudging, down to the last, when I gave up affluence and power, to enable them to come into office, and embraced (with my eyes open to the consequences) the course of ending my days under the pressure of all kinds of difficulty. My eyes were not, indeed, open to that other consequence which has ensued—namely, that I was connected with a set of men who would take advantage of my leaving the House of Commons and the power I then had, and would further take a still more base advantage—namely, of treating me as they durst not treat any one whose principles they were secured by, I mean that advantage has been taken of the perfect knowledge they had that no personal injustice, be it ever so aggravated, would ever drive me to act contrary to my principles and attack them. This, they and the party were sure of, and on this they have basely reckoned throughout.[4]

Ministers reckoned on no such forbearance from Brougham and they were relieved that illness kept him out of town for the duration of the 1836 session. In July, Joseph Parkes, a prominent Whig radical in the House of Commons, reported that Brougham was better, but keeping his thoughts to himself: 'of his future plans or plots we hear nothing'.[5] Brougham resumed his seat in the Lords in 1837. For the whole of the session he took little interest in its proceedings. Behind the scenes he was busy ingratiating himself with the radicals, corresponding with Francis Place on the deficiencies of the new electoral system and encouraging John Arthur Roebuck, one of the Young Turks of the left, to organize a distinct radical party in the lower

House. In the summer of 1837 the elections caused by Queen Victoria's accession had cut deeply into the government ranks and although the radicals suffered losses as severe as the Whigs', the government's precarious majority over the Conservatives revived their aspirations to independence and whetted Brougham's appetite for mischief. The new parliament met before Christmas and its proceedings were at once enlivened by two contrary declarations. First, Lord John Russell, in a speech which earned him the nickname of 'Finality Jack', avowed his opinion that the 1832 reform act had settled the limits of the franchise for a generation. It was a bold statement, since it was certain to antagonize many radicals and the government would be outnumbered in any division should they join forces with the Tories. It was followed by a more startling declaration. On 1 December Brougham announced in the Lords that he had come to be dissatisfied by the 1832 act and that henceforth he would be found enlisted under the banner of household suffrage (that is, without a rating or rental qualification), triennial parliaments, equal electoral districts and the secret ballot. Ellice called the declaration, which amounted nearly to the programme of the nascent Chartist movement, 'a new comet in the history of the times' and interpreted it as an overt bid for the leadership of the radical movement.[6]

Leadership of the radicals was beyond Brougham. Irreconcilably divided into separatists and ministerialists, they were scarcely capable of being led. And if there were to be a lead, the partisans in both camps, Roebuck and Place in the one, John Stuart Mill and Albany Fonblanque in the other, looked to Durham to provide it. That the left should make a hero of Durham was hard on Brougham. Durham had only twice before 1834 evinced any interest in reform—in 1821, when he introduced a motion for universal suffrage, then not again until 1831, when he sat on the committee which drafted the Whig reform bill. His elevation in radical eyes derived from his quarrel with Brougham in the autumn of 1834, when, to the astonishment and disgust of his former colleagues, he advertised himself as the 'architect of reform'. They more readily recalled his sulking and intermittent presence in cabinets (when he condescended to take a break from lavish entertaining at Lambton Castle or yachting at Cowes) and his endless pestering for an earldom. Brougham thought it folly for liberals to put their faith in such a man.

Ld D never said one word on reform since his famous universal suffrage bill in 1821, never spoke for Ld J. Russell's motions, indeed never took any part in Parlt, & then as soon as Canning was minister he joined him, and got a *peerage*, the only thing he ever cared for. In truth, so great an aristocrat I never saw in the world . . . I dispute not his taste. Only dont let that *kind* of man be puffed as a *popular character* and the only *democratic* statesman of the day . . . I dont blame him for doing absolutely nothing all the time *we* were working for the Irish Caths, agt the Six Acts (on which he never opened his mouth), agt the Holy Alliance, for reform and for retrenchment. He had a right to go wherever he pleased and do nothing if he liked. But then dont let such a man, merely because he now makes big and pharisaical professions, be called the only man who serves the people—above all dont let him brag of his struggles in Parlt, and puff himself as doing any thing there, when he never does and never did any one thing. And how mighty easy after all would it have been for him, in no profession, independent in fortune, risking nothing by opposing the Court, to have come forward as Denman, Scarlett . . . and I did at all hazards?[7]

That Durham was the wrong man to lead the radicals did not make Brougham the right one. Of course it was difficult for him to understand that his personal shortcomings had destroyed his political usefulness, but the radicals' distrust of him had deeper roots. His conversion to democracy was too sudden to convince them that it represented anything more than a swipe at the Whigs. Once before, after his election defeat at Liverpool, when he was similarly ill-disposed towards the Whigs, they had tried him and been disappointed. They were not ready to try him again.

Brougham was bent on revenge, but since the radicals would not serve as his tool and the Tories, waiting for the reaction in their favour to gather strength in the constituencies, held back from outright assaults on the government, he found himself stranded in savage isolation. Although he continued to sit on the ministerial benches, within a whisper of Lord Melbourne, his waspish exchanges with the prime minister added to the gaiety of the nation. 'There can be in *Parliament* only two parties,' Brougham had written a year earlier, 'and I must be either for a Government or against it.'[8] The session had barely begun when there occurred a memorable collision between him and Melbourne, one of the most purely personal in the annals of parliament.[9] Brougham was addressing the House on the Duchess of

Kent's annuity bill when he referred to her as the 'Queen-mother'. Melbourne, sitting next to him, interjected to say 'No, no; not Queen-mother, but the mother of the Queen'. Brougham, who was always impatient of being corrected, rounded on Melbourne with the peculiarly sarcastic drawl and expressive eye that he used on such occasions. 'Oh! I know the distinction between the two phrases as well as my noble friend does; but he is a much more expert courtier than I am.' The Tory peers, enjoying the allusion to the prime minister's intimate and constitutionally suspect friendship with the new young queen, pealed with laughter, and they continued to laugh when Brougham went on, in tones of mock solemnity, to elaborate the charge.

I am rude and uncultivated in speech. The tongue of my noble friend has been recently so well hung and attuned to courtly airs, that I could not attempt to enter into competition with him on such subjects as these. The notions of my noble friend are more strictly poised and governed on these points than mine are.

Brougham's sneers brought Melbourne to his feet. 'My Lords, I took the liberty to suggest that there was a difference, not an immaterial one in the present case, between the expressions "Queen-mother" and the "mother of the Queen". The noble and learned lord said that was a distinction only to be made in courts—a distinction only recognised where there is glosing and flattery—where tongues are better hung, as the noble and learned lord expressed it. I do not know what the noble and learned lord means when he says that my tongue is better hung; I cannot speak of the hanging of the tongue; and as to glosing and flattering, I must be allowed to say that I know no man in this country who can more glose and flatter, and bend the knee, than the noble lord himself—not one.' It was a spirited reply, although what it cost Melbourne to be vindictive was evident from the faltering stammer of his delivery. Brougham returned to the attack, no longer in accents of banter, but with a withering malevolence which stilled the laughter from the opposition benches.

I positively and solemnly deny, and I call on the noble viscount to produce his proofs, that I ever in my life did, and more than that, that I ever in my nature was capable of doing, that which the noble viscount has chosen tonight, unprovoked, to fling out as a charge against me.

Lord Melbourne interposed: 'No, no; not unprovoked!'

> Yes, unprovoked; I say utterly unprovoked. I spoke in as good-humoured a tone, with as perfectly inoffensive a meaning, as it was possible for man to speak or for man to feel, when the noble viscount observed, with a contemptuous sort of air, that I should not say 'Queen-mother', but 'mother of the Queen'; as much as to intimate, 'Oh! you know nothing of these things; you don't speak the language of courts.' I said, far be it from me to enter into competition with the noble viscount, whose tongue is now attuned and hung to courtly airs. The noble viscount answers that, by saying he cannot enter into competition with me in the hanging of the tongue. It was not the hanging of the tongue I spoke of—it was the attuning of the tongue—the new tune, with recent variations.

Finished with Melbourne, Brougham succumbed to his fatal weakness, the rage to justify himself.

> The imputation or insinuation that I ever, in the discharge of my duty, stooped to glose, or to bow before or to flatter any human being, much more any inmate of a court, is utterly, absolutely, and I will say, notoriously, without foundation.

The earnest gravity, worthy of Malvolio, with which the words were uttered brought a hush to the chamber. Brougham's bad temper and righteous indignation so far exceeded their cause that men were entitled to wonder whether he any longer acknowledged the civilities of political debate or, indeed, was able in his mind to distinguish personal from political opposition.

The question was raised again by the part which he played in the centrepiece of the 1838 session of parliament, the debates on Lord Durham's mission to British North America and his handling of the crisis brought on by a rebellion in the largely French-speaking province of Lower Canada. The root of the trouble was the inability of the elected assembly, representing the French majority in the province, to control the English-speaking executive, which was appointed by the governor. Durham's report, which pointed the way to responsible government in the colonies, that form of parliamentary government in which ministers are drawn from the legislature and are therefore answerable to it and removable by it, secured his posthumous fame. Every Canadian schoolboy knows Lord Durham. Yet although responsible government was taking root in England, the imperial parliament could not be brought to extend it to Canada, especially to a province in which the Catholic, agrarian, French-speaking majority would have swamped the Protestant, commercial, English-speaking minority. In the spring of 1837 Melbourne's government, in ten resolutions accepted by parliament, denied to the elected assembly of Lower Canada the right to withhold taxation from the executive. The following November a band of French Canadians attempted to raise a rebellion, and although their unco-ordinated rioting was quickly subdued, the colonial office in London recognized that it had a crisis on its hands. Early in 1838 the government brought in a bill to suspend the colonial constitution and to send Lord Durham to govern Canada with virtually unlimited powers.

Throughout the period of the crisis in Canada Brougham held to a more or less consistent line. He was the only member of the House of Lords to dissent from the ten resolutions and he voted against the 1838 act. That he knew much about Canada must be doubted. At the end of 1837 he turnd down an invitation from the Westminster Reform Society to preside at a meeting on the recent rebellion because, as he told Wellesley, 'I am in a great degree ignorant of the present state of that Question and unable as yet to determine how far blame should be distributed'. He was satisfied, however, that the outbreak of war vindicated his opposition to the ten resolutions in the previous summer and he told Wellesley that he meant to stick by his principles.[10]

The chief principle was to embarrass Melbourne's government. News of the insurrection reached London on 22 December. Three days later Brougham wrote to Francis Place requesting a meeting to discuss 'the feeling likely to be excited by this Canada War'. His professed object was to prevent the public from running wild about blood. His deeper, barely articulated, ambition was to hound the Whigs, 'but a war is above my mark, even to purchase their perpetual exclusion'.[11] Radicals who had pinned their hopes on Durham were dismayed, two weeks later, to learn that he had agreed to come to the aid of his old party and go to Canada. They turned, faute de mieux, to Brougham. 'As we are deserted by Durham,' Roebuck said, 'we must trot out the old horse.'[12] Brougham was eager for a gallop. He told Place that he would exact a strict account of the Canadian business from the government and Place supplied him with 'a stock of ammunition'.[13]

On 17 January the government brought in its emergency bill. Peel and the Tories supported it and, indeed, by their amendments strengthened Durham's powers. Peel's action ensured that the bill would be passed. The next night in the Lords, nevertheless, Brougham lacerated the government in a speech which delighted the radicals, but no one else. In the course of it he directed one of his best *mots* at Lord Glenelg, the colonial secretary, who for sheer laziness alone deserved his reputation as the weakest member of Melbourne's cabinet. The events in Canada, Brougham feared, would give the minister many a sleepless day. The jibe was a rare glance of wit in an unrelenting tirade against the government. The 'laughter' inserted by the press reporters, Brougham informed Macvey Napier, the editor of the *Edinburgh Review*, was either unreal or sardonic. 'I was stern, bitter and inexorable throughout.'[14]

Brougham claimed that his reluctance to admonish the government was overcome only by a sense of public duty. 'Be assured,' he wrote to Lord Wellesley, 'that I could take no less hostile position to the Govt. I could not attack *gently & kindly* such misconduct as loss of a Province & provoking a Civil War. If I spoke at all my course was necessarily harsh & uncompromising. I assure you I deliberated, in this connection, whether I could avoid speaking. But after what I had said & recorded last Session [against the ten resolutions], I should have been ruined forever in character had I flinched.'[15] That Brougham spoke more in sorrow than anger was not apparent to eye-witnesses. James Grant, a lively and acute sketcher of parliamentary scenes, was reminded of 'a cross-tempered remorseless pedagogue, unsparingly applying the birch—regardless alike of their piteous looks and whining cries—to the persons of some half-dozen of his urchins'.

> If anything could have given additional effect to the heaviness of every successive blow, it would have been the appearance and manner of his lordship. It did not seem to require an effort. His heart was evidently in the work: there were no indications of a reluctant application of the rod . . . with Lord Brougham the thing was manifestly a labour of love. You saw in the leer of his eye, in the general expression of his features, in the exulting tone of his voice, that to behold Ministers writhing about him, was to him a positive luxury, and one of the highest order.[16]

The speech had no power to alter government policy, but the

government was shaken and Brougham was exhilarated by its discomfiture. For the next few months he went about, Greville wrote, 'in a state of furious mental activity, troubled neither with fear nor shame, and rejoicing in that freedom from all ties which renders him a sort of political Ishmael, his hand against everybody, and everybody against him, and enables him to cut and slash, as his fancy or his passion move him, at Whig or Tory'.[17] And all the while he waited for some misadventure across the Atlantic to trip up the government.

His opportunity came in July. The act suspending the colonial constitution had empowered Lord Durham to govern within the existing laws of the colony. In transporting to Bermuda eight alleged ringleaders of the rebellion, without trial, Durham overreached himself. He had no authority to imprison offenders outside the colony. His action brought Brougham and the Tory peers into union against the government. Brougham introduced a bill whose substance was to indemnify those colonial officials, including Durham, who had transgressed the law. But since the law officers of the Crown had no intention of bringing charges, its only real purpose was to censure the government and destroy Durham. Durham had known that he was acting illegally. He had done so because the inflamed state of opinion in Lower Canada made a fair trial impossible. From the letters he received from Melbourne and Glenelg he expected that the government would defend his action as a necessity in an emergency. Frightened by the opposition of Brougham and the Tories, Melbourne deserted him and accepted the indemnity bill. Durham, dismayed at being so ignobly sacrificed, resigned his commission and returned to England. Brougham had gained his object, but the affair brought him little credit. His speech introducing the bill, although sound on the main point of law at issue, was elsewhere riddled with legal errors and misconceptions about Canada. 'Brougham is evidently all astray as to Lord Durham in Canada,' concluded Roebuck, an expert on Canadian affairs, 'misled by a desire to find Durham in the wrong, and by a passion for talking on all matters, whether he understands them or not.'[18] Lord John Russell, distressed that Durham's indiscretion had been elevated into a major crime, spoke against Brougham publicly for the first time in his life. Durham, he told the House of Commons, had behaved honourably in an abnormal situation. He had tried to reconcile the ways of mercy with the safety of the province. 'He need care for no violence or invective, for no refinement of sympathy, for no bitterness of sarcasm, accompanied by professions of friendship, attempting to disguise but not succeeding in disguising the petty and personal feelings at the bottom of all these attacks, for he will have deserved well of his country, well of his sovereign and well of posterity.'[19] Durham's service to the Whig party shone bright against Melbourne's cowardice and Brougham's spite. 'If the Devil wanted an holiday,' Sydney Smith wrote shortly after Durham's return from Canada, 'how safely he might trust the diffusion of evil to Brougham, and what a relief for Mankind when the Devil came back and resumed his occupations.'[20]

For Brougham the 1838 session of parliament was one long, unbridled vendetta against the Whig ministers. But he had forfeited all moral authority. Worse, he had lost his party. In England party is everything. Without it, as Macaulay said, though a man may do wonders, he is a mere tongue.[21] Brougham raised a tempest of humane sentiment by a series of speeches at Exeter Hall and in the House of Lords on the state of West Indian slavery and the speeches regained for him a brief hour of public adulation. They did not succeed in persuading parliament to shorten the slaves' period of apprenticeship. 'The great meteor of the year has been Brougham,' Greville wrote, 'who, by common consent, has given proofs of the undiminished force of his wonderful capacity, and who has spoken with as much, if not with greater, eloquence than at any previous period in his life. But while he has excited no small degree of wonder and admiration, he has not raised his reputation for wisdom or honesty.'[22] Brougham flattered the Tories and they, titillated to watch him flail the Whig ministers, invited him to their parties. 'But though they talk with expressions of regret of his having radicalised himself, and he would probably, if he saw an opening, try to wriggle himself out of Radicalism and into Toryism, they will take care, in the event of their return to office, not to let such a firebrand in amongst them.'[23]

*   *   *

Not content to scourge ministers in parliament, Brougham took up his pen against them. In 1838 he published four volumes of his speeches and prefaced each speech with an introduction in which the Whigs were excoriated for their sins while his own virtues were extolled. The introductions were written in the third person, but the prose was unmistakably Brougham's. For sheer effrontery, they are unsurpassable. Brougham had acted with the Whig leaders for a quarter of a century. He had enjoyed their friendship, shared their confidence and joined in their labours. Yet in page after page he tarred them with the blackest pitch for having, during the whole of that span, behaved as base, fawning place-hunters 'with one eye turned to the Court, and one askance to the Country'.[24] In the first volume of his *Historical Sketches of Statesmen who Flourished in the Time of George III*, published a year later, the war was waged more subtly. Driven out of his party, Brougham discovered that it was the party system itself which vitiated popular government.[25] The system withdrew able men from service to the country and placed them for great portions of their lives in opposition. It turned politics into a sport and duped the people into believing that the competitors were fighting for them. Party was 'hurtful to the interests of the country, corrupting to the people, injurious to honest principle'. Brougham may have come to believe all manner of cant, but it stretches credulity to imagine that he had forgotten that opposition was as valuable a service for the statesman as government. Party is the ripe fruit of a mature political civilization. Brougham derided it as a device, to be borne only by nations still in their infancy, for enabling the aristocracy to stifle the voice of the people. He would have made more sense if he had aimed his fire at the aristocracy without identifying it with party.

Brougham's own publications reached a small audience and, since they were scarcely able to influence the course of English politics, he itched to get the *Edinburgh Review* into his own hands and transform it into an organ for exposing the cupidity and sham liberalism of his former friends. It was an evil day for Macvey Napier, the editor, when the Great Seal was taken out of commission and given to Cottenham. Melbourne congratulated himself on having broken with a termagant mistress and married the best of cooks, but Napier was not so fortunate. As John Morley said, the termagant was left on his hands.[26] Yet the antecedents of the struggle between Brougham and Napier for control of the *Edinburgh* lay farther back, in the year 1829, when Napier succeeded Jeffrey as editor and Thomas Macaulay became the member of parliament for Calne.

Brougham and Jeffrey had been friends from their boyhood days in Edinburgh. They had their quarrels, since Jeffrey suffered as much as anyone else from Brougham's domineering, but they were quarrels tamed by long friendship and mutual respect. When Napier became editor, Brougham, acting from an inflated sense of his importance, affected to withdraw from the review. 'I doubt if I could suddenly transfer myself to my own brother,' he explained to Jeffrey. 'It is rather a little *feeling* than any reason, and it will wear away speedily, I doubt not.'[27] Jeffrey passed the note on to Napier. 'I cannot say that I perfectly understand it; but I believe we must let it alone a while. He will no doubt contribute, and I am confident will very soon be as unreserved with you as he has been with me; but he is not to be urged when his humour or caprice leads him to hold back.'[28] Probably, Jeffrey suggested, Brougham was waiting to see what kind of number Napier first got out. 'I anticipate he will either fly off, or come cordially around before the next. At all events, let me beg that you would not turn your thoughts to giving up the Review, if otherwise prosperous, on this account. If a necessity should arise for resisting Brougham, and this leads to a rupture, it will be much easier and better for the cause to throw him off than the Review.'[29]

It is little cause for wonder, when a man of Jeffrey's experience could weigh up oppositions apparently so unbalanced, that Brougham should consider himself to be indispensable to the review. Recently, however, a new planet had swum into the sky to challenge his ascendancy. Macaulay's essay on Milton appeared in the journal in 1825. It created an overnight sensation and drew from Jeffrey the famous statement, 'The more I think, the less I can conceive where you picked up that style'. Brougham could not bear competition from a young lion, especially one whose contributions became the review's chief ornaments. His own essays, richer in knowledge and more rigorous in analysis, were never ornamental. He prided himself on being 'of the science school' of political and historical writing; Macaulay he relegated to the anecdotal school.[30] Macaulay, for his part, joined in the cry that 'long, dull articles' were ruining the review and he was flattered to be told by Napier that his articles were the only thing that kept the work up at all.[31]

So the affection which each had shown to the other when they met, the one a great man of the world, the other a precocious schoolboy, on Brougham's frequent visits to the Macaulay household, soured into mutual antipathy. Brougham's envy was the cause. He complained that Macaulay was taking up too much of the review and he used his influence to keep Jeffrey from offering the editorship to him. He could not, however, prevent Lord Lansdowne from bringing Macaulay in as the Whig member for Calne in 1829. Brougham, who thought, with some justice, that Denman, so long a battler in the Whig cause, deserved better than to be passed over in favour of a young sprig of a Tory family, could not keep his anger to himself. He berated Lansdowne in the robing-room of King's Bench and when Macaulay entered the House of Commons to take his oath, he cut him dead. 'We never spoke in the House, excepting once, that I can remember,' Macaulay told his sister, 'when a few words passed between us in the lobby. I have sat close to him when many men of whom I knew nothing have introduced themselves to me to shake hands, and congratulate me after making a speech, and he has never said a single word.'[32]

No sooner had Brougham begun to write for Napier (he withdrew for only one number) than he put the rivalry between himself and Macaulay to the test. Napier had asked Macaulay for an essay on the July revolution in France. Brougham, who for no good reason regarded France as his domain, demanded the subject for himself. The Whigs had just made gains at the elections. They were looking forward to office. What if Macaulay should queer the pitch?

I must beg, and indeed, make a point of giving you my thoughts on the Revolution, and, therefore, pray send off your countermand to Macaulay. My reason is this: all our movements next session turn on that pivot, and I can trust no one but myself with it, either in or out of Parliament. Jeffrey always used to arrange it so upon delicate questions, and the reason is obvious. Were it possible (which it plainly is not) to disconnect me and the party from the E.R., I should care little how such questions might be treated there; but as it is, I and the party I lead are really committed.[33]

Napier, still finding his feet as editor and anxious lest a blunder harm the Whig party, bowed to Brougham's bullying. Macaulay was irate. 'It is not very agreeable to me to find that I have thrown away the labour—the not unsuccessful labour, as I thought—of a month, particularly as I have not many months of perfect leisure.' Why, he asked Napier, had Brougham not shown a desire to write on the subject earlier, since he must have known that it would appeal to many people?

I am therefore a good deal vexed at this affair. But I am not in the least surprised at it. I see all the difficulties of your situation.

337

Indeed, I have long foreseen them. I always knew that, in every association, literary or political, Brougham would wish to domineer. I knew, also, that no Editor of the Edinburgh Review could, without risking the ruin of the publication, resolutely oppose the demands of a man so able and powerful . . .

My expectations have been exactly realized. The present constitution of the Edinburgh Review is this, that at whatever time Brougham may be pleased to notify his intention of writing on any subject, all previous engagements are to be considered as annulled by that notification. His language, translated into plain English, is this: 'I must write about this French Revolution, and I will write about it. If you have told Macaulay to do it, you may tell him to let it alone. If he has written an article, he may throw it behind the grate. He would not himself have the assurance to compare his own claims with mine. I am a man who acts a prominent part in the world; he is nobody. If he must be reviewing, there is my speech about the West Indies. Set him to write a puff on that. What have people like him to do, except to eulogise people like me?' No man likes to be reminded of his inferiority in such a way; and there are some particular circumstances in this case which render the admonition more unpleasant than it would otherwise be. I know that Brougham dislikes me; and I have not the slightest doubt that he feels great pleasure at having taken this subject out of my hands, and at having made me understand—as I do most clearly understand—how far my services are rated below his.[34]

Macaulay did not blame Napier, but he saw no reason to make sacrifices for a review which lay under 'an intolerable dictation'. Napier's pleadings succeeded in retaining Macaulay's services; they did nothing to assuage his anger. It was nonsense to say that a 'Whig manifesto' on France was necessary before the meeting of parliament. 'Your intentions towards me,' he told Napier, 'I know, are perfectly kind and fair. I have no such confidence with respect to his. I would sacrifice much to your convenience. But I cannot tell you how my whole heart and soul rise up against the thought of sacrificing anything to his love of domination.'[35]

It was a piece of good fortune that Brougham did not prevail against Macaulay and drive him from the *Edinburgh*, for it is doubtful whether any other journal, certainly not the Tory *Quarterly* nor the radical *Westminster*, would have published the essays which, even more than the *History of England*, have secured Macaulay's place in English literature.*

Napier, like Jeffrey before him, learned to tolerate Brougham, but no editor ever endured more torment. Brougham scolded and storm-ed, he hectored and found fault, exhausting the vocabulary of opprobrium and never ceasing to threaten desertion or prophesy ruin if he did not get his way. For so long as his way ran along the Whig path, he was no more than a thorn in Napier's side, painful without being poisonous. When Melbourne dropped him, Brougham changed direction and espoused the novel doctrine that the *Edinburgh* was not, nor had ever been, a Whig organ. The assertion constituted a revolution in his mind. He had justified taking subject after subject into his own hands—the July revolution in France was merely one of many—on the ground that the journal must trumpet the correct Whig line. As late as March 1835, when he still entertained hopes of being recalled to office, he asked Napier to reserve for him a few pages on the treachery of the Stanleyite deserters 'from our colours'.[36] But Melbourne had not despaired of reuniting the party and Brougham was furious to discover that Napier had compacted with him to keep silent about the renegades. He accused Napier of reckoning his assistance 'a very secondary object' and preparing to put him on the shelf.

This is the common lot of those who, in any concern, outlive their

---

* It is pleasant to record that their literary quarrel did not prevent Brougham and Macaulay from acting fairly towards one another in the conduct of their public duties. One of Brougham's first acts as lord chancellor was to present a living of £300 a year to Macaulay's brother and Macaulay commented that 'nothing could be done more handsomely' (Macaulay to Napier, 17 December 1830. *Napier Correspondence*, 98–9). More handsome still was Macaulay's defence of Brougham in the House of Commons against Croker's charge that Brougham had reneged on his pledge to the Yorkshire electors and gone to the House of Lords to gain place. 'The noble Lord had but a few days for deliberation, and that at a time when great agitation prevailed, and when the country required a strong and efficient Ministry to conduct the government of the State. At such a period a few days are as momentous as months would be at another period. It is not by the clock that we should measure the importance of the changes that might take place during such an interval. I owe no allegiance to the noble Lord who has been transferred to another place; but as a member of this House I cannot banish from my memory the extraordinary eloquence of that noble person within these walls—an eloquence which has left nothing equal to it behind: and when I behold the departure of the great man from amongst us, and when I see the place in which he sat, and from which he has so often astonished us by the mighty powers of his mind, occupied this evening by the honourable member who has commenced this debate, I cannot express the feelings and emotions to which such circumstances give rise.' (Trevelyan, *Macaulay*, i, 157–8).

contemporaries, and no one, I must say it for myself, in this world has less of personal punctilio about him, or cares less for such trifles when in pursuit of a great object. But at the same time, I really do feel that I ought not to be merely made a hack of, and 'offered' such and such books; that is, whatever nobody else likes to do. Yet it does so happen that of late years this is my position. Dr Southey, I assure you, is considered in a very different way by the Quarterly Review.[37]

Brougham told Napier that henceforth he would review only such subjects as suited his tastes and that he would no longer interpose an obstacle to the conductors of the review, who must be left to the direction of jobbing ministers. That Napier was hurt by the letter astonished him. He wished Napier well and even the review, 'while it supports its old honest principles and does not let itself be turned into a tool of Holland House, or any other class of place-loving politicians'.[38]

There was some truth to Brougham's argument that the *Edinburgh* had never been a *tool* of the Whig party, though he had to go back to the Cevallos article of 1808 to find the strongest evidence for his case. But it had never pretended not to serve the Whig *cause* and Napier was simply maintaining a tradition when he removed personal attacks on ministers from Brougham's articles. On one occasion he chided Brougham for inserting a passage accusing ministers of taking their opinions from underlings. What, Napier asked, would he have thought if so mean a charge had been laid against him? Brougham's answer was breath-taking.

> What you put as a case, I deny the application of, namely any one charging me, as Chancellor, with listening to underlings. A personal attack on *me* in the Edinburgh Review would have been indecent . . . I *enabled* it to go on; indeed, I believe I have written somewhere about a *fifth* of it with my own hand. I need not say that this gives me a very singular claim respecting it.[39]

Neither Jeffrey nor Napier ever disputed the claim, only the tyranny with which Brougham pressed it. By late 1837 Napier and Brougham were in direct opposition. Brougham asked for an all-out attack on ministers to be combined with support for household suffrage and the secret ballot. The review, in other words, was to be made an instrument of his effort to assume leadership of the radical movement.

Napier had borne much to placate Brougham and he had been severely criticized for allowing him to monopolize the writing of political articles during Lord Grey's administration. To be asked now to abandon the whole character of the review broke his patience. 'I tell your Lordship the truth,' he wrote to Brougham, 'when I say that your advice will always have due weight with me; but you must give me leave to add that there may sometimes be adverse views to deal with, and that something must be left to my own judgment and sense of propriety.'[40]

From every quarter Napier was advised to retain Brougham's services, but not to yield to him. John Allen, one of the ancient Whig friends whose company Brougham had forsworn, felt sympathy for his old friend in his political decline.

> I can easily conceive [he wrote to Napier early in 1838] how you will have perpetually recurring difficulties with Lord Brougham, but the Review is too useful an instrument to be thrown away. He may coax or bluster, but he will not break with you. In your situation I would reject all personalities and extravagant opinions, but refuse nothing in itself reasonable or plausible, because it went beyond the doctrines hitherto maintained in the Review. Great allowance must be made for his situation. After all the services he has rendered to public liberty, it is a cruel state to be in a manner proscribed by all his former associates, and it is no alleviation to his mind that he has incurred this misfortune by his own faults.[41]

Allen knew, nevertheless, how dangerous Brougham could be. He warned Napier to be on his guard. 'You know one of the great defects of his character is to over-value the immediate object he has in hand; to be carried away by the passion of the moment; and under that impulse to say and do what he has reason afterwards to regret. His passion at present is to punish ministers for their neglect of him, to turn them out, and to annoy them by all the means in his power.'[42]

Napier continued to humour Brougham. In the summer of 1838, for the last time, he stood in the middle while Brougham and Macaulay fired shots at each other. Brougham had just published a piece on the Earl of Chatham and to accommodate it Napier had turned down Macaulay's request to write on the same subject. Macaulay was not alone in thinking that Brougham treated Chatham too tenderly, leaving out his charlatanry and passing over the supposed 'madness' of his later years. Brougham assured Napier that he had done right to preserve Chatham from Macaulay, who was a slave of the Holland House set.

As to Macaulay, I only know that he left his party, which had twice given him seats in Parliament for nothing, while they were labouring for want of hands in Parliament, and jumped at promotion and gain in India. But what think you of his never having called on me since his return? . . . As he is the second or third greatest bore in society I have ever known, and I have little time to be bored, I don't at all lament it . . . That you have done anything very adventurous in encountering the wrath of the Macaulay party, I really do not much apprehend. That he has any better right to monopolise Lord Chatham, I more than doubt. That he would have done it better, I also doubt: for if truth, which he never is in search of, be better in History than turning sentences, and producing an effect by eternal point and glitter, I am assured that the picture I have done, poor as it is, may stand by any he or Empson could have done. But that is a trifle, and I only mention it to beg of you to pluck up a little courage, and not be alarmed every time any of the little knot of threateners annoy you. *They want to break off all kind of connection between me and the Edinburgh Review.* I have long seen it . . . they will never cease till they worry you out of your connection with me, and get the Review into their own hands, by forcing you to resign it yourself. A *party and a personal* engine is all they want to make it. What possible right can any of these silly slaves have to object to my opinion being—what it truly is—against the Holland House theory of Lord Chatham's madness. I *know* that Lord Grenville treated it with contempt. I know others now living who do so too, and I know that so stout a Whig as Sir P. Francis was clearly of that opinion, and he knew Lord Chatham personally. I had every ground to believe that Horace Walpole, a vile, malignant, and unnatural wretch, though a very clever writer of Letters, was nine-tenths of the Holland House authority for the tale. I knew that a baser man in character, or a meaner in capacity than the first Lord Holland existed not, even in those days of job and mediocrity. Why, then, was I bound to take a false view because Lord Holland's family have inherited his hatred of a great rival?[43]

Napier, who must have been amused to read that it was Brougham's enemies who were trying to get hold of the review, showed the letter to Macaulay and received a spirited reply.

As to Brougham's feelings towards myself, I know and have known for a long time that he hates me. If, during the last ten years, I have gained any reputation either in politics or in letters, if I have had any success in life, it has been without his help or countenance, and often in spite of his utmost exertions to keep me down. It is strange that he should be surprised at my not calling on him since my return. I did not call on him when I went away. When he was Chancellor and I was in office, I never once attended his levée. It would be strange indeed if now, when he is squandering the remains of his public character in an attempt to ruin the party of which he was a member then, and of which I am a member still, I should begin to pay court to him. For the sake of the long intimacy which subsisted between him and my father, and of the mutual good offices which passed between them, I will not, unless I am compelled, make any public attack on him. But this is really the only tie which restrains me, for I neither love him nor fear him.[44]

In the autumn of 1838 Napier removed from one of Brougham's historical sketches some strictures on the party system. Brougham protested in good humour. 'Surely, surely, there cannot be the slightest possible objection to a mere sentence or two of moralising . . . All the world allows a man to say a word or two on Party.' He would have a look at Speaker Hanmer's correspondence, which Napier had suggested he might review. 'But, if so many subjects are *tabooed*, it is not so easy, and far from comfortable. I can say nothing on Party, yet must treat of its use and abuse practically. I can say nothing against the Whigs, and yet must speak of all their most jobbing characters—and so of other subjects. However, I will try how I move in shackles and, *if I can*, I will dance a hornpipe as you and your Whig zealots desire.'[45]

Brougham's quarrels with Napier were not entirely the tantrums of a rejected man. Cockburn criticized the *Edinburgh* for falling too much under the thumb of Melbourne's government[46] and no one can read its pages without regretting that under Napier it lost the lustre and freshness of its early days. The purpose for which the journal had been founded, to ruffle the complacency of the establishment, had passed to John Stuart Mill's *Westminster Review*. Shackled to a ministerial organ Brougham was not content to remain for long. He wrote four articles in 1839. In 1840 he wrote only one and it, apart from an 1846 essay on the law courts, ended his connection with the review.

* * *

From 1839 until the fall of Melbourne's government two years later Brougham was much more in the company of Tories than of Whigs. The Duke of Wellington frequently entertained him; Lord Lyndhurst became a regular companion; and Croker, with whom he started a correspondence in 1839, took to praising him in the *Quarterly Review*. There was speculation that Brougham hoped to become a Tory lord chancellor. He joined in the opposition's baiting of ministers when Melbourne exploited the Queen's inexperience to cling to office during the Bedchamber crisis of 1839, and when Peel at last brought down the Whigs in 1841, he rejoiced that '*now* we shall have some regard paid to principles and measures, and hear no more of what has been so ruinous,—"Anything to keep out the Tories" '.[47] But neither Wellington nor Peel had ever done or said anything to feed his ambition and the change of government brought no change to his personal prospects. Added to his public misfortune was private grief. His young daughter, Eleanor-Louise, died in November 1839, and his mother a few weeks later. His daughter's death struck him too dumb for tears or any public show of bereavement. Henry Reeve, clerk of appeal in the Judicial Committee of the Privy Council, saw him on the morrow of her funeral as frisky as usual and unusually civil. 'Since Brougham has been broken-hearted,' he wrote in his diary, 'he is really so pleasant to mankind in general that one wishes he had a calamity two or three times at least in the course of a Session.'[48] Two years later Brougham was still engulfed in melancholy, from which he was able to distract himself only by ceaseless work and an abiding passion for politics. By then, of course, he knew that he was really no longer a contender in the great political game, the scramble for office. What a spectacle of pathos he presented to the world, one morning in September 1841; when he sat with his lady in a carriage on a hill in Putney to watch the new Tory ministers pass by on their way to be sworn in at Claremont!

16

Recessional

A politician who has once swayed cabinets and held senates in thrall comes with difficulty to understand that his sun has set. In 1842 Brougham began a correspondence with Sir Robert Peel, Melbourne's successor in Downing Street. The elections of 1841 had furnished Peel with a handsome majority in the House of Commons. What Brougham thought or did was of no consequence to the Conservative government. Brougham thought that, it must be. No prime minister, he imagined, could be comfortable without the benefit of his opinions. In 1844, for example, he wrote to Peel to advise him not to relinquish the income tax (the idea had not entered Peel's mind) and to assure him that he would vote for its continuation. 'It is better by far you should know my feelings & sentiments on so material a point while you may be making up your mind on it.'[1] Nearly forty years before, Brougham had won a famous victory against the income tax, and the passing of time had not changed his view that the tax was iniquitous. The difference was that in the 1840s Brougham was all for men, not measures. He supported Peel's government because he would not hold out an olive branch to the Whigs. Private friendships were repaired—the Greys were happy to receive him at Howick and Melbourne made him his executor—but Brougham's memories of 1835 were too painful to enable him to return to political alliance with the Whig party. He told Napier that a man must belong to another planet to wish the Whigs back in office[2] and it gave him immense pleasure to inform Lord Wellesley that 'there never was a party more reduced to insignificance than our friends the Whigs now are'.[3] The liberal direction of Peel's economic and social policy made it easier for him to support a Conservative government with an untroubled conscience. Brougham had been an earnest and constant friend of the Irish Catholics from his earliest days in politics, and when, in 1845, Peel introduced legislation to place the finances of the Catholic seminary at Maynooth on a permanent parliamentary foundation, he denounced the 'blockheads & idiots' on the Tory back benches who voted against it.[4] Justice to Ireland was not his only concern. The Maynooth bill, which was carried by Whig votes in the lobby, imperilled the future of Peel's government. More than half of the Conservative party in the House of Commons voted against it. And when, a few months later, potato famine in Ireland drove Peel to abandon a cardinal article of the Tory faith, the protection of England's cornfields by tariffs on imported grain, the party broke under the strain.

Questions of trade and finance had never occupied a prominent place in Brougham's mind, but since 1815, when the radicals began to focus the nation's attention on the evil of protecting landowners' profits by keeping up the price of bread to the poor, he had, however mutely, taken the side of the free-traders. He accepted, too, the argument that free trade would relieve distress in the manufacturing districts by enabling foreign markets to buy English industrial products. He therefore welcomed Peel's 'conversion' to free trade. What alarmed him, as all but the extreme radicals were alarmed, were the probable political consequences of Peel's boldness. His first fear was that the repeal of the Corn Laws would appear to be a victory of the Anti-Corn Law League and its strident style of mass agitation. 'There is one mode of carrying it,' he wrote to Peel at the end of 1845, 'which I am not for—Mob. To mob I am in all its hideous & despicable features a sworn enemy. I broke with the Whigs because they were undertaking the Govt without a reliance except on the mob—the mob in Ireland, the mob in England, and I regard the battle we now have to fight is with the mob.'[5] How the Whigs would have smiled at Brougham's new version of his quarrel with them and how the radicals would have congratulated themselves on keeping their distance from him! Mob-rule, at any rate, was a long way off. Brougham's second fear was more immediate, that the battle over the Corn Laws would open an irreparable breach between the Conservative government and the great landed interest in the country and, by splitting the Conservative party, let in a government of the Whigs.

Throughout the session of 1846, while the protectionist die-hards of the Conservative party were rallying their forces against the government, Brougham, taking upon himself the role of mediator, strove furiously to persuade them that it was folly to break up the party in a vain endeavour to prolong an economic system that had outlived its day. But neither he nor anyone else could stem the flow of anger which welled up in the agricultural constituencies and kept Conservative backbenchers up to the mark. The Corn Laws were abolished, but only because the whole of the Whig party marched into the division lobbies with the government. Two-thirds of the Conservative party in the House of Commons voted against the measure and their defiance dealt Peel's ministry its death-blow. In the last week of June Brougham moved heaven and earth to prevent the Whigs from coming into office. His plan, hatched with Lord Lyndhurst, was for Peel and Sir James Graham, the virtual deputy leader of the Conservatives, to resign, thereby enabling the Tory protectionists to have their pound of flesh. The rest of the cabinet could then remain in office, under Lord Stanley's leadership, and a united Tory party could continue to govern the country. It was a shallow plot, designed, some people thought, to restore Brougham to the Woolsack, and it ended in failure.

Lord John Russell became prime minister. He and Brougham had enjoyed a long friendship and Russell alone had stood by Brougham in 1835, when he recommended that the dislodged lord chancellor should be given a secretaryship of state or the Rolls to compensate for the loss of the Great Seal. Russell's promotion might therefore have been expected to diminish Brougham's hostility to the new Whig government. In 1844, however, Russell, in common with everyone else, had declared against Brougham's bill to create a new permanent judge in the Judicial Committee of the Privy Council, to be titled vice-president of the council and to receive an annual salary of £2,000. The bill was lost because it was universally ridiculed as a shameless device of Brougham's to secure himself a permanent place. Brougham did not forgive Russell for believing the 'slander'. Early in July 1846, when the new Whig government was a week old, he wrote to John Murray of Russell's 'crime' in falling for the 'silly lie' merely 'to toad eat the slanderous portion of his Whig creatures'.[6] For a time Brougham hoped that a reunited Conservative party might displace the Whigs, but the divisions within Toryism went far deeper than resentment at Peel's throwing over protection and the wounds inflicted during the bitter debates of 1846 could not be healed overnight. Russell remained prime minister until 1852, sustained in office by the votes of the Peelite Conservatives, whose breach with the Protectionists widened, rather than narrowed, over the years. Brougham, a life-long free-trader, found himself in the unenviable position of acting with the reactionary Protectionist party in parliament. In 1849, in a futile attempt to oust the Whigs, he betrayed his convictions and voted with the Protectionists against the government's bill (a logical corollary to the repeal of the Corn Laws) to abolish the ancient Navigation Laws, one of the last relics of the bygone mercantilist era. 'There is no wonder,' Russell remarked, 'that Brougham thinks he knows something of the Navigation Laws, as he has been fishing for seals so long.'[7]

Failure to unseat the Whig government in 1849 seems at last to have convinced Brougham that his power to influence the course of party politics was spent. Nor was he willing to dress himself in the bigoted anti-Catholicism with which the Protectionists sought to cover their intellectual nakedness. When Russell resigned office in 1851, but returned after the Protectionists' confession that they were too weak to form a government, Brougham did not shed tears at the event. 'With my own feelings and opinions, both as to Protection and as to No-Popery,' he wrote to a friend, 'I feel truly grateful for the self-denial of those who have preferred running no risks.'[8] He had little confidence in Lord Stanley, the Protectionist leader, who had moved steadily to the right since his days as a Whig minister in Grey's government. Brougham who in more than two decades of Conservative leadership failed to gain a reputation for political gravity, described Stanley, as 'one of the cleverest and lightest and most ill-furnished heads in England, with a great many good qualities more or less unavailing'.[9] When Stanley, who inherited the earldom of Derby in the summer of 1851, formed a government in 1852, Brougham, who was nearing his seventy-fourth birthday, neither sought nor was offered a place in it.

*   *   *

For some men—Canning is, perhaps, the supreme 19th-century example—the game of politics is everything. It was never so with Brougham and, although he could not extinguish his brooding disappointment at being excluded from office after 1835, he found distraction from the disappointment in a variety of activities. In 1844 he founded the Law Amendment Society, whose quarterly journal, the *Law Review*, was the nursery of many mid-century reforms in the law. It was edited by James Stewart, who sat in parliament as a Whig from 1837 to 1841, but its animating spirit was Brougham. Not all of Brougham's brainwaves were taken seriously—the proposal to establish 'reconciliation courts' where parties could appear before an action was brought and another to extend the informal procedure followed in county courts to the superior courts were considered to be impractical—and his bill to codify the criminal law, introduced in 1844, was a crude piece of drafting which confirmed the opinion that he had neither the mind of a codifier nor the skill of a conveyancer. But his act of 1845 abolishing arrest for debt and one of 1851 compelling both parties in civil actions to give evidence were valuable improvements to the law. Brougham told Peel, when the debt act was before parliament, that he was merely the instrument of the whole legal profession.[10] It would be more just to say that he was its prime mover. The *Law Review* was endlessly imaginative in ideas, now suggesting that England learn from Scotland and create the post of public prosecutor, now recommending that trial by jury be abolished in cases involving debt or breach of contract, now urging a thorough purification of the administration of justice by local magistrates. To judge Brougham's accomplishments piece by piece would be to miss the great importance of the Law Amendment Society as a fertilizing agency. 'The real aim of the essay or the article,' the *Quarterly Review* wrote in praise of Brougham, 'was attained by the inquiry it stimulated or the example it set. He led the way and others followed, who without him would not have moved at all.'[11]

All his life Brougham had been a journalist and he was used to writing rapidly. 'I have written a longish pamphlet since I came in,' he wrote to Napier on one occasion, 'namely in eight and a half hours . . . As I was in a fervour of composition, like Dryden on his Ode (to compare great things with small), I could not stop, but it rather exhausted me, for it was sixty pages of writing.'[12] Brougham's facility of expression enabled him to get up two, three, sometimes four long articles for the *Edinburgh* issue after issue. When his connection with the *Edinburgh* ended, he continued to write, for the *Law Review* and, after 1845, occasionally for the *Quarterly*. The standards required by the great 19th-century reviews far exceeded what would be expected of a journalist today. But reviews are, by their nature, ephemeral. Only the very best of them, like Macaulay's essays, endure. Brougham longed for a more solid literary reputation. In 1838 he confessed to Napier what had always been his 'chief ambition as to literary character (after eloquence, of course)—I mean the rank and station of an historian'.

I have some little knack of narrative, the most difficult by far of all styles, and never yet attained in perfection but by Hume and Livy; and I bring as much oratory and science to the task as most of my predecessors, nor does the exceedingly flimsy and puerile work of [Archibald] Alison, &c., deter me from my favourite subject— French Revolution. I shall think well before I undertake it, but also before I give it up.[13]

Whether because Carlyle's *French Revolution*, published in 1837, drove him from the field, Brougham never fulfilled his ambition. Over the last thirty years of his life he nevertheless turned out a stream of books on an astonishing range of subjects. The first volume of his *Discourse on Natural Theology*, with an edition of Paley's famous work, appeared in 1835 and it was followed by the four volumes of his *Collected Speeches* with introductions (1838–45), *Historical Sketches of Statesmen in the Time of George III* (three series, 1839–45), *Demosthenes upon the Crown* (translated, with notes, 1840), *Political Philosophy* (1842–43), a novel, *Albert Lunel* (1844), *Lives of Men of Letters and Science in the Reign of George III* (1845), *History of England and France under the House of Lancaster* (1852), *Tracts, Mathematical and Physical* (1860) and the three volumes of memoirs (1863).

Brougham was the least fastidious of writers. Not for him the endless, soul-racking crossing out of sentences, nor the fretful waiting for the muse to descend. 'In the employment of a literary man,' runs a passage in *Albert Lunel*, 'nothing is of such importance as a constant supply of work and of a kind which he can at all times perform. The nearer he brings his work to the common kinds of day labour, the labour at least of artizans, the better for him . . . The evils of a literary life resolve themselves almost entirely into the ups and downs of imaginative composition, the uncertainty of finding a demand for the exertions of genius, the greater uncertainty of being able to make these exertions, the occasional idleness and consequent want which are the result. Hence the anxieties, the sufferings, the various fortunes, the too often unequal spirits, even the recourse to dissipation for relief, which chequer the lives of literary men.'[14] Although all his books, apart from the biographical sketches, were critical and commercial failures, his confidence in his literary powers was boundless. 'My six weeks here have not been idle certainly,' he wrote to Napier from Cannes in the autumn of 1838, 'for I have also finished four long Dialogues on Instincts and a full abstract and commentary on Cuvier's Osteology and Geology, and other matter, for my concluding volume of Natural Theology. Pray attend to my theory of Instinct. It is full of novelty, and there are some mathematical novelties of importance.'[15] When a year passed without a review of the volume in the *Edinburgh*, Brougham protested. 'It should be done without any praise at all, even if it deserved it, but it should really have the benefit of being known. The Principia [a commentary on Newton] is the only deep and learned commentary on the greatest and most inaccessible work of man, and yet I undertake to say it, it enables any one to read and follow it.'[16] Napier was accustomed to Brougham's frank expressions of vanity. Peel may have been more surprised to hear from him in 1844 that the essay on Voltaire, nearly finished, was 'very full in all parts' and 'the first real & fair & if I may say so, learned appreciation of him, for it requires Natural Philosophy as well as Greek and Latin to estimate him'.[17]

The world took a different view of Brougham's literary talent. His knowledge of Greek was too slender to prepare him for the task of translating Demosthenes and the *De Coronâ* was slated in the press, especially the *Times*, which gave its reviewer six successive days to expose Brougham's misunderstandings of meanings and historical errors. Campbell read the *Political Philosophy* with pleasure and profit, but he could find no one else who had;[18] nor could Macaulay, who remarked that Brougham's absurdities were 'merely pitiable while he confines himself to the pen'.[19] According to Campbell, the German edition of the *Political Philosophy* was in demand at two successive Leipzig fairs, but in England it fell still-born from the presses. The first printing was damasked (the pages stamped by a machine with small squares) and sent as lining-paper to the trunk-makers.[20] The *Natural Theology*, which suffered the most from the critics, was said by one peer to be 'so full of Ologies' that he could not read it,[21] and Disraeli, himself incompetent to judge the scientific value of the work, borrowed the world's condemnation of it to poke fun at Brougham in one of his 'Runnymede Letters'.

> At present, I am informed that your Lordship is occupied in a translation of your Treatise of Natural Theology into German, on the Hamiltonian system. The translation of a work on a subject of which you know little, into a tongue of which you know nothing, seems the climax of those fantastic freaks of ambitious superficiality which our lively neighbours describe by a finer term than quackery.[22]

Albert Lunel, Brougham's only foray into fiction, was written as a monument to his daughter, Eleanor-Louise, who is the model of the novel's suffering heroine. It gains some interest from being a kind of *roman à clef* in which Brougham himself, Croker and Lyndhurst appear in a most flattering light, but as fiction it is worthless. The narrative lacks pace, the dialogue is stilted, there is no demonstration of character issuing in action, and for plot there is substituted a succession of preposterous coincidences. Brougham called the novel a 'philosophical romance', and indeed it is nothing more than a series of tableaux, settings for contrived discussions of all manner of subjects—literature, religion, politics, ethics and history. For the historian there is a minor point of interest. In the 1840s and 1850s, as Protestants took alarm at the number of converts who followed John Henry Newman to Rome, a spate of anti-Catholic novels descended on England. Although, a few years later, Brougham was to find the 'No Popery' of the Protectionists indigestible, *Albert Lunel* is a subdued version of the anti-Catholic literature of the period: he uses Albert, a Protestant converted to truth from Roman error, to attack Catholicism, especially the monastic life, for its attempt to confine the exercise of human reason and suppress the free play of human passions. Brougham had the novel privately printed, but on the advice of several friends he suppressed it. The volumes remained out of sight at Brougham Hall until he died, when his son, in an act of misplaced filial affection, put them on the market.

Brougham was at his best as a sketcher of famous men's lives. History, he believed, should make the reader delight in good actions and execrate evil ones. The historian's duty was to preach the virtues of peace, progress in the arts and sciences, the diffusion of national prosperity and the improvement of national institutions.[23] History was neither the merely aesthetic production of the *belletrist* nor the sterile exhumation of the past. It was an agent for moral improvement. Much as he admired Hume, Gibbon, Robertson and Voltaire, Brougham aspired to take the writing of history beyond the mere chronicling of wars and dynasties. The experiment, as he called it, of 'writing lives and histories so as to keep up the interest and yet treat the crimes of those vulgarly called great men so as to excite disgust when atrocious and contempt when mean—and so as, also, to give a proper *relief* to the truly important events and circumstances and sink the less material things to their right level' was new. It would succeed only if several men tried it.[24] He made the experiment by fixing his attention on the reign of George III, 'the Augustan age of modern history', when the most finished orators, the most accomplished captains, the greatest statesmen and the founders of modern science and political economy all flourished. It was also the age which placed the rights of the people on a new and firm foundation and began the work of diffusing culture and knowledge among the people.

Brougham's brief lives are too short to entitle him to the rank of historian. They were also written about the very recent past, often, as John Allen said, under the influence of 'temporary feelings'.[25] Done in ink-wash, rather than oils, they are somewhat bare of facts. At times Brougham seems to judge men according to their likeness to himself. Consider his estimate of Chatham.

> A mind eminently fertile in resources; a courage which nothing could daunt in the choice of his means; a resolution equally indomitable in their application; a genius, in short, original and daring, which bounded over the petty obstacles raised by ordinary men—their squeamishness and their precedents, and their forms, and their regularities—and forced away its path through the entanglements of this base undergrowth to the worthy object ever in view, the prosperity and renown of his country. Far superior to the paltry objects of a grovelling ambition, and regardless alike of party and of personal considerations, he constantly set before his eyes the highest duty of a public man, to further the interests of his species.[26]

Occasionally Brougham's passion to instruct submerges historical accuracy. George III is said to have interfered in government business 'more than any prince who ever sat upon the throne of this country since our monarchy was distinctly admitted to be a limited one'[27] and the inexpert reader might be forgiven for not knowing that between the distinct admission and George III's accession only two sovereigns occupied the throne. The candour which Brougham promised in the introduction to the first volume of the *Statesmen* is consistently Whiggish. There are other blemishes: the reluctance to point an argument by examples, the failure to trace the *progress* of a man's career, and a certain monotony of arrangement. But when Brougham knows absolutely what he is writing about he is very good indeed. Where is there to be found a better portrait of George III?

Of a narrow understanding, which no culture had enlarged; of an obstinate disposition, which no education, perhaps, could have humanized; of strong feelings in ordinary things, and a resolute attachment to all his own opinions and predilections, George III possessed much of the firmness of purpose, which, being exhibited by men of protracted mind without any discrimination, and as pertinaciously when they are in the wrong as when they are in the right, lends to their characters an appearance of inflexible consistency, which is often mistaken for greatness of mind, and not seldom received as a substitute for honesty . . . In other respects, he was a man of amiable disposition, and few princes have been more exemplary in their domestic habits, or in the offices of private friendship. But the instant that this prerogative was concerned, or his bigotry interfered with, or his will thwarted, the most unbending pride, the most bitter animosity, the most calculating coldness of heart, the most unforgiving resentment, took possession of his whole breast, and swayed it by turns.[28]

When Jeffrey read the essay, 'George IV and Queen Caroline', first published in the *Edinburgh Review* in 1838, he was lavish in his praise. 'The characters have the copiousness and the colouring of Clarendon, with a great deal, too, of his generous candour, on some points, and the traces of his deep partialities on others; and there are bits *excavated* with the sharp style of Tacitus.'[29] Not every sketch merits such applause. But the judgements are so piquant and the prose so spritely that it is, perhaps, surprising that a century-and-a-half has passed without their being reprinted.

*　　*　　*

Much of Brougham's writing was done at Cannes, where from 1838 until his death he spent a part of each year, almost always the autumn, when parliament was in recess, and frequently part of the spring as well. Brougham was on his way to Savoy in December, 1834, when the cholera forced him to break his journey at Cannes, then a tiny, unregarded fishing village, famous only as the spot where Napoleon first touched French soil on his return from Elba. So charmed was he by the still beauty of the place that he decided to build himself a château there. By October 1838 the house was ready to be lived in, and although the Hollands found it exceptionally ugly and everything in extreme bad taste,[30] Brougham was happy with it and with the fine view of the Mediterranean which it commanded.

354

I never saw a better, not to say, a finer country house [he wrote to Napier]. Fine exterior, magnificent rooms, four and five on a floor, staircase such as I never saw in any house, beautiful terraces on the roof, orange groves, almond trees, vineyards, and a fine pine forest behind, of which part belongs to me, and the rest I am in treaty for. Then I dip my feet in the blue Mediterranean, my groves reaching to its edge. I found our hay harvest got in, peas nearly over (first crop), cherries set, apricots fit for tarts, artichokes ripe, and green almonds at the dessert.[31]

Away from England, which he took to calling 'Fog-land', Brougham refreshed himself each year in the sweet climate of Provence. He set an example which the English aristocracy followed. Cannes became a favourite watering-hole and the town honoured him by naming the central square after him and erecting there a statue to his memory.

Brougham was seldom idle at Cannes. He rose most mornings at six, took an early constitutional, and spent the rest of the day in concluding scientific experiments, usually optical, writing or entertaining visitors. French statesmen, scientists and men of letters flocked to his door. France had always excited his interest and compelled his affection. The French returned the compliment. Brougham's French was more droll than he allowed—a Paris wit once said that 'in addition to his other gifts, he must have the gift of unknown tongues'[32]—but at least he was able to deliver lectures in the language at the Institute, which elected him a member in 1838. He was overbearing when conversation turned to French affairs. Creevey, who listened to a conversation between Brougham and Talleyrand in 1831, when Talleyrand was ambassador to London, reported that 'it appeared most clearly that Vaux had been intimately acquainted with every leading Frenchman in the Revolution, and indeed with every Frenchman and every French book that Tally mentioned'.[33] But Brougham was one of the very few English politicians to form a genuinely intimate friendship with King Louis-Philippe and members of the French assembly. Residence at Cannes stimulated his interest in French politics, which came to occupy more and more of his thoughts as his influence in English party politics waned. In the early 1840s the French and English governments were earnestly attempting to establish freer trade and a closer partnership between the two countries. (It was then that the phrase, *entente cordiale*, was first used, either by the foreign secretary, Lord Aberdeen, or by

Louis-Philippe.) Brougham flattered himself that his unofficial links with the French government did good. He wrote to Lord Grey in February 1843 that he had been 'very glad to *assist* (as the French call it) at the debates, because I was enabled to do some little good in setting them right as to English matters of which their ignorance is profound';[34] later in the same year he was shown a letter written by a French correspondent of Lord Redesdale 'which was gratifying as confirming very remarkably the good effects of my pacific & *kindly* speeches in Paris'.[35]

When the revolution of 1848 broke out in Paris, Brougham was at Cannes. The formation of a provisional government and the calling of elections to a constituent national assembly stirred strange notions in his brain: he would put himself forward as a candidate for the department of the Var, where his château stood. The inhabitants of the village greeted his candidacy with approval, but there was a difficulty, one which a former lord chancellor might have foreseen. Brougham was not a French citizen. He therefore went to Paris and applied to the minister of justice for naturalization. He received the following reply.[36]

> I must apprise you of the consequences of the naturalisation you demand, should you obtain it. If France adopts you for one of her sons, you cease to be an Englishman; you are no longer Lord Brougham, you become citizen Brougham. You lose forthwith all titles of nobility, all privileges, all advantages, of whatever nature they may be, which you possessed, either in your quality of Englishman, or by virtue of rights hitherto conferred upon you by British laws or customs, and which cannot harmonise with our law of equality between all citizens . . . It is in this sense that you must write to me. I must presume that the late British Chancellor is aware of the necessary consequences of so important a demand. But it is the duty of the Minister of Justice of the French Republic to warn you officially.

Brougham sent off another letter to the minister remarkable for its obtuseness.

> I never doubted that by causing myself to be naturalised a French citizen I should lose all my rights as a British Peer and a British subject in France. I will retain my privileges as an Englishman only in England; in France I should be all that the laws of France accord

to the citizens of the Republic. As I desire above all the happiness of the two countries, and their mutual peace, I thought it my duty to give a proof of my confidence in the French institutions, to encourage my English countrymen to confide in them as I do.

Once again the matter had to be explained to him.

My letter has not been understood. Yours, to my great regret, does not permit me to comply with your demand . . . I used the clearest and most positive expressions in my letter. France admits no partition—she admits not that a French citizen shall at the same time be the citizen of another country. In order to become a Frenchman, you must cease to be an Englishman. You cannot be an Englishman in England, and a Frenchman in France; our laws are absolutely opposed to it. You must necessarily choose.

Brougham withdrew his application. In the House of Lords he rounded on the provisional government in Paris with such vehemence that Lord Lansdowne, unwilling to let the occasion for merriment slip, expressed his great satisfaction to learn that the strange rumour then afloat of the noble lord's wish to transfer his eloquence from Westminster to the Place de la Concorde was groundless. Unfortunately for Brougham the comedy did not end there. His correspondence with the French government was published in the French press, whence it was picked up by English journalists. On 18 April the *Times* had a field day.

All who remember English history for the last forty years, speak of Henry Brougham as the most eccentric figure in that eventful period. So much of greatness in words, and so little dignity in action, have never been found in the same individual. Now shaking the House of Commons with his eloquence, and now exciting the laughter of schoolboys, still it is the same marvellous man. Lord Brougham has just thrown the highest somersault that he has ever accomplished. It is not sufficient for him to have played the Edinburgh Reviewer, the English Barrister, to have propounded startling theories in science, to have been created an English peer, to have translated Demosthenes, and to have passed himself as the greatest orator of his age—like Alexander, he sighed for other worlds, not to conquer, but in which to display his eccentricities . . . A National Convention is still open to the *Citoyen Brougham*. He may yet rival Vergniaud in eloquence, and employ the remainder of his life in reconstituting civilisation in France. For this turbid pre-eminence we find him almost ready to sacrifice ermine, coronet, pension, and all. When sacrificed at last before the rising demagogues of the new Mountain, and led off to the Place de la République in a cart, he will devote the brief minutes of his passage to chanting, with sincere enthusiasm and strong Northumbrian burr,

'——*Mourir pour la Patrie,*
C'est le sort le plus beau et le plus digne d'envie.'

By 1848 Brougham was beyond injury from such ridicule. He had long before reached the happy point, as Macaulay expressed it, where it was equally impossible for him to gain character or to lose it.[37] Within a month the farce was forgotten.

Brougham's faculties were undimmed, his constitution hale. Although he ceased to play a part in the Judicial Committee of the Privy Council after 1850, he continued to attend the appellate and ordinary sessions of the House of Lords with great regularity. In 1856 he made his last spirited speech in that House, when he lent his authority to the majority which resisted the innovation of life peerages. Much of his time was occupied in reminiscent correspondence; and he was equally happy in indulging his scientific curiosity. Henry Reeve came across him at Brougham Hall experimenting with fire-balloons[38] and in 1860 he published a collection of essays entitled *Tracts, Mathematical and Physical.* They included the 1794 paper on porisms which had earned Brougham election to the Royal Society, but there were also papers written in the 1850s, and the contents list, which ranges over the integral calculus, the architecture of bees' cells, light and colour, the forces of attraction, problems in Kepler and meteoric stones, is wonderful proof of the mental zest which he retained throughout his life.

Macaulay made a note of Brougham in his diary in 1856. 'Strange fellow! His powers gone. His spite immortal. A dead nettle.'[39] The words were untrue and unkind. William Forsyth, who spent long periods with Brougham in Westmorland, found his memory for past events sharp and his acerbity softened by old age. During all their conversations he never heard him say an ill-natured word of anyone.[40] In 1857 Brougham had his seventy-ninth birthday, yet in that year he formed a committee to establish a National Association for the Promotion of Social Science. Until 1865 he was its president and each year he travelled, to Birmingham or Edinburgh or wherever the annual congress was convened, to deliver the presidential address. After the first congress, held at Birmingham in September 1857, he complained to Gladstone of the 'horrid name' which the newspapers were attaching to the Association. 'Sociological! I have intimated to my colleagues that it must be either Latin or Greek, but not such an obvious hybrid.'[41] He was elected chancellor of his old university at Edinburgh in 1859 and he confessed to Gladstone that he had written an inaugural address of 'formidable proportions'.

> But I wished to treat of some important matters, & it is like anything I now do. It is a Swan's voice, or valedictory. (I heartily wish I could bring myself to believe this and so relieve my mind and *my purse*) . . . The subjects I dwell upon are the crimes of great (falsely called) men and of really great historians in not calling things by their proper *names*. So Henry V, Q. Elizabeth, Lorenzo de Medici, are called up for Judgment, but above all Napoleon, whom I really consider the worst man that ever lived.[42]

Brougham travelled to Manchester for the Social Science congress in 1866 and in the same year he attended the prize-giving at London University. For limited periods his mind was still able to concentrate. He wrote a concise and pointed preface to the *Life of Lord Plunket*, an old ally from his House of Commons days, in 1867. Some years before, however, friends had begun to mark the change in him. Sir Frederick Pollock visited him at Brougham Hall in 1861. 'I think he remembered me; but he seemed very feeble, his face was of ashen grey, and he said only a few words. He looked like a shadow of the past.'[43] Some days were better than others. Charles Knight saw him after a gap of years at the Social Science meeting at London in 1862. 'Though his face was furrowed, there was something like the old lustre in his eyes, and the smile that has so often told of the kindliness that was as natural as the power of sarcasm still lingered about his mouth.'[44] Prosper Merimée found him at Cannes 'very weak and tottery, but as great a busybody as ever, inquisitive to a degree'.[45] By 1867 the good days were becoming rarer. William Forsyth saw him for the last time in London, where Brougham was stopping on his way from the north of England to Cannes.

> When the servant opened the door he told me that Lord Brougham would not recognise me, but begged me to go in and see him. He

then opened the door of the dining-room and I saw Lord Brougham sitting in an arm-chair near the fire. His hair was white as snow, and so were his shaggy eyebrows. I did not like to advance, for I was painfully conscious that he no longer knew me, as he made no sign of recognition, but continued to stare fixedly at me without moving. I turned away with a presentiment that I should never see him again in this life, and a few months afterwards the news of his death at Cannes reached England.[46]

Brougham died in his sleep on 7 May, 1868, and was buried, by his request, in the little cemetery at Cannes.

Lord Melbourne once wrote in his commonplace book that no man could be worth anything until he discovered that he was a fool. Those men who never made the discovery spent the whole of their lives 'desperate and inveterate cases of folly, self-conceit, and impertinence'.[47] Perhaps Brougham fell into the category. His friends and colleagues, without exception, located the source of his shifting in moral imperfections, in his deceitfulness and vanity. Hence his political ruin. It is the custom of men to esteem moral above intellectual virtues. The English especially prefer manners to opinions. A man who would make his way in public life must first be approved so that he might become useful. When Brougham's spleen was resting, he was the most amiable of men. At other times his combativeness was ill-mannered: he loved a duel and it cannot be said that he always minded when the button fell from his foil. He over-estimated his knowledge, prodigious though it was, and the error led him into bullying. But his contempt for men's ignorance was nothing compared to his scorn for their thinking it bliss. It is true, as Campbell said, that, for all the words and theories that poured from his pen, he nowhere extended the bounds of knowledge. His writings have fallen into neglect, for the most part justified. But in their time they helped to enlarge the community in which things were known. Brougham has only a small claim on posterity's attention as a writer and none at all as a thinker. So much may be allowed without going the length of Campbell's judgement that he accomplished nothing as a states-man.[48] His activity was miscellaneous, but his achievements were not random. They were rooted in the conviction that knowledge and justice are the parents of human freedom. Wilberforce is remembered and revered, along with men like Shaftesbury and Cobden, because they directed their fire at a single target. They stood on the perimeter of the party battle-ground. Brougham attempted what is virtually impossible in English, or any other, politics, simultaneously to be a party leader and a spokesman for advanced opinions. It is a commonplace to say that by trying to do everything he ended up doing nothing. The well-known fable of his having his photograph taken is worth repeating.

Lord Brougham was at his chateau at Cannes when the first introduction of the daguerreotype process took place there, and an accomplished neighbour proposed to take a view of the chateau, with a group of guests in the balcony. The artist explained the necessity of perfect immobility. He only asked that his Lordship and friends would keep perfectly still for five seconds; and Brougham vehemently promised that he would not stir. He moved too soon, however, and the consequence was—a blur where Lord Brougham should have been; and so stands the daguerreotype view to this hour. There is something mournfully typical in this. In the picture of the century, as taken from the life by history, this man should have been a central figure; but now, owing to his want of steadfastness, there will be for ever—a blur where Brougham should have been.[49]

What Caribbean slave who heard dim reports of Henry Brougham across the seas, what Indian defendant who gained redress in the Judicial Committee of the Privy Council, what Lancashire operative who first had the mysteries of steam power explained to him in a mechanics' institute, what fair-minded Whig, indeed, who rejoiced when the long night of Tory rule ended, did not see a clearer image? For Brougham's epitaph there are words which he wrote of a far, far greater man, but a man whose pursuit of justice and the life of reason he took as an example from his youth. Substitute for 'light accomplishments' the words 'worldly vanities' and what Brougham pronounced of Voltaire may, in a spirit of generosity, be said of him.

If ever the time shall arrive when men, intent solely on graver matters, and bending their whole minds to things of solid importance, shall be careless of such light accomplishments . . . then the impression which this great genius has left will remain; and while his failings are forgotten, and the influence of his faults corrected, the world, wiser and better because he lived, will continue to celebrate his name.[50]

NOTES

CHAPTER ONE

1 Sefton to Creevey, 19 November 1830. H. Maxwell (ed.), *The Creevey Papers. A Selection from the Correspondence & Diaries of the Late Thomas Creevey*, London, 1903, ii, 214.
2 Sefton to Creevey, 18 November 1830. *Ibid.*, ii, 214.
3 *Ibid.*, i, 108.
4 'Rousseau', *Men of Science and Letters in the Reign of George III*, in *Collected Works*, ii, 155–6.
5 H. Brougham, *The Life and Times of Henry Lord Brougham*, London, 1871, i, 11–12.
6 *Ibid.*, i, 18–19.
7 H. Cockburn, *Memorials of his Time* (new edn), Edinburgh, 1910, 3–4, 10.
8 *Ibid.*, 10.
9 Lord Campbell, *Lives of Lord Lyndhurst and Lord Brougham*, London, 1869 edn, 225.
10 D. le Marchant, *Memoir of John Charles, Viscount Althorp, Third Earl Spencer*, London, 1876, 74–5.
11 Earl Russell, *Recollections and Suggestions, 1813–1873*, London, 1875, vi.
12 R. J. Mackintosh (ed.), *Memoirs of the Life of the Right Honourable Sir James Mackintosh*, 2nd edn, London, 1836, i, 29.
13 Horner to J. Hewlett, 17 July 1798. L. Horner (ed.), *Memoirs and Correspondence of Francis Horner*, London, 1843, i, 65–6.
14 Brougham, *Life and Times*, i, 69–70.
15 Brougham to Lord Grey, [12 September 1814]. Brougham, *Life and Times*, ii, 109.
16 L. J. Jennings (ed.), *The Croker Papers*, London, 1844, iii, 308.
17 Horner to J. Loch, 25 August 1798. R. H. H. Buddle Atkinson and G. A. Jackson (ed.), *Brougham and his Early Friends. Letters to James Loch, 1798–1809*, London, 1908, i, 41–2.
18 H. Brougham, *An Inquiry into the Colonial Policy of the European Powers*, Edinburgh, 1803, ii, 435.
19 Cockburn, *Memorials*, 69.
20 H. Cockburn, *Life of Lord Jeffrey with a Selection from his Correspondence*, Edinburgh, 1852, 56.
21 T. Sadler (ed.), *Diary, Reminiscences, and Correspondence of Henry Crabb Robinson*, 3rd edn, London, 1872, ii, 226.
22 M. Napier (ed.), *Selection from the Correspondence of the Late Macvey Napier*, London, 1879, 279.

23 James Ferguson to J. Loch, 15 October 1798. *Brougham and Early Friends*, i, 45–8.
24 E. B. Ramsay, *Reminiscences of Scottish Life and Character*, Edinburgh, 1874, 101–26.
25 Brougham to Allen, [31] March 1800. Brougham/Allen MSS. Add.Mss. 52,177, ff.4–5.
26 Louisa Adam to J. Loch, 25 February 1800. *Brougham and Early Friends*, i, 107; Brougham to Stuart, 31 March 1800. *Ibid.*, i, 225.
27 Campbell, *Lyndhurst and Brougham*, 233.
28 Cockburn, *Memorials*, 111.
29 Cockburn, *Life of Jeffrey*, 77.
30 *Ibid.*, 85–6.
31 Brougham to Loch, 6 April 1801. *Brougham and Early Friends*, i, 238.
32 Clephane to Loch, 11 April 1801. *Ibid.*, i, 245–6.
33 Brougham to Loch, 5 June 1801. *Ibid.*, 276.
34 H. Brougham, 'Voltaire', *Collected Works*, ii, 14. The tragedy was *Oedipe*.
35 Brougham to Loch, 6 April 1802. *Brougham and Early Friends*, i, 319–21.
36 Brougham to Loch, 7 November 1802. *Ibid.*, i, 351.
37 Brougham to Loch, 16 December 1802. *Ibid.*, ii, 9–11.
38 Brougham to Loch, 19 June 1803. *Ibid.*, ii, 67–9.
39 Brougham to Loch, 12 December 1803. *Ibid.*, ii, 101–2.
40 Brougham to Loch, 19 June 1803. *Ibid.*, ii, 67–9.
41 N. C. Smith (ed.), *The Letters of Sydney Smith*, Oxford, 1953, i, 91.
42 Smith to Caroline Fox, [April 1803]. *Ibid.*, i, 77.
43 R. and S. Wilberforce, *The Life of William Wilberforce*, London, 1838, ii, 194.
44 Horner to Loch, 7 November 1802. *Horner Memoirs*, i, 204–5.
45 Brougham to Loch, 6 April 1802. *Brougham and Early Friends*, i, 319–21.
46 Colonial Policy, ii, 468–9.
47 *Ibid.*, ii, 443–4.
48 Lady Holland, *A Memoir of the Rev. Sydney Smith*, London, 1879 edn, 12.
49 J. Clive, *Scotch Reviewers. The Edinburgh Review, 1802–1815*, London, 1957, 192.
50 *Horner Memoirs*, i, 201.
51 Brougham to Loch, 28 January 1803. *Brougham and Early Friends*, ii, 32.
52 *Horner Memoirs*, i, 278.
53 Brougham to Horner, 27 June 1803. Horner MSS. II, 14.
54 Clive, *Scotch Reviewers*, 62.
55 Jeffrey to Loch, 21 June 1804. *Brougham and Early Friends*, ii, 129–30.
56 Jeffrey to Horner, 20 July 1810. Cockburn, *Life of Jeffrey*, ii, 129.
57 Brougham to Grey, 13 October 1811. Brougham, *Life and Times*, i, 527–31.
58 H. Martineau, *Autobiography*, London, 1877 (3rd edn), i, 322.
59 *Horner Memoirs*, i, 205.
60 Romilly to Dumont, 31 May 1803. S. Romilly, *Memoirs of the Life of Sir Samuel Romilly Written by Himself; with a Selection from his Correspondence*, London, 1840, ii, 104–5.
61 *Letters of Smith*, i, 91.

62 Cockburn, *Life of Jeffrey*, ii, 83.
63 *Romilly Memoirs*, ii, 23.
64 *Letters of Smith*, i, 82.
65 H. Cockburn, *Journal of Henry Cockburn, Being a Continuation of the Memorials of his Time. 1831–54*, Edinburgh, 1874, ii, 88.
66 *Horner Memoirs*, i, 41.
67 K. Miller, *Cockburn's Millennium*, London, 1975, 46–7.
68 *Brougham and Early Friends*, i, 343–6.
69 Brougham to Loch, 28 January 1803. *Ibid.*, ii, 31–5.
70 Brougham to Loch, 25 October 1803. *Ibid.*, ii, 83–4.
71 Cockburn, *Life of Jeffrey*, i, 142.
72 *Ibid.*

CHAPTER TWO

1 H. A. Cockburn (ed.), *Some Letters of Lord Cockburn with Pages Omitted from the Memorials of his Time*, Edinburgh, 1932, 83.
2 Campbell, *Lyndhurst and Brougham*, 250–1.
3 Brougham to Stuart, 31 July 1804. *Brougham and Early Friends*, ii, 141–5.
4 Ward to 'Ivy', February 1810. S. H. Romilly (ed.), *Letters to 'Ivy' from the First Earl of Dudley*, London, 1905, 92.
5 *Horner Memoirs*, i, 258–9.
6 Viscountess Knutsford, *Life and Letters of Zachary Macaulay*, London, 1900, 21.
7 Horner to Jeffrey, 29 March 1804. Horner MSS. II, 47.
8 Brougham to Leigh Hunt, 1812. Hunt MSS. Add.Mss. 38,108, ff.124–5.
9 Knutsford, *Macaulay*, 482, quoting the *Christian Observer* from 1839.
10 R. and S. Wilberforce, *Life of Wilberforce*, iii, 187.
11 Brougham to Allen, [1807]. Brougham/Allen MSS. Add.Mss. 52,177, ff.86–7.
12 Wilberforce to Lord Harrowby, 29 September 1804. R. and S. Wilberforce (ed.), *The Correspondence of William Wilberforce*, London, 1840, i, 328–31.
13 *Ibid.*
14 Brougham, *Life and Times*, i, 294–5.
15 Wilberforce to Brougham, 23 September 1812. *Ibid.*, ii, 49.
16 Brougham to J. Murray, 2 April 1805. *Ibid.*, i, 313–17.
17 Brougham to Loch, 30 May 1798. *Brougham and Early Friends*, i, 33–6.
18 Currie to Creevey, 2 October 1804. *Creevey Papers*, i, 30.
19 Horner to Murray, 8 June 1804. Horner MSS.
20 R. Furneaux, *William Wilberforce*, London, 1974, 227.
21 *Correspondence of Wilberforce*, ii, 51–3.
22 A. Aspinall, *Lord Brougham and the Whig Party*, Manchester, 1927, 13
23 Croker to Brougham, 14 March 1839. *Croker Papers*, ii, 350–2.
24 Jeffrey to his brother, 2 March 1800. Cockburn, *Life of Jeffrey*, i, 105.
25 *Letters of Smith*, i, 102.
26 J. Morley, *Studies in Literature*, London, 1904, 291.

27 L. Strachey and R. Fulford (ed.), *The Greville Memoirs, 1814–1860*, London, 1938, ii, 150–2. Diary entry, 7 June 1831.

28 Macaulay to Napier, 17 December 1830. *Napier Correspondence*, 98–9.

29 'Mr Horne Took', *Historical Sketches of Statesmen Who Flourished in the Time of George III*, London, 1839 and 1843, ii, 107.

30 *Memoir of Althorp*, 137n.

31 *Ibid.*

32 P. Quennell (ed.), *The Journal of Thomas Moore, 1818–1841*, London, 1964, 14. Journal entry, 27 November 1818, quoting Samuel Rogers.

33 *Letters of Smith*, i, 107–8.

34 *Correspondence of Wilberforce*, ii, 77–80.

35 Brougham to Allen, undated. Brougham/Allen MSS. Add.Mss. 52,177, ff.82–3.

36 Brougham to Lord Holland. Holland House MSS. Add.Mss. 51,561, ff.21–3.

37 Brougham, *Life and Times*, i, 377n.

38 *Ibid.*, i, 367.

39 Horner to Murray, 2 June 1806. Horner MSS.

40 Brougham to Lord Rosslyn, 12 December 1806. Brougham, *Life and Times*, i, 376–7.

41 Horner to Murray, 27 October 1806. *Horner Memoirs*, i, 378–9.

42 Special pleading long ago disappeared from the law. The best statement of what it entailed was given by Lord Campbell in a letter to his brother: 'You desire me to give you some notion of *special pleading*. It is the business of the special pleader to draw all the written proceedings in a suit at law. First, the declaration, which contains a statement of the cause of action, or the injury of which the plaintiff complains: that the defendant has seduced his wife; has trespassed upon his land; has given him a beating; has sold him an unsound horse, etc. Next comes the plea, setting forth the defendant's answer, who says that he is not guilty, or that the land is his own, or that the plaintiff made the first assault, or that he did not warrant the horse as sound etc. The *replication*, the *rejoinder*, etc., contain what each party has to allege, till at last they take issue upon some point of fact and the cause is submitted to a jury. If it is thought that what is stated in the *declaration*, though true, would not be sufficient in law to sustain an action, or in the *plea* to establish a defence, then there is a demurrer, and the cause is decided by the judges. There is the most scrupulous nicety required in these proceedings. For instance, there are different kinds of actions, as assumpsit, detinue, trespass, case, etc. The difficulty is to know which of these to bring, for it seldom happens that more than one of them will lie. There is still more difficulty in the defence, to know what is a good justification and how it ought to be pleaded, to be sure that you always suit the nature of the defence to the nature of the action, and to take advantage of any defect on the opposite side. Special pleaders in general are not at the bar. One or two who remain pleaders permanently are considered as something between attorneys and barristers, but the common way is for a young man to plead a few years *under the bar*, as they call it, before being called. It is easier to get this kind of business than

briefs in the court, and you thus gradually form and extend your connections. This is a very bad plan for the profession; in the first place, the special pleaders take much lower fees than if they were at the bar, and thus carry away a great deal of business; and in the next place, by continuing in this low illiberal drudgery so long, their minds are contracted and they are mere quibblers all their lives after.' Sir W. Holdsworth, *A History of English Law*, London, 1952 edn, xiii, 451.

43 Brougham, *Life and Times*, i, 400.
44 J. B. Atlay, *The Victorian Chancellors*, London, 1906, i, 184.
45 Lord Holland, *Memoirs of the Whig Party*, London, 1852–4, ii, 228–9.
46 Brougham to Allen, [3 June 1807]. Brougham/Allen MSS. Add.Mss. 52,178, ff.3–4.
47 Brougham to Allen, [6 June 1807]. *Ibid.*, ff.7–8.
48 Grey to Brougham, 16 June 1807. Grey MSS.
49 *Brougham and Early Friends*, ii, 347.
50 Brougham to Allen, [27 May 1807]. Brougham/Allen MSS. Add.Mss. 52,177, ff.30–1.
51 Brougham to Allen, [January 1807]. *Ibid.*, ff.88–91.
52 Brougham, *Life and Times*, i, 382–5.
53 *Ibid.*, i, 399.
54 *Ibid.*
55 Brougham to Grey, 31 May 1808. *Ibid.*, i, 400–2.
56 Brougham to Grey, 2 July 1808. *Ibid.*, i, 404–6.
57 Brougham to Allen, [30 June 1808]. Brougham/Allen MSS. Add.Mss. 52,178, ff.71–2.
58 Grey to Brougham, 29 September 1808. Grey MSS.
59 'Spain and the War', *Edinburgh Review*, October 1808, reprinted in H. Brougham, *Contributions to the Edinburgh Review*, London, 1856, ii, 214–16.
60 C. W. New, *The Life of Henry Brougham to 1830*, Oxford, 1961, 47.
61 Smith to Lady Holland, 10 January 1809. *Letters of Smith*, i, 152; Jeffrey to Horner, 6 December 1808. *Horner Memoirs*, i, 437–8.
62 Horner to Murray, 9 December 1808. Horner MSS.
63 Brougham to Napier, 27 October 1839. *Napier Correspondence*, 308–9.
64 Horner to Murray, 9 December 1808. Horner MSS.
65 Brougham to Allen, [6 September 1808]. Brougham/Allen MSS. Add.Mss. 52,178, ff.79–82.
66 Croker to J. Lockhart, 17 August 1834. *Croker Papers*, ii, 229–30.
67 'The First Edinburgh Reviewers', *Works*, i, 7.
68 7 October 1831, *Hansard*, 3rd Series, viii, 268.
69 Brougham to Allen, [spring, 1807]. Brougham/Allen MSS. Add.Mss. 52,178, ff.35–6.
70 Brougham to Allen, [January 1808]. *Ibid.*, ff.61–2.
71 Brougham to Dr Shepherd, 19 September 1814. Brougham, *Life and Times*, ii, 108.
72 Smith to Jeffrey, 26 December 1809, and to Lady Holland, 20 June 1810. *Letters of Smith*, i, 178, 189.
73 Horner to Jeffrey, 16 July 1810. *Horner Memoirs*, ii, 51–3; Smith to Lady Holland, December 1808. *Letters of Smith*, i, 151.

74 Brougham to Allen, [January 1808]. Brougham/Allen MSS. Add.Mss. 52,178, ff.65–6.
75 Jeffrey to Horner, 21 December 1809. *Horner Memoirs*, ii, 12–3.
76 Brougham, *Life and Times*, i, 503.
77 Grey to Brougham, 22 November 1809. *Ibid.*, i, 476–7.
78 Grey to Brougham, 16 December 1815. Grey MSS.
79 Croker to Lockhart, 17 August 1834. *Croker Papers*, ii, 230.

CHAPTER THREE

1 Jeffrey to Brougham, 25 July 1808. Brougham MSS.
2 Baring to C. Wood, 15 February 1855. Earl of Northbrook (ed.), *Journals and Correspondence of Francis Thornhill Baring, Lord Northbrook*, London, 1902, ii, 55–7.
3 'Lord Brougham', in N. St John-Stevas (ed.), *Bagehot's Historical Essays*, New York, 1965 (Doubleday edn), 124.
4 Elliot to J. Loch, 15 May 1808. *Brougham and Early Friends*, ii, 302.
5 J. Ward to 'Ivy', [October 1809]. *Letters to 'Ivy'*, 81.
6 Ward to 'Ivy', [1808]. *Ibid.*, 54.
7 Brougham to Holland, 5 October 1808. Holland House MSS. Add.Mss. 51,561, ff.61–5.
8 Brougham to Holland, 28 October 1808. *Ibid.*, Add.Mss. 51,561, ff.66–7.
9 S. Keppel, *The Sovereign Lady. A Life of Elizabeth Vassall, Third Lady Holland*, London, 1947, 143.
10 Brougham to Grey, 5 January 1814. Brougham, *Life and Times*, ii, 99–102.
11 Smith to J. Murray, 7 January 1810. *Letters of Smith*, i, 199.
12 Lord Holland, *Further Memoirs of the Whig Party, 1807–21*, London, 1905, 45n.
13 Smith to J. Murray, 7 January 1810. *Letters of Smith*, i, 199.
14 Lauderdale to Grey, 16 November 1807. Grey MSS.
15 Lauderdale to Grey, 20 November 1809. *Ibid.*
16 *Romilly Memoirs*, ii, 127–8.
17 Brougham to Grey, 31 May 1808. Brougham, *Life and Times*, i, 400–2.
18 Rosslyn to Brougham, 7 January 1810. *Ibid.*, i, 493–7.
19 Brougham to Allen, [January 1810]. Brougham/Allen MSS. Add.Mss. 52,178, ff.105–6.
20 'Mr Pitt', *Statesmen of George III*, i, 196.
21 Ward to 'Ivy', [13 May 1812]. *Letters to 'Ivy'*, 157.
22 P. Medd, *Romilly*, London, 1968, 93.
23 Smith to L. Horner, 26 August 1812, *Horner Memoirs*, ii, 436.
24 W. Thomas, *The Philosophical Radicals, Nine Studies in Theory and Practice, 1817–1841*, Oxford, 1979, 49–50.
25 W. H. Grimmer, *Anecdote of the Bench and Bar*, London, 1858, 137.
26 Countess of Airlie, *In Whig Society, 1775–1818*, London, 1921, 56–7.
27 W. Wordsworth, 'A Poet's Epitaph'.
28 'John Allen', *Statesmen in the Time of George III*, iii, 347–8.
29 Brougham to Allen [January 1810]. Brougham/Allen MSS. Add.Mss. 52,178, ff.105–6.

30 Quoted in A. Sampson, *The New Anatomy of Britain*, London, 1971, 402.
31 Horner to Mrs Brougham, 6 March 1810. Brougham, *Life and Times*, i, 500.
32 Jeffrey to Brougham, 19 March 1810. *Ibid.*, i, 504.
33 *Hansard*, 1st Series, xvii, 658–75.
34 Campbell, *Lyndhurst and Brougham*, 264,262.
35 Miller, *Cockburn's Millennium*, 28.
36 Aspinall, *Brougham and the Whig Party*, 23.
37 Brougham to Creevey, 1810. *Creevey Papers*, i, 119–20.
38 *Ibid.*
39 Ward to 'Ivy', May 1810. *Letters to 'Ivy'*, 106–7.
40 *Free Thoughts on Public Affairs, or Advice to a Patriot*, London, 1806, in *Collected Works*, iii, 14.
41 Brougham to Creevey, 1810. *Creevey Papers*, i, 119–20.
42 Brougham to Allen, 1 January 1810. Brougham/Allen MSS. Add.Mss. 52,178, ff.101–2.
43 Brougham to Holland, 3 January 1810. Holland House MSS. Add.Mss. 51,561, ff.78–80.
44 Brougham to Allen, 26 December 1809. Brougham/Allen MSS. Add.Mss. 52,178, ff.97–100.
45 'Parliamentary Reform', *Edinburgh Review*, February 1811, 353.
46 *Ibid.*, 361–2.
47 Brougham to Grey, [15 December 1809]. Brougham, *Life and Times*, i, 490.
48 Brougham to Grey, 16 November 1809. *Ibid.*, i, 475.
49 Brougham to Grenville, 18 April 1810. Brougham/Grenville MSS. Add.Mss. 58,965, ff.2–9.
50 Brougham to Grey, 2 August 1812. Brougham, *Life and Times*, ii, 26.
51 Brougham to Holland, 8 October [1811]. Holland House MSS. Add.Mss. 51,561, ff. 97–8.
52 Brougham to Holland, 6 April [1811]. *Ibid.*, Add.Mss. 51,561, ff.91–2.
53 Brougham to Allen, 21 June 1811. Brougham/Allen MSS. Add.Mss. 52,178, ff.138–9.
54 Brougham to Grey, 2 August 1812. Brougham, *Life and Times*, ii, 25.
55 Horner to Murray, 22 January 1812. *Horner Memoirs*, ii, 108–9.
56 Brougham to Allen, [28 October 1812]. Brougham/Allen MSS. Add.Mss. 52,178, ff.164–71.
57 Horner to Murray, 22 January 1812. *Horner Memoirs*, ii, 108–9.
58 *Romilly Memoirs*, ii, 279.
59 Ward to 'Ivy', 6 July 1812. *Letters to 'Ivy'*, 167.
60 Brougham, *Life and Times*, ii, 1–2.
61 Brougham to Hunt, undated. Hunt MSS. Add.Mss. 38,108, ff.40–1.
62 Romilly diary, 3 April 1806. *Romilly Memoirs*, ii, 140–1.
63 *Collected Speeches*, i, 14–47.
64 Rosslyn to Grey, 22 February 1811. Grey MSS.
65 Murray to Brougham, 26 February 1811. Brougham, *Life and Times*, i, 520–1.

66 Brougham to Holland, [27 February 1811]. Holland House MSS. Add.Mss. 51,561, ff.87–8.
67 Brougham to Allen, [24 February 1811]. Brougham/Allen MSS. Add.Mss. 52,178, ff.134–5.
68 Diary, 8 August 1812. E. Hughes (ed.), *The Diaries and Correspondence of James Losh, 1811–1833*, London, 1962–63, i, 15.
69 *Horner Memoirs*, ii, 136.
70 A. Polson, *Law and Lawyers, or, Sketches and Illustrations of Legal History and Biography*, London, 1840, i, 22.
71 Brougham to Creevey, [May 1812]. *Creevey Papers*, ii, 154.
72 *Edinburgh Review*, July 1812, 35.
73 Brougham to Allen, 25 September 1812. Brougham/Allen MSS. Add.Mss. 52,178, ff.162–3.
74 Brougham to Hunt, [August 1812]. Hunt MSS. Add.Mss. 38,108, ff.53–4.
75 Brougham to Grey, 8 August 1812. Brougham, *Life and Times*, ii, 39–40.
76 Brougham to Peel, August [1843]. Peel MSS. Add. Mss. 40,532, f.172.
77 Brougham to Grey, 28 September 1812. Brougham, *Life and Times*, ii, 55–7.
78 *Collected Speeches*, i, 485–6.
79 Creevey to his wife, 17 October 1812. *Creevey Papers*, i, 172.
80 Brougham to Hunt, [October 1812]. Hunt MSS. Add.Mss. 38,108, ff.59–60.
81 Horner to Murray, 21 October 1812. *Horner Memoirs*, ii, 132–4.
82 Brougham to Hunt, [October 1812]. Hunt MSS. Add.Mss. 38,108, ff.59–60.

CHAPTER FOUR

1 Brougham to J. Allen, [28 October 1812]. Brougham/Allen MSS. Add.Mss. 52,178, ff.164–71.
2 Brougham to Grey, 10 September 1812. Brougham, *Life and Times*, ii, 50.
3 Ward to 'Ivy', [20 October 1812]. *Letters to 'Ivy'*, 173.
4 Brougham to Allen, [28 October 1812]. Brougham/Allen MSS. Add.Mss. 52,178, ff.164–71.
5 Brougham to Creevey, 1812. *Creevey Papers*, i, 174.
6 Lamb to Grey, 3 November 1812; Grey to Lamb, 12 November 1812. Grey MSS.
7 Brougham to Grey, 16 December 1812. Brougham, *Life and Times*, ii, 74–5.
8 See Aspinall, *Brougham and the Whig Party*, 31 and Clive, *Scotch Reviewers*, 81–2.
9 Introduction to speech on parliamentary reform, *Collected Speeches*, ii, 548–9.
10 Brougham to Allen, [3 November 1812]. Brougham/Allen MSS. Add.Mss. 52,178, f.172.
11 Brougham to Grey, 14 November 1814. Brougham, *Life and Times*, ii,

268–9; T. Sadler (ed.), *Diary, Reminiscences, and Correspondence of Henry Crabb Robinson*, 3rd edn, London, 1982, i, 240.

12 *Letters to 'Ivy'*, 197–8.
13 Brougham to Creevey, 24 November 1814. *Creevey Papers*, i, 206–8. The 'Grenville winter' is a reference to the Talents' term of office in 1806–07.
14 Brougham, *Life and Times*, ii, 249.
15 G. Wallas, *The Life of Francis Place, 1771–1854*, London (4th edn), 1925, 96.
16 New, *Brougham*, 152.
17 See Thomas, *Philosophic Radicals*, 21–44.
18 Brougham to L. Hunt, [30 September 1812]. Hunt MSS. Add.Mss. 38,108, ff.57–8.
19 A. Aspinall, 'The Westminster Election of 1814', *English Historical Review*, October 1925, 566.
20 Brougham to Creevey, 29 June 1814. *Creevey Papers*, i, 195.
21 New, *Brougham*, 138.
22 Cockburn, *Memorials*, 271.
23 *Romilly Memoirs*, ii, 139–40.
24 Brougham to Dr Shepherd, 19 September 1814. Brougham *Life and Times*, ii, 108–9.
25 Brougham to Creevey, 24 November 1814. *Creevey Papers*, i, 206–8.
26 Brougham to Grey, 7 November 1814. Brougham, *Life and Times*, ii, 131–3.
27 Brougham to Creevey, 14 July 1815. *Creevey Papers*, i, 243–4.
28 Brougham, *Life and Times*, ii, 290–1.
29 Littleton diary, 13 December 1831. A. Aspinall (ed.), *Three Early Nineteenth Century Diaries*, London, 1952, 164.
30 'Johnson', *Collected Works*, ii, 304–77.
31 Brougham to Forsyth, 13 September 1859. W. Forsyth (ed.), *Letters from Lord Brougham to William Forsyth*, London, 1872, 49–50.
32 Brougham to Peel, [1844]. Peel MSS. Add.Mss. 40,482, ff.38–9.
33 Brougham to Creevey, 14 July 1815. *Creevey Papers*, i, 243–4.

CHAPTER FIVE

1 Brougham to Grey, 27 January 1815. Brougham, *Life and Times*, ii, 280–1.
2 Creevey to Dr Currie, 13 April 1805. *Creevey Papers*, i, 34.
3 Brougham to Hunt, undated. Hunt MSS. Add.Mss. 38,108, ff.136–7.
4 Brougham to Leigh Hunt, undated. *Ibid.*, ff.147–8.
5 Brougham to Grey, 5 December 1815. Brougham, *Life and Times*, ii, 297–9.
6 Grey to Brougham, 16 December 1815. Grey MSS.
7 Brougham to Creevey, 14 January 1816. *Creevey Papers*, i, 247–9.
8 Lady Holland to Grey, 21 December [1816]. Grey MSS.
9 Brougham to Creevey, 14 January 1816. *Creevey Papers*, i, 247–9.
10 Bennet to Creevey, 21 July 1816. *Ibid.*, i, 257–8.
11 *Collected Speeches*, i, 604. Introduction to the speech.
12 *Ibid.*, i, 621–2.

13 Brougham to Hunt, [March 1816]. Hunt MSS. Add.Mss. 38,108, ff.157–8.
14 Brougham to Grey, 2 August 1812. Brougham, *Life and Times*, ii, 28.
15 Cockburn, *Memorials*, 289.
16 Brougham, *Life and Times*, ii, 312.
17 Place memorandum, March 1816. Place MSS. Add.Mss. 27,850, f.288.
18 A. Mitchell, *The Whigs in Opposition, 1815–1830*, Oxford, 1967, 97n.
19 Whishaw to Thomas Smith, 27 March 1816. Lady Seymour (ed.), *The 'Pope' of Holland House. Selections from the Correspondence of John Whishaw and his Friends, 1813–1840*, London, 1906, 149.
20 Romilly diary, 20 March 1816. *Romilly Memoirs*, ii, 236–7.
21 Brougham to Hunt, [21 March 1816]. Hunt MSS. Add.Mss. 38,108, ff.161–9.
22 Aspinall, *Brougham and the Whig Party*, 63.
23 *Ibid.*, 65.
24 Bennet to Creevey, 21 July 1816. *Creevey Papers*, i, 257–8.
25 H. K. Olphin, *George Tierney*, London, 1934, 173.
26 Brougham to Creevey, undated. *Creevey Papers*, i, 252–3.
27 Smith to Lady Grey, [January] 1819. *Letters of Smith*, i, 314–15.
28 Western to Creevey, 17 February 1816. *Creevey Papers*, i, 251–2.
29 Western to Creevey, [20 March 1816]. *Ibid.*, i, 249–50.
30 Wallas, *Life of Place*, 117.
31 Brougham to Hunt [29 February 1816]. Hunt MSS. Add.Mss. 38,108, ff.157–8.
32 Aspinall, *Brougham and the Whig Party*, 69.
33 *Ibid.*, 74.
34 Brougham to Grey, October 1817. Brougham, *Life and Times*, ii, 331.
35 *Collected Speeches*, i, 566–8.
36 *Correspondence of Whishaw*, 174.
37 Bennet to Creevey, 20 July 1817. *Creevey Papers*, i, 264–5.
38 For these negotiations see Mitchell, *Whigs in Opposition*, 32–4.
39 Creevey to Bennet, 30 December 1818. *Creevey Papers*, i, 290–1.
40 S. J. Reid, *Life and Letters of the First Earl of Durham, 1792–1840*, London, 1906, i, 106.
41 C. W. New, *Lord Durham*, Oxford, 1929, 21–2.
42 Brougham to Lambton, undated. Durham MSS.

CHAPTER SIX

1 Brougham to Lansdowne, [3 August 1817]. Aspinall, *Brougham and the Whig Party*, 82–3.
2 Wallis, *Life of Place*, 109.
3 *Ibid.*, 96.
4 Brougham to Lambton, [July 1818]. Durham MSS.
5 *Collected Speeches*, iii, 17–67.
6 Brougham to Creevey, 21 August [1822]. *Creevey Papers*, ii, 45–6.
7 S. Bamford, *Passages in the Life of a Radical*, London, 1840–44, ii, 15.

8 D. Owen, *English Philanthropy, 1660–1960*, Cambridge, Massachusetts, 1964, 182–208.

9 New, *Brougham*, 224.

10 Campbell, *Lyndhurst and Brougham*, 361.

11 Smith to Whishaw, 13 April 1818. *Letters of Smith*, i, 289.

12 Brougham to Creevey, undated. *Creevey Papers*, i, 254. Maxwell wrongly gave the date of 1816 to the letter.

13 New, *Brougham*, 184.

14 For a discussion of this matter see Thomas, *Philosophical Radicals*, 57–94.

15 Mackintosh, *Life of Mackintosh*, ii, 353.

16 Darlington to Brougham, 15 January 1818. Brougham MSS.

17 Brougham to Creevey, undated. *Creevey Papers*, i, 120, where the letter is wrongly placed with another.

18 Tierney to Grey, [3 February 1818]. Grey MSS.

19 Brougham to Holland, [July 1818]. Holland House MSS. Add.Mss. 51,561, ff.127–8.

20 Brougham to Lambton, [21 June 1818]. Durham MSS.

21 New, *Durham*, 19–20.

22 Brougham to Creevey, undated. *Creevey Papers*, i, 254.

23 Rosslyn to Grey, 6 March 1818. Grey MSS.

24 Diary, 24 March 1820. *Diaries of Losh*, i, 110.

25 Denis le Marchant to Francis Baring, 7 July 1826. *Journals of Baring*, i, 46–7.

26 Brougham to Grey, 7 November 1818. Brougham, *Life and Times*, ii, 338–9.

27 Brougham to Creevey, 19 August 1822. *Creevey Papers*, ii, 44.

28 Martineau, *Autobiography*, i, 310–12.

29 J. Grant, *The Bench and the Bar*, London, 1837, i, 138, 140.

30 Smith to Lady Holland, 20 August 1819. *Letters of Smith*, i, 335–6.

31 Smith to Lady Grey, [4 Jamuary 1819]. *Ibid.*, i, 309.

32 Whishaw to Thomas Smith, 17 July 1819. *Correspondence of Whishaw*, 205.

33 Smith to Jeffrey, 30 July 1819. *Letters of Smith*, i, 331.

34 Smith to Lady Grey, 15 August 1819. *Ibid.*, i, 334.

35 Whishaw to Thomas Smith, 17 July 1819. *Correspondence of Whishaw*, 205.

36 Creevey to Miss Ord, 9 and 10 May 1823. *Creevey Papers*, ii, 71–2.

37 Creevey to Miss Ord, 25 June 1825. *Ibid.*, ii, 89.

38 Brougham to Holland, [25 June 1818]. Holland House MSS. Add.Mss. 51,561, ff.130–5.

39 Brougham to Holland, [19 September 1819]. *Ibid.*, Add.Mss. 51,561, ff.162–4.

40 C. J. Bartlett, *Castlereagh*, London, 1966, 187.

41 The Office of 'The Times', *The History of The Times*, London, 1935, i, 240.

42 Brougham to Grey, 25 August 1819. Grey MSS.

43 *Diaries of Losh*, ii, 160.

44 Brougham to Allen, 23 October 1819 (postmark). Brougham/Allen MSS. Add.Mss. 52,178, ff.205–6.

CHAPTER SEVEN

1 Princess Caroline to the Prince of Wales, 14 January, 1813. Brougham, *Life and Times*, ii, 157–63.
2 *Ibid.*, ii, 169.
3 Brougham to Grey, 24 July 1814. *Ibid.*, ii, 241–2.
4 *Ibid.*, ii, 260–1.
5 *Ibid.*, ii, 182.
6 *Ibid.*, ii, 157–63.
7 Mackintosh, *Life of Mackintosh*, ii, 263–4.
8 Creevey to his wife, 21 June 1814. *Creevey Papers*, i, 197–8.
9 Aspinall, *Brougham and the Whig Party*, 102.
10 Brougham, *Life and Times*, ii, 354.
11 A. G. Stapleton, *Canning and his Times*, London, 1859, 266.
12 *Croker Papers*, i, 172.
13 Aspinall, *Brougham and the Whig Party*, 108.
14 Denman's memoir, 'The Year 1820'. Sir J. Arnould, *Memoir of Thomas, First Lord Denman*, London, 1873, i, 138–9.
15 Brougham to Queen Caroline, 4 June 1820. Brougham, *Life and Times*, ii, 362–3.
16 Brougham to Hutchinson, 4 June 1820. *Ibid.*, ii, 364–5.
17 Creevey to Miss Ord, 11 August 1821. *Creevey Papers*, ii, 23–4.
18 Canning to Huskisson, 2 October 1820. Stapleton, *Canning*, 300.
19 E. Lytton Bulwer, *England and the English*, 1970 edn, Chicago, 42.
20 'George IV', *Statesmen of George III*, 17.
21 *Memoir of Denman*, i, 139.
22 Creevey to Miss Ord, 3 September 1821. *Creevey Papers*, ii, 28–9.
23 Brougham, *Life and Times*, ii, 376–7.
24 Furneaux, *Wilberforce*, 387.
25 *Ibid.*, 387.
26 'George IV', *op. cit.*, 14–15.
27 Creevey to Miss Ord, 11 August 1821. *Creevey Papers*, ii, 23–4.
28 Brougham, *Life and Times*, ii, 382.
29 *Memoir of Denman*, i, 161.
30 *Times*, 15 August 1820.
31 *Greville Memoirs*, i, 105.
32 *Memoir of Denman*, i, 174.
33 *Hansard*, 2nd Series, iii, 112–210.
34 Campbell, *Lyndhurst and Brougham*, 312.
35 Brougham, *Life and Times*, ii, 400.
36 Hazlitt, *Commonplaces*, London, 1823, No. LXXIII.
37 *Hansard*, 2nd Series, iii, 892.
38 2 November 1820. *Ibid.*, 1457–8.

CHAPTER EIGHT

1 B. Disraeli (ed. W. Hutcheon), *Whigs and Whiggism*, London, 1913, 414. Disraeli did not use the phrase specifically of Brougham's handling of the Queen's business, but generally of his career.

2 Campbell, *Lyndhurst and Brougham*, 324.
3 Ellice to Grey, [6 August 1825]. Grey MSS.
4 *Dictionary of National Biography*.
5 Lord David Cecil, *Lord M*, London, 1955 (Reprint Society edn), 348.
6 P. C. Scarlett, *A Memoir of the Right Honourable James, First Lord Abinger*, London, 1877, 193.
7 Smith to Lady Grey, 27 March 1821. *Letters of Smith*, i, 377.
8 Sir W. F. Pollock, *Personal Remembrances*, London, 1887, i, 20.
9 *Memoir of Abinger*, 78–9.
10 T. Macaulay to Z. Macaulay, 1 September 1827. G. O. Trevelyan, *The Life and Letters of Lord Macaulay*, Oxford, 1978 (World's Classics edn), i, 134–5.
11 J. Grant, *The Bench and the Bar*, London, 1837, i, 110.
12 *Ibid.*, i, 110–18.
13 Campbell, *Lyndhurst and Brougham*, 331–2.
14 Earl Russell, *Recollections and Suggestions, 1813–1873*, London, 1875, 137; Campbell, *Lyndhurst and Brougham*, 330. The speech was published as the pamphlet, *The Speech of Henry Brougham, Esq., in the Case of the King v. Williams*, London, 1822.
15 Campbell, *Lyndhurst and Brougham*, 331.
16 Brougham, *Life and Times*, ii, 430.
17 3 February 1825, *Hansard*, 2nd Series, xii, 63–5.
18 Campbell, *Lyndhurst and Brougham*, 346.
19 H. Perkin, *The Origins of Modern English Society, 1780–1880*, London, 1969, 50.
20 Lord North's in 1782, Shelburne's in 1783, Addington's in 1804, and the Duke of Wellington's in 1830.
21 Grenville to the Marquis of Buckingham, 9 May 1820. Duke of Buckingham and Chandos, *Memoirs of the Court of George IV, 1820–1830*, London, 1850, i, 21.
22 Mrs Arbuthnot, Journal, 13 May 1820. F. Bamford and the Duke of Wellington (ed.), *The Journal of Mrs Arbuthnot, 1820–1832*, London, 1950, i, 18–19.
23 Brougham, *Life and Times*, ii, 402.
24 Creevey to Miss Ord, 15 January 1821. *Creevey Papers*, ii, 2.
25 Brougham to Lambton [February 1818]. Durham MSS.
26 *Journal of Mrs Arbuthnot*, 7 February 1822, i, 140.
27 Wynn to the Marquis of Buckingham, 31 January 1824. Buckingham, *Court of George IV*, 39–42.
28 Brougham to Grey, 26 January 1824. Brougham, *Life and Times*, ii, 464–5.
29 Brougham to Allen [2 September 1822]. Brougham/Allen MSS. Add.Mss. 52,719, ff.23–7.
30 Grey to Brougham, 5 September 1822. Grey MSS.
31 *Ibid.*
32 Mitchell, *Whigs in Opposition*, 37.
33 Cockburn, *Memorials*, 398.
34 Cockburn to T. Kennedy, 14 April 1825. H. Cockburn, *Letters Chiefly Connected with the Affairs of Scotland, 1818–1852*, London, 1874, 131–2.

35 Brougham to Z. Macaulay, 16 September 1823. Knutsford, *Macaulay*, 391.
36 Brougham to Gladstone, 2 February 1863. Gladstone MSS. Add.Mss. 44,114, ff.317–18.
37 *Collected speeches*, ii, 51–100.
38 *Ibid.*, ii, 127–8.
39 *Ibid.*, ii, 47. Introduction to speech of 1 June.
40 Trevelyan, *Macaulay*, i, 103–4.
41 Russell, *Recollections and Suggestions*, 136–7, 55–6.
42 Disraeli, *Whigs and Whiggism*, 255.
43 D. le Marchant, *Memoir of John Charles, Viscount Althorp, Third Earl Spencer*, London, 1876, 217–18.
44 Lord Colchester (ed.), *Lord Ellenborough. A Political Diary 1828–1830*, London, 1881, ii, 413–14.
45 Gladstone memorandum, 18 January 1836. Gladstone MSS. Add.Mss. 44,777, ff.23–8.
46 Trevelyan, *Macaulay*, ii, 212.
47 Russell, *Recollections and Suggestions*, 55–6.
48 Hazlitt, *Spirit of the Age*, 335.
49 Cockburn, *Memorials*, 204.
50 T. Taylor (ed.), *The Autobiography and Memoirs of Benjamin Robert Haydon*, London, 1926 edn, ii, 553.
51 Brougham to Forsyth, 17 December 1863. *Letters to Forsyth*, 107.
52 Cockburn, *Some Letters of Lord Cockburn with Pages Omitted*, 110; Cockburn, *Memorials*, 199.
53 Grenville to Brougham, 7 June 1825 (copy). Grenville/Brougham MSS. Add.Mss. 58,965, ff.77–9.
54 Trevelyan, *Macaulay*, i, 72.
55 *Collected Speeches*, ii, 543. Introduction to speech on parliamentary reform. reform.
56 Gladstone memorandum, 28 April 1838. Gladstone MSS. Add.Mss. 44,819, f.39.
57 Hazlitt, *Spirit of the Age*, 327–32.

CHAPTER NINE

1 *Journal of Mrs Arbuthnot*, 20 March 1825, i, 383.
2 29 January 1828, *Hansard*, 2nd Series, xviii, 57–8.
3 *Collected Speeches*, iii, 71–98.
4 *Ibid.*, iii, 99–152.
5 He gave details of this system in his address to the Manchester Mechanics' Institute, July 1825. *Ibid.*, iii, 153–78.
6 *Practical Observations*, 109–10.
7 C. Knight, *Passages of a Working Life During Half a Century*, London, 1864, i, 276.
8 *Ibid.*, ii, 44–7.
9 *Ibid.*, ii, 196–7.

10 *Diary of Crabb Robinson*, ii, 67.
11 Knight, *Passages*, ii, 55.
12 Holland to Brougham, 31 December 1831. Brougham, *Life and Times*, iii, 453–4.
13 Knight, *Passages*, ii, 62–3.
14 Brougham to Peel, 14 October 1842. Peel MSS. Add.Mss. 40,482, ff.6–9. The almanac continued to be published for thirty-seven years.
15 Brougham to Allen, [September 1827]. Brougham/Allen MSS. Add.Mss. 52,179, ff.49–52.
16 Knight, *Passages*, ii, 178.
17 *Penny Magazine*, 31 March 1832.
18 W. N. Molesworth, *The History of England from the Year 1830 to 1874*, London, 1875, i, 228; G. Boyce, J. Curran and P. Wright (ed.), *Newspaper History from the Seventeenth Century to the Present Day*, London, 1978, 100.
19 Brougham to Allen, [7] September 1827. Brougham/Allen MSS. Add.Mss. 52,179, ff.59–61. Dumont regularly prepared Bentham's scripts for publication.
20 Brougham to Creevey, 1830. *Creevey Papers*, ii, 206.
21 Brougham to Hunt, undated. Hunt MSS. Add.Mss. 38,109, ff.63–4.
22 Martineau, *Autobiography*, ii, 176–7.
23 *Ibid.*, i, 221.
24 *Ibid.*, i, 176, 312.
25 Campbell, *Lyndhurst and Brougham*, 338.
26 A. M. Gilbert, *The Work of Lord Brougham for Education in England*, Pennsylvania, 1922, 73.
27 *Times*, 9 February 1825.
28 New, *Brougham*, 362.
29 V. H. H. Green, *The Universities*, London, 1969, 104.
30 Brougham to Rogers, 20 August 1825. P. W. Clayton, *Rogers and his Contemporaries*, London, 1889, i, 418–19.
31 Drummond to Macaulay, 22 May 1826. Knutsford, *Macaulay*, 435–6.
32 Brougham to Lambton, 8 August 1825. Durham MSS.
33 Extracts from the letter are printed in New, *Brougham*, 380–1.
34 *Ibid.*, 382.
35 T. Carlyle, 'Signs of the Times' (1829), *Essays*, ii, 80.
36 Aspinall, *Politics and the Press*, 12.
37 *Quarterly Review*, October, 1825, 410.
38 A. P. Stanley, *Life and Correspondence of Thomas Arnold*, London, 1844, 157–8.
39 New, *Brougham*, 342.
40 H. Belloc, 'The Liberal Tradition', *Essays*, London, 1897.
41 W. Cobbett, *Rural Rides*, London, 1830, ii, 365.
42 *Maclean's Monthly Sheet of Caricatures*, 1 October 1832.
43 *Collected Works*, vii, 371–418.
44 Brougham to Peel, 26 October 1842. Peel MSS. Add.Mss. 40,482, ff.13–16.
45 Brougham to Allen, September 1827. Brougham/Allen MSS. Add.Mss. 52,179, ff.49–52.

46 Smith to Lady Grey, 15 July 1829. *Letters of Smith*, ii, 494.

47 Quoted in S. Bennett, 'Revolutions in Thought', in J. Shattock and M. Wolff (ed.), *The Victorian Periodical Press: Samplings and Soundings*, Leicester and Toronto, 1982, 228. Bennett's essay provides a detailed examination of the SDUK's commercial operations and concludes that the society played an important part in the growth of a mass reading public between 1825 and 1845.

CHAPTER TEN

1 E. Lytton Bulwer, *England and the English*, Chicago, 1970 edn, 286–7.

2 Peel to Croker, 23 March 1820. *Croker Papers*, i, 170.

3 Brougham to Allen, [25 August 1822]. Brougham/Allen MSS. Add.Mss. 52,179, ff.21–2.

4 Brougham to Allen, [6 September 1822]. *Ibid.*, ff.28–9.

5 Brougham to Lansdowne, 18 December 1822. Lansdowne MSS.

6 17 April 1823, *Hansard*, 2nd Series, viii, 1091.

7 Creevey to Miss Ord, 18 April 1823. *Creevey Papers*, ii, 67–8.

8 Lady Holland to Henry Fox, 18 April 1823. Ilchester, *Lady Holland to her Son*, 20.

9 4 February 1823, *Hansard*, 2nd Series, viii, 54. Lord John Russell described the speech as one of Brougham's 'brightest flights' (*Recollections and Suggestions*, 137) and James Losh called it 'one of his most powerful specimens of what has been called the *terrible* in eloquence' (*Diaries of Losh*, i, 177–8).

10 Diary, 4 February 1823. Earl of Ilchester (ed.), *The Journal of the Hon. Henry Edward Fox, afterwards 4th and last Lord Holland, 1818–1830*, London, 1923, 156.

11 Maria Copley to Creevey, 6 March 1823. *Creevey Papers*, ii, 64–5.

12 Russell to Thomas Moore, 23 February 1826. Rollo Russell (ed.), *Early Correspondence of Lord John Russell, 1805–40*, London, 1913, i, 245.

13 Brougham to Zachary Macaulay, 1827. Knutsford, *Macaulay*, 445–6.

14 Olphin, *Tierney*, 227–8.

15 3 February 1825, *Hansard*, 2nd Series, xii, 72.

16 Brougham, *Life and Times*, ii, 468.

17 Reid, *Durham*, i, 166.

18 Grey to Brougham, 21 December 1825. Grey MSS.

19 Brougham to Grey, 16 November 1824. Brougham, *Life and Times*, ii, 467–8.

20 Brougham to Allen [25 February 1827]. Brougham/Allen MSS. Add. Mss. 52,179, ff.40–4.

21 For Brougham's close relations with Thomas Barnes, editor of the *Times*, *see* the newspaper's official history, *The History of the Times*, i, *passim*.

22 *See* Aspinall, *Brougham and the Whig Party*, 140–2 and Mitchell, *Whigs in Opposition*, 195–6.

23 New, *Brougham*, 309.

24 *Greville Memoirs*, 23 September 1834, iii, 88.

25 New, *Brougham*, 311.
26 Macdonald to Lansdowne, 14 April 1827. A. Aspinall (ed.), *The Formation of Canning's Ministry, February to August 1827*, London, 1937, 78–80.
27 Brougham, *Life and Times*, ii, 490.
28 Hon. Mrs Hardcastle, *The Life of John, Lord Campbell*, London, 1881, i, 440.
29 Mrs Taylor to Creevey, 21 April 1827. *Creevey Papers*, ii, 113.
30 New, *Brougham*, 312.
31 *Ibid.*, 313.
32 Brougham to Creevey, 21 April 1827. *Creevey Papers*, ii, 114–15.
33 Creevey to Sefton, 31 May 1827. *Ibid.*, ii, 118–19.
34 Brougham to Creevey, 27 April 1827. *Ibid.*, ii, 115.
35 Burdett to Lansdowne, 21 April 1827. Aspinall, *Canning's Ministry*, 146–7.
36 Mitchell, *Whigs in Opposition*, 199.
37 Cockburn to Thomas Kennedy, 26 April 1827. Cockburn, *Letters Chiefly Connected with Scotland*, 153.
38 Ellice to Grey, 21 May 1827 (postmark). Grey MSS.
39 Russell to Grey, 8 September 1827. *Ibid.*
40 Bedford to Russell, 29 April 1827. S. Walpole, *The Life of Lord John Russell*, London, 1889, i, 134–5.
41 *Greville Memoirs*, 9 January 1830, i, 334–5.
42 Brougham to Grey, 12 August 1825; Grey to Brougham, 12 August 1825. Brougham, *Life and Times*, ii, 469–71.
43 Brougham to Allen, [August] 1827. Brougham/Allen MSS. Add.Mss. 52,179, ff.47–8.
44 Arbuthnot to Peel, 6 July 1827. C. S. Parker, *Sir Robert Peel from his Private Papers*, London, 1899, i, 491–2.
45 He wrote to his brother a few days after the King sent for Canning that he expected to be given it (New, *Brougham*, 315).
46 Aspinall, *Canning's Ministry*, liii.
47 Brougham, *Life and Times*, ii, 436.
48 Creevey to Sefton, 23 September 1827. *Creevey Papers*, ii, 129.
49 James, *Curiosities of Law*, 224.
50 Bexley to Herries, 1 September 1827. E. Herries, *Memoir of the Public Life of the Right Hon. John Charles Herries*, London, 1880, i, 210–11.
51 Brougham to Allen [4 September 1827]. Brougham/Allen MSS. Add.Mss. 52,179, ff.55–8.
52 Aspinall, *Brougham and the Whig Party*, 157.
53 J. A. Roebuck, *History of the Whig Ministry of 1830, to the Passing of the Reform Bill*, London, 1852, i, 460.
54 Lansdowne to Brougham, 6 September 1827. Brougham, *Life and Times*, ii, 489–90.
55 Brougham to Grey, 13 August 1827. *Ibid.*, ii, 485–6.
56 Mitchell, *Whigs in Opposition*, 207.
57 Brougham to Allen, 7 September 1827. Brougham/Allen MSS. Add.Mss. 52,179, ff.59–61.
58 Grey to Brougham, 19 August 1827. Grey MSS.

59 Rosslyn to Grey, 22 August 1827. *Ibid.*
60 Brougham to Allen, [7 November 1827]. Brougham/Allen MSS. Add.Mss. 52,179, ff.65–9.
61 Rosslyn to Grey, 7 November 1827. Grey MSS.
62 Rosslyn to Brougham, 31 October 1827. Brougham, *Life and Times*, ii, 493–5.
63 Brougham to Allen, 7 September 1827. Brougham/Allen MSS. Add.Mss. 52,179, ff.59–61.
64 Rosslyn to Brougham, 20 October 1827. Brougham, *Life and Times*, ii, 491–2.
65 Ellice to Grey, 16 December [1827]. Grey MSS.
66 Creevey to Miss Ord, 14 October 1827. *Creevey Papers*, ii, 132–3.
67 Rosslyn to Grey, 7 December 1827. Grey MSS.
68 Grey to Creevey, 13 December 1827. *Creevey Papers*, ii, 139–41.
69 Bedford to Grey, 10 December 1827. Grey MSS.
70 Aspinall, *Brougham and the Whig Party*, 285.
71 Brougham to Cleveland, [February 1828] (copy). Grey MSS.
72 Grey to Cleveland, 14 February 1828 (draft). *Ibid.*
73 Grey to Cleveland, 15 February 1828 (draft). *Ibid.*
74 Brougham to Allen, [September 1828]. Brougham/Allen MSS. Add.Mss. 52,179, f.64.
75 Brougham to Cleveland, 25 February 1828 (copy). Grey MSS.
76 Creevey to Miss Ord, 15 February 1828. *Creevey Papers*, ii, 149–50.
77 Grey to Cleveland, 3 March 1828 (copy). Grey MSS.
78 Brougham to C. Grey, 8 June 1852. *Ibid.*
79 C. Grey to Brougham, 12 June 1852 (copy). *Ibid.*

CHAPTER ELEVEN

1 Diary, 3 August [1828]. *Diaries of Losh*, ii, 68.
2 Diary, 28 March 1828. *Ibid.*, ii, 59.
3 *Greville Memoirs*, 2 January 1828, i, 192–4.
4 Brougham to T. Barnes, 2 March 1828. *History of the Times*, i, 259.
5 Althorp to Russell, 13 January 1828. *Early Correspondence of Russell*, i, 271–2.
6 Creevey to Miss Ord, 27 February 1828. *Creevey Papers*, ii, 154.
7 Aspinall, *Brougham and the Whig Party*, 166–7.
8 Roebuck, *Whig Ministry*, i, 49–50.
9 Introduction to his law reform speech, *Collected Speeches*, ii, 287–91.
10 Holdsworth, *History of English Law*, xiii, 306; Atlay, *Victorian Chancellors*, 285.
11 *Collected Speeches*, ii, 312.
12 Diary, 29 February 1828. *Croker Papers*, i, 407–8.
13 Campbell, *Lyndhurst and Brougham*, 360.
14 Brougham to Allen, August 1828. Brougham/Allen MSS. Add.Mss. 52,179, ff.79–80.
15 Losh diary, 1 June 1828. *Diaries of Losh*, ii, 63–4.

16 J. Abercromby to Devonshire, 3 February 1830. Aspinall, *Brougham and the Whig Party*, 172.
17 Althorp to Grey, 6 March 1830. *Memoir of Althorp*, 243–5.
18 T. Macaulay to H. Macaulay, 29 August 1831. Trevelyan, *Macaulay*, i, 223–4.
19 *Ibid.*
20 Hazlitt, *Spirit of the Age*, 333.
21 Mackintosh, *Life of Mackintosh*, i, 174–5.
22 30 June 1830, *Hansard*, 2nd Series, xxv, 823–5.
23 Croker diary, 2 July 1830. *Croker Papers*, ii, 68.
24 *Collected Speeches*, ii, 131–57.
25 Aspinall, *Brougham and the Whig Party*, 175.
26 The story of Brougham's adoption may be followed in detail in N. Gash, 'Brougham and the Yorkshire Election of 1830', *Proceedings of the Leeds Philosophical and Literary Society*, May 1956, 19–35.
27 Aspinall, *Brougham and the Whig Party*, 176.
28 Brougham, *Life and Times*, iii, 38.
29 *Memoir of Denman*, i, 312.
30 Brougham, *Life and Times*, iii, 40.
31 *Ibid.*, iii, 42.
32 Campbell, *Lyndhurst and Brougham*, 366–7.
33 Althorp to Brougham, 26 August 1830. Brougham, *Life and Times*, iii, 43.
34 *Edinburgh Review*, July 1830, 582.
35 Campbell, *Lyndhurst and Brougham*, 367.
36 Ord to T. Kennedy, 23 September 1830. Cockburn, *Letters Chiefly Connected with Scotland*, 236–7.
37 Gash, *op. cit.*, 31.
38 M. Brock, *The Great Reform Act*, London, 1973, 74.
39 Howick journal, 27 August 1830. Grey MSS.
40 Durham to Grey, 4 October 1830. *Ibid.*
41 Ellice to Grey, [28 October 1830]. *Ibid.*
42 Mitchell, *Whigs in Opposition*, 243.
43 [A. Somerville], *The Autobiography of a Working Man*, London, 1848, 143.
44 Campbell, *Lyndhurst and Brougham*, 372–3; 16 November 1830, *Hansard*, 3rd Series, i, 562–3.
45 Bedford to Russell, 17 November 1830. *Early Correspondence of Russell*, i, 313–14.
46 17 November 1830, *Hansard*, 3rd Series, i, 567–8.
47 Disraeli, *Whigs and Whiggism*, 255.
48 Althorp to Russell, November 1830. *Early Correspondence of Russell*, i, 312.
49 Aspinall, *Brougham and the Whig Party*, 187.
50 Brougham, *Life and Times*, iii, 80.
51 *Ibid.*, iii, 79.
52 Creevey diary, September 1818. *Creevey Papers*, i, 287.
53 *Greville Memoirs*, 20 November 1830, ii, 64–5.
54 *Ibid.*
55 Le Marchant diary, 30 November 1830. A. Aspinall, *Three Diaries*, 4.

56 Brougham, *Life and Times*, iii, 80–1.
57 Lord Broughton, *Recollections of a Long Life*, London, 1911, iv, 256.

CHAPTER TWELVE

1   Cockburn to Sir T. Dick-Lauder, 30 December 1830. *Letters of Cockburn*, 29–30.
2   Peel to H. Hobhouse, 24 November 1830. Peel MSS. Add.Mss. 40,401, ff.290–5.
3   Smith to J. Murray, 3 January 1831. *Letters of Smith*, ii, 515.
4   *Letters of Cockburn*, 29–30.
5   Brougham to J. Losh, August 1831, in E. Hughes, 'The Bishops and Reform, 1831–33: Some Fresh Correspondence', *English Historical Review*, July 1941, 463–4.
6   *Greville Memoirs*, 1 December 1830, ii, 76.
7   Bishop of Durham to J. Losh, 10 September 1831. Hughes, 'Bishops and Reform', 465–7.
8   Littleton diary, 18 July 1831. Aspinall, *Three Diaries*, 107–8.
9   Ellenborough diary, 22 November 1830. *Ibid.*, 22.
10 Atlay, *Victorian Chancellors*, 293.
11 *Correspondence of Whishaw*, 34–5.
12 26 November 1830, *Hansard*, 3rd Series, i, 673–5.
13 *Greville Memoirs*, 16 and 19 March 1834, iii, 24–5.
14 *Ibid.*, 20 August 1833, ii, 407.
15 Pollock to his son, 17 March 1869. Lord Hanworth, *Lord Chief Baron Pollock. A Memoir*, London, 1929, 176.
16 Ellenborough diary, 4 December 1830. Aspinall, *Three Diaries*, 29.
17 Campbell, *Lyndhurst and Brougham*, 386.
18 *The Examiner*, 11 September 1831.
19 Le Marchant diary, June 1833. Aspinall, *Three Diaries*, 332.
20 Creevey to Miss Ord, 21 November 1827. *Creevey Papers*, ii, 137–8; *Greville Memoirs*, 8 August 1832, ii, 316.
21 Creevey to Miss Ord, 12 March 1831. *Creevey Papers*, ii, 222; *Greville Memoirs*, 15 March 1831, ii, 130–1.
22 Ellenborough diary, 17 March 1831. Aspinall, *Three Diaries*, 68.
23 A. D. Kriegel (ed.), *The Holland House Diaries, 1831–1840*, London, 1977, 43.
24 *Times*, 12 October 1831.
25 *Greville Memoirs*, 24 February 1831, ii, 120.
26 [T. Barnes], *Parliamentary Portraits*, London, 1815, 25.
27 Creevey to Miss Ord, 27 February 1831. *Creevey Papers*, ii, 219–20.
28 Brougham to Grey, [February 1831]. Grey MSS.
29 Creevey to Miss Ord, 19 February 1831. *Creevey Papers*, ii, 219.
30 Grey to Brougham, 25 February 1831. Grey MSS.
31 Brougham, *Life and Times*, iii, 92–3.
32 Grey to Durham, 24 February 1831. Durham MSS.
33 J. R. M. Butler, *The Passing of the Great Reform Bill*, London, 1914, 184n.
34 Brougham to Losh, August 1831. Hughes, 'Bishops and Reform', 464–5.

35 Le Marchant diary, March 1831. Aspinall, *Three Diaries*, 15.
36 Brougham, *Life and Times*, iii, 115.
37 *Ibid.*, iii, 116.
38 Brougham, *Recollections*, iv, 108.
39 Brougham, *Life and Times*, iii, 117; *Greville Memoirs*, 24 April 1831, ii, 138.
40 Brougham, *Life and Times*, iii, 118.
41 Russell, *Recollections and Suggestions*, 74. According to S. J. Reid (*Life of Durham*, i, 259), some persons attributed the phrase to Edward Ellice.
42 *Greville Memoirs*, 10 October 1831, ii, 205; *Memoir of Althorp*, 352.
43 *Holland House Diaries*, 64–5.
44 Campbell, *Lyndhurst and Brougham*, 398.
45 7 October 1831, *Hansard*, 3rd Series, viii, 220–75.
46 Littleton diary, 8 October 1831. Aspinall, *Three Diaries*, 147.
47 *Holland House Diaries*, 64–5.
48 *Ibid.*
49 Hughes, 'Bishops and Reform', 464.
50 Brougham to Russell, September [1831]. *Early Correspondence of Russell*, ii, 27.
51 Hughes, 'Bishops and Reform', 465.
52 Trevelyan, *Macaulay*, i, 174.
53 *Holland House Diaries*, 106.
54 Althorp to Lord Spencer, 12 July 1831. *Memoir of Althorp*, 328–9.
55 *Holland House Diaries*, 39.
56 *Ibid.*, 83.
57 Butler, *Great Reform Bill*, 264–5.
58 *Holland House Diaries*, 75–6.
59 *Ibid.*, 83.
60 Grey to Sir H. Taylor, 19 November 1831. *Correspondence of Grey and William IV*, i, 431.
61 *Holland House Diaries*, 83–4.
62 Palmerston to Melbourne, 20 November 1831. L. C. Sanders (ed.), *Lord Melbourne's Papers*, London, 1889, 142.
63 Lamb to Melbourne, undated. *Ibid.*, 144–5.
64 *Holland House Diaries*, 110.
65 Diary, 15 March 1832. *Diaries of Losh*, ii, 135.
66 Ilchester, *Lady Holland to her Son*, 134.
67 Brougham to Napier, 4 January 1836. *Napier Correspondence*, 174–5.
68 *Holland House Diaries*, 83–4.
69 Brougham to Grey, 29 and 31 December 1831. Brougham, *Life and Times*, iii, 151–8.
70 *Ibid.*, iii, 193.
71 *Holland House Diaries*, 176.
72 Creevey to Miss Ord, 9 May 1832. *Creevey Papers*, ii, 245.
73 Le Marchant diary, May 1832. Aspinall, *Three Diaries*, 245.
74 17 May 1832, *Hansard*, 3rd Series, xii, 995.
75 Taylor to Brougham, 7 June 1832. Brougham, *Life and Times*, iii, 213–14.
76 *Ibid.*, iii, 206. Talking to Lord Stanley in 1861, Ellice said that Brougham's doubt was 'absurd': 'he had the list made out: the names

contained in it were 97: out of those only 11 would have been permanent additions to the peerage: the rest being sons of peers, or heirs of peers, or childless men of fortune'. J Vincent (ed.), *Disraeli, Derby and the Conservative Party. Journals and Memoirs of Edward Henry, Lord Stanley*, Sussex, 1978, 175.

CHAPTER THIRTEEN

1 'First Letter to C'. *Romilly Memoirs*, iii, 377–88.
2 Creevey to Miss Ord, 9 February 1831. *Creevey Papers*, ii, 218.
3 Le Marchant diary, 22 February 1831. Aspinall, *Three Diaries*, 10.
4 *Holland House Diaries*, 220–1.
5 Campbell, *Lyndhurst and Brougham*, 388.
6 T. Martin, *A Life of Lord Lyndhurst*, London, 1883, 311–12.
7 Taylor to Brougham, 14 July 1833. Brougham, *Life and Times*, iii, 295–8.
8 Detailed treatment of Brougham's work in this field may be found in P. A. Howell, *The Judicial Committee of the Privy Council, 1833–1876*, Cambridge, 1979, and D. B. Swinfen, 'Henry Brougham and the Judicial Committee of the Privy Council', *Law Quarterly Review*, July 1974, 396–411.
9 *Greville Memoirs*, 11 January 1833, ii, 342.
10 *Ibid.*, 24 January 1833, ii, 345.
11 *Ibid.*, 2 May 1833, ii, 370–1.
12 Howell, *op. cit.*, 230.
13 A. S. Turberville, *The House of Lords in the Age of Reform, 1784–1837*, London, 1958, 219.
14 Campbell, *Lyndhurst and Brougham*, 413.
15 Ellice to Grey, 22 September [1833]. Grey MSS.
16 Grey to Melbourne, [August] 1832. *Ibid.*
17 Le Marchant diary, 27 March 1834. Aspinall, *Three Diaries*, 377.
18 *Greville Memoirs*, 20 August 1833, ii, 406–7.
19 Grey to Brougham, 19 June 1833. Grey MSS.
20 *Holland House Diaries*, 243.
21 Le Marchant diary, 27 March 1834. Aspinall, *Three Diaries*, 377.
22 Brougham, *Life and Times*, iii, 357–63.
23 Littleton diary, 6 April 1833. Aspinall, *Three Diaries*, 318–19.
24 Creevey to Miss Ord, 8 May 1834. *Creevey Papers*, ii, 274–5.
25 Brougham, *Life and Times*, ii, 365–7.
26 Aspinall, *Brougham and the Whig Party*, 194.
27 T. Raikes, *A Portion of the Journal Kept by Thomas Raikes, Esq., from 1831 to 1847*, London, 1858, i, 144.
28 *Holland House Diaries*, 253–5.
29 Grey to Brougham, 1 June 1834. Grey MSS.
30 Grey to Althorp, 30 June 1834. *Memoir of Althorp*, 498–9.
31 Russell, *Recollections and Suggestions*, 127n.
32 Althorp to Grey, 7 July 1834. *Memoir of Althorp*, 505–7.
33 Littleton to Wellesley, 23 June 1834. E. Littleton, *Memoir and Correspondence Relating to Political Occurrences in June and July 1834*, London, 1872, 37.

34 Littleton to Fazakerley, 11 July 1834. *Ibid.*, 90.
35 *Greville Memoirs*, 13 and 19 July 1834, iii, 58 and 61–2.
36 Creevey to Miss Ord, 4 August 1834. *Creevey Papers*, ii, 285–6.
37 Creevey to Miss Ord, 11 August 1834. *Ibid.*, ii, 286–7.
38 *Holland House Diaries*, 257–8.
39 Hatherton, *Memoir of 1834*, 21–2.
40 Countess Grey to Creevey, 18 September 1834. *Creevey Papers*, ii, 287.
41 Creevey to Miss Ord, 24 September 1834. *Ibid.*, ii, 287–8.
42 Brougham to Althorp, 9 July 1834. *Memoir of Althorp*, 510–11.
43 Althorp to Brougham, 10 July 1834. *Ibid.*, 511–12.
44 Creevey to Miss Ord, 24 September 1834. *Creevey Papers*, ii, 287–8.

CHAPTER FOURTEEN

1 *Holland House Diaries*, 258.
2 Sir H. Taylor to Brougham, 10 July 1834. Brougham, *Life and Times*, iii, 401–5.
3 Brougham to Wellesley, [12 July 1834]. Wellesley MSS. Add.Mss. 37, 311, ff.249–52.
4 Taylor to Brougham, 12 July 1834. Brougham, *Life and Times*, iii, 406–8.
5 *Ibid.*, iii, 410.
6 *Greville Memoirs*, 21 July 1834, iii, 63–4.
7 *Ibid.*, iii, 59–60.
8 *Journal of Thomas Moore*, 220.
9 Place to J. Parkes, 17 July 1834. Place MSS. Add.Mss. 35,149, f.308.
10 *Practical Observations*, 147–8.
11 *Collected Works*, vii, 400.
12 *Greville Memoirs*, 23 July 1834, iii, 64.
13 *Collected Speeches*, iii, 475–525.
14 *Ibid.*, iii, 298–9.
15 *Times*, 29 May 1834.
16 *History of the Times*, i, 289–90.
17 *Globe*, 2 June 1834.
18 *History of the Times*, i, 290.
19 *Ibid.*, i, 291.
20 Althorp to Brougham, 4 June 1834. Aspinall, *Politics and the Press*, 256.
21 *History of the Times*, i, 300–2.
22 Brougham to Wellesley, [July 1834]. Wellesley MSS. Add.Mss. 37,311, ff.201–4.
23 Aspinall, *Politics and the Press*, 237.
24 Barnes to Le Marchant, 1834. *Ibid.*, 440.
25 *Greville Memoirs*, 18 September 1834, iii, 83.
26 *Times*, 19 July 1834.
27 *Ibid.*, 26 August 1834.
28 *History of the Times*, i, 317.
29 *Times*, 17 September 1834.
30 Aspinall, *Politics and the Press*, 246.

31 *Letters of Smith*, ii, 592.
32 Brougham, *Life and Times*, iii, 336–7.
33 D. Southgate, *The Passing of the Whigs*, London, 1962, 55n.
34 Reprinted from the *Examiner* in A. Fonblanque (ed.), *England Under Seven Administrations*, London, 1837, iii, 99–101.
35 'The Crisis Examined', *Whigs and Whiggism*, 38.
36 Brougham to Wellesley, undated. Wellesley MSS. Add.Mss. 37,311, ff.175–6.
37 *Collected Speeches*, iii, 77–86.
38 Fonblanque, *Seven Administrations*, iii, 115.
39 Durham to Russell, 7 November 1834. *Early Correspondence of Russell*, ii, 54–6.
40 Reid, *Durham*, ii, 73.
41 Ellice to Grey, [4 November 1834]. Grey MSS.
42 Brougham to Duncannon, January 1835. Aspinall, *Politics and the Press*, 457–9.
43 Creevey to Miss Ord, 22 October 1834. *Creevey Papers*, ii, 289.
44 Sefton to Grey, 7 November 1834. Grey MSS; *Greville Memoirs*, 23 September 1834, iii, 87.
45 Cockburn, *Journal*, i, 68–9.
46 Aspinall, *Three Diaries*, xxxii, n.
47 Melbourne to Grey, 14 November 1834. Grey MSS.
48 Ellice to Grey, [November 1834]. *Ibid.*
49 Brougham to Wellesley, [November 1834]. Wellesley MSS. Add.Mss. 37,311, ff.186–7.
50 Campbell, *Lyndhurst and Brougham*, 460.
51 *Greville Memoirs*, 17 November 1834, iii, 97.
52 Rogers to R. Sharp, 26 November 1834. Clayden, *Rogers and his Contemporaries*, ii, 106–7.
53 Brougham to Wellesley, [January 1835]. Wellesley MSS. Add.Mss. 37,311, ff.211–12.
54 Melbourne to Grey, 23 January 1835. *Melbourne Papers*, 237.
55 Russell, *Recollections and Suggestions*, 139.
56 Grey to Melbourne, 1 February 1835. *Early Correspondence of Russell*, ii, 86–7.
57 Russell, *Recollections and Suggestions*, 140.
58 *Ibid.*, 138.
59 Melbourne to Brougham, 14 February 1835. *Melbourne Papers*, 257–8.
60 Melbourne to Brougham, 17 February 1835. *Ibid.*, 258–63.
61 Cockburn, *Journal*, 2 May 1835, i, 93–4.
62 Ilchester, *Lady Holland to her Son*, 160.

CHAPTER FIFTEEN

1 J. Parkes to Durham, 13 August 1835. Reid, *Durham*, ii, 73.
2 *Memoir of Althorp*, 548–9.
3 Campbell, *Lyndhurst and Brougham*, 476.

4 Aspinall, *Brougham and the Whig Party*, 221.
5 Reid, *Durham*, ii, 87.
6 Ellice to Grey, [2 December 1837]. Grey MSS.
7 Thomas, *Philosophical Radicals*, 360.
8 Aspinall, *Brougham and the Whig Party*, 220.
9 The best account of this episode is in J. Grant, *Random Collections of the Lords and Commons*, London, 1838, i, 66–74.
10 Brougham to Wellesley, 31 December 1837. Wellesley MSS. Add.Mss. 37,312, ff.91–2.
11 Brougham to Place, 25 December 1837. Place MSS. Add.Mss. 35,151, ff.45–6.
12 Broughton, *Recollections*, v, 116.
13 Brougham to Place, 6 January 1838. Place MSS. Add.Mss. 35,151, ff.58–9; Place to Parkes, 18 January 1838. *Ibid.*, Add.Mss. 35,151, ff.70–1.
14 Brougham to Napier, 23 January 1838. *Napier Correspondence*, 231–2.
15 Brougham to Wellesley, [23 January 1838]. Wellesley MSS. Add.Mss. 37,311, ff.424–5.
16 Grant, *Lords and Commons*, i, 29–31.
17 *Greville Memoirs*, 18 February 1838, iv, 24.
18 Reid, *Durham*, ii, 213.
19 New, *Durham*, 434.
20 Smith to Lady Grey, September 1838. *Letters of Smith*, ii, 672.
21 Macaulay to Napier, 1 September 1838. *Napier Correspondence*, 270.
22 *Greville Memoirs*, 23 August 1838, iv, 89–90.
23 *Ibid.*, 4 March 1838, iv, 34–5.
24 *Collected Speeches*, i, 473
25 'Effects of Party', *Statesmen of George III*, i, 310–13.
26 Morley, 'Memorials of a Man of Letters', *Studies in Literature*, 292.
27 *Napier Correspondence*, 62n.
28 Jeffrey to Napier, 1829. *Ibid.*, 62–3.
29 Jeffrey to Napier, 5 November 1829. *Ibid.*, 69.
30 Brougham to H. Reeve, 1 January 1860. *Reeve Memoirs*, ii, 37–8.
31 Trevelyan, *Macaulay*, i, 274–5.
32 *Ibid.*, i, 173.
33 Brougham to Napier, 8 September 1830. *Napier Correspondence*, 88.
34 Macaulay to Napier, 16 September 1830. *Ibid.*, 89–91.
35 Macaulay to Napier, 16 October 1830. *Ibid.*, 91–4.
36 Brougham to Napier, 4 March 1835. *Ibid.*, 156.
37 Brougham to Napier, 9 June 1835. *Ibid.*, 159–60.
38 Brougham to Napier, 15 June 1835. *Ibid.*, 160–2.
39 Brougham to Napier, 26 September 1835. *Ibid.*, 168–71.
40 Napier to Brougham, 6 November 1837. *Ibid.*, 212–13.
41 Allen to Napier, 10 January 1838. *Ibid.*, 229.
42 Allen to Napier, 12 March 1838. *Ibid.*, 240.
43 Brougham to Napier, 4 July 1838. *Ibid.*, 260–1.
44 Macaulay to Napier, 20 July 1838. *Ibid.*, 261–5.
45 Brougham to Napier, 13 September 1838. *Ibid.*, 275–6.
46 Cockburn, *Journal*, ii, 72.

47 Brougham to Napier, 30 August 1841. *Napier Correspondence*, 356–8.
48 Reeve, *Memoirs*, i, 107.

CHAPTER SIXTEEN

1   Brougham to Peel, [September 1844]. Peel MSS. Add.Mss. 40,482, ff.73–8.
2   Brougham to Napier, 16 October 1842. *Napier Correspondence*, 405–6.
3   Brougham to Wellesley, 29 August 1842. Wellesley MSS. Add.Mss. 37,313, ff.190–1.
4   Brougham to Lady Grey, 5 April 1845. Grey MSS.
5   Brougham to Peel, 26 December 1845. Peel MSS. Add.Mss. 40,482, ff.236–8.
6   Brougham to Murray, 9 July 1846. Brougham/Murray MSS. Add.Mss. 40,687, ff.93–6.
7   Walpole, *Russell*, ii, 99.
8   Brougham to Lord Granton, 4 March 1851. E. G. Collieu, 'Lord Brougham and the Conservatives', in H. R. Trevor-Roper (ed.), *Essays in British History Presented to Sir Keith Feiling*, London, 1964, 217.
9   *Memoir of Denman*, ii, 328.
10 Brougham to Peel, [23 July 1845]. Peel MSS. Add. Mss. 40,482, ff.210–11.
11 *Quarterly Review*, January, 1869, 60.
12 Brougham to Napier, 9 September 1839. *Napier Correspondence*, 299. The pamphlet was the 'Letter on National Education to the Duke of Bedford'.
13 Brougham to Napier, 28 February 1838. *Ibid.*, 238–9.
14 *Albert Lunel*, Vol. III, Chapter 3.
15 Brougham to Napier, 2 October 1838. *Napier Correspondence*, 276.
16 Brougham to Napier, 9 September 1838. *Ibid.*, 299–300.
17 Brougham to Peel, 18 December 1844. Peel MSS. Add.Mss. 40,482, ff.111–12.
18 Campbell, *Lyndhurst and Brougham*, 493–4.
19 Macaulay to Napier, 20 October 1843. *Napier Correspondence*, 447–8.
20 Campbell, *Lyndhurst and Brougham*, 439–44. The *Collected Speeches* met the same fate.
21 *Holland House Diaries*, 309.
22 *Whigs and Whiggism*, 253.
23 'Robertson', *Collected Works*, ii, 269–70.
24 Brougham to Russell, 19 August 1828. *Early Correspondence of Russell*, i, 278–9.
25 Allen to Napier, 18 April 1840. *Napier Correspondence*, 322–4.
26 *Statesmen of George III*, i, 24–5.
27 *Ibid.*, i, 9.
28 *Ibid.*, i, 6.
29 Jeffrey to Napier, 17 March 1838. *Napier Correspondence*, 241.
30 *Holland House Diaries*, 382; Lady Holland to Henry Fox, 2 April 1839. Ilchester, *Lady Holland to her Son*, 175.

31 Brougham to Napier, 26 April 1838. *Napier Correspondence*, 244–6.
32 Stanley diary, 30 July 1850. Vincent, *Disraeli, Derby and the Conservative Party*, 30.
33 Creevey to Miss Ord, 20 September 1831. *Creevey Papers*, ii, 236.
34 Brougham to Grey, 2 February [1843]. Grey MSS.
35 Brougham to Grey, [November 1843]. *Ibid.*
36 The correspondence is printed in Campbell, *Lyndhurst and Brougham*, 552–4.
37 Macaulay to Napier, 4 November 1838. *Napier Correspondence*, 283.
38 *Reeve Memoirs*, i, 209.
39 Trevelyan, *Macaulay*, ii, 336.
40 *Letters to Forsyth*, 11.
41 Brougham to Gladstone, 28 September 1857. Gladstone MSS. Add.Mss. 44,114, ff.44–5.
42 Brougham to Gladstone, 9 April 1860. *Ibid.*, Add.Mss. 44,114, ff.184–5.
43 Sir W. F. Pollock, *Personal Reminiscences*, London, 1887, ii, 99.
44 Knight, *Passages*, iii, 225.
45 E. Miller, *Prince of Librarians. The Life & Times of Antonio Panizzi*, London, 1967, 317n.
46 *Letters to Forsyth*, 19.
47 *Melbourne Papers*, 91.
48 Campbell, *Lyndhurst and Brougham*, 213–14.
49 Reid, *Durham*, ii, 215. The writer of the anecdote, which was written shortly after Brougham's death, is not given.
50 'Voltaire', *Collected Works*, ii, 112.

BIOGRAPHICAL NOTES

Allen, John (1771–1843), physician and man of letters; born outside Edinburgh; after 1805 habitué of Holland House; contributor of historical and political essays to the *Edinburgh Review*; warden (1811–20) and principal (1820–43) of Dulwich College; eulogised by Brougham in his *Sketches of Statesmen*.

Burdett, Sir Francis (1770–1844), radical and, in last years, Tory MP; first elected in 1796, sat for Middlesex from 1807 to 1837; champion of free speech against Pitt's government and a radical parliamentary reformer; leading opponent of flogging in the services; favourite pastime was fox-hunting.

Cockburn, Henry Thomas, Lord Cockburn (1779–1854), barrister, judge and memorialist; born at Edinburgh and contemporary of Brougham at the university; life-long friend of Jeffrey and contributor to the *Edinburgh Review*; prominent speaker at Whig public meetings in Scotland; one of the drafters of the Scotch reform bill in 1831.

Croker, John Wilson (1780–1857), Tory politician and man of letters; MP from 1807 to 1832; chief political writer for the *Quarterly Review* during its first forty years; famous for an insensitive attack on Keats' *Endymion* (1818) and an edition of Boswell's *Johnson*; founder of the *Athenaeum*; the source for the character of Rigby in Disraeli's *Coningsby*.

Denman, Sir Thomas, 1st Baron Denman (1779–1854), barrister, judge and Whig politician; MP from 1818–26 and 1830–32; attorney-general in 1830–32; Chief Justice of King's Bench from 1832 to 1850.

Ellice, Edward (1781–1863), Whig politician; MP from 1818 to 1826 and from 1830 to 1863; nicknamed 'the Bear'; brother-in-law of Lord Grey and chief whip in Grey's government.

Folkestone, Viscount, 3rd Earl Radnor (1779–1869), Whig politician; MP from 1801 to 1828; leading figure in the 'Mountain'; prominent opponent of flogging in the services and government prosecutions for libel.

Fonblanque, Albany (1793–1872), journalist; founding contributor to the *Westminster Review* and a member of the Benthamite circle; editor and proprietor of the radical *Examiner* from 1830 to 1847; one of that rare species of writer whose journalism has survived.

Greville, Charles Cavendish Fulke (1794–1865), clerk of the Privy Council from 1821 to 1859; writer of the finest political diaries in English literature; connoisseur of the turf and owner of race-horses.

Horner, Francis (1778–1817), lawyer and Whig politician; barrister on the western circuit; MP in 1806–12 and 1813–17; expert on economic affairs and chairman of the bullion committee (1810) which recommended a return to cash payments.

Le Marchant, Sir Denis (1795–1874), barrister and civil servant; Brougham's private secretary (1830–34); secretary to the board of trade (1836–41 and 1848–50); chief clerk of the House of Commons (1850–71).

Littleton, Edward John, 1st Baron Hatherton (1791–1863), Whig politician; MP from 1812 to 1835, when he was raised to the peerage; chief secretary of Ireland (1833–34); never again held political office.

Loch, James (1780–1855), barrister and Whig politician; born at Edinburgh and boyhood friend of Brougham; called to the English bar in 1806; MP from 1827 to 1852; named his first son Henry Brougham Loch.

Losh, James (1763–1833), coal-owner and barrister on the northern circuit; Unitarian; prominent in Newcastle reform and literary circles; founding member of the Newcastle Mechanics' Institute; recorder of Newcastle (1832–33).

Mackintosh, Sir James (1765–1832), barrister and man of letters; friend of Brougham at Edinburgh University, where he read medicine; Whig MP from 1813 to 1832; founding member of the 'King of Clubs' dining club, which first met at his London house; contributor to the *Edinburgh Review*; famous for the Whig answer to Burke in 1791, the *Vindiciae Gallicae*.

Murray, John (1779–1859), barrister and Whig politician; born at Edinburgh and member of the 'Spec' at the same time as Brougham; early contributor to the *Edinburgh Review*; MP from 1832 to 1839; lord advocate (1835–39).

Pollock, Sir Jonathan Frederick (1783–1870), barrister and Tory politician; called to the bar in 1807 and went the northern circuit; MP from 1831 to 1844; attorney-general (1834 35 and 1841–44); appointed Chief Baron of the Exchequer in 1844.

Ponsonby, George (1755–1817), lawyer and Whig politician; MP from 1776 to 1817; chancellor of the exchequer in 1782; lord chancellor of Ireland (1806–07); Whig leader in the House of Commons from 1807 to 1817.

Robertson, William (1721–1793), historian and Presbyterian minister; established his name as an historian with his *History of Scotland* (1759); principal of Edinburgh University (1762–92); moderator of the Church of Scotland (1763–79).

Roscoe, William (1753–1831), historian and Whig politician; leading light in Liverpool political and literary circles; become first president of the Royal Liverpool Institution in 1817; MP for Liverpool from 1806 to 1807.

Scarlett, James, 1st Baron Abinger (1769–1844), barrister and politician; called to the bar in 1791 and went the northern circuit; Whig MP from 1819 to 1822 and 1823 to 1831; attorney-general under Canning (1827) and Wellington (1829–30); opposed the reform bill and sat as a Tory MP from 1832 to 1834; Chief Baron of the Exchequer 1834–44.

Stuart, Sir Charles, 1st Baron Stuart de Rothesay (1779–1845), diplomat; born at Edinburgh and life-long friend of Brougham; ambassador to Paris (1815–30) and St Petersburg (1841–45).

Ward, John William, 1st Earl of Dudley (1781–1833), politician; MP from 1802 to 1818 and from 1819 to 1823; Pittite and follower of Canning; foreign secretary under Canning and Goderich in 1827; occasional contributor to the *Quarterly Review*.

Wellesley, Richard Colley, 1st Marquess Wellesley (1760–1842), politician and colonial governor; brother of Wellington; governor-general of India (1797–1805); foreign secretary (1809–12); twice (1811 and 1812) failed to get the premiership; lord-lieutenant of Ireland (1821–28 and 1833–34).

Whishaw, Thomas (1764–1840), barrister and habitué of Holland House; friend of Brougham and Bentham; commissioner of public accounts (1806–35); sat on the first council of University College and was a member of the committee of the SDUK.

Whitbread, Samuel (1758–1815), Whig politician; son of the Bedfordshire brewer; MP from 1790 to 1815; leading figure in the 'Mountain'; friend of Sheridan and devoted last years of his life to rebuilding the Drury Lane Theatre.

Wilson, Sir Robert Thomas (1777–1849), general in the French wars and Whig politician; MP from 1818 to 1831; active promoter of the Whig/Canningite coalition in 1827.

SELECT BIBLIOGRAPHY

Manuscript Sources

Brougham/Allen MSS (British Library)
Brougham/Grenville MSS (British Library)
Brougham/Murray MSS (British Library)
Durham MSS (Durham County Record Office)
Gladstone MSS (British Library)
Grey MSS (Durham County Record Office)
Holland House MSS (British Library)
Horner MSS (London School of Economics)
Leigh Hunt MSS (British Library)
Place MSS (British Library)
Peel MSS (British Library)
Russell MSS (Public Record Office)
Wellesley MSS (British Library)
Willis Print Collection (Greater London Record Office)

Printed Sources

Airlie, Mabell, Countess of, *In Whig Society, 1775–1818*, London, 1921
Anderson, O., 'The Wensleydale Peerage Case and the Position of the House of Lords in the Mid-nineteenth Century', *English Historical Review*, July 1967
Anon., *Opinions of Lord Brougham on Politics ... &c. as Exhibited in his Parliamentary and Legal Speeches and Miscellaneous Writings*, London, 1837
Arnould, Sir J., *Memoir of Thomas, First Lord Denman*, 2 vols, London, 1873
Aspinall, A., *Lord Brougham and the Whig Party*, Manchester, 1927
—— (ed.), *The Formation of Canning's Ministry, February to August 1827*, London, 1937
——, *Politics and the Press, c.1780–1850*, London, 1949
—— (ed.), *Three Early Nineteenth Century Diaries*, London, 1952
——, 'The Westminster Election of 1814', *English Historical Review*, October 1925

——, 'Lord Brougham's "Life and Times" ', *English Historical Review*, January 1944

Atlay, J. B., *The Victorian Chancellors*, vol. 1, London, 1906

Bagehot, W., 'Lord Brougham', in St John-Stevas, N. (ed.), *Bagehot's Historical Essays*, New York edn, 1965

Bamford, F., and Wellington, Duke of (ed.), *The Journal of Mrs Arbuthnot, 1820–1832*, 2 vols, London, 1950

[Barnes, T.], *Parliamentary Portraits; or Sketches of the Public Characters of Some of the Most Distinguished Speakers of the House of Commons*, London, 1815

Bartlett, C. J., *Castlereagh*, London, 1966

Bennett, S., 'Revolutions in Thought', in J. Shattock and M. Wolff (ed.), *The Victorian Periodical Press: Samplings and Soundings*, Leicester and Toronto, 1982

Boyce, G. *et al.* (ed.), *Newspaper History from the Seventeenth Century to the Present Day*, London, 1978

Brightfield, M. F., *John Wilson Croker*, London, 1957

Brock, M., *The Great Reform Act*, London, 1973

Brooke, J., and Sorenson, M. (ed.), *The Prime Ministers' Papers: W. E. Gladstone. II: Autobiographical Memoranda, 1832–1845*, London, 1972

Brougham, H., *An Inquiry into the Colonial Policy of the European Powers*, Edinburgh, 1803

——, *Speeches of Henry, Lord Brougham*, 4 vols, London, 1838

——, *Historical Sketches of Statesmen who Flourished in the Time of George III*, 3 vols, London, 1839–43

——, *Contributions to the Edinburgh Review*, 3 vols, Edinburgh, 1856

——, *The Life and Times of Henry, Lord Brougham*, 3 vols, London, 1871

——, *Albert Lunel*, 3 vols, London, 1872

——, *Collected Works*, 11 vols. London, 1855–1861

Buddle Atkinson, R., and Jackson, G. (ed.), *Brougham and his Early Friends. Letters to James Loch, 1795–1809*, 3 vols, London, 1908

Butler, J. R. M., *The Passing of the Great Reform Bill*, London, 1914

Campbell, Lord, *Lives of Lord Lyndhurst and Lord Brougham*, London, 1869

Cannon, J., *Parliamentary Reform, 1640–1832*, Cambridge, 1972

Cecil, Lord David, *Melbourne*, London, 1955 edn (comprising *The Young Melbourne* and *Lord M*)

Clarkson, T., *Strictures on a Life of William Wilberforce*, London, 1838

Clayden, P. W., *Rogers and his Contemporaries*, 2 vols, London, 1889

Clive, J., *Scotch Reviewers. The Edinburgh Review, 1802–1815*, London, 1957

——, 'The Edinburgh Review: the Life and Death of a Periodical', in Briggs, A. (ed.), *Essays in the History of Publishing*, London, 1974

Cockburn, H., *Life of Lord Jeffrey with a Selection from his Correspondence*, vol. 1, Edinburgh, 1852

——, *Letters Chiefly Connected with the Affairs of Scotland, 1818–1852*, London, 1874

——, *Journal of Henry Cockburn, Being a Continuation of the Memorials of his Time, 1831–54*, 2 vols, Edinburgh, 1874

——, *Memorials of his Time*, new edn, Edinburgh, 1910

Cockburn, H. A. (ed.), *Some Letters of Lord Cockburn with Pages Omitted from the Memorials of his Time*, Edinburgh, 1932

Collieu, E. G., 'Lord Brougham and the Conservatives', in Trevor-Roper, H. R. (ed.), *Essays in British History Presented to Sir Keith Feiling*, London, 1965

Coupland, R., *Wilberforce. A Narrative*, Oxford, 1923

Creston, D., *The Regent and his Daughter*, London, 1932

Dinwiddy, J. R., 'Sir Francis Burdett and Burdettite Radicalism', *History*, February 1980

Disraeli, B. (ed. W. Hutcheon), *Whigs and Whiggism*, London, 1913

Flick, C. T., *The Birmingham Political Union and the Movements for Reform in Britain, 1830–1839*, Connecticut, 1979

Fonblanque, A., *England Under Seven Administrations*, 3 vols, London, 1837

Fonblanque, E. Barrington de, *The Life and Labours of Albany Fonblanque*, London, 1874

Forsyth, W. (ed.), *Letters from Lord Brougham to William Forsyth*, London, 1872

Fulford, R., *The Trial of Queen Caroline*, London, 1967

——, *Samuel Whitbread, 1764–1815: a Study in Opposition*, London, 1967

Furneaux, R., *William Wilberforce*, London, 1974

Garratt, G. T., *Lord Brougham*, London, 1935

Gash, N., 'Brougham and the Yorkshire Election of 1830', *Proceedings of the Leeds Literary and Philosophical Society*, May 1956

Gilbert, A. M., *The Work of Lord Brougham for Education in England*, Pennsylvania, 1922

Godsell, P. (ed.), *Letters and Diaries of Lady Durham*, Toronto, 1979

Grant, J., *Random Collections of the House of Commons*, London, 1836

——, *The Bench and the Bar*, 2 vols, London, 1837

——, *Random Collections of the Lords and Commons*, 2 vols, London, 1838

Grey, H., Earl (ed.), *The Correspondence of the late Earl Grey with His Majesty King William IV and with Sir Herbert Taylor*, 2 vols, London, 1867

Grimmer, W. H., *Anecdotes of the Bench and Bar*, London, 1858

Hanworth, Lord, *Lord Chief Baron Pollock. A Memoir*, London, 1929

Hardy, T. D., *Memoirs of the Right Honourable Henry Lord Langdale*, 2 vols, London, 1852

Harvey, A. D., *Britain in the Early Nineteenth Century*, London, 1978

Hawes, F., *Henry Brougham*, London, 1957

Haydon, B. R. (ed. T. Taylor), *The Autobiography and Memoirs of Benjamin Robert Haydon*, new edn, London, 1926

Hazlitt, W., *The Spirit of the Age: or Contemporary Portraits*, London, 1825

Holdsworth, W. (ed. A Goodhart and H. Hanbury), *A History of English Law*, vol. 13, London, 1952

Holland, Lady, *A Memoir of the Rev. Sydney Smith*, London, 1878 edn

Holland, Lord, *Memoirs of the Whig Party*, 2 vols, London, 1852–54

—— (ed. Lord Stavordale), *Further Memoirs of the Whig Party, 1807–21*, London, 1905

Hone, J. A., *For the Cause of Truth. Radicalism in London, 1796–1821*, Oxford, 1982

Horner, L. (ed.), *Memoirs and Correspondence of Francis Horner*, 2 vols, London, 1843

Howell, P. A., *The Judicial Committee of the Privy Council, 1833–1876. Its Origins, Structure and Development*, Cambridge, 1979

Hughes, E. (ed.), *The Diaries and Correspondence of James Losh, 1811–1833*, 2 vols, London, 1962–63.

——, 'The Bishops and Reform, 1831–33: Some Fresh Correspondence', *English Historical Review*, July 1941

Hunt, L., *Autobiography*, London, 1860

Hunt, T. (ed.), *The Correspondence of Leigh Hunt*, 2 vols, London, 1862

Ilchester, Earl of (ed.), *The Journal of the Hon. Henry Edward Fox, afterwards 4th and last Lord Holland, 1818–1830*, London, 1923

——, *Elizabeth, Lady Holland, to her Son, 1821–1845*, London, 1946

James, C., *Curiosities of Law and Lawyers*, 2nd edn, London, 1891

Jennings, L. J. (ed.), *The Croker Papers. The Correspondence and Diaries of the Late Right Honourable John Wilson Croker*, 3 vols, London, 1884

Keppel, S., *The Sovereign Lady. A Life of Elizabeth Vassall, third Lady Holland, with her Family*, London, 1974

Knight, C., *Passages of a Working Life During Half a Century*, 3 vols, London, 1864

Knutsford, Viscountess, *Life and Letters of Zachary Macaulay*, London, 1900

Kriegel, A. D. (ed.), *The Holland House Diaries, 1831–1840*, London, 1977

Laughton, J. K., *Memoirs of the Life and Correspondence of Henry Reeve*, 2 vols, London, 1898

Le Marchant, D., *Memoir of John Charles, Viscount Althorp, Third Earl Spencer*, London, 1876

Lytton Bulwer, E., *England and the English*, London, 1874 edn

Mackintosh, R. J. (ed.), *Memoirs of the Life of the Right Honourable Sir James Mackintosh*, 2 vols, 2nd edn, London, 1836

Martin, T., *A Life of Lord Lyndhurst*, London, 1883

Martineau, H., *Autobiography*, 3rd edn, London, 1877

Maxwell, H. (ed.), *The Creevey Papers. A Selection from the Correspondence & Diaries of the Late Thomas Creevey*, 2 vols, London, 1903

Medd, P., *Romilly. A Life of Sir Samuel Romilly, Lawyer and Reformer*, London, 1968

Mill, J. S., *Autobiography*, New York, 1957 edn

Miller, E., *Prince of Librarians. The Life and Times of Antonio Panizzi of the British Museum*, London, 1967

Miller, K., *Cockburn's Millennium*, London, 1975

Miller, M. R., *Thomas Campbell*, Boston, 1978

Mitchell, A., *The Whigs in Opposition, 1815–1830*, Oxford, 1967

Mitchison, R., *A History of Scotland*, London, 1970

Molesworth, W. N., *The History of England from the Year 1830–1874*, vol. 1, London, 1875

Morrison, B., 'Upper Grub Street', *Encounter*, July 1979

Nash, T. A., *The Life of Richard, Lord Westbury*, 2 vols, London, 1888

New, C. W., *Lord Durham. A Biography of John George Lambton, First Earl of Durham*, Oxford, 1929

——, *The Life of Henry Brougham to 1830*, Oxford, 1961

[Newman, J. H.], *The Tamworth Reading Room*, London, 1841

Northbrook, Earl of (ed.), *Journals and Correspondence of Francis Thornhill Baring, Lord Northbrook*, 2 vols, London, 1902

Office of 'The Times', *The History of The Times*, vol. 1, London, 1935

Olphin, H. K., *George Tierney*, London, 1934

Owen, D., *English Philanthropy, 1660–1960*, Massachusetts, 1964

Perkin, H., *The Origins of Modern English Society, 1780–1880*, London, 1969

Plunket, D., *The Life, Letters and Speeches of Lord Plunket*, 2 vols, London, 1867

Pollock, W. F., *Personal Remembrances*, 2 vols, London, 1887

Polson, A., *Law and Lawyers, or, Sketches and Illustrations of Legal History and Biography*, 2 vols, London, 1840

Prest, J., *Lord John Russell*, London, 1972

Quennell, P. (ed.), *The Journal of Thomas Moore, 1818–1841*, London, 1964

Raikes, T., *A Portion of the Journal kept by Thomas Raikes, Esq., from 1831 to 1847*, 2 vols, London, 1858

Ramsay, E. B., *Reminiscences of Scottish Life & Character*, Edinburgh, 1874

Reeve, H. (ed.), *Memoir and Correspondence relating to Political Occurrences in June and July 1834 by the Right Hon. Edward John Littleton, First Lord Hatherton*, London, 1872

Reid, S. J., *Life and Letters of the First Earl of Durham, 1792–1840*, 2 vols, London, 1906

Retourney, H., *Cannes. Lord Brougham et la Centenaire*, Marseille, 1879

Roberts, M., *The Whig Party, 1807–1812*, London, 1939

Roebuck, J. A., *History of the Whig Ministry of 1830, to the Passing of the Reform Bill*, 2 vols, London, 1852

Rogers, C., *Traits and Stories of the Scottish People*, London, 1867

Romilly, S. H. (ed.), *Letters to 'Ivy' from the First Earl of Dudley*, London, 1905

Romilly, S., *Memoirs of the Life of Sir Samuel Romilly Written by Himself; with a Selection from his Correspondence*, 3 vols, London, 1840

Russell, Earl, *Recollections and Suggestions, 1813–1873*, London, 1875

Russell, R. (ed.), *Early Correspondence of Lord John Russell, 1805–1840*, 2 vols, London, 1913

Sadler, T. (ed.), *Diary, Reminiscences, and Correspondence of Henry Crabb Robinson*, 2 vols, 3rd edn, London, 1872

St Leonards, Lord, *Misrepresentations in Campbell's Lives of Lyndhurst and Brougham Corrected by St Leonards*, London, 1869

Sanders, L. C. (ed.), *Lord Melbourne's Papers*, London, 1889

Scarlett, P. C., *A Memoir of the Right Honourable James, First Lord Abinger*, London, 1877

Seymour, Lady (ed.), *The 'Pope' of Holland House. Selections from the Correspondence of John Whishaw and his Friends, 1813–1840*, London, 1906

Smith, N. C. (ed.), *The Letters of Sydney Smith*, 2 vols, Oxford, 1953

Southgate, D., *The Passing of the Whigs, 1832–1886*, London, 1962

Stapleton, E. J. (ed.), *Some Official Correspondence of George Canning*, 2 vols, London, 1887

Stanley, A. P., *Life and Correspondence of Thomas Arnold*, London, 1844

Strachey, L., and Fulford, R. (ed.), *The Greville Memoirs, 1814–1860*, 8 vols, London, 1938

Sudley, Lord (ed.), *The Lieven–Palmerston Correspondence, 1828–1856*, London, 1943

Swinfen, D. B., 'Henry Brougham and the Judicial Committee of the Privy Council', *Law Quarterly Review*, July 1974

Thale, M. (ed.), *The Autobiography of Francis Place*, Cambridge, 1972

Thomas, W., *The Philosophical Radicals. Nine Studies in Theory and Practice, 1817–1841*, Oxford, 1979

Trevelyan, G. O., *The Life and Letters of Lord Macaulay*, 2 vols, Oxford, 1978 edn

Turberville, A. S., *The House of Lords in the Age of Reform, 1784–1837*, London, 1958

Wallas, G., *The Life of Francis Place, 1771–1854*, 4th edn, London, 1925

Walpole, S., *The Life of Lord John Russell*, 2 vols, London, 1889

Wardroper, J., *Kings, Lords and Wicked Libellers. Satire and Protest, 1760–1837*, London, 1973

Webb, R. K., *The British Working Class Reader, 1790–1848*, London, 1955

Wellesley, Lord, *The Wellesley Papers*, 2 vols, London, 1914

West, E. G., *Education and the Industrial Revolution*, London, 1975

Wheatley, Vera, *The Life and Work of Harriet Martineau*, London, 1957

Wilberforce, R. I. and S., *The Life of William Wilberforce*, 5 vols, London, 1838

—— (ed.), *The Correspondence of William Wilberforce*, 2 vols

Wilson, R. (ed. H. Randolph), *Canning's Administration: Narrative of its Formation*, London, 1872

INDEX

Abercromby, James, 103, 117n., 174
Aberdeen, Lord, 62, 355
Adam, Dr, 5–6
Addington, Henry (Lord Sidmouth), 2, 171, 219
African Institution, 91–2, 175–6
Alexander I, Tsar, 208
Allen, John, 11, 20, 22, 27, 34, 39, 40, 44, 48, 50, 51, 61, 67, 71, 78, 80, 86, 139, 173, 192, 193, 203, 212, 222, 223, 238, 322, 341, 353
Allen, William, 88, 121, 122
Althorp, Lord, 72, 202, 211, 214, 221, 230, 231, 233, becomes Whig leader, 240–1; 245, and offer of Great Seal to Brougham, 249–50; 287, 288–9, and fall of Grey's government, 295–302; and formation of Melbourne's government, 303–4; 305, 310, 312, goes to the Lords, 319–20; 325, 326
Anglo-American rivalry, 42, 73, 81, 87
Arbuthnot, Charles, 172
Arbuthnot, Mrs Charles, 183
Argyll, Duke of, 29
Arnold, Thomas, 4, 192, 200, 270
Attwood, Thomas, 270

Babington, Thomas, 29, 123, 125, 176
Bagehot, Walter, 50, 56, 256
Baillie, Dr, 96
Baines, Edward, 242–3
Bamford, Samuel, 127
Banks, Sir Joseph, 16, 26
Baring, Alexander, 74, 106
Baring, Sir Francis, 55
Barnes, Thomas, 64, 260, 272, 294, 309–13
Bathurst, Lord, 171, 225
Bedford, Duke of, brings Brougham into parliament, 58–9; gives up nomination to Camelford, 79–80; 121, 216, 248
Belloc, Hilaire, 201

Bennet, Henry, 103, 104, 111, 113, 115, 117, 151
Bentham, Jeremy, 86, introduced to Brougham, 88–9; 114, 205, 207n., on Brougham's law reform speech, 234–5; 260, 277, attack on Brougham, 284; 305
Benthamites, 50, 88–9, 102–3, 114–5, 123, 129, 188, 234, 270, 305
Bentinck, Lord George, 320
Bessborough, Lady, 58
Bexley, Lord (Nicholas Vansittart), 171, 220, 228, 232
Bickersteth, Henry, 234
Birkbeck, George, 184–5, 197, 202
Black, Joseph, 6
Braxfield, Judge, 13
Bright, John, 25
British and Foreign School Society, 121–2
Brooks's Club, 36, 107, 118, 215–6, 233, 320
Brougham, Eleanor-Louise, 344, 352
Brougham, Henry, accepts the Woolsack, 1; antecedents, 2; growing up in Scotland, 2–4; on Rousseau, 3; at Edinburgh High School, 4–6, 28; at Edinburgh University, 6–11, 28; papers for Royal Society, 7–8; reads for the bar, 8, 11; member of the 'Spec', 9–10; and oratory, 10; first years as advocate, 11–14; the Colonial Policy, 14–19; on marriage, 14; on history-writing, 17; on slavery, 18–19; helps found Edinburgh Review, 19–23; goes to London, 23–7; discontent with the law, 25–6; on the value of study, 28–9; works with the 'Saints', 29–32; on religion, 29–30; tour in Europe, 31–3; flirts with the Tories, 32–4; forms Whig ties in London, 34–6; and the 'Talents' government, 36–41; mission to Portugal, 37–8; fails to enter parliament, 38; early law career in

Brougham, Henry – cont.
England, 38–9; as pamphleteer and
'hack', 39–41; and orders-in-council,
41–4; law career, 43–4; Cevallos article, 45–53, 69; and politics of the
Edinburgh Review, 49–54; on the Whig
'valuables', 51–3; and the Whigs, 55–7;
quarrel with Lady Holland, 58; MP for
Camelford, 59–61; outset of parliamentary career, 61–5; maiden speech, 65;
and slave-trade bill, 65–6; and 1810
session, 66–9; and the Whigs (1811–
12), 70–2; repeal of orders-in-council,
73–4; defends the Hunts, 74–8; his
courtroom manner, 78; his rapid political rise, 78–9; surrenders Camelford,
79–80; Liverpool election (1812), 80–4;
anger at the Whigs, 84–5; rejects election for Middlesex, 86; defends Luddites, 86–7; forms Benthamite ties,
88–91; and Westminster election
(1814), 89–92; and slave trade, 91–3;
visit to France (1814), 93; on his illness,
93–7; MP for Winchilsea (1815), 97;
strategy for post-war politics, 99–103;
and Whig leadership, 103–4; and the
Holy Alliance, 104–5; and repeal of
income tax, 106–7, 111; attacks the
Prince Regent, 108–10; wooed by
Place, 109–11; and 1816 session, 111–
14; and 1817 session, 115–17; and 1818
session, 117–19; and education reform,
120–8; Westmorland election (1818),
128–32; marries, 133–5; and 'Peterloo',
137–9; the royal divorce trial, 140–59;
on the northern circuit, 160–4; courtroom manner, 162–4; and the Durham
clergy, 164–8; fails to get silk, 168–70;
and the agricultural interest, 172; and
the Whig leadership, 174; rector of
Glasgow University, 174–5; and trial of
John Smith, 176–9; his parliamentary
oratory, 179–82; and education in the
1820s, 183–204; row with Canning,
206–7; and the Irish Catholics, 209–12;
and Canning's government, 212–19;
and Goderich's government, 220–6;
quarrel with Grey, 226–9; his reputation (1830), 230–2; and 1828 session,
232–3; law reform speech (1828), 233–
8; surrenders Winchilsea, 239–40; passed over by Althorp for Whig leadership, 240–1; and Yorkshire election

(1830), 242–5; and parliamentary reform, 245–8; and formation of Grey's
government, 248–52; and Church patronage, 253–4; first days on the Woolsack, 254–5; in Chancery, 255–9; and
Horse Guards incident, 257–8; and
drafting of the reform bill (1831), 260;
and *Times* attacks on Grey, 260–2; and
the reform bill, 262–3, 264–76; his
reform speech (1831), 266–8; and peer-
creation, 269–74, 276; on illness, 272–
3; law reforms, 278–85; and abolition of
slavery, 286; and parliamentary grant
to education, 286; irritates colleagues,
287–92; and Whigs' Irish policy, 289–
302; and fall of Grey, 292–302; and
formation of Melbourne's government,
303–4; and poor law (1834), 305–9;
quarrel with Barnes and the *Times*,
309–13; tour of the North (1834),
314–20; quarrel with Durham, 316–19;
and Melbourne's dismissal, 320; omitted from Melbourne's government,
321–4; and Melbourne's government,
325–34; and the radicals, 326–8; row
with Melbourne, 328–30; and the
Canada crisis, 330–4; and the *Edinburgh Review*, 339–43; and the Tories,
344; and Peel's government, 345–7;
and the Protectionists, 347–8; and the
Law Amendment Society, 348–9; his
writings, 349–54; on history, 352–4; at
Cannes, 352–3; and France, 355–8; last
years, 358–60; death, 360
Brougham, James, 250, 288
Brougham, William, 260–1
Brougham Hall, 2, 26, 58, 65, 93, 94, 135,
190, 272, 352, 358, 359
Buchan, Lord, 47
Bulwer, Lytton, 149, 205
Burdett, Sir Francis, 52, 53, 71, 78, 89,
103, 113, 185, 211, 215–16
Burke, Edmund, 1–2, 16, 62
Burns, Robert, 3, 24
Buxton, Fowell, 35, 175–6
Byron, Lord, 47, 48, 205

Calcraft, John, 105
Cambridge University, 6
Campbell, Lord, 11, 25, 28, 65, 128, 165,
238, 244, 279, 285, 326, 351, 360
Campbell, Thomas, 195–7
Canada, rebellion in, 330–4

Cannes, 354–6, 359–61

Canning, George, 2, 22, 51, 62, 69, 74, 79, and Liverpool election, 80–3; similarities to Brougham, 88; 94, 126, 140, 146, 147, 173, and Brougham's oratory, 179–80; 181, 182, 183, and his government, 205–29; 348

Carlisle, Lord, 216

Carlyle, Thomas, 199–200, 350

Caroline, Queen, 139, and her trial, 140–59, 160, 164, 171, 174, 179, 180, 244

Carnot, Lazare, 93

Cartwright, Major, 86, 90, 114

Castlereagh, Lord, 69, 74, 94, 105, 107, 126, Brougham on his suicide, 132; 153, 172–3, 206

Catholic Association, the, 209–12, 219, 238–9

Catholic emancipation, Whig attitudes to (1810), 67, (1812) 79; 88, Brougham on Eldon and, 169–70; 171, 205–6, Brougham on (1825), 209–12; 213–14, and the Whig 'Malignants', 216–17, 224, 228; 220, carried into law, 238–9; 328

Catholic relief, 37, 48, 53, 81, 345–6

Cavendish, Lord George, 103–4

central criminal court, 279

Chancery, Court of, 235, 255–9, 277–9

Chadwick, Edwin, 305

charitable abuses, 123–8

Charles X, King, 104

Charlotte, Princess, 114, 140, 144–5

Chatham, Earl of, 231, 341–2, 353

Clarkson, Joseph, 121

Clephane, Andrew, 14

Cleveland, Lord, 226–8, 239–40

Cobbett, William, 50, 52, 53, 75, 100, 114, 202

Cobden, Richard, 360

Cochrane, Lord, 89–90, 93, 102, 116

Cockburn, Henry, 5, 8, 9, 10, 12, 13, 24, 28, 66, 175, on Brougham's oratory, 180–1; 216, on Grey in office, 253; on Brougham, 319; 323, 343

coercion in Ireland, 289–302, 311

Coleridge, Samuel Taylor, 205

Corn Laws, 102, 346–7

Cottenham, Lord, 325–6

Cowper, Lord, 231

Cox Francis, 196–7

Creevey, Thomas, 1, 66–7, 79n., and

Liverpool election, 80–2; 85, 93, 94, 97, 103, 104, names Tierney 'Mrs Cole', 117; 118, 129, 130, 131, 132, on dinner with the Broughams, 135; 145, on Brougham and Caroline, 149, 151, 152; 171, 194, 215, 219, 225, on Brougham and Grey (1828), 227–8; on Brougham's pretensions to leadership (1828), 233; 275, on Brougham's plotting to overthrow Grey, 298, 300; on Brougham in Scotland (1834), 319; 355

Croker, John Wilson, on Whigs and Tories, 34; on quarterly reviews, 49, 54; on Brougham and Caroline, 146; 237, attacks Brougham (1830), 255, 339n.; 344, 352

Currie, Dr, 33

Curtis, Sir William, 107

Cuvier, Georges, 93

Darlington, Lord, 97, 130, 136, 226, 239

Delicate Investigation, the, 141, 143, 144

Demerara, 176–9, 209

Denman, Thomas, 151, 153, 154, 157, 173, 198, 244, 250, 270, 328

de Quincey, Thomas, 130–1

Devonshire, Duke of, 130, 216, 249

Disraeli, Benjamin, 32, 62, on Brougham's oratory, 179; on offer of attorney-generalship to Brougham, 249; 304, on Brougham's tour of Scotland (1834), 314, 315; on Brougham's writings, 351

Drummond, 198

Duncannon, Lord, 214, 260, 317

Durham, John Lambton, Lord, early friendship with Brougham, 118–9; 124, 130–1, 172, 198, 211, 233, 246–7, and Brougham and the *Times*, 260–2; 273, 289, excluded from Grey's cabinet (1834), 293, exclusion angers Barnes, 309–10; and row with Brougham (1834), 316–19; Brougham's attack on, 327–8; and Canada crisis, 330–4

Durham clergy, 164–8, 179

Edinburgh, 2, 23–4, 92, 106, 314, 316–17, 319, 359

Edinburgh High School, 5–6, 7, 24

Edinburgh Review, its foundation, 19–23; 31, 33, 34, 36, 39, 42, 43, and political bias, 45–54; 59, 64, 66, 67, 79, 86, 91, 92, 94, 121, 142, 176, 185, 191, 207n.,

Edinburgh Review – cont.
227, 245, 246, 253, 273, under Napier, 335–43
Edinburgh University, 3, 6, 8–11, 197
education reform, 48, 87, 88, 101, 120–8, 286
Eldon, Lord, 68, 137, 147, on Brougham and Caroline's trial, 155–6; 167, refuses Brougham silk, 168–70; 171, 200, 208, 212, 222, 232, 256, and Chancery, 258–9; 277, 280
elections, of 1807, 38–40; of 1812, 285; of 1830, 1, 241–2, 245–6; of 1832, 285; of 1837, 327
Eliot, Gilbert, 56
Ellenborough, 1st Baron, 76–7, 86–7
Ellenborough, 2nd Baron, 254, 256, 258
Ellice, Edward, 160, 216, 225, 246, 260, 286, 291, 317, 320
Enlightenment, in Scotland, 2–4
Erskine, Henry, 12, 13, 77, 78
Erskine, Thomas, Lord, 25, 63–4, 155
Eskgrove, Lord, 12
Essex, Lord, 215
Eversley, Viscountess, 35

Ferdinand VII, King, 104, 207
Ferguson, Adam, 17
Fitzgerald, Vesey, 238–9
Fitzherbert, Mrs, 154, 157
Fitzwilliam, Lord, 137, 138, 242
flogging, 70, 74–8, 173
Folkestone, Lord, 70, 78, 103, 111
Fonblanque, Albany, 207n., 314–15, 327
Forsyth, William, 96, 181, 358, 359–60
Fox, Caroline, 17
Fox, Charles James, 16, 22, 34, 36, 38, 45, 52, 62, 70, 91, 120, 181, 266, 319
Fox, Henry, 208
Fox, Joseph, 121
free trade, 17, 33, 37, 116–17, 210, 346–7
French revolution, 5, 12–13, 47, 48, 49

Gascoigne, Thomas, 80–2
Gascoyne, General, 264
George III, King, 48, 139, 147, 353
George IV, King, 53, 71, Hunt's libel of, 77; 79, 90, 104, Brougham's attack on (1816), 107–9, 112; 114, 115, 139, and Caroline's trial, 140–59; Brougham on his tour of Scotland, 165–6; 172–3, 212, 222, 241
Gladstone, William, 64, 130, 182, 359

Glasgow University, 174–5, 183–4, 197
Glenelg, Lord, 332–3
Goderich, Frederick Robinson, Lord (Lord Ripon), 174, 206, 220–5, 292
Goldsmid, Sir Isaac, 196
Graham, Sir James, 247, 260, 263, 292, 347
Grant, Charles, 9
Grant, James, 134, 162, 332
Grant, Robert, 9
Great Seal, the, 1, 115, 150, 169, 249–51, 254–5, 259, 270–1, 275, 314, 320, 325, 347, 348
Grenville, Thomas, 170
Grenville, Lord, 37, 68, 74, 79, 228
Greville, Charles, 154, 214, assessment of Brougham, 231–2; 251, 255, 257, on Brougham in the Lords, 259–60; 266, 283, 287, 298, 304, 312, 333, on Brougham (1838), 334
Grey, Lord, 1, 22, 33, 35, 38, 39, 40, 44, 45, 49, 53, 57, 58, 59, 67, 70, 75, 77, 79, 81, 85, 87, 93, 94, 97, 99, 102, 103, 106, 109, 112, 116, 118, 130, 132, 138, 172, 174, 175, 203–4, 206, on Ireland (1825), 211–2; 214, on Canning's government, 216–19, 222–5; row with Brougham (1828), 226–9; 230, 233, 239–41, and formation of his government, 247–51; 253, and 1st reform bill, 260–6; 268, and 2nd reform bill, 270–6; 280, 285–91, and fall of his government, 292–300; 303–4, 311, 314, 316–19, recommends Brougham to Melbourne, 321; 323, 345, 356
Grey, General, 228–9
Grote, George, 188
Gurney, Joseph, 196

Hamilton, Alexander, 100
Harewood, Lord, 242
Haydon, Benjamin, 181
Hazlitt, William, 28, 67, on Caroline's trial, 158–9; 180, on Brougham, 182; 240
Herries, Sir John, 220–1
Hewlett, John, 24
Hicks Beach, Michael, 19
Hill, Matthew, 188–90
Hodgskin, Thomas, 185
Holland, Lady, 19, 36, falls out with Brougham, 58; 103, 134, 207, 272–3, on Brougham's fall, 323

Holland, Lord, 17, 33, 36, 37–8, on Brougham and 1807 elections, 39; 45, chastised by Brougham, 57–8; 59, 65, 67, 70, 78, 93, 104, 130, Brougham complains to of ill treatment, 136–7; 174, 191, 221, 224, 226, 248, 252, 253, 258, 266, 270, 272–3, 278, 287, on Brougham during cabinet crisis (1834), 293; on Brougham and the fall of Grey, 299–300; 303, 354

Holland House, 1, 11, 36, 47, 58, 103–4, 114, 248, 304, 320, 340, 342

Holy Alliance, the, 104–5, 207–8, 328

Hone, William, 116

Horner, Francis, on Brougham's powers, 7; 8, 9, 10, 11, 13, 17, 19–23, 24, 26, 29, 34–5, 36, 38, 48, 51, 52, 56, 62, 72, 78, 82, 84, 89, 121, 123, 132–3, 184

Horner, Leonard, 184

Horse Guards, the, 257–8

Howe, Lord, 268

Howick, Lord, 246

Hume, Joseph, 197–8

Hunt, Henry ('Orator'), 55, 114, 137–8

Hunt, Leigh, 29, 52, 64, and libel prosecution, 74–8; 80, 82, 100, praises Brougham in the *Examiner*, 109; 114, 194, 207n.

Huskisson, William, 94, 174, 206, 241

Hutchinson, Lord, 147–9

income and property tax, 54, 62, 87, 101–2, repeal of, 106–7; 112, 345

Irish Church, reform of, 282, 286–7, 289–92

'Ivy' (Helen d'Arcy Stewart), 57

Jeffrey, Francis, 8, 10, 11, 13, 19–23, 26–7, 29, 31, 34, 47, 50, 51, on Whig tactics, 52–3; 55, 65, 134, 253, 336 n., 339, 340, 352

Jersey, Lady, 114, 154, 176

Johnson, Samuel, 24, 94–5

Judicial Committee of the Privy Council, 235–6, 279–80, 282–5, 347, 358, 361

Kemble, John, 35

Key, Sir John, 263

King, Lord, 135

'King of Clubs', 36

King's College, 197–9

Knaresborough, constituency of, 239

Knight, Charles, 187–93, 202, 311, 359

Lamb, George, 129, 272

Lancaster, Joseph, 88, 121

Lansdowne, Henry Petty, Lord, 9, 120, 171, 206, 208, 213–17, 220–1, 226, 233, 283, 336–7, 357

Lansdowne House, 1, 252

Laplace, Pierre, 6, 93

Lauderdale, Lord, 33, 57, 58, 59, 85

Law Amendment Society, 279, 348–9

law reform, 179, 220, Brougham's speech on (1828), 233–8; ·258–9, and Brougham as lord chancellor, 277–85; 348–9

Leach, Sir John, 150, 157, 284

Le Marchant, Denis, 6, 256, 263, 275, 286–7, 288, 309–12

Leopold, Prince, 145

libel laws, 70–1, 73, 74–8, 87, 101–2, 111

Lincoln's Inn, 26, 44, 189, 254

Lindsay, Lady Charlotte, 88

Littleton, Edward (Baron Hatherton), 295–300

Littleton, Lord, 94

Liverpool, Lord, 17, 107, 112, 146, 147, 148, 149, 150, 157, 171, 183, 212

Liverpool election (1812), 80–3, 84–5

Loch, James, 14, 15, 21, 26, 36

local courts bill (1833), 279–82

Lockhart, John, 54, 65

London University, 8, 184, 195–9, 203–4

Londonderry, Lord, 265

Lonsdale, Lord, 128–9, 139

Losh, James, 78, 131, 230–1, 263, 269, 270

Louis-Philippe, King, 355, 356

Lowe, Robert, 120

Lowther, Lord, 34, 37–8, 128–31, 200

Luddite trials, 86–7

Lushington, Stephen, 226

Lyndhurst, Lord, 8, 169, 256, 265, 274, 277, and local courts bill (1833), 290–2; 320, 325, 344, 347, 352

Macaulay, Thomas, 35, 62, 155, 181, 240, 266, 270, 334, literary rows with Brougham, 335–43; 349, 351, 358

Macaulay, Zachary, 30–1, 176, 197–8

Macdonald, Sir James, 214

Mackintosh, Sir James, 6–7, 16, 36, 63, 129, 144, 174, 189, 197, on *caractère*, 241

Malthus, Thomas, 305–6

Malthusianism, 113, 185–6, 202–3, 305–8

Marshall, John, 242

Martineau, Harriet, 22, on Brougham in society, 133; 134, antipathy to Brougham, 194–5
Maynooth College, 345–6
Mechanics' Institutes, 8, 184–7, 200, 203, 361
Melbourne, William Lamb, Lord, 6, 63, 84–5, 160–1, 179, 216, 269, 271, 286, 295–6, 300, 302, 304, excludes Brougham from his government, 320–3; 325–6, and the 'Queen-mother', 329–30; 331–4, 339, 343, 344, 345, 360
Melville, Henry Dundas, Lord, 12, his impeachment, 32; 49, 63, 66, 99
Merimée, Prosper, 359
Milan commission, 145, 150, 152
Mill, James, 2, early association with Brougham, 88–90; 103, 114, 121, 197, 207n., 260, 284
Mill, John Stuart, 205, 207n., 327, 343
Minto, Lord, 155
Moore, Sir John, 49
Moore, Thomas, 241, 304
Morley, John, 35, 335
Morpeth, Lord, 244, 246
'Mountain', the, 49, 52, 56, 67, 70–1, 97, 102–4, 115, 117, 141, 151, 173
Muir, Thomas, 13
municipal corporations, reform of, 287, 325
Murray, John, 8, 23, 72, 77, 347
Murray, John (publisher), 188, 190

Napier, Macvey, 272, 332, 335–43, 345, 350–1, 355
Napoleon (Bonaparte), 31, 37, 41, 45, 49, 74, 92, 93, 99–100, 104, 145, 354
National Association for the Promotion of Social Science, 358–9
National Society, 122
Newman, John Henry, 200–1, 352
Newton, Sir Isaac, 3–4, 8, 191, 351
North, Lord, 240
northern circuit, 78, 118, 136, 160–2, 169, 238, 320

O'Connell, Daniel, 209, 238–9, 285, 289, 294–8
orders-in-council, 41–5, 62, 73–4, 170, 244
Ossulton, Lord, 94
Oxford University, 6, 68–9

Palmerston, Lord, 6, 179, 269, 272
Parke, Judge, 44
Parkes, Joseph, 234, 326
parliamentary reform, 37, 48, 53, 67, Brougham on (1811), 68; 69–70, 84, 86, 87, and Westminster election (1814), 90; 115–16, 128–30, 139, 173, 179, 209, 216–18, 230, 245–8, (1831–32), 262–76; 327–8
Peacock, Thomas, 199
Peel, Sir Robert, 94, 96, Brougham's attack on (1819), 126–7; 174, 179–80, 196, 200, 203, 205, 206, 213, 234–5, 239, 260, 280, 285, 292, 321, 332, 344, Brougham's support of, 345–7
Perceval, Spencer, 1, 43, 62, 73, 79, 144
Pergami, Bartolommeo, 145, 152
Peterloo massacre, 55, 137–9, 168
Phillpotts, Henry, 167–8
Pigou, Georgiana, 134
Pitt, William, 1, 17, 18, 25, 30, 31, Brougham's leaning towards, 32–4; 36, 37, 62, 63, Brougham attacks in the *Edinburgh Review*, 66–7; 75, Brougham attacks on the hustings (1812), 81–2; 101, 105, 120, 219, 266
Place, Francis, early association with Brougham, 88–91; 103, 107, woos Brougham, 109–11; distance from Brougham, 113–14, 115–16; and the Lancasterian Association, 121–2; 185, 196, 233, 304, 326–7, 331
Playfair, John, 6, 7
Polignac, Count, 241
political unions, 270–1, 304
Pollock, Sir Frederick, 160–2, 256, 359
Ponsonby, George, 49, 56, 70, 72, 90, 103, 104, 111
Ponsonby, Lord, 29
poor law, 185–6, 305–11
Portland, Duke of, 48
press, freedom of, 87, 102, 104
Protectionists, the, 346–8

Quarterly Review, 34, 47, 49–50, 54, 122, 188, 200, 338, 340, 344

radicals, the, 49–59, 90–1, 102–4, 109–16, 129, 326–8
Ramsay, Dean, 10
Redesdale, Lord, 210, 280, 356
Reeve, Henry, 344
reform act (1832), 260, 262–76, 285

Ricardo, David, 171
Richmond, Duke of, 264–5, 269, 292
Robertson, William, 2, 4, 6, 15, 28, 352
Robinson, Henry Crabb, 10, 87, 190
Roebuck, John Arthur, 221, 233–4, 326, 331, 333
Rogers, Samuel, 140, 231, 321
Romilly, Sir Samuel, 13, 23, 49, 52, 56, 71, 74, 75, 80, 84, 92, 94, 97, 117, 121, 123, 125, 132–3, 136, 240, 277, 324
Roscoe, William, 66, 80–2
Rose, George, 43, 73
Rosslyn, Lady, 57, 216
Rosslyn, Lord, 37–8, 57, 60–1, 77, 131, 223–5
Rousseau, Jean-Jacques, 3
Royal Lancasterian Society, 88, 121–2
Royal Society, the, 7, 16
Russell, Lord John, 6, 128, 165, 173, 174, 179, 180, 202, 209, 216, 218, 260, 266, 269, 286, 289–92, 294, 320–1, 327, 333

St Vincent, Lord, 37
'Saints', the, 29–31, 121, 198
Salisbury, Lord, 64
Scarlett, Sir James, 136–7, 160–1, 165, 168, 169, 173, 237, 320, 328
Scott, John, 74–5
Scott, Sir Walter, 3, 65, 174
Scott, Sir William, 180
Sefton, Lord, 1, 35, 80–1, 118, 214, 233, 250, 257, 260–1, 275, 287, 291, 319
Shaftesbury, Lord, 360
Shelburne, Lord, 62
Shelley, Percy Bysshe, 132
Sheridan, Richard Brinsley, 56, 62, 89–91
Shepherd, Dr, 80
Six Acts, the (1819), 139, 328
slavery, 17–19, 29, 33, 86, 175–9, 209, 238, 242–5, 286, 334, 361
slave trade, 17–19, 30–1, 37, 65–6, 75, 81, 88, 91–3, 175
Smith, Adam, 3, 14, 15, 17
Smith, John, 176–9, 209
Smith, Sydney, 2, 17, 19–23, 34, 40, 47, 51, 58, 62, 112, 129, 134–5, 161, 203, 253, 258–9, 314, 334
Society for the Diffusion of Useful Knowledge, 8, 96, 133–4, 184, 187–95, 197, 200–4, 226, 238, 256, 311–2
Somerville, Alexander, 247
Spa Fields riots, 115

Spalding, Mary Ann (Mrs Brougham), 134–5
Speculative Society, the, 9–10, 14
Spencer, Lady, 36
Spencer, Lord Robert, 59
standing army, 102, 105
Stanley, Lord (Lord Derby), 269, 287, 289–92, 347–8
Stephen, James, 10, 29, 31, 43, 283
Stewart, Brigadier-General, 75
Stewart, Dugald, 6, 14
Stewart, James, 348
Stuart, Charles, 11, 28
Sugden, Sir Edward, 256

Talleyrand, Charles Maurice de, 355
Tarleton, General, 81–2
taxes on knowledge, 188, 193, 311–2
Taylor, Sir Herbert, 275–6, 282
Test and Corporation Acts, 216
Thanet, Lord, 130
Thirlwall, Connop, 192
Thomson, John, 9
Thornton, Henry, 30–1, 33
Tierney, George, 56, 70, 72, 84–5, 103, becomes Whig leader, 117–19; 150, 171, 173, 211, 216, 220, 228, 261
Tindal, Nicholas, 38–9, 152–3, 161
Tooke, Horne, 35, 188
Tooke, William, 188
Tory party, 2, 12–13, 29, 32–4, 79, 131–2, 137, 170–4, 232, 239, 280–1, 344, 346–8
trade unions, 270–1, 304

Verona, Congress of, 208
Victoria, Queen, 327, 344
Vienna, Congress of, 92–3
Vincent, Sir Francis, 40
Voltaire, François Marie Arouet de, 3–4, 8, 14–15, 203, 351, 352, 361

Walter, John, 309
Ward, John, 29, 57, 62, 74, 85, 87
Warren, Samuel, 160, 281
Watt, James, 183–4
Waverers, the, 269–73
Wedderburn, Lord, 25
Wellesley, Lord, 295–301, 303, 311–12, 321, 331–2, 345
Wellington, Duke of, 64, 93, 94, 180, 183, 207, 213, 219, 221, 226, 228, 230, 232, 239, 241, 247, 251, 275, 276, 277–8, 290–1, 285, 344

Western, Sir Charles, 106, 112, 113
Westminster by-election (1814), 89–91, 93
Westminster Review, 50, 207n., 338, 343
Westmorland, Lord, 232
Westmorland elections, 118–19, 128–32
Wharncliffe, Lord, 264–5
Whately, Richard, 192
Whig party, 2, in Scotland, 12–13; 29, Brougham's early acquaintance with, 34–6; 40–1, 43, 48–9, Brougham's dissatisfaction with, 51–3; Francis Baring on, 55–6; 57, (1810–12), 67–72; 78, Brougham's despair of, 79; Brougham's anger at, 84–6; 99, Brougham's attempt to organize (1815), 100–4; 11, 115, 130, 137–9, 141, 170–1, and prospects of office (1822), 172–4; and formation of Canning's government, 212–18; 223, 228–9, 232–3, 239, 240–1, 246–7, 285, 292, 322, 339–41

Whishaw, Thomas, 108, 117, 134, 255
Whitbread, Samuel, 35, 49, 56, 71, 87, 90, 97, 109, 111, 121, 122, 132–3, 141, 143
Wilberforce, William, 17, 30–2, 33, 35, 37, 65, 92, 121, 123, 127, 129, 151, 175–6, 360
William IV, King, 230, 241, 247, 249, 251, 263–6, 268, 270–1, 274–6, 282, 289, 291–4, 297, 299, 303–4, 314–15, 318, 320, 323
Williams, John, 152
Wilson, Sir Robert, 75, 118, 213, 215
Wood, Alderman, 147–8, 151
Winchilsea election (1815), 97
Wordsworth, William, 130
Wynn, Charles, 108, 172

York, Duke of, 49, 52
Yorkshire election (1830), 1, 132, 242–246
Young, Thomas, 47, 191–2